1949

THE FIRST ISRAELIS

TOM SEGEV

Arlen Neal Weinstein

English Language Editor

An Owl Book

Henry Holt and Company   New York

To my mother. She came to Israel 50 years ago as a refugee from Germany, but just like many of the first Israelis never learned Hebrew properly and could not read this book until it came out in English.

Henry Holt and Company, Inc.
Publishers since 1866
115 West 18th Street
New York, New York 10011

Henry Holt® is a registered trademark
of Henry Holt and Company, Inc.

Library of Congress Cataloging-in-Publication Data
Segev, Tom.
[1949, ha Yiśre 'elim ha-rishonim. English]
1949, the first Israelis / Tom Segev; Arlen Neal Weinstein,
English language editor.—1st Owl books ed.
p. cm.
"An Owl book."
Previously published: New York: Free Press: London: Collier
Macmillan, c1986.
Includes bibliographical references and index.
ISBN 0-8050-5896-6
1. Israel—History—1948–1967. 2. Israel-Arab War, 1948–1949—
Armistices. 3. Palestinian Arabs—Government policy—Israel.
4. Immigrants—Israel—Social conditions. 5. Israel—Ethnic relations.
6. Orthodox Judaism—Israel—Relations—Nontraditional Jews.
7. Religion and state—Israel. 8. National characteristics, Israeli.
I. Weinstein, Arlen Neal. II. Title
DS126.5.S41513   1998   97-42451
956.9405'2—dc21   CIP

First published in the United States in 1986 by The Free Press

First Owl Books Edition 1998

Printed in the United States of America
All first editions are printed on acid-free paper.∞

1 3 5 7 9 10 8 6 4 2

Contents

Preface: *Ten Years Later*

S ome time after this book first came out, a friend surprised me with an Arabic edition, published in Beirut by the Institute for Palestinian Studies. I had no prior knowledge of the translation and of course the Institute, affiliated with the Palestine Liberation Organization, had not asked for permission, nor had it offered to pay royalties. Still, I was quite pleased that the book had found its way across the line of fire. Subsequently, when I met a member of the Institute, I said to him, "I know you—you stole my book." "True," the man answered, "but you stole my country." This exchange, I think, more or less sums up the level of discussion between Israelis and Palestinians in the 1980s. We have certainly come a long way since. Indeed, the first Israelis would hardly recognize their country now.

For me, the story of those first Israelis is basically one of success; I tend to think of them with compassion and not a little envy for their part in the historic task of creating a new state. Yet when my book appeared in Israel a decade ago, it caused a stormy controversy. Reactions ranged from shame to dismay to rejection, for the book shattered a firmly established self-image and exposed as myths a large number of long-accepted truths. Its effect was all the more devastating since it was based almost entirely on official documents.

History plays a role of immense importance in Israel's political and cultural discourse. Indeed, the very existence of the country is based on a certain interpretation of Jewish history, namely the Zionist one. According to the official version of that history—for many years the only version—Israel's history was one of exemplary equality and justice. *1949*, however, suggested that the story was far less noble and heroic than Israelis had been led to believe. For it is true: Israel *does* bear part of the responsibility for the tragedy of the Palestinian refugees; it has *not* taken up every chance to make peace with its Arab neighbors; and the government *did* at times discriminate against new immigrants from Arab countries. It is not surprising, then, that many critics were outraged; some described my book as a display of post-Zionist self-hatred.

The appearance of *1949* coincided with a period of tremendous fragility in Israeli life, marked by the ongoing war in Lebanon and triple-digit inflation, to name just two sources of instability. Shortly after the book came out *Koteret Rashit*, a now-defunct newsweekly, published a nationwide poll which revealed that eight out of ten Israelis said they were personally happy, but six out of ten believed that most other Israelis were not. This contradiction seemed to suggest that while people felt content in their own lives, they were uncertain about the general well-being of Israeli society. Had such a poll been conducted in 1949, it might well have indicated the opposite: that the first Israelis were often unhappy in their personal lives but believed in their country and its future. They had a dream. This is perhaps the most profound difference between Israelis then and now.

But the loss of the dream has not been an unequivocal negative, for self-knowledge has taken its place. The people of Israel have grown up. Their maturity has come in the wake of peace agreements with Egypt and Jordan and negotiations with the Palestinians: they feel more secure today and their economic situation has also improved dramatically. Unlike the first Israelis, who saw themselves collectively, most now tend to think of themselves as individuals. The tribalism which may have been imperative in the early days of Israel has since lost much of its urgency, as has political ideology in general. More and more Israelis live not for the sake of history or the future but for the present, for life itself. Having grown up, they have also learned to apply some degree of self-criticism. It is probably no coincidence that many of the so-called "new historians" were trained at American universities; one of the most crucial lessons they brought home was the importance of challenging and criticizing accepted truths.

As far as I know, the term "new historiography" was first used in Israel in connection with my book. But I was not a new—that is, alternative or revisionist—historian in any sense. It was my good fortune that a great deal of previously inaccessible archival material had just been made available for research. And I was thus in a position to tell a story no one had told before. My use of this material made me, more precisely, a "first" historian of that particular period, just as much of what was later called new historiography is more properly "first" historiography. In truth, before the archives were accessible, Israel had a national mythology; only after the archives were opened could real history be written, and for the first time. The true new historians will be those who reevaluate and revise what we have done.

In recent years the Israeli government has declassified the minutes of cabinet meetings held in 1949. Most of these documents were not officially available to me when I worked on this book, although I was able to see parts of them unofficially. Declassifying these minutes indicates a commendable degree of liberalism, although some sections are still secret—specifically, those which contain evidence on atrocities committed by Israeli soldiers against Palestinian civilians during the war of 1948, or those which record high-level discussions among cabinet ministers about the need to expel the Arab population. So even now Israelis are not allowed to know the whole truth about their past.

Readers should be aware that in addition to the new archival material, numerous other books uncovering Israel's early history have been published in the last decade. The following list highlights only some titles of interest: Itzhak Levi's memoirs of the 1948 War of Independence contain a remarkable account of the Dir Yassin massacre. Benny Morris revisits the origins of the Arab refugee problem in his book *The Birth of the Palestinian Refugee Problem*. A number of other historians, including Baruch Kimmerling, Ilan Pape, Zaki Shalom, Itamar Rabinowitz, Arye Shalev, and Avi Shlaim have reexamined diverse aspects of the Israeli-Arab conflict and challenged Israel's official history. Several new books have been written about Israel's Arab citizens, the most noteworthy by Uzi Benziman and Attalah Mansour.

The painful story of the Yemenite children that was first described in *1949* has recently become a heated political issue, characterized by much demagoguery and even some violent outbursts. Two official commissions of inquiry, in addition to the one mentioned in my book, have been set up to look into the matter.

The treatment of new immigrants has also been taken up in a number of works by Dvora Hakohen, Tsvi Tsameret, and others. The treatment of Holocaust survivors has been studied by Hanna Yablonka as well as in my own *The Seventh Million*.

As Israel celebrates fifty years of independence, its society remains deeply divided over basic conflicts. Indeed, Israel seems more bitterly riven today than ever before, caught in a *Kulturkampf*, a war between basic moral and political values. Prime Minister Yitzhak Rabin lost his life in that war. Israel's first native-born prime minister, Rabin was also the first leader to tell his people that Israel's existence was no longer in danger and hence the time had come to take the risks of peace. His was the voice of optimism; his assassin acted out of pessimism. Their two positions express the conflict at the heart of Israel today.

Bitter as these differences are, I nevertheless believe that the last decade has brought Israelis a better understanding of themselves. And that is a crucial step to understanding the other, particularly when the other is an enemy of long standing. Today, I would tell my colleague at the Institute for Palestinian Studies, such a reckoning is as essential for Palestinians as for Israelis. Leaving behind the mythological past is a painful but necessary task, one of the most challenging confronting "the first Palestinians" as they begin to gain national self-determination, nearly fifty years after the first Israelis gained theirs.

1949: The First Israelis was commissioned by the Domino Press, Jerusalem, and publisher and agent Deborah Harris deserves my first thanks. The English version was updated and slightly abridged. It is based on hundreds of files containing thousands of documents. I located them at the Israel State Archives, the Central Zionist Archive, the archives of the Israel Defense Forces and the Haganah, the Ben-Gurion estate at kibbutz Sde-Boker, the Israeli Labor Party, kibbutz Hameuhad, Beit Jabotinsky, Yad Vashem, the Municipality of Jerusalem, and the Central Archives of Jewish History. Together with the files I received some excellent advice for which I am deeply grateful. I also owe a debt of deep gratitude to three friends who read the manuscript: Yosef Avner, Abraham Kushnir, and Nahum Barnea. They were of great help.

Introduction

O<small>N ONE OF</small> the first days of 1949, and one of her first days in Israel, Mrs. Rivka Waxmann, a new immigrant from Poland, went out shopping on Herzl Street in Haifa and happened to notice a soldier emerge from a jeep and walk up to the ticket window of the Ora Movie Theater. Mrs. Waxmann froze on the spot muttering, then shouting, "Haim?" The soldier turned toward her and for the next few seconds the two figures stared at one another in stunned disbelief. Then the woman stretched out her arms and flung herself at the young man. She was his mother.

The last time Mrs. Waxmann had seen her son was eight years earlier, when he was fourteen. They were separated by the war, and until meeting him in the street in Haifa she believed that Haim had perished in the Holocaust. The afternoon daily *Maariv*, then barely a year old, published the story on the same day; it had symbolic value.[1]

Thousands of people, young and old, had been torn from their loved ones during the Nazi occupation and never knew what had become of them—in the ghettos, the deportations, the death camps, the forests. In Israel, they found one another purely by chance, or through advertisements in the papers or with the aid of the heartrending radio program called *Who Recognizes, Who Knows?* "Aryeh (Leibush) Kantrowitz, now in kibbutz Hazorea, is looking for his mother Fanya, née Margolin," the announcements would run. "Bluma Langer, née Wasserstein, formerly of Kovno, now in the immigrant hostel in Raanana, is looking for her husband, Aharon Langer. Leah Koren of Lublin, now in Israel, is looking for her sister Sheina Friedman, nee Koren." All were recent immigrants on the threshold of a new life.

The story of the first Israelis is a tale of great hope and faith that things can only get better—and will be. It is about a people who dreamed of an enlightened and just society guaranteeing every man and woman happiness in the spirit of law and morality, justice and peace. In presenting his first government to the Knesset, Israel's parliament, Prime Minister David Ben-Gurion declared that the State of Israel would not rest content with having its citizens eat, drink and bear children. "Our activities and policy are guided not by economic considerations alone," he said, "but by a political and social vision that we have inherited from our prophets and imbibed from the heritage of our greatest sages and the teachers of our own day." Ben-Gurion spoke of the need to "alter man's relationship to society," by means of mutual cooperation in the spirit of pioneering, socialist Zionism. Accordingly he added that "the government sees it as the duty of the state to provide full moral, legal, and financial support for the sake of fostering these values [the moral values of the prophets] as the way . . . to educate youth and forge the image of the Jewish nation that is true to its ancient source of the vision of the End of Days."[2]

The papers of the day printed photos of men and women pioneers, beautiful people, shot from the angle of the soil—as though against the background of the future. The Philips Company had drawings of people in this same style in gigantic ads it published in the press: a young couple—she full-bodied, he muscular, people of labor—a map of the country in the background, with the inspirational line below: "Dawn is breaking now."[3] Self-conscious bathos was the style of the hour.

The seventy-fifth birthday of President Haim Weizmann, once a leading statesman but by then a mere figurehead, almost blind and deeply disappointed, was celebrated in a series of official ceremonies conducted with an almost regal air. The same kind of national excitement, military grandeur and Zionist sentimentality accompanied the reburial of the remains of Theodor Herzl, the founder of the Zionist movement. His remains were brought over from Vienna; it was considered an historic event. "Here he comes," shouted the daily *Maariv* in a huge headline. Herzl had never lived in Israel, but according to the papers he was "returning to us" at last.[4]

Everyone was aware of being a part of history in the making; everyone wanted to carve out a small place for himself in the annals of that history.

When an alarm clock factory was opened in Haifa, the photographs published in *Davar Hashavua* (*Davar's* weekend magazine) were captioned: "The first alarm clock assembled in Israel was sent as a gift to the President of the state, Haim Weizmann; the second alarm clock was sent to Prime Minister David Ben-Gurion."[5]

Ben-Gurion was placed on the first train that wound its way up to Jerusalem after the war. Dozens of officials crowded in behind him to peer at the cameras that would immortalize the event for the papers and posterity. And they were truly moved, those witnesses to the first event of its kind in 2,000 years. Every paper in Israel printed that shot.

While the war was still at its height, the country established its first governing institutions: ministries were founded and officials and generals appointed, ambassadors were sent out to every capital that would have them, Supreme Court judges were chosen. The Provisional State Council paved the way for the Knesset, bowing to the will of its Speaker, Yosef Shprintsak, a shrewd, diminutive man with an ever-present cigar, even then an experienced parliamentarian by virtue of his activities in the Zionist movement. A visitor from abroad who happened into his office one day was astonished by the mountain of minutes piled up there. "Can it possibly be that you've already managed to say so much?" he asked.

"That's because we've held our peace for two thousand years," Shprintsak quipped.

Among other things, its members debated the size and structure of the Knesset. The delegates of the small factions wanted the institution to have as many representatives as possible (171); those of the large factions wanted to have relatively few (70). They compromised on 120, which was the membership of the Great Knesset during the Second Temple period. Similar decisions faced them every day. "This is a precedent for generations to come," sighed one of the leaders of *MAPAI* (the leading Social Democratic Labor party) during the debate on the structure of the government, and another lamented: "I don't have very much experience in building countries."[6] MAPAI had dominated all the institutions of the Jewish community in the country for many years. Its leaders had guided the struggle against British rule; their actions then prefigured the creation of the state and the War of Independence.

The first Knesset was a homogeneous body—the overwhelming majority were men (there were only 11 women in the House) and 70 percent had been born in Eastern Europe, chiefly in Russia or Poland. Most of them were either political activists, functionaries or lawyers, and most were in their fifties or sixties.

Half the members of the first Knesset had been delegates to the thirty-second Zionist Congress, which had met in Basel in 1946. One-third of the MKs had also served in the Fourth Representative Assembly, the highest elected body of the Jewish community in Palestine under the British Mandate.

All these factors contributed to the continuity of a stable democratic parliamentary system, giving the impression that no revolution had actually taken place. "I cannot stand the conservatism of my revolutionaries . . .," Ben-Gurion used to moan.[7]

The ideology of Israel's social and political establishment contained an extraordinary hybrid of Eastern European rabbinic traditions combined with the Marxist message of the enthusiastic, conspiratorial Russian revolutionism.

The men of the early waves of Zionist immigration, up to the 1920s, were proud of their achievements and zealously attached to the tradition they had created from personal struggle and backbreaking labor. Yet at times their staunch conservatism was intolerable to those who sought to add, innovate and mend. "A sort of Israeli Mayflower elite emerged," wrote economist David Horowitz, "whose moral authority was so great that it became a closed caste, excluding not only new people but also new ideas."[8]

The attachment of that older generation to its posts clogged the passages through which the younger generation tried to break into positions of responsibility and accounted also for the advanced age of those in power. Fanatic nationalism, social pathos and the feeling of still being in the underground endowed this establishment with a highly distinctive character—puritan-ical, heroic, stubborn, ideologically revolutionary, yet profoundly conservative in its modes of action and thought.

David Ben-Gurion, of course, bore the ultimate responsibility for the system's continuity and stability, and symbolized them as well. By 1949 the man with the shock of white hair, a native of Plonsk, Poland, was 63 years old, with many years of politics behind him. His leadership and political power reflected his abilities and his courage in making decisions. Those around him tended to treat him as the source of all authority, the man who creates precedents and epitomizes values; some even saw him as the personification of history.*

Ben-Gurion's diaries, letters and other documentary material reflect his involvement with the minutest details of major national decisions, as well as countless other matters. This entry from his diary on Friday, March 11, 1949 indicates how deep was his involvement in all the issues of the day.

> This morning (Chief of Staff) Yaakov Dori telephoned me to say that at midnight last night our flag was flown on the Red Sea Bay. We have reached Eilat. . . . Is it now the turn of the West Bank? The Rhodes [armistice] talks will be decisive. . . . We have to plan the absorption of 800,000 immigrants within four years. How many industrial plants will be needed, what types of industry will be developed, which lands shall we settle, how much money will be needed, what equipment will be required, what the import and the export. . . . We have to discuss with each local and municipal council what are its development plans, those that need government assistance and those that do not. What of the machinery in the factories, is there a way of renewing or developing it? What are the industries that can be transferred to Jerusalem . . .? A road to be constructed from Beersheba to the south, via the Dead Sea. . . . There is a plan to pump up the water of the Dead Sea and transport it directly to the Mediterranean. . . . Workers' committees should be created to support the state, on the basis of the government's plan for occupational training, improvement of the standard of living, improvement of production, labor laws. . . . And time must be

---

*The following episode illustrates the magnitude of his influence. In April 1949 Ben-Gurion held a political consultation. The minutes of this meeting show that he left before it ended. After he left, the people assembled started a prolonged discussion about the possible meaning of one of the comments he had made. Some interpreted his words one way and some another, each of them quoting him verbatim to reinforce his interpretation. Among them were such people as Moshe Dayan.[9]

found! How to manage within the limits of 24 hours a day?! I should establish a rigid daily schedule—for the Ministry of Defense (meetings with the General Staff, principal officials of the Ministry, the navy and air force); for economic planning (meetings with the Treasury, Labor, Agriculture, Industry and Rationing); coordination of Government Ministries; contact with the workers, with the academic and free professions, with army commanders; visits to camps, factories and settlements; receiving people, reading material, writing. Liaison officers will be needed: with the Ministries (at least bi-weekly reports on each Ministry); with the state of labor (regular reports, at least 2 or 3 a week, about the labor and unemployment situation); housing (execution of plans, preparations and shortages); settlement; Arabs; state of industry; finance; a science council; arms industry; state of supplies; police and internal security; foreign affairs (talks with Arab countries, relations with major powers, Russia and America, and with countries of the East and West, connections with Jewish Agency and Jewish communities in the Diaspora, with the ... Labor movement); the press—Israeli, Jewish, general*. We must begin to formulate a number of laws: 1. civil equality, freedom of religion; freedom of conscience, language, education and culture, equality for women; freedom of association and expression; universal suffrage. 2. General conscription law. 3. Nationalization of water sources, natural resources, unused lands. 4. Control of imports and prices. 5. Taxes—progressive, inheritance, increment. 6. Encouragement of childbirth. 7. General education. 8. Demobilization benefits. 9. Labor laws. 10. Admission of civil servants . . ."[10]*

*The absence of MAPAI in this list is not accidental. At this time Ben-Gurion engaged in little party activity. He rarely appeared before the party's central bodies and each appearance was an event. The role of the party in the decision making process had greatly diminished since the creation of the state.

Ben-Gurion's diaries contain whole pages of statistical data, which he copied with meticulous zeal. The recording into his notebooks alone must have consumed hours daily. He used to make notes in his diary even in the course of meetings and conferences. Whenever he finished one notebook he would append to it a table of contents and index. In addition, he wrote hundreds of letters, on almost every subject. While the War of Independence was being fought, he sent a letter to the editor of MAPAI's daily *Hador*, in connection with an article on Aesop's fables which had appeared in that paper. He listed seven errors in that article, starting with the Hebrew spelling of Aesop's name.[11] He wrote to a little girl called Ronnie Baron of Tel Aviv, saying that if he had a private car of his own he would gladly have taken her every day to and from kindergarten, but as Minister of Defense he could not accede to her request and allow her uncle to take her in his army vehicle, "because that car belongs to the nation and the state."[12] Hundreds of citizens received such letters from him.

While winning the war, establishing the first governing institutions, electing the first Knesset and beginning to legislate the
first laws, the first Israelis also established new settlements to
absorb immigrants—at a rate of one every three days, or a total
of about 100 a year. At the same time they built housing projects
for veterans, set up new industrial enterprises, health services
and educational networks, opened the Weizmann Institute of
Science, the Faculty of Medicine and the Faculty of Law at the
Hebrew University, and published the first volume of the *Ency-
clopaedia Hebraica*—each day bringing achievements and innovations of dashing boldness and breathtaking momentum.
Those first Israelis had good reason to feel optimistic and sure of
their footing.

But in their staunch faith, they more than once turned a
blind eye to the true state of affairs. Six out of every ten Israelis
believed that the death notices for men who fell in battle should
not be published in the papers or posted in the streets, as was the
custom, lest the general mood be adversely affected.[13] Thousands of families throughout the country were in mourning for
the war dead, as 6,000 Israelis—one of every hundred citizens—
had lost their lives during 14 months of the fighting between
November 1947 and January 1949. Tens of thousands were
wounded, and tens of thousands of others, demobilized soldiers,
now had to reenter society. Between shell shock and the shock
of returning home, they had difficulty adjusting; many felt alienated from the society they had just fought to defend. The story of
the first Israelis is therefore also a story of great distress and human misery.

During the first half of January 1949, a reporter from the
afternoon daily *Yediot Aharonot* took a stroll through the narrow alleys of Jaffa. "I was confronted by a truly startling sight,"
he subsequently wrote, "people carrying suitcases, packages
of meager household goods, blankets, mattresses, furniture, followed by clamorous women and children. . . . Where to? To seek
a night's shelter."[14] They were new immigrants. Hundreds of
them, the reporter wrote, came to Jaffa daily, searching for
apartments deserted by their Arab tenants.* Most of these

---

*The Arabs of Jaffa had left the city some eight months earlier. One of
them described their departure in almost the same words used by the Israeli
journalist to describe the entry of the immigrants: "The sight of crowds of people, women and children floundering under the burden of suitcases and pack-

apartments had already been claimed, but the immigrants kept coming anyway. Tens of thousands of them lived in tent camps. And then there were the Arabs who remained in the country, a defeated, humiliated, terrified people.

Confined to one of the prisons at the time was Abu Laban, a leader of the Arab community of Jaffa. He was being held in administrative detention contrary to the ruling of the Supreme Court, which had ordered his release. In addressing that fact, the daily *Haaretz* wrote in its editorial: "We are in the decisive stages of the history of the young state, in which its image will be established and its traditions forged, and it will be an ominous sign if in the struggle between the authority of the law and the power of administrative fiat, the law does not emerge the winner."[16]

Unlike the Labor Union's *Davar*, which was suffused with naive, almost solemn faith, trapped in the rhetoric of the great vision, the privately owned *Haaretz* was scowling, skeptical, often given to pettiness and arrogance, and frequently found itself caught in the rut of criticism.

One of the very few articles to appear in that revolutionary year bearing the signature of Gershom Schocken, the editor of *Haaretz*, demanded that the symbol of the state be changed forthwith on the grounds that it was "aesthetically abominable and an example of the Israeli government's lack of taste, lack of culture, and lack of aesthetic sense." Schocken railed about the design of the *menorah* (seven-branched candelabrum), the letters and the olive branches (which he deemed too large), "all of it within a placard worthy of the trophies awarded to the winners of sports competitions."[17] The paper's readership wrote letters to the editor complaining of overcrowded buses, of the municipal administration that did not clean the streets, of the constant shortage of coins used for small change and of the low cultural level of the officials who had decided to impose a luxury tax on classical records. During the summer *Haaretz* devoted abundant space to a spate of sexual offenses that plagued the country and pronounced it "among the manifestations of demoralization

---

ages as they moved ploddingly toward the port of Jaffa in an inauspicious tumult, left an indelible impression on me." Much later, the writer of these lines became known worldwide as Abu Iyad, Deputy to the Chairman of the PLO, Yasser Arafat.[15]

caused by war among both winners and losers to the same degree."[18] Within eight months of the Proclamation of Independence in May 1948, the paper published an article containing one of the more lasting innovations of the time: the word Zionism used to connote empty bombast.[19]

The country was touched by a genuine readiness to sacrifice, and there was more than a modicum of true, supremely patriotic pioneering for the sake of the commonweal. But it coexisted with a very human desire to pursue the good life and concern for personal welfare, every man for himself, often at the expense of others. Some looted in wartime, others thieved after the war, and before long a black market was thriving. The first Israelis were thus no more virtuous or idealistic than those who came after them.

A few months after the establishment of the state, David Ben-Gurion warned that "We will disappoint the Zionist movement and miss the mark if suddenly we should begin philosophizing about who I am and what I am. Right now the only question that stands before us is a pragmatic one, and we must solve it. . . ."[20] He tended to focus on the problems of the state rather than on those of the individual, and in this respect he was followed by most of the writers of that generation, who wrote—and thought—in the first person plural. The great human drama of the time was depicted not as a conflict between the individual and society but as a series of collective confrontations: between Jews and Arabs, between veterans and immigrants, and between the religious and the secular camps—all taking place against the backdrop of the clash between the noble vision and the mundane reality of daily life.

Ben-Gurion tried to cope with the weaknesses of the vision in his own inimitable way: twice that year he summoned a large group of writers and intellectuals for a talk and demanded—as if he were a union boss—that collectively they boost the spirit of the country. Some of them were struggling with basic existential questions, bemused vagabonds wandering between the Jewish past and the Israeli present, between the negation of the Diaspora and a sense of Jewish solidarity, between humanism and morality and the government's *Realpolitik*, always searching for identity and a path. One of Ben-Gurion's guests even questioned whether there was still any purpose to the people. That was Martin Buber. "Do we still have a purpose?" he mused aloud, and the Prime Minister cut him off impatiently. The exchange between them had the ring of a dialogue between priest and prophet.

"We spoke of 'redemption,' the redemption of the soil, the redemption of labor," said Buber. "We even spoke of the redemption of man in Israel. The matter was rooted in the concept of faith, but we destroyed that element of it. We spoke of redeeming the soil and we meant making it Jewish soil. Jewish soil to what end?"

"To bring forth bread out of the earth!" Ben-Gurion replied.

"What for?" Buber continued.

"To eat!"

"What for?" Buber kept pressing.

"Enough!" Ben-Gurion pronounced, quite enraged by then. "He asks questions to which there are no answers. Isn't it enough to bring forth bread out of the earth? That's not enough. For the sake of independence? Again, that's not enough. For the sake of redeeming the Jewish people? Even that isn't enough. And Professor Buber continues to ask why. Maybe he has a final answer, though I doubt it. So I ask him: What are all these questions for?"

Ben-Gurion did not deny the right to doubt. "One can ask," he admitted, "but first of all we must build the state!"[21]

As Israel's Declaration of Independence was being drafted, Felix Rosenbluett (who was soon to change his name to Pinhas Rozen and become the new country's Minister of Justice) demanded that the document cite the country's borders. Ben-Gurion objected, and the exchange between the two men was recorded as follows:

> Rozen: "There's the question of the borders, and it cannot be ignored."
> Ben-Gurion: "Anything is possible. If we decide here that there's to be no mention of borders, then we won't mention them. Nothing is *a priori* [imperative]."
> Rozen: "It's not *a priori*, but it is a legal issue."
> Ben-Gurion: "The law is whatever people determine it to be."[22]

Ben-Gurion assumed that the country's borders would reflect the results of a war that was already in progress and that these frontiers would ultimately be broader than the lines stipulated by the United Nations in its Partition Resolution of 1947.* The first Israelis constantly shuttled between these two poles, one wholly legalistic and cognizant of the impossible, the other wholly pragmatic and convinced that everything is possible.

On November 29, 1947, the UN General Assembly voted to partition Palestine into two states, one Jewish and the other Arab.

The Zionist dream was to become a reality many generations after the Jewish people had lost its political sovereignty and was exiled from its land. But that vote did not in itself ensure the existence of the new states. Between November 29, 1947, and the Declaration of Independence on May 14, 1948, the country was swept by a wave of terror and bloodshed in which thousands lost their lives and hundreds of thousands (most of them Arabs) were forced to abandon their homes. As long as the violence continued, the viability of the Jewish state was left open to doubt. And when Israel's independence was finally declared in May 1948, it was at the height of a war that would go on for another six months, during which it was sometimes highly questionable whether Israel would emerge the victor.

Even when victory came into view and the state's first governing institutions were established, it was still doubtful whether Israel would be a state based on the rule of law. For, during its first months, the nascent country's citizens had difficulty closing ranks around common precepts—so much so that some observers feared the outbreak of a civil war. A few weeks after the proclamation of the state, the *Altalena*, a ship carrying immigrants and arms to the dissident right-wing, anti-British terror organization *Irgun Zvai Leumi* (IZL), appeared off the coast, and Ben-Gurion, who claimed it had been sent "to destroy the Israeli army and murder the state," ordered it to be shelled (after most

*In the months that followed, a distinction was drawn between the areas originally allocated to the Jewish state in the Partition Plan and the newly conquered areas, particularly in Galilee, which were labeled "the administered territories." Shortly thereafter a district court judge in Haifa, Moshe Etsioni, ruled that the sovereignty of the State of Israel was based first and foremost on the natural and historical right of the Jewish people, so that the borders cited in the UN Resolution did not in fact determine the frontiers of the state. On the basis of this ruling, the court indicted a resident of the Arab village of Shfaram accused of smuggling who argued in his defense that his case was beyond the jurisdiction of an Israeli court because the crime was committed outside the borders of Israel.[23]

of the immigrants had been removed to safety).[24] The ship went up in flames and sank, taking a painful toll in dead and wounded. Then, in July 1948, Ben-Gurion clashed with the Left when a number of high ranking army officers demanded the promotion of colleagues associated with the left-wing MAPAM party. When Ben-Gurion rejected the demand and a few officers resigned in protest, the prime minister dubbed their move "a political mutiny."[25] A few days later, in another context, the engineer Meir Tubiansky was taken to a deserted house near the main road to Jerusalem and after a travesty of a trial, during which he was not permitted to present a case in his own defense, was shot for spying on behalf of the British. No record was kept of the proceedings; the "charges" and the "sentence" were not committed to paper until after the "defendant" was dead. Both the "trial" and the "execution" were perpetrated on the initiative of Isser Be'ery, one of the heads of Israel's secret service. During the same period, the right-wing, anti-British underground was still operating in Jerusalem, and in September members of the *Lehi* (the so-called Stern Gang) murdered the UN mediator Count Folke Bernadotte for having drawn up a proposal for a peace settlement that would have deprived Israel of some of the territorial gains it achieved as a result of its War of Independence.

All these events took place within a period of less than six months and marked the transition from chaos to law and order in a new state. The following year, 1949, was very different from its predecessor. With the struggle to establish the state and the war to defend it—and extend its borders—drawing to an end, the emphasis shifted to a series of decisions that would set the style and tone of life in Israel and forge the first Israelis into a unified, though pluralistic society; the first decisions of 1949 were of a patently political and military nature.

PART I

Between Jews
and Arabs

1

The Green Line

O N THE EVENING of December 31, 1948, James McDonald, an American diplomat serving in Israel, dropped his preparations for the New Year's party he was to throw the next day in Tel Aviv, and left posthaste for the Galei Kinneret Hotel in Tiberias, where David Ben-Gurion was vacationing. McDonald, subsequently America's first Ambassador to Israel, carried an ultimatum from President Truman demanding that Israel withdraw the force which had crossed the international border with Egypt and penetrated into the Sinai Peninsula. The American initiative had come in response to a request from London and was strongly worded: if Israel refused to withdraw its forces from Sinai, the United States would "re-examine" its relations with Israel. Ben-Gurion read the letter slowly while the American envoy sat waiting for a reply. Finally the Prime Minister remarked that the tone of the communication was harsh, but he promised to pull his forces back to the Israeli side of the border, thereby forfeiting any chance of capturing the Gaza Strip.[1]

When word of McDonald's visit reached his headquarters, the commander of the southern front, Yigal Allon, tried to save the operation in Sinai by rushing back to Tel Aviv to talk with Acting Chief of Staff Yigael Yadin, then with Foreign Minister

Sharett, and finally with Ben-Gurion himself. Allon did manage to elicit the prime minister's approval for one more operation—an attack on the town of Rafah—but the action failed, though they managed to cut off the Egyptian troops in the Gaza Strip. The Israeli army now held the entire northern Negev, with the exception of the Gaza Strip and the so-called Faluja Pocket. A few thousand Egyptian soldiers were still trapped in that pocket, one of whom happened to be Gamal Abdel Nasser. The Israelis could not overcome them. "The Egyptians have learned to fight," Ben-Gurion reported to the Cabinet, and that same day the ministers decided to accept a ceasefire.[2] Ben-Gurion regarded this as a great accomplishment, despite the fact that Gaza and Faluja had not fallen. "This is an important stage in the achievement of peace and fortifying the position of the State of Israel," he wrote in his diary. "If we reach an agreement with the Egyptians—and that "if" is not lightly stated—it will be easier for us to reach an agreement with Transjordan and the others. . . ."[3]

One evening during that week, Ben-Gurion took the time to attend a showing of a Soviet war film, to which he had been invited by the Soviet minister Pavel Ivanowich Yershov. "In the midst of the bombing by the Soviet planes," the prime minister later wrote, "an air-raid siren went off. Yershov, who was seated beside me, wanted to stop the showing. I objected, and the show went on. About half an hour later the all-clear sounded. But afterwards I learned that the airport at Lydda had been bombed and the mess hall of the 82nd Battalion was hit. One soldier was killed and two were injured. The film—pure propaganda."[4] That same week the port of Tel Aviv was shelled and Jerusalem was bombed from the air, causing the destruction of a wall of the Shaarei Tsedek Hospital and injury to a few pedestrians.[5] Firing was still going on at the southern front, too, despite the government's decision. "Yigael [Yadin] suspects our soldiers of not having stopped either, though Yigal Allon received an explicit order from him this morning," Ben-Gurion wrote. "Yadin believes that when [Allon] got back down south, the members of the 'clan'—[Itzhak] Rabin, Itzhak Sade, and others—told him to continue. . . ."[6]

But these were the last shots, and the war with the Arab states ended with two air battles in which five British planes were shot down; one British pilot was killed and two were taken prisoner. Israel claimed that the British planes had penetrated its airspace and were shot down over its territory, but that was untrue. Ben-Gurion copied into his diary the cable he received from the south stating that Allon had ordered the remains of the planes towed out of Egyptian territory and scattered over Israeli territory "for obvious reasons."[7]*

A few hours after this incident, Ben-Gurion returned to Tiberias in very good spirits. "It's been a marvelous day," he wrote in his diary. "Has the war ended today?"[9] Four days later the Civil Defense Command cancelled the order requiring the windows and street lights in residential areas to be blacked out, and although the blackout remained in force in industrial and business establishments, the immediate danger had passed. In the Yellow Room of the Hotel des Roses in Rhodes, preparations had in the meantime been completed for the opening of armistice negotiations on the new border between Israel and Egypt, which was to become known as the Green Line.

David Ben-Gurion would have preferred to hold the armistice talks in Jerusalem, or on the Israeli-Egyptian border, or at sea, on board an American vessel flying the UN flag, rather than on the Island of Rhodes. However, he did not press the point.[10] The northern cliff of the historic island still seemed to be haunted by the spirit of Count Folke Bernadotte, the UN mediator who had been assassinated in Jerusalem four months earlier.[11] The Swedish diplomat had set up his headquarters on the island, describing it as an ideal spot for peace negotiations, far removed from the hatred and gunfire, yet close enough to international lines of communication.[12] Moshe Dayan, too, would one day recall it as a place where "thousands of butterflies of all sizes and colors fluttered among the bushes, as if it had been the scene for a fairytale. . . ."[13] The Hotel des Roses was known for its rustic old-style atmosphere, an appropriate setting for journalists and diplomats, millionaires and spies to rub elbows over glasses of whisky and lemonade. Itzhak Rabin, then a Lt. Colonel who was flown to Rhodes straight from the battlefield in the Negev,

---

*The attack on the British planes was essentially an act of mischief by a few trigger-happy pilots. Ezer Weizmann, who flew one of those planes, later wrote in his memoirs that he did it because he was "blue" about having missed out on the glory of that day. "Here the war was over," he wrote, "here it was breathing its last breath . . . and I was left out of the celebration," so out he went to seek his prey.[8]

would fondly recall the juicy steaks he ate there,[14] and Director General of the Israel Foreign Ministry, Walter Eitan, would note the sweets which were flown in by the Egyptians from the famous confectioners, "Groppi" of Cairo.[15] The UN mediator who conducted the talks was Dr. Ralph Bunche, a black American, brilliant and humane, whose achievements would later win him the Nobel Peace Prize. He and his aides occupied one wing of the hotel, while the Egyptians and the Israelis were assigned another wing, with the Egyptians occupying the floor above the Israelis. Violent winds and rainstorms greeted the visitors upon their arrival in Rhodes, Thursday, January 13.

Ben-Gurion was not in a conciliatory mood. He said during one of the discussions with his aides:

> Before the founding of the state, on the eve of its creation, our main interest was *self-defense*. To a large extent, the creation of the state was an act of self-defense. . . . Many think that we're still at the same stage. But now the issue at hand is conquest, not self-defense. As for setting the borders—it's an open-ended matter. In the Bible as well as in our history there are all kinds of definitions of the country's borders, so there's no real limit. No border is absolute. If it's a desert—it could just as well be the other side. If it's a sea, it could also be across the sea. The world has always been this way. Only the terms have changed. If they should find a way of reaching other stars, well then, perhaps the whole earth will no longer suffice.[16]

In his diary Ben-Gurion laid down a more precise definition: "Peace is vital—but not at any price."[17]

The first encounter between the Israeli and the Egyptian delegations was not very promising. At first the Egyptians tended to ignore the Israelis. Walter Eitan did notice, however, that some of them, overcome by curiosity, would turn their heads for a quick glance whenever they ran into each other in the hotel lobby. At first Bunche did not succeed in getting them to meet face to face. Finally, however, the Egyptians agreed to meet the Israelis in his suite. The mediator sat on a sofa with the delegations facing him—the Israelis to his right, the Egyptians to his left. The Egyptians made a point of addressing him, as though the Israelis were not there. Slowly but surely the atmosphere thawed as the delegates began speaking to each other in English and French, and affectionately showing one another snapshots of their families.[18] Eitan headed the Israeli delegation, which included

Reuven Shiloah, one of Ben-Gurion's closest advisors and a pioneer of Israel's Intelligence community, and Eliyahu (Elias) Sasson, director of the Middle East division at the Foreign Ministry. Sasson, a Damascus-born journalist and public figure was one of the first diplomats of the Jewish Agency to visit Arab capitals, a regular caller at the palaces of their sultans and kings; he was both a man of peace and a dreamer. Acting Chief of Staff Yigael Yadin headed the military delegation, accompanied by Rabin and two other officers.

At the beginning Bunche alone was aware of the two delegations' basic positions, and he would make sure to present them to each side gradually and with the utmost care. Bunche made each side believe that agreement was imminent. Thus the Israelis gained the impression that the Egyptians might be willing to withdraw from the Gaza Strip, provided the local population was not placed under Israeli rule. Later it was learned that the distance between the two parties was much greater than had been realized. Israel insisted that Egypt give up the Strip, and the Egyptians demanded that Israel give up Beersheba. This was especially important to the Egyptians, because they had never admitted that the town had fallen to the Israelis; the Egyptian public was yet to hear about it from its government. The two parties rejected each other's counterproposals with nerve-racking stubbornness. Bunche tried everything to bring them closer. At one point he invited both delegations to his suite and showed them ceramic plates which he had especially ordered in a local factory, with the inscription, "Armistice Talks, Rhodes, 1949." "If you come to an agreement," he said, "you'll each receive such a plate as a souvenir. If you don't—I'll smash them on your heads." Eitan reported to Foreign Minister Sharett that "it was a most extraordinary occasion," and promised a further report on what he termed "the comic aspect of it." As for the Egyptians' stubbornness, he wrote that it made him want to scream.[19]*

---

*Walter Eitan, a native of Munich, Germany, had studied at Oxford. His telegrams to Sharett reflect considerable arrogance, and a rather petty bureaucratic mind. The Israeli delegates in Rhodes telegraphed home profusely, to clarify every single detail and ask for instructions. They rarely ventured a decision or proposals of their own. Tel Aviv wired back several times a day, a total of thousands of telegrams, letters and other memos. They generally corresponded in English, whether for practical reasons, having no Hebrew telex, or because they felt that a diplomatic communication should properly be made in English.

As negotiations proceeded, the Israeli government decided to give up the demand that the Egyptians leave Gaza, but refused to give in with regard to the area around the archeological site at Auja al-Khafir, which the Israelis called Nitsana. Giving up Gaza was not easy. The army and *MAPAM*, the left-wing opposition, viewed it as a humiliating and dangerous concession, and so, of course, did *Herut*, the right-wing opposition. There had, indeed, been little hope that Egypt would willingly vacate the Strip, and the Israeli government therefore preferred to face reality rather than risk the collapse of the talks.

The next two weeks in Rhodes were taken up by haggling over details, and finally, on February 24, the agreement was signed. Ben-Gurion wrote: "After the creation of the state and our victories in battle—this is the great event of a great and marvellous year."[20]

The armistice agreement with Egypt was based primarily on the existing military situation. Israel had to agree to an Egyptian military presence in the Gaza Strip, and to withdraw her own forces from the area of Beit Hanoon and the sector near the Rafah cemetery. However, she was allowed to keep seven outposts along the Strip. The Egyptian brigade which had been surrounded in Faluja was released, and the area was turned over to Israel.* Israel was obliged to agree to demilitarize the area around Nitsana, but her demand that the demilitarization extend to both sides of the border was accepted. Nitsana was to serve as the seat of the mixed armistice commission, but Israel objected to the area being placed under UN jurisdiction. The Egyptian demand that Beersheba be part of the reduced troops area was rejected; however, Revivim, a kibbutz 25 kilometers south of Beersheba, was included in it. The signing of the armistice agreement with Egypt greatly improved the prospect of signing similar agreements—and possibly even peace treaties— with other Arab states. Itzhak Rabin commented, "I believed that we were moving forward to peace. We all believed it."[21]†

---

*The following year Gamal Abdel Nasser, later President of Egypt, returned to the site, by arrangement with the armistice commission, to help locate the graves of Israeli soldiers who had fallen there and been buried by the Egyptians.

†After the agreement was signed, Eitan sent Tel Aviv a detailed suggestion how to brief the press. He recommended de-emphasizing the Israeli gains so as not to provoke the Egyptians. He also proposed concealing certain Israeli concessions.[22]

Some four weeks after the agreement with Egypt, a similar one was signed with Lebanon. The negotiations that led up to it were not difficult. Some informal talks had been held before, but the Lebanese did not want to be the first. "Reach an agreement with one of the other Arab states first," they told the Israelis: "Lebanon will be the second." The negotiations were held on the border between the two countries, near Rosh Hanikrah. They would meet alternately in the customs house on the Lebanese side, and in the police station on the Israeli side. The two buildings were some 500 meters apart, situated on rocky cliffs overlooking the Mediterranean—a breathtaking view; the road between the buildings wound through mine fields.

The two delegations often talked to each other in Arabic. The Israeli delegation was headed by Lt. Colonel Mordehai Makleff, later the third Chief of Staff of the Israeli army, who was accompanied by Yehoshua Felmann (Palmon) and Shabtai Rozen from the Foreign Ministry. The UN representatives, Henri Vigier and William Riley, were not called upon to intervene as much as Bunche had to in Rhodes. "The site tends to encourage personal relations between the delegations," Rozen reported. "Since one acts as the host and the other as its guest, the talks are accompanied by lavish refreshments, as is customary in the East, and people get to know each other."[23] Rozen drew a lesson for the future from this encounter—direct talks are preferable to mediated negotiations. When alone with the Israelis, he wrote Sasson, the Lebanese would act as if they were not Arabs, and had been drawn into the war against their will. "For internal reasons—so they say—they cannot openly avow their hatred of the Syrians and their objection to the presence of a Syrian army in their country, but they are eager to have the agreement restrict the free movement of the Syrian army in Lebanon. . . . I believe that as soon as a convenient opportunity presents itself they will propose renewing trade relations with us."[24]

When the negotiations began, the Israeli army was in control of a narrow strip in Lebanon, just west of the northern Galilee, which enclosed fourteen villages, the northernmost of which was not far from the Litani River. There were hardly any disagreements between the negotiating teams. The two states agreed that the international border would serve as the armistice line, and that as soon as the agreement was signed Israel would vacate the territory she had conquered. Nevertheless, it was three weeks before the agreement was signed, because Israel at first tried to link her withdrawal with a Syrian withdrawal from Lebanon, and—even more significantly—with Syria's withdrawal from Israeli territories Syria had occupied during the war along the Jordan River and the eastern bank of the Sea of Galilee. Some of the Israeli diplomats disagreed with that plan.

This was, in effect, a dispute between the Foreign Ministry and the army. Yigael Yadin wrote Walter Eitan to say that the diplomats "do not understand" the military problems of the northern border and its importance; he demanded that they be briefed accordingly.[25] Rozen reported that according to his impression, ". . . the Lebanese government is very eager to come to an agreement with us."[26] However, the negotiations had reached a dead end. Within a few hours it became apparent that there was only one way of reaching an agreement.

On March 17 Ben-Gurion wrote in his diary: "In my opinion we should sign regardless of the Syrian withdrawal. 1. It strengthens our political position in general, and especially with regard to Eilat (which had just been taken). 2. It increases our pressure on the Syrians. 3. It facilitates a move onto the West Bank—if it should be necessary."[27] That evening, Chief of Staff Dori and Moshe Dayan, as well as Eitan and Rozen came to see him to sort out the disagreement between the army and the Foreign Ministry. Meanwhile, Ralph Bunche and the US government were exerting massive pressure. They warned that if the negotiations failed Israel would be blamed. It would gravely damage her international standing and might very well damage her chances of being accepted as a member of the United Nations. Ben-Gurion concluded: "I'm in favor of signing the armistice agreement with Lebanon."[28]*

---

*This, however, did not put an end to the old dream of annexing southern Lebanon to Israel and establishing a Christian state in the north—or, at least, of dividing Lebanon and establishing a Christian state in the south. Ben-Gurion aimed at it from the beginning of the war. "The Moslem rule in Lebanon is artificial and easily undermined. A Christian state ought to be set up whose southern border would be the Litani River. Then we'll form an alliance with it."[29] Ben-Gurion raised this idea repeatedly in the coming years. Sharett noted in his diary that the Chief of Staff (Dayan) supported (Ben-Gurion): "In his view, all we need to do is to find a Christian Lebanese officer, perhaps no higher than a captain, and win him over or buy him with money, so that he would declare himself the savior of the Maronite population. Then the Israeli army would enter Lebanon, occupy the territory in question and establish a Christian government which would form an alliance with Israel."[30] Sharett himself considered this an "awful" idea.

Shortly after the conclusion of the agreement with Egypt and before the conclusion of the one with Lebanon, similar talks began with Transjordan. These talks, too, opened in Rhodes and were mediated by Ralph Bunche. There, at the Hotel des Roses, the agreement was signed, after little more than an opening ceremony concluding with the signing of the agreement, which lasted altogether only seven minutes. Not much happened between the Israelis and the Jordanians in Rhodes. "The main problem with the Jordanian delegation is its idiotic personnel," wrote Moshe Dayan.[31] The diplomats dispatched by King Abdullah got on his nerves: "They are bound by their instructions and will not budge from them," he complained. Indeed, they made no decisions and Dayan did not waste time talking to them. The decisive talks had already been held in Europe and Jerusalem and in a series of top secret and lavishly catered meetings held in the King's palaces.

Dayan had played a key role in these talks. The son of Shmuel Dayan—a member of the first Knesset—Moshe Dayan was in effect born into the labor party which gave him an important advantage in the army, many of whose commanders were leftist supporters of MAPAM, and therefore were distrusted by Ben-Gurion. Dayan kept in direct touch with the Prime Minister, going over the heads of his own superior officers, usually without informing them beforehand. Ben-Gurion regularly consulted him. The man with the black eye-patch was then 33 years old. Born in kibbutz Deganiah, Dayan, the soldier, farmer, secret poet, amateur archeologist, politician and statesman, always spoke briefly and to the point, confining himself to what needed, or did not need, to be done that day. This was an ideological age, characterized by much rhetoric, but Dayan was not inhibited by any ideology. He therefore appeared to be moved by purely practical considerations. Generally, but not always, they appeared to be correct. When he was stationed in Jerusalem, Dayan contacted Abdullah Tall, then Commander of the Transjordanian forces in the city. At first they met through the good offices of the UN, in order to solve various local problems and make everyday life in the city easier while the war still went on. In time, they began to meet face to face, just by themselves. Sometimes they met in the Assyrian convent near the Jaffa Gate, at other times in the Mandelbaum house on the outskirts of the orthodox quarter of Mea Shearim. On occasion they met standing between the front lines, amid the land mines at the foot of the Old

City wall. Later they established a direct telephone line. At the end of November 1948 they agreed on a "sincere ceasefire"— along certain lines. In effect, this was the beginning of the division of Jerusalem. Concurrent with the Jerusalem meetings between Dayan and Tall, similar talks between Jordanian and Israeli representatives were held in Paris and London. All of these laid the groundwork for the direct talks to be held in the palaces of King Abdullah.

Contacts between the Zionist movement and the old Bedouin ruler, who was also Britain's protégé, had in fact begun long before. Abdullah had known Moshe Sharett for fifteen years and had also met frequently with Zionist and later Israeli emissary Eliyahu Sasson. Shortly before the establishment of the state, Golda Meirson (Meir) went to see him, disguised as a man, hoping to come to an arrangement which would prevent the war. The King did not like her. Later, when he heard that she had been sent to Moscow as Israeli Ambassador, he commented: "Good. Leave her there."[32]

The meetings in El Shuna and Amman produced multiple reports, some of them contradictory, and others closer to folk tales than history. One of the first meetings with the King after the war was arranged with the intention of bringing about the release of some 700 Israelis who had been captured by the Jordanians in the Etsion bloc and Jerusalem. The King would regale his Israeli guests with royal dinners and entertain them at great length with Oriental witticisms and Arabian legends, deep into the night. After dinner he would amuse them with all kinds of riddles and jokes. Sasson always laughed and obediently praised the King as was expected of guests. Dayan viewed the King's talkativeness as a wearisome nuisance. Eliyahu Sasson was ten years older and intimately familiar with the ways of the East. He was having such a good time that he seemed to have forgotten all about the captives. From time to time Dayan would urge him to get on with it. It was after midnight. The agreement, complete with all the technical details—including the travel expenses for the captives—had all been settled with Tall, and according to Dayan, had also been settled between Tall and the King. But still the King had not said a word about it: "Finally, when I felt that the right time had come," recalled Sasson, "I said to Dayan, now let's get up. So he and I stood, and the King rose too and we all began to walk to the door. I knew that we would probably embrace before parting. That's what had happened at our previous visits. And then, when the King came to embrace me, I quickly slipped my hand under his cummerbund and held on to him. This is an old custom in Arabia. If you manage to do it you'll be given anything you ask for. Abdullah raised his hands and said: 'Elias, ask only for the possible.' That is to say, I'm in your hands, and you can ask whatever you want. I said: 'I'll ask only for the possible.' Some scene it was with everyone standing around and looking on, including Dayan and Tall. I said: 'Your Majesty, you're holding 700 men, women and children, old men and soldiers. Your government has to spend a lot of money to feed them. What for?—Give them to us.' And the King agreed."[33]

Abdullah was known for his friendly attitude and good will toward his Israeli guests; "He kept talking Zionism," Eitan reported to Sharett after one of the meetings with the King.[34] Sometimes they read poetry together, sometimes they exchanged gifts. And at least once they raised the possibility that the Israeli air force would help the Jordanians conquer Damascus: all that needed to be done was to paint the Israeli planes with Jordanian colors.[35]

The Israelis would drive to the meetings with Abdullah in Tall's armored car, dressed in UN uniforms. Dayan replaced his black eye-patch with dark sunglasses, lest he be recognized. If they were late coming back and it was already daylight, they would lie on the floor of the car and Tall would cover them with red *keffiehs* (Arab headgear). In their secret reports Abdullah Tall was codenamed "William," after William Tell. King Abdullah was nicknamed Meir, an anagram of his former title of Emir. Nevertheless, those who needed to know about those clandestine diplomatic ventures knew exactly who was there and what was said. The King's enemies received current reports from Tall, whose loyalty to his sovereign was rather dubious. Years later, when the British Foreign Office and the US State Department opened their files for research, it was learned that both the British and the American ambassadors had been able to brief their governments in detail about these contacts. Only the press, in Israel and abroad, knew nothing about them. It was probably the biggest story missed that year.* Ben-Gurion doubted the rele-

---

*The story was published in detail some ten years later, in the memoirs of Abdullah Tall. They were translated into Hebrew and published by the military publishing house; Moshe Dayan related his version of the story in a series of articles published by the newspaper *Yediot Aharonot*.[36]

vance of this activity. "I doubt if there is any practical point in these talks at all," he wrote in his diary. He thought little of Abdullah, and always wrote the word "king" in quotation marks. Once he wrote: "The old man reminds me of Nahum Sokolow when he was President of the Jewish Agency. Talks pleasantly with no control and without authority. . . ."[37] Sokolow, a journalist and Zionist leader, had been known as a big talker. Sasson was more optimistic. "The King feels that we as friends will have no difficulty in finding a common language," he wired Sharett. "I'm asking therefore that the King be treated generously, patiently, and that we explain things to him as friends with mutual interests and that we wish him well. We should not behave as statesmen who insist on their rights. This is the way we have always behaved with him, and I believe we must continue like this. I have no doubt that in the end we shall get what we want."[38]

Several months before, David Ben-Gurion proposed that Israel attack the Arab Legion and occupy all of Jerusalem, Bethlehem and Hebron, where about 100,000 Arabs lived. "I presumed that most of the Arabs of Jerusalem, Bethlehem and Hebron would flee . . . and then the entire country, as far as the Jordan, north or south of Jericho, as well as all of the western bank of the Dead Sea would be ours," he wrote. But the Cabinet rejected the proposal; years later Ben-Gurion would maintain that this rejection was a fatal error.[39]*

By the time they began negotiating, Israel and Jordan had already unofficially agreed that the territory would be divided between them, and so would the city of Jerusalem. They had also agreed in principle that the Palestinians would have no say in the matter. At the beginning of the negotiations, Abdullah suggested a settlement based on the UN Partition Resolution and the Partition Plan outlined by Count Bernadotte shortly before his assassination in Jerusalem. The Israelis wanted to base the agreement on the military status quo. Abdullah hoped to annex

*In the course of the war Ben-Gurion recorded in his diary all sorts of wild ideas which seemed to possess his mind. "When we destroy the Arab Legion and bomb Amman we'll also finish off Transjordan, and then Syria will fall," he wrote one day. "If Egypt dares to go on fighting—we'll bomb Port Said, Alexandria and Cairo."[40] That was the day he envisioned "the new order" in Lebanon. Some time later he wrote: "Perhaps we shall also bomb Damascus."[41] But several months later he noted: "I'm not particularly sorry that we did not take the West Bank. But I'm very sorry that we did not capture Jerusalem and then go as far as the Dead Sea."[42]

the southern Negev to his kingdom, but agreed to share it with Israel. While he was still talking about it, the Israeli army sent two brigades down to the Red Sea, in order to enhance their political position. On March 10 they reached an abandoned police station at Umm Rashrash, and on its flagpole raised a makeshift white sheet with two blue stripes and a Star of David—hand drawn with ink, as they had forgotten to bring a national flag with them.

Israel now controlled the entire Negev, except for the Gaza Strip; a new city would soon be built at the southern tip, which would be called Eilat. Ben-Gurion's praise was jubilant: "This could well be the greatest event of the last few months, if not of the entire war of liberation and the conquest. And not a drop of blood was spilt."[43] Abdullah conceded his defeat and did not break off the talks. He was greatly concerned about the Gaza Strip. "Keep it," he said to the Israelis, "or give it to the devil—so long as you don't leave it for the Egyptians."[44] The King hoped that Israel would eventually allow him to annex the Strip to Jordan. Israel made some territorial demands of its own, such as free passage to Mount Scopus, to the Mount of Olives cemetery and to the Wailing Wall in the Old City of Jerusalem.

·Eventually it was agreed that Wadi Arah, in the north, with its Hadera-Afulah road, would be turned over to Israel; this meant that Jordan had literally handed over thousands of Palestinian Arabs to Israel without ever consulting them. The armistice agreement set up a variety of arrangements in Jerusalem, including free passage to the Wailing Wall, but Jordan never kept that part of the agreement. The Negev remained in Israeli hands. Abdullah gave in on it, for fear that if he rejected Israel's demands, she would proceed to occupy the entire region of Samaria, as she had the Negev.

Four months after the signing of the agreement with Jordan, a similar agreement was reached with Syria. The preliminary talks that led up to it were the longest and hardest of them all. In the course of the war the Syrians had managed to seize territories beyond the international border. When the negotiations opened, they were holding the area around Mishmar Hayarden, the sector between the international border and the Sea of Galilee, south of Ein Gev, and other areas. Israel demanded that Syria withdraw to the international border and the Syrians refused. Shortly before the talks began there was a military coup in Damascus. The new ruler was a colonel by the name of Husnei

Zaim. Some time after he seized power, Zaim proposed a meeting with Ben-Gurion with the aim of reaching a peace agreement. Moreover, he stated that he would be willing to give permanent residence to between 300,000 and 350,000 Palestinian refugees in his country. On April 16 Ben-Gurion wrote in his diary: "The Syrians have offered to make separate peace with Israel. Cooperation and a joint army. . . . But they want to change the border—to cut across the Sea of Galilee. I instructed . . . that the Syrians be told plainly—first of all, an armistice agreement based on the international border. Then talks about peace and an alliance. We'll be willing to cooperate fully."[45] Two weeks later Ben-Gurion wrote: "It's been agreed to meet with Zaim, and Reuven Shiloah and Yigael Yadin will be proposed [for the meeting], but Zaim may insist on the Prime Minister or the Foreign Minister. Sharett is willing to meet, but not this week."[46]

Two days later, the US Ambassador in Syria, James Kiley, reported that Zaim repeated his offer to settle 350,000 or more Palestinian refugees in his country.[47] That week Ben-Gurion heard from the US Ambassador in Israel, James McDonald, that Zaim and the US Ambassador in Syria were asking the State Department to urge Ben-Gurion to agree to the proposed meeting. Ben-Gurion related, "I said that if Zaim would commit himself in advance to evacuate our territory and withdraw to the international border, I'd be willing to meet with him."[48] The Americans could not believe their ears. Secretary of State Dean Acheson, suspected that Zaim's proposal had not been forwarded to Ben-Gurion. He instructed Ambassador McDonald to tell Ben-Gurion that the United States wanted the meeting to take place.[49]

UN Representative William Riley tried to persuade Foreign Ministry official Shabtai Rozen to press for the meeting, and Rozen reported this at length to Ben-Gurion. Ben-Gurion, as usual, summed things up succinctly: "Riley spoke to Rozen. Zaim wants to develop Syria and accept 300,000 refugees. Riley asks if we would agree to sign an armistice agreement now, on the basis of the existing situation [later there would be further talks on the basis of the UN Partition Resolution]. Rozen replied that our answer was negative."[50] Thus far, no one in the Israeli administration had given serious thought to Zaim's offer to take in 300,000 refugees. Their attention was riveted on the border problem. Only Abba Eban, in the United States, wished to know "why we are unimpressed" by the prospect that Syria would absorb the refugees—the fact that the offer was made struck him as very significant.[51] The American representative in Syria continued to lavish praise on Zaim, on whom he hung "the last hope," provided Israel was willing to compromise, or at least if Ben-Gurion was willing to meet him. Everyone who has met Zaim, reported the American diplomat, was impressed by his sincerity and his open-mindedness toward Israel.[52]

> June 1, 1949. Eban to Sharett: ". . . Bunche, Riley, still believe Zaim–Ben-Gurion meeting could produce first peace treaty between Israel and Arab state. They would be prepared to arrange meeting if we agree. . . ."[53]
> June 2, 1949. Sharett to Eban: ". . . Ben-Gurion against meeting Zaim before Bunche . . . [submits] his proposals."[54]
> June 5, 1949. Sharett to Eban: ". . . Bunche beseeching we not give up meeting. . . . [His representative] freely granted [that] we have been hundred percent right procedurally but Syrians suffer unconquerable inferiority complex vis-à-vis us, therefore we should bear with them. . . ."[55]

After prolonged hesitations and consultations with Ben-Gurion, Sharett announced that he was willing to go to Syria to meet with Zaim and discuss two subjects with him, armistice and peace, in that order. Once an armistice agreement was achieved, including a Syrian withdrawal to the international border, it would be possible to talk about peace. The Syrians were not interested in such a discussion. Sharett hastened to conclude that the whole thing was a fraud. He commented: "Apparently they assumed . . . that we would list such subjects as medieval Arab poetry or Bedouin lore, or maybe even Cartesian philosophy or Japanese art. . . ."[56] A few weeks later Zaim was deposed and executed.*

The armistice talks with the Syrians were held in Hirbet Warda, the no-man's-land, between Mahanayim and Mishmar Hayarden. The Israeli delegation was led by Lt. Colonel Morde-

---

*Ben-Gurion assumed that Zaim was genuinely interested in peace. Shortly before the armistice agreement was signed he noted in his diary:

The fact that Zaim is ready for an armistice which entails complete withdrawal to the border, proves that for some reason he wishes to have good relations with us. Is it because of the conflict with Iraq? The interests of France—Zaim's ally—also favor peace between Syria and Israel. If—as Makleff believes—an armistice agreement is signed this week, it would be desirable to send Sasson to Damascus to inspect the situation. Eitan too believes that the first peace may be with Syria and that Zaim's ambition is to be the first Arab statesman to meet us.[57]

hai Makleff. As in the talks with Lebanon, UN officials Henri
Vigier and William Riley were present, but the main effort was
made by Ralph Bunche, operating from New York. He maneu-
vered as he knew best, often deceiving both parties and finally
bringing them to the point of compromise. The Syrians withdrew, and the territories they vacated were demilitarized.

Ben-Gurion followed the talks closely and made many of the
decisions. He rarely consulted Sharett, but instead preferred the
advice of Moshe Dayan and Reuven Shiloah. Ben-Gurion felt
that his Foreign Minister spent too much time talking and
thinking. Sharett was a rather pathetic figure who paid much attention to both his dress and speech. He was meticulous over
the pettiest of details, mostly concerned with his own dignity,
and an obedient yes-man to Ben-Gurion whom he regarded with
vast admiration and awe. Sharett was more moderate than Ben-
Gurion, more cautious and yielding, and often more judicious.
But he rarely stood up for his own opinions; his moderation, cau-
tion, flexibility and judiciousness served him mostly in selling
Ben-Gurion's policies. This is what happened in the case of the
proposed meeting with Zaim. He himself attached "tremendous
importance" to the Syrian leader's offer to take in refugees, but
the decision was not his.[58]

Reuven Shiloah, like Moshe Dayan, was one of the most interesting people among the policy makers, and like him enjoyed
free access to Ben-Gurion. His opinions were generally, though
not always, listened to. In the Zaim affair they were not: he had
favored the meeting.[59] Shiloah too was one of the most important people at that time, but unlike Dayan, he stayed behind the
scenes, far from both the media and politics. He tended to keep
himself all but invisible, never saying too much, always inquisi-
tive. At the beginning of the War of Independence he was with
Ben-Gurion in the "Red House," the headquarters at that time.
He carried out any number of secret missions and was one of the
founders of the Israeli Intelligence and Espionage services. He
had an analytical and methodical mind and his advice, like that
of Moshe Dayan, was always brief and to the point, which Ben-
Gurion appreciated.

The negotiations leading up to the armistice agreements
were accompanied by a public debate, which reached its climax
in the election campaign for the first Knesset. "All the parties
are ready to make peace," stated Moshe Sharett (MAPAI), "and
we are all equally ready to continue the war, if peace is not

achieved. But the question is whether we should strive for peace on terms which we can live with, or continue to fight for the conquest of the entire country."[60] Menahem Begin (Herut) countered, "There is a peace which leads to war, and there is a true peace, a permanent peace. In Munich, too, 'peace' was supposedly won, yet that 'peace' led to the worst war of all."[61] Herut objected to giving up any part of the historical Land of Israel, and certainly any part of its western portion, west of the Jordan River. Begin's speeches were full of nationalist rhetoric: "They have carved up not the territory," he cried after the agreement with Egypt and before the one with Jordan, "but our very soul!"[62] Other members of his party spoke in similar terms. The poet Uri Tsvi Greenberg observed:

> Right now we might—without exaggeration, if we'd only been ready in time—be across the Jordan and on the slopes of Lebanon and en route to the Nile. And then, instead of a worthless armistice, we would have obtained peace on very comfortable terms to us. . . . The Rhodes talks . . . are a Jewish tragicomedy. . . . The real Jerusalem is only that which is within the walls. . . . What's the point of a State of our own without Jerusalem? Abdullah, King of Jerusalem means an Arab Palestine with a temporary, autonomous Jewish ghetto.[63]

Ben-Gurion replied that it was better to have a Jewish state without all the land of Israel than all the land without a Jewish state. A Jewish state in all the land would be impossible if it wished to be a democracy, he explained—because there were more Arabs than Jews in Palestine. "Would you like in 1949 to have a democratic State of Israel throughout the land; or do you want a Jewish state throughout the land and for us to drive out all the Arabs; or do you want to have democracy in this state?" As for him, he said he preferred a democratic Jewish state, even if it did not possess all the land.[64]

Yet this was not his line of thinking when he proposed the conquest of the West Bank to the Cabinet. He had assumed then that the Arabs would flee or be driven out, and that Jews would come to take their place, ensuring a Jewish majority in the country. Ben-Gurion frequently adapted arguments, explanations and ideological justifications to the political situation which he had created. Herut, on the contrary, demanded to shape reality to correspond to their ideology, and so did the leftist MAPAM (an acronym of the Hebrew for the United Labor Party), which was formed as a socialist party in 1948, based mainly on the *Hasho-mer Hatsair* youth and kibbutz movement. The provisional gov-ernment included two MAPAM ministers, Mordehai Ben-Tov and Aharon Cizling. With the war going on they tried to smooth over their differences, but the minutes of the provisional gov-ernment's meetings show that the MAPAM ministers often adopted clearly oppositional postures which were often more hawkish than those of Ben-Gurion and his party, MAPAI; many of the higher-ranked officers in the army belonged to MAPAM.

MAPAM's position in those days reflected a rather bizarre mixture of military activism, verging on expansionism, and a deep commitment to Jewish–Arab co-existence in peace. They also fostered an anti-imperialist attitude which was not yet di-rected against the United States, but focused on Britain, in spite of the fact that Britain's imperial power was quickly eroding. In their opinion Israel ought to seize the West Bank, and create an independent state for the Palestinian population, which would ensure that it was ruled by "progressive elements," who would make peace with Israel. To achieve this, the party proposed that Israel recruit Israeli–Arab fighters and help them win a state of their own.[65]

Ben-Gurion's response to MAPAM was that it was none of Is-rael's business to create a state for the Palestinian Arabs. "We are not contractors for the construction of an independent Arab state," he said. "We believe it's the business of the Arabs."[66] In his diary he set forth a simple rule: "Peace with the existing, not the imaginary, Arabs. No war for a Palestinian Arab state, no war to place a particular Arab group in power over it. If such a war is needed, let it be a war between Arabs and Arabs and not with us."[67]*

In fact, the "existing Arab" was Abdullah, whom Ben-Gurion had little use for. "He's a worthless man," he noted in his diary,

---

*The Arabs, too, were divided on this issue. Abdullah sought to annex the West Bank, whereas Egypt created a "Palestinian government," otherwise known as the "Gaza government," which claimed to represent the Palestinian Arabs. It enjoyed the protection of Egypt, but had no power whatever. By the end of 1949 all that was left of it was a "Prime Minister" with a secretary, who passed the time issuing communiqués to the press. On the West Bank, Abdul-lah's influence was increasing. He derived his authority from a Palestinian leadership conference which took place in December 1948, the so-called Jericho conference. Abdullah based his claim on this "conference" and Israel recognized it.

and once again compared him to Nahum Sokolow.[68] Yet the contacts with the King went on steadily. Among other issues, there were discussions about regulation of everyday life in divided Jerusalem. This included the possibility of annexing the Jewish Quarter of the Old City to Israel, and giving Jordan an access road to the Mediterranean. In the course of these negotiations, the King received Moshe Sharett, the Foreign Minister, at his palace, and proposed to come to the Israeli side of Jerusalem to have dinner with Ben-Gurion.[69] At one point they drew up a draft for a five-year non-aggression pact.[70] On February 13, 1951, Ben-Gurion would write in his diary: "Transjordan is not something natural and lasting, but one man, who may die at any moment." A week later the King came to pray on the Temple Mount in Jerusalem. An assassin, waiting for him in the crowd, shot him dead.

The armistice agreements put an end to the war that had lasted over a year. Ending it was the most important achievement so far. With the signing of the agreements, Israel was in control of a greater territory than had been allotted to her in the UN Partition Resolution, with far fewer Arab inhabitants than had been projected by the Resolution. The agreement with Egypt referred only to the northwestern part of the Negev; it enabled Israel to occupy its southern part. The agreements with Jordan and Syria also enlarged the state's territory.*

Yet the agreements left many loopholes. The border along the Gaza Strip was penetrable and permitted the infiltration of terrorists. In time this would generate retaliatory actions, leading, in turn, to renewed warfare. The partition line agreed upon between Israel and Jordan was entirely arbitrary, often in total disregard of the disrupted population on the spot. As a result of this agreement, thousands of Arab villagers found themselves living on the Israeli side of the line, while some of their lands remained on the Jordanian side. On the other hand, some lands be-

---

*The United Nations Special Committee on Palestine (UNSCOP), which had prepared the Partition Resolution of 1947, had allotted 62 percent of the territory of Palestine to the Jewish state and 38 percent to the Arab one. The November 29 Resolution itself altered this ratio in favor of the Arabs, giving them 45 percent as opposed to 55 percent to the Jews. Following the conclusion of the armistice agreements, Israel retained nearly 80 percent of the territory and the Arabs about 20 percent. Moshe Sharett, who revealed these figures to his colleagues in MAPAI's secretariat, asked them to keep them secret, "or they might serve as a dangerous weapon against us, like oil on the fire."[71]

longing to Arabs living on the Jordanian side remained in Israeli hands. The border between the two countries, like the one with Egypt, was easily breached by infiltrators, and the settlements established along the border were exposed to constant harassment. Jerusalem was divided with barbed-wire fences and minefields and rows of windowless structures. There were frequent outbursts of gunfire across the boundary line. Mount Scopus was an isolated Israeli enclave, connected to the other side only by a fortnightly convoy. The Hebrew University buildings and the Hadassah hospital stood vacant and began to crumble. In effect, it was no longer possible to bury the Jewish dead on the Mount of Olives, nor visit the ancient cemetery or the Wailing Wall, even though article eight of the agreement was to allow for this.* As for the Israeli–Syrian armistice agreement, no one could tell exactly what areas had been marked as demilitarized zones between the two states, and what the demilitarization entailed. In the course of the years there were many outbursts of hostility along this border, and life in the settlements along it was extremely difficult. The new status quo, then, was far from satisfactory, and the longer it continued, the deeper grew the hostility between the Israelis and the Arabs.

Shortly before the signing of the agreement with Syria, Israel and the Arab states were called upon to take part in a "Conciliation Commission," held in Lausanne, Switzerland, under the auspices of a special UN committee, consisting of representatives from the United States, France and Turkey. The conference produced a plethora of reports, letters and telegrams containing literally tens of thousands of words, but in reality nothing much happened there. Prolonged efforts were required to induce the delegates from Israel, Egypt, Jordan and Syria to agree to an agenda, known as the "Lausanne Protocol." And that was the ex-

---

*In the course of the negotiations various proposals for a redivision of the city were made, including suggestions for the exchange of certain neighborhoods. The Jordanians hoped to get back the Katamon and Baq'a quarters and the "German colony," as well as Talpiot and Ramat Rachel. In return, they were willing to give up the Jewish Quarter in the Old City and certain parts of northwestern Jerusalem. There was a proposal to create a demilitarized zone between the Israeli and the Jordanian side of the city, running through King David Street; the YMCA building and the King David Hotel were to have international, extraterritorial status. When the partition of Jerusalem was drawn on paper the pencil used was too thick—in reality the area it covered was several meters wide. That area ended up as no-man's-land.

tent of it. The Arab states agreed to negotiate with Israel on the basis of the UN Partition Resolution of 1947. Israel responded with the demand that Egypt evacuate the Gaza Strip and Jordan the West Bank—since the UN Assembly had determined that no Arab armies were to remain in the country. The Arabs replied that the problem of the refugees had to be dealt with first—also in accordance with UN Resolutions. Israel maintained that the problem of the refugees had to be solved in the context of an overall peace accord. And so it went. Everybody said exactly what they were expected to say as the talks went round and round in endless circles.

One day, in the latter half of August 1949, Eliyahu Sasson and Reuven Shiloah met with the head of the Egyptian delegation to the Conciliation Commission, Abd el Monaim Moustapha. Their talks lasted seven hours. Sasson later described it in one of his regular letters to Moshe Sharett. This was not the first such meeting between Israelis and an Egyptian diplomat; its course, content and results indicated once again that there was no problem of communication between Israel and the Arab countries. The Arabs "recognized" Israel and were ready to discuss peace, but Israel did not accept the conditions.

The Egyptians demanded that the Negev, as well as the West Bank, become an independent Arab state, serving as a buffer between Egypt and Israel as well as Egypt and Transjordan. The Egyptian diplomat explained that such a buffer zone would permit the settlement of many refugees, including those who were then in Egypt and the Gaza Strip, and possibly others from other areas. The entire northern Negev could be settled, said the Egyptian. With financial aid from the United States and the Arab countries, the project was feasible. Moreover, he felt that the proposal had another advantage. It could be presented as being based on the 1947 Partition Resolution. In exchange, he offered a peace treaty.

Sasson and Shiloah pointed out to the Egyptian that the UN Partition Resolution allotted the Negev to the Jewish State. The Egyptian replied that was an issue he was aware of, but on the other hand, the Partition Resolution had allotted Galilee to the Arabs, and Israel was obviously determined not to give that up. Sasson and Shiloah replied that neither would Israel be willing to give up an inch of the Negev. "In that case," the Egyptian diplomat responded, "there is nothing to talk about, and the two countries had better put their case before the UN General Assembly." He promised that Egypt would abide by the Assembly's decision, and if called upon to do so, would evacuate the Gaza Strip. But then there would be no basis for understanding, for peace and cooperation between the two countries, and war could break out. Not a war of firearms, but a cold war, a political and economic war. At this point, Sasson noted, the Egyptian became rather impassioned. "Understand me," he said, "Egypt does not wish to have a border with Israel. Egypt would have been happy had Israel never existed. It did everything to prevent Israel's independence. Egypt is convinced that an Israeli state, entirely alien to the Arabs, in the midst of an ocean of Arabs, would inevitably be a permanent source of conflict, complications and instability in the Middle East." "Perhaps," he added, "Egypt is mistaken in its assessment of Israel's nature and her intentions. But words alone cannot, at least for the present, erase that possibly erroneous impression in Egypt. Egypt will not feel secure with three or four million educated, energetic and self-sacrificing Jews living across her Negev border." This was why he wanted to establish a "buffer state" in the Negev.

The Israelis tried to convince him that he was mistaken. "Your fears are groundless," they told him. The Egyptian reiterated that he might be mistaken, but that his country had to take the worst possibilities into consideration. The Israelis also told him that even if the UN Assembly resolved that she must give up the Negev, Israel would have to disregard it, because the Negev is essential to her.* The Egyptian said: "Do as you please!" Sasson: "This argument about the Negev made it impossible for us to discuss other issues with him. When we tried to do so, he said there was no point. When we wanted to arrange another meeting, he said he was always willing to meet with us, but if that was our position, it would be better not to talk politics at all."[73]†

*Ben-Gurion believed that the entire Negev would be densely populated. In his diary he listed the natural resources hidden in its soil. The Ben-Gurion Institute in Sde-Boker, which is in charge of his estate, crossed out one word in this list; judging from its length it could well have been uranium.[72]

†Shiloah and Sasson talked in a similar vein with Samir a Rifai, later Prime Minister of Jordan. They met with him in Abdullah's winter palace at Shune. Abdullah welcomed them but later withdrew and did not take part in the talks. The Jordanian statesman, like the Egyptian, told the Israelis that the Negev was a wedge in the Arab territorial space. If Jordan obtained the Negev, she

A few weeks after the UN Partition Resolution, Ben-Gurion had promised his party that "major changes" would take place in the demographic composition of the country. He was referring to the Arabs, whom he expected to leave. In his view, this was a desirable development.[75] Indeed, tens of thousands of Arabs abandoned their homes during those months. A few weeks before the Declaration of Independence, Ben-Gurion said: "Now history has shown who is really attached to this country, and for whom this country is a luxury which is easily given up. So far, not a single Jewish settlement, however remote, helpless or isolated, has been abandoned. The Arabs, on the other hand, have abandoned entire cities, like Tiberias and Haifa, with the greatest of ease, after their very first defeat. Despite the fact that they did not have to fear destruction or massacre. Indeed, it has now been made amply clear which people is deeply attached to this country."[76] At the time of these statements, the chronicles of Zionist settlement had already noted several instances of abandoned Jewish settlements. The Partition Resolution had already placed several Jewish settlements outside of the area allotted to the Jews. In the course of the war several Jewish settlements could not withstand the Arab attacks and their inhabitants either fled or surrendered. The armistice agreements had also stipulated that certain places be given up.[77] Many Arabs did indeed leave their homes, but not the country. They found shelter among relatives in areas which seemed more secure. Many had left their homes before the war, and yet others fled in terror after the massacre of Deir Yassin.* Some Arabs left, believing that they would return in a few days bringing up the rear of the victorious Arab armies. Some left despite attempts made by certain

---

could justify her pacifist policy in the eyes of the Arab world. Ben-Gurion: "Our people explained to him that it was out of the question. We would make no territorial concessions. We would only agree to free access to the sea. Territory was out."[74]

*This massacre occurred when members of the Irgun Zvai Leumi (IZL) and Lehi (the so-called Stern Gang), both Jewish right-wing terrorist organizations, attacked the Arab village of Deir Yassin located on the outskirts of Jerusalem, at the height of the war, on April 9, 1948, only four weeks before the Declaration of Independence. Over two hundred villagers, many of them women and children, were killed. The rest were paraded through the streets of Jerusalem and then forced to cross over to the Arab part of the city. The Jewish Agency strongly denounced this action. The massacre at Deir Yassin, like that of the Jews of Hebron nearly twenty years earlier, became a landmark in the chronicles of the Israeli–Arab conflict and a symbol of the horrors of war.

Israeli leaders who tried to persuade them to remain. Some fought against the Israeli army and fled only after they had been defeated in battle. Still others must have heard the same reports about the Israeli troops that also reached the Prime Minister. "I'm shocked by the deeds that have reached my ears," he said to members of his party, some time after the war had reached its climax.[78]

During those months, he had been informed of murderous acts—or "slaughter," as he put it—and rape, which were committed by Israeli soldiers. Such reports intensified the panic and flight of the Arabs.[79]*

Tens of thousands of Arabs remained in their homes—only to be driven out by the Israeli army.

The minutes of the Ministerial Committee for Abandoned Property record the following:

> E. Kaplan reported that "the conquest of Lydda and Ramlah has now, for the first time, confronted us with the problem of possessing an area occupied by a very large number of Arabs. The total number of inhabitants in these two towns and the adjoining villages is estimated at several tens of thousands."
>
> B. Shitrit had "visited occupied Ramlah and observed the situation close up. The army proposed to capture all the men who are capable of bearing arms (except for those who signed the letter of surrender), take them as far as the Arab border and set them loose. Mr. Shitrit contacted the Foreign Minister and asked him

---

*Reports of atrocities committed by Israeli soldiers during the course of the conquest, and also afterwards, preoccupied the government in several of its sessions. The information which reached the ministers shocked them and led to one of the most severe comments ever made in a Cabinet meeting. Aharon Cizling, Minister of Agriculture, said,

> I've received a letter on the subject. I must say that I have known what things have been like for some time and I have raised the issue several times already here. However after reading this letter I couldn't sleep all night. I felt the things that were going on were hurting my soul, the soul of my family and all of us here. I could not imagine where we came from and to where are we going. . . . I often disagreed when the term Nazi was applied to the British. I wouldn't like to use the term, even though the British committed Nazi crimes. But now Jews too have behaved like Nazis and my entire being has been shaken. . . . Obviously we have to conceal these actions from the public, and I agree that we should not even reveal that we're investigating them. But they must be investigated. . . .[80]

Yaakov Shimshon Shapira was designated to conduct this investigation.[81] When he brought his findings before the government it was decided to appoint a special committee which would "advise the government on methods to prevent acts of atrocity by the army against the civilian population."[82]

to formulate a policy. The Foreign Minister's reply was that
those inhabitants who wished to remain could do so, provided
the State of Israel did not have to support them. Those who
wished to leave could also do so."

E. Kaplan: "Discussed the problem of the population of Ramlah and
Lydda with the Minister of Defense [Ben-Gurion] and received
an answer which to a certain extent contradicts that of the Foreign Ministry. The Minister of Defense replied that the young
men should be taken captive, the rest of the inhabitants ought
to be encouraged to leave, but those who remain, Israel will
have to provide for."[83]

Two days later Ben-Gurion wrote: "The Arab Legion has
wired that there are 30,000 refugees moving along the road between Lydda and Ramlah, who are infuriated with the Legion.
They're demanding bread. They should be taken across the Jordan river."[84]*

Hundreds of thousands of Arabs had already fled, or had been
driven out of, the country when the army—following a proposal
made by the Minister of Agriculture in July—issued the following order:

Except in the course of actual fighting, it is forbidden to destroy,
burn or demolish Arab towns and villages, or to expel Arab inhabitants from their villages, neighborhoods and towns, or uproot inhabitants from their homes without express permission of an order

---

*Years later Itzhak Rabin recalled a meeting at which he asked Ben-Gurion
what was to be done with the inhabitants of Lydda and Ramlah. According to
him, Ben-Gurion responded with a gesture which Rabin interpreted as indicat-
ing expulsion. And that, he said, was what happened in Lydda: the people were
marched to the border. Ramlah learned the lesson and its inhabitants agreed to
leave of their own accord, on condition that they be given vehicles to take
them, and this was done. These details were to be included in Rabin's memoirs, but were barred from publication in Israel. Some time later they were
quoted in the New York Times and caused a furor. Yigal Allon firmly denied
them. However, the instruction "to encourage the inhabitants to leave" seems
to suggest that Rabin's version was true, as does also the following comment
by the Minister of Agriculture, Aharon Cizling, at a Cabinet meeting:

I have to say that this phrase [regarding the treatment of Ramlah's inhabitants] is a
subtle order to expel the Arabs from Ramlah. If I'd received such an order this is how
I would have interpreted it. An order given during the conquest which states that
the door is open and that all the Arabs may leave, regardless of age and sex, or they
may stay, however, the army will not be responsible for providing food. When such
things are said during the actual conquest, at the moment of conquest, and after all
that has already happened in Jaffa and other places. . . . I would interpret it as a warning, "Save yourselves while you can and get out!"[85]

from the Minister of Defense, in each and every case. Anyone violating this order will be liable to prosecution.[86]

Some time later, the Ministers were informed that all the inhabitants of Beersheba—women, children "and some of the men"—had been transferred "at their own request" to Egyptian territory. The Minister of Finance asked if it was true that the army had deported several hundreds of the inhabitants of Ashdod who had met it with white flags. The Military Governor Elimelih Avner replied that he was in possession of a report which stated that the army found Ashdod entirely abandoned.[87] In Galilee it was mainly the Moslems who were expelled. An officer from the police national headquarters, who had visited the villages of Elabun and Mrar in November 1948, reported:

> All the inhabitants of Elabun were deported, except for four villagers who are Greek Orthodox, and a small number of old people and children. The total number of inhabitants left in the village is 52. The priests complained bitterly about the expulsion of the villagers and demanded their return. . . . In Mrar, most of the inhabitants remained, except for many of the Moslems.[88]

Ben-Gurion tended to ignore the human tragedy of the Palestinian Arabs. He viewed their plight with the same pragmatic purposefulness which generally characterized his national policy: "Land with Arabs on it and land without Arabs on it are two very different types of land," he told his party's central committee, as if he were a real-estate agent discussing business.[89] A month later he called in his advisors to discuss the inclusion of Arab villages in Israeli territory, following the agreement with Jordan.

The minutes of that meeting record:

Ben-Gurion: "Do we want the Arabs who live in the territory ceded by Abdullah to remain or to leave?"

Sasson: "I think it's better that they remain, for several reasons."

Lifshitz, an aide: "I think it's better that they leave."

Ben-Gurion: "I want to think about it some more."[90]*

---

*By the armistice agreement with Jordan, Israel had undertaken the responsibility not to harm the villagers who would now be under her jurisdiction, and in fact most of them were left in peace. But while the negotiations were taking place it was assumed that these Arabs would be expelled. "I imagine that the intention is to get rid of them," said Moshe Sharett. "The interests of security demand that we get rid of them."[91] A Foreign Ministry file contains an extraordi-

The Israeli policy regarding the refugees took shape gradually. Three weeks after the Declaration of Independence, while the war was still raging and the country was rapidly emptying out its Arab inhabitants, Foreign Minister Sharett had been made aware of an announcement made over the radio by the spokesman of the Jewish Agency. It was announced that Israel would be willing to take back the refugees, and even to compensate them. Sharett hastily instructed his Director General not to repeat such announcements. "We must not be understood to say that once the war is over they can return," he warned, but added: "We'll keep every option open."[93] Ten days later Sharett wrote Dr. Nahum Goldmann that "the most spectacular event in the contemporary history of Palestine, in a way more spectacular than the creation of the Jewish state, is the wholesale evacuation of its Arab population. . . . The opportunities opened up by the present reality for a lasting and radical solution of the most vexing problem of the Jewish state, are so far-reaching, as to take one's breath away. The reversion to the *status quo ante* is unthinkable," he declared.[94]

In a June session of the provisional government, Ben-Gurion said that even after the war he would oppose the return of the refugees. Sharett repeated those words to Count Bernadotte.[95] "He was hard as a rock," Bernadotte noted later.[96] Yet in September Ben-Gurion still said to the US Ambassador in Israel, James McDonald, that "the door was not shut" on the possible return of refugees; "in the context of negotiations for a peace treaty, everything will be negotiable," he promised.[97]

Yosef Weitz, head of the Jewish National Fund, pleaded with him to take a firm and unequivocal stand against any possibility of restoring the Palestinian refugees to their homes. In the latter half of September, Weitz proposed a series of measures which would drive the refugees far from the border areas, deep into the

---

nary document in connection with this, by Walter Eitan, in which he wrote to his minister:

> I don't know how Shiloah and Dayan felt about this, but certainly Yadin and I had qualms, and, if you like, moral reservations, about what we were doing. . . . In spite of all guarantees and fine phrases, it was as clear to the Transjordanians as to us that the people of these villages were likely to become refugees. . . . The people who are letting these Arab villagers down are of course the Transjordanians, but that does not make it any more agreeable for us. We are partners in this deal, and it is we, not the Transjordanians, who will be blamed for its results.[92]

Arab hinterland. "They must be harassed continually," he in-sisted.[98] Ben-Gurion instructed him to study the subject to-gether with Zalman Lifshitz, surveyor and cartographer, and Ezra Danin, Arabist and secret advisor. The three were described as the "Transfer Committee." In October, they brought their findings to Ben-Gurion: "(a) The Arabs themselves are responsi-ble for their flight; (b) They must not be allowed to come back, because they will be a fifth column and generate dissent. Their economy has been destroyed and their rehabilitation would cost the state huge sums, far beyond its means. . . ."

The committee recommended that if Israel were compelled to take back refugees, she must categorically refuse to return them to their villages—only to the towns, where they should not exceed 15 percent of the Jewish population. They estimated the number of refugees at about half a million or more.[99] At the end of October, Ben-Gurion received a report from Galilee: "In all the villages where we fought the population has already fled, but many more will still flee."[100]

As time went on and the number of refugees increased, oppo-sition to their return hardened, and Israeli spokesmen began to express it in so many words. "What happened happened, and there's no bringing back the past," said Dov Yosef, the military governor of Jerusalem, to the UN Reconciliation Commis-sion.[101] The US delegate to that commission reported to his su-periors in Washington that he kept reiterating to the Israelis that their attitude was cruel, but they remained unmoved.[102] Mean-while, the Middle East department of the Foreign Ministry was rife with speculations about the future. The department staff es-timated that the refugees would "manage." As they put it, "the most adaptable and best survivors would manage by a process of natural selection, and the others will waste away. Some will die but most will turn into human debris and social outcasts and probably join the poorest classes in the Arab countries."[103] Ben-Gurion informed the Minister for Immigration, Moshe Shapira, that the "Government line is that they may not return."[104] That was in April 1949. The "Transfer Committee" had already concluded its plans for the resettlement of the refugees in the Arab countries, when it suddenly received a new and top secret order: Foreign Minister Sharett asked that the committee pre-pare a plan for "the eventuality that the government will be compelled to return some of the refugees to Israel." This plan, he told them, "must determine the maximum acceptable number

of returnees, the method of selecting them and the areas and settlements in which they might be allowed to resettle."[105] Some
months later Weitz wrote Sharett to say that the refugee problem was causing him "great anxiety"; he feared they were already coming back.

> Every day our men encounter familiar faces, people who had been
> absent, and now they are walking about freely and, step by step, re-
> turning to their villages. I fear that while you are discussing the is-
> sue in Lausanne and in other places, the problem is (unfortunately)
> solving itself—the refugees are coming back! And our government
> has taken no action to stop the infiltration. There seems to be no
> authority, either military or civilian. We've loosened the rope, and
> the Arab, with his sly cunning, senses it and knows how to take ad-
> vantage of it.

Weitz warned that the idea that the refugee problem would solve
itself in time was an illusion. "The ring of embittered Arabs surrounding us with hatred and vengeance on all sides will not be
loosened for many years to come, and will act as a barrier to a
genuine peace between us and our neighbors."* Weitz concluded that it was necessary to issue a "firm and unequivocal"
statement to the effect that not a single refugee would be allowed back, except within the framework of family reunification, but nevertheless the government of Israel would undertake
a major part of the cost of resettling them in the Arab countries.
"And if the Minister of Finance should ask, where is the money
to come from?" Weitz went on, "the answer is obvious: the people of Israel will give! . . . If we were willing to purchase peace at
the cost of many dear lives, would we refrain from purchasing it
with money?!"[107]†

Weitz knew what he was talking about. A few days after his
letter to Sharett, the latter told the US Ambassador, McDonald,
that in the past few months some 24,000 refugees had returned
to Israel. The Ambassador interpreted this as a softening of the

---

*In one of the Cabinet meetings, Aharon Cizling, Minister of Agriculture,
said: "We still do not properly appreciate what kind of enemy we are now nur-
turing outside the borders of our state. Our enemies, the Arab states, are a mere
nothing compared with those hundreds of thousands of Arabs who will be
moved by hatred and hopelessness and infinite hostility to wage war on us, regardless of any agreement that might be reached. . . ."[106]

†Ben-Gurion held that this was an unnecessary expenditure, as the refugee
problem would solve itself. "In his opinion," Weitz noted in his diary, "time
will cure all, and all will be forgotten."[108]

Israeli position.[109] Six weeks later Sharett informed McDonald that Israel would be willing to take back 100,000 refugees, on the condition that return would be part of a general and final solution of the entire refugee problem. McDonald thought that this was "a step in the right direction"; the Americans held, however, that Israel should take back 250,000 refugees.[110]

The proposed initiative to absorb 100,000 refugees* was the outcome of a misunderstanding resulting from the proposal to annex the Gaza Strip to Israel as part of a peace settlement with Egypt. Israel had agreed to the proposal. Moshe Sharett told the Foreign Affairs and Security Committee of the Knesset that the government hoped to obtain "considerable advantages" from the annexation of the Strip, such as the additional territory, the removal of the Egyptian presence from Israel's border to the other side of the Sinai desert, and the elimination of the possibility that the Strip would be annexed by Jordan, or anyone else.[111] Some time later it was learned that the government had wrongly estimated the number of refugees in the Gaza Strip. When the government had agreed to annex it, it figured that the Strip's total population numbered no more than 180,000; later it turned out that the correct figure was 310,000, 230,000 of whom were refugees. At that point Sharett suggested that there should be no more talk about the Gaza Strip. The announcement that Israel was willing to accept 100,000 refugees had therefore in effect represented a withdrawal from its earlier willingness to accept more than twice that number.

Sharett tried to represent the entire matter as a "tactic" to the Foreign Affairs and Security Committee, but he was not believed. When the issue came up in the Knesset the debate was exceptionally heated, marked by much shouting and frequent insults. Ben-Gurion employed his favorite diversionary tactic of changing the subject, and began speaking about the conduct of the Opposition on the eve of the war. Within minutes everyone was heatedly and loudly arguing about that, and the subject of the refugees seemed to be forgotten.[112] The US Consul in Jerusalem reported to the Secretary of State in Washington that the fury caused by the government's decision to permit the return of refugees was an artificial one, created purposefully by the gov-

*The figure of 100,000 was not the outcome of a study or a real estimate. It was arbitrarily fixed, perhaps from force of habit, as in the years before the creation of the state the demand was often made to permit 100,000 Jewish DPs to settle in the country. That figure, too, was an arbitrary one.

ernment itself. But a few days later the US Chargé d'affaires corrected the Consul's observation. "The fury was genuine," he stated.[113]*

Even inside MAPAI there was a tempestuous argument. Its Knesset members and leaders were in a state of shock, and some even proposed voting against the government. "This is a hair-raising proposal," one of them said, and then proceeded to state that "accepting Arab refugees is a prescription for war, because the front will adjoin every house in Israel. The refugees will not be a fifth column—they will be the first column!" Another warned that public opinion was entirely opposed to the government and called for a way out of the situation. Moshe Sharett tried to reassure them. It was not a question of 100,000, but that number minus those who had already made their way back; thus it was a question of some 65,000, at the most, and it was not intended to return them to their homes, but to resettle them wherever the government saw fit, perhaps in some remote region, out of sight. "I am willing to pay sixty-five thousand Arabs for peace and a solution to the border problem," he said, greatly agitated. His colleagues answered that the Arabs would not agree to end the conflict in return for Israel's acceptance of 65,000 refugees. "For them it would be tantamount to a second defeat. They can divide sixty-five thousand refugees among them and they don't need this gesture on our part."[115] "If they don't want it, we won't pay," replied Sharett. And, of course, that's how it stayed.† Before long the entire affair was forgotten, much like that bizarre notion "to hasten the peace" by means of a Palestinian puppet government-in-exile, to be headed by Attorney Nimer Houari.**

*The US Consul in Jerusalem had doubts about the value of the Israeli proposal to accept 100,000 refugees. In a letter to Secretary of State Acheson, the Consul, William Burdett, reported on a meeting of the Israel–Jordan armistice commission which dealt with the case of some 1,000 villagers whom Israel had expelled from Baq'a el Gharbieh and forced across the border. Moshe Dayan commented that the United Nations could compel Israel to take the refugees back, but if they did, "they would be sorry." The Consul felt that those words cast a new light on the true value of the Israeli proposal.[114]

†Sharett had been forced to deal with the rebellious party on his own—Ben-Gurion did not come to help him out. When Yosef Weitz complained to Ben-Gurion about the decision to accept refugees, Ben-Gurion maintained that the decision was made "against his judgment." "In any case," Ben-Gurion said, "they are not returning yet."[116]

**Houari led a right-wing Arab youth movement, the *Nejjada*. Eliyahu Sasson proposed making him the "Prime Minister" of a government-in-exile,

The question then remains whether Israel ever intended to take back tens of thousands of refugees, or whether it was a mere "tactic." There was scarcely a chance that the Arabs would have accepted the proposal, and it was similarly unlikely that public opinion in Israel would have let the government carry out its promise. In any event, there were some in the Foreign Ministry who considered the project seriously. There was the committee appointed by Sharett to study it, and there were some who hastily drafted a loyalty oath to be signed by the returning refugees: "In return for being accepted by the Government of Israel as a citizen with all the rights of citizenship," read one of the drafts, "I hereby swear and declare that I seek peace and will be loyal to the State of Israel, abide by her laws and obey the orders of her government, be willing to fight her enemies and give my life for her." The officials debated the exact wording of the oath. "With regard to the first sentence," wrote one of them to the other, "I don't think that it's desirable to link the Arab's declaration of loyalty as a citizen of Israel to any commitment on our part. The declaration is unilateral: not a contract between the Arab and the State of Israel." They corresponded on the subject as if it were about to become a reality.[118] Yet one day Ben-Gurion noted in his diary: "Abba Eban came. He sees no point in chasing after peace. The armistice agreement is sufficient for us. If we chase after peace the Arabs will demand a price: either territory, return of refugees, or both. It's best to wait a few years." The Prime Minister noted those words without making any comment of his own.[119]

A few weeks later, the Lausanne conference adjourned with no results. Moshe Sharett did not regret its failure: "Any bad compromise which would serve as the basis for a permanent peace accord could be a fatal error," he wrote Abba Eban. Evidently, he did not believe in the possibility of a good compromise, because the price would have been too high.[120]

While still doing his best to arrange a meeting between Zaim and Ben-Gurion, the US representative in Damascus attempted to predict what would be the verdict of history: Israel may discover that she has won the war with Palestine, he wrote to his

---

supported by Israel, and Sharett made no objection. Houari came to Lausanne and Sasson paid his hotel bill—probably the sole practical aspect of the affair. Eventually Houari was allowed to settle in Nazareth and was made an Israeli judge.[117]

chief, the US Secretary of State, but lost the peace.[121] The United States administration applied considerable pressure on Israel to show greater flexibility. Various American diplomats ascribed the deadlock to both sides, but believed that the chance for peace depended on Israel. Mark Ethridge, the US delegate to the Lausanne conference, wrote President Truman that Israel's inclination to base her future on her military security, while forgoing the chance of making peace, seemed "unbelievable," in view of her being such a tiny state. According to him, he had tried to explain to the Israelis that they were endangering their own future and that of the entire Western world, but his efforts had been in vain.[122]

By August the American Secretary of State had come to the conclusion that chances of reaching a compromise were nil. Mr. Acheson told the US ambassadors in the Middle East that Israel had finally opted for the status quo. He did add, however, that the Arab governments also preferred the existing state of affairs, having submitted to the hawkish public opinion they had themselves created—just as the government of Israel had done.[123] A few weeks earlier Reuven Shiloah had explained to Ben-Gurion that President Truman was now inclined to support the Arabs, because he sympathized with the suffering of the Palestinian refugees, just as he had earlier supported the Zionist cause because he had sympathized with the Jewish refugees, survivors of the Holocaust.[124] Truman had personally intervened to save the Rhodes talks. He wrote to both Ben-Gurion and Israel's President Haim Weizmann. Ben-Gurion noted in his diary that the American President's letter was worded in "harsh and threatening" language. Truman demanded that Israel compensate the Arabs for the loss of the territories which had not been assigned to her by the UN Partition Resolution. Ben-Gurion wrote:

> The State of Israel was not established as a consequence of the UN Resolution. Neither America nor any other country saw the Resolution through, nor did they stop the Arab countries (and the British mandatory government) from declaring total war on us in violation of UN Resolutions. America did not raise a finger to save us, and moreover, imposed an arms embargo, and had we been destroyed they would not have resurrected us. Those boundaries determined in the UN Resolution were based on peace accords, the validity of international law, and the Arabs' acceptance of them. But the Arabs rejected it. There are no refugees—there are fighters who sought to destroy us, root and branch. The Arab states came at

their request, and they still refuse to make peace or to recognize us, and are openly threatening revenge. Shall we bring back the refugees so that they can exterminate us for the second time, or should we ask America to take pity on us and send an army to protect us? America is immense. We are a tiny and helpless nation. We could not withstand American might, but our self-preservation is more important to us than obedience to America. The rebuke and the threatening style [of Truman's letter] are incomprehensible.[125]

Sometime during this exchange, a phrase was coined which would serve Israel countless times in the future: "International law does not require that Israel commit suicide."[126]*

In time, Ben-Gurion would be accused of sacrificing opportunities for peace in order to preserve the tension which was needed to unify Israeli society and keep MAPAI in power. Some would claim that Israel missed a number of opportunities to make peace.

The minutes of the closed sessions, the secret telegrams exchanged by government leaders, as well as Ben-Gurion's personal diary, all indicate, however, that there was genuine willingness to reach a settlement, but not at any price: "Please indicate how much political importance you ascribe to a successful conclusion of negotiations," wired Director General Eitan to Foreign Minister Sharett, shortly after the talks with Egypt began.[129] Both in the armistice agreements and at Lausanne, the Israeli delegates concentrated on the price that would have to be paid for peace. They were tough hagglers; time after time they became so involved with the minor details that they lost sight of the overall picture and were unable to distinguish between the major and lesser issues. In seeking to extract from

---

*While the negotiations were going on, the US delegate at Lausanne accused the American Ambassador in Israel of failing to use his influence to advance the positions of the US State Department in Israel. James McDonald, formerly High Commissioner for Refugees in Geneva, was known to be a great friend of Israel. Now President Turman left the reprimanding of McDonald up to his Secretary of State.[127] One day that summer, Eliyahu Sasson left Lausanne for Paris to meet McDonald, who was staying there on his way back from Tel Aviv to Washington. "I don't know if it was worth the effort, but I did it for old times' sake," he wrote Sharett. He reported that McDonald was depressed. "He said he feared his standing in the White House, and even more in the State Department, was in jeopardy, that he was being used as a messenger boy and was not being consulted about policy. During his stay in Washington he would try to find out whether there was any point left in his remaining at his present post."[128]

these negotiations various territorial advantages and defense guarantees, a hill here, a road there, the suspension of the actual fighting seemed to count for little. "The armistice agreement with Lebanon gained us nothing. On the contrary, it was Lebanon who gained," commented Ben-Gurion.[130] Only Eliyahu Sasson perceived that in these negotiations lay the chance of achieving lasting Jewish–Arab coexistence. He maintained that Israel must strive to integrate into the Arab world.[131] Sasson arrived in Rhodes toward the end of the talks with Egypt, and made a great contribution to their ultimate success by means of informal conversations with the Egyptians, in which he projected a sense of mutual confidence, friendliness, moderation and ease. He warned that his colleagues' rigidity would make future relations between Israel and Egypt much more difficult. "The Egyptians kept reiterating that they regarded the armistice agreement as only the first step toward the future," he stated in one of his telegrams, demanding greater generosity.[132] "It is essential that both you and Ben-Gurion devote all your strength toward peace, just as you did toward defense," he wrote Sharett. But he was not heeded because he was not considered to be a practical man.[133]

The price the Arabs wanted for peace was indeed very high. They demanded the Negev and the return of the refugees. One could interpret this hard-line position as an indication of the Arabs' unwillingness really to negotiate. However, one could view their position as just an opening bid later to be modified during the normal course of negotiations. Israel's position was based on several erroneous assumptions, some of which could have been recognized at the time. Ben-Gurion assumed that time was on Israel's side. If she could hold out, grow strong and build up a deterrent force, the Arab states would have to recognize her and the armistice boundaries. In time, the refugees would become absorbed wherever they happened to be, and thus the source of conflict would completely disappear. This was an error. As far as the Arabs were concerned, the armistice lines were lines of defeat. They could never agree to make them borders of peace. It also became apparent that the longer the Palestinians felt they had been abandoned, and the longer they remained in exile, the stronger their national consciousness grew and the more diminished the chances of resettling them in Arab countries. Some warned Ben-Gurion that this would happen, but he ignored their pleas, and failed to take into account the unifying power of exile and homesickness.

Ben-Gurion also believed that the right thing to do was to obtain an accord with Egypt, the biggest Arab state, yet he gambled on the King of Jordan. That, too, was an error. The agreement with Israel was so humiliating for Jordan, that the King had tried to keep its details secret even from his own ministers, and the more he was humiliated, the harder it became for Egypt to compromise with Israel. Thus the price of peace went up as time went on. Time was not on Israel's side.

Would the Israeli government have shown greater moderation had it been aware that its tough posture was laying the foundation for a long-standing, perhaps even eternal, enmity between Israel and the Arabs? Perhaps not. For beside the rationalist pragmatism which characterized Ben-Gurion's government, there were the alienation and suspicion, the hostility and fear which distorted the thinking of both the government and the public. The government was generally responsive to the public. At all times it was subjected to loud and persistent criticism. The Opposition, on both Left and Right, repeatedly charged it with being soft and having a defeatist mentality. Such charges could be heard inside MAPAI, too. The last five years had been stamped by the Holocaust, Arab terror and British repression. The War of Independence had been very fierce, and had greatly deepened the hostility between the two peoples. Having been considered an unavoidable war for actual survival, it became a glorious war of conquest. All these factors promoted rigidity instead of moderation. At times the government found that the public mood was much more hawkish than that of the ministers, and the ministers could not ignore the public.

But the government also had those who thought and talked as conquerors, with their many victories heightening their ambitions. David Horowitz, of the Ministry of Finance and later Governor of the Bank of Israel stated:

> It depends largely on us, whether King Abdullah will last, because he's primitive and backward. The standard of living is low: There are no parties, there is no democracy. There is nothing. That's because they're living at a pre-capitalist level. As for us, if we triple the population in a few years, our GNP will equal that of the entire Arab world put together. We shall have an industrialized country. . . . Time is on our side. In another five years we shall be a tremen-

dous power in this region and we shall be able to absorb easily two million people. We'll be an economic, social and military force. We shall be the major factor in the development of this area, and as a result the focus will be on us. . . . Abdullah, more than anyone else, will be dependent on us.

Horowitz favored the annexation of the West Bank to Jordan, because it would become a burden on its economy. As a result, Jordan would depend on Israel as the market for its agricultural produce, thereby becoming politically dependent as well. Yigael Yadin warned against letting Jordan annex strategic territories, but Horowitz thought in different terms: "It is known that in a modern state military potential is a function of industry and men. Our men are on a completely different cultural and moral level. The immigration is causing us to grow at great speed, and even if the Arabs should develop at an incredibly feverish pace they will be unable to keep up with us. . . ." Ben-Gurion asked, "Where do we get Jews from?" but Horowitz replied that once there was (industrial) development, Jews would come from many countries, including the United States.[134] Some time later Horowitz suggested bribing the leaders of the Arab countries to adopt a more favorable position toward Israel.[135] Yadin asked, as though he were attending the Versailles conference: "Will we have to waive their war debts?" He proposed a long-term strategy of setting the Arab countries against each other. "We can use the accepted method of divide and conquer," he said, "and I think that we will get good results."[136]

In addition to the political discussions they also frequently considered military action. Yadin: "The border with Jordan should be on the first mountain range. There is really no other logical border; if we can't obtain this by negotiation, with a clear presentation of the issue, then we must do so with military force, and the time to do so is approaching."[137]

In March, Ben-Gurion wrote to the Committee of Settlements in the Jordan Valley: "We have not, of course, forgotten El Kasr and Kafr Samra, and we're still demanding their liberation in our diplomatic negotiations. . . . If we cannot liberate these places peacefully then we will liberate them by other means."[138] In April he said, "There is really only one type of pressure: if Syria refuses to sign the armistice agreement on the basis of the international border, we shall have to seize it by force."[139] Six weeks later, Dayan proposed the occupation of Mount Scopus.[140] The military option was always a possibility for them, so there was no rush to achieve their goals through negotiations. Even Sasson told Ben-Gurion that there was no reason to fear an Arab attempt to reopen hostilities, even if there was no peace.[141] The more they trusted their ability to realize the goals of the state "by other means," the less they were inclined to compromise. None of the participants in those discussions ever proposed considering what they could actually give up in return for peace.

During those months, Israeli representatives often met with Arab officials who said they wanted peace. The files of the Foreign Ministry, as well as the Prime Minister's diaries, are full of detailed reports about such meetings. Therefore, contact with the Arabs, in itself, was not considered a great achievement. Ben-Gurion did not feel that he might be missing something if he declined to meet with the Syrian ruler. It was assumed that there would be further opportunities to do so in the future.

Before long there was a school of thought in the Foreign Ministry which counseled that any peace agreement would not be worthwhile at present. Foreign Minister Sharett told the MAPAI members of the Knesset that in the Foreign Ministry there were "some very creative people, who contribute a good deal to the formation of the Ministry's general philosophy," and they tend to be satisfied with the armistice agreements. Thus they suggest "to stop reiterating declarations about our desire for peace, since the Arab world interprets them as a sign of weakness and as an indication of our willingness to surrender. We should say the opposite: We do not need peace. We are satisifed with the present agreement. Perhaps the Arabs need peace." Sharett went on to explain at length why Israel could not afford to remain in "malignant isolation" for long, and how she could profit from peace in the areas of tourism and commerce, citing the use of the Suez Canal as an example. Yet he also stated, "I quite agree that from a tactical point of view we should desist from those declarations about our striving for peace and our desire for peace . . . as if it were a daily prayer."[142] Ben-Gurion told a correspondent from the London Times: "Though I would get up in the middle of the night to sign a peace treaty, I am in no rush. I can wait ten years. We are under no pressure."[143]

On December 9, 1949, the UN General Assembly resolved that Jerusalem should be a "separate body," governed by an international authority. The resolution was carried by a large majority; it called for a response. Ben-Gurion proposed that the government transfer the Knesset from Tel Aviv to Jerusalem, thereby demonstrating that Jerusalem was inseparable from the State of Israel. His proposal was accepted. Only two ministers objected: Moshe Shapira, Minister of the Interior and Immigration, a member of the religious *Hapoel Hamizrahi* party, and Eliezer Kaplan, Minister of Finance, from MAPAI, who were both well known for their dovish views. Kaplan was also the chief speaker in the subsequent debate, which was held by the MAPAI Knesset members before the proposal was brought before the House. "I believe that this move to Jerusalem is a fatal error and an unnecessarily provocative act against the United Nations," he said. "What we ought to do is intensify the pace of construction and industry in Jerusalem, but not do anything demonstrative which involves such a risk." All the speakers, including Ben-Gurion, treated the UN Resolution with the utmost concern. They assumed that the UN might try to impose its rule in Jerusalem despite Israel's objections. They even considered the possibility that the UN would create an international army and take the city by force. Ben-Gurion acknowledged, "Obviously, if it comes to a confrontation with a military force sent by the UN, we shall give in." He supposed however that this would not happen. The possibility that the UN would punish Israel and impose economic sanctions seemed more plausible. "We should remember that we have bread for only three months," one MK pointed out, and another one added: "Leaving Jerusalem on her own, even if we send in water, is a very dangerous option." They felt that they faced a fateful decision—to give up Jerusalem or to fight for it. Some compared it with the dilemma that had faced them prior to the Declaration of Independence. Golda Meir explained, "My own motivation in all these debates was fear. I always feared that if we did not decide as we did, things would be worse." Ben-Gurion added, "I know no one more fearful than myself, and I admit that I'm afraid of this decision."

Ben-Gurion was worried that the Soviets, the Vatican and the Arabs would use the move to Jerusalem as an excuse to force more territorial concessions on Israel. The MAPAI MKs debated the issue in two lengthy sessions. Pinhas Lubianiker (Lavon) stated, "I think that Jerusalem, quite apart from the UN resolution, is a bad place for a national capital. Practically speaking, I think some of the ministries could be in Jerusalem, but there are others which it would be absurd to move there. Transferring the Knesset is absurd . . . moving the Treasury to Jerusalem is insane."* Ben-Gurion had to speak once more before he could persuade his party members to support his position. He did his best to point out the gravity of the situation. "From the moment they remove Jerusalem from the jurisdiction of the State of Israel we'll be without hope and there will be war," he said. His conclusion: "We must challenge the UN." Eventually he succeeded in getting his way—24 members voted for it, 12 either opposed, abstained or voted for other proposals.†

A few days later Ben-Gurion wrote in his diary: "During the last three years I have had to make several bitter and difficult decisions, even fateful ones. I doubt if I've ever faced a more difficult decision than to challenge the UN while facing the Catholic, the Soviet and the Arab world. . . ."[146] Among those who had supported Ben-Gurion were Golda Meir and Levi Eshkol. Toward the end of the week he received a telegram from Moshe Sharett, who was then in New York. The Foreign Minister had not taken part in the decision to move the Knesset to Jerusalem and he opposed the move. After the decision had been made, Sharett resigned. "With the debate in the UN ahead of us, I'm afraid I can no longer be helpful since I cannot wholeheartedly defend the step that has been taken," he wired. Ben-Gurion instructed that Sharett be told that all those who "took part in May 14" (the date of the Declaration of Independence) must "remain undivided." Sharett immediately obeyed: "I accept your verdict," he told his master.[147]

---

*In the eyes of the politicians from Tel Aviv, Jerusalem was a remote little village. Yosef Shprintsak, Speaker of the Knesset, who opposed moving it to Jerusalem for political reasons, frequently complained about how uncomfortable the ride was to there. The cold weather also disturbed him. As far as he was concerned, the whole thing was an intolerable nuisance. Had he been consulted, he said, he would have proposed waiting a year or two to let the Knesset develop in a "suitable climate," in Tel Aviv.[144]

†In the debate among the MAPAI MKs it was suggested that if the party did not propose moving the Knesset to Jerusalem Herut would do so, and MAPAI would be afraid to oppose it, since they might be accused of being weak. It was best, therefore, to make the proposal on their own behalf. Ben-Gurion noted: "Begin, of course, demanded a debate on the government's policy and a no-confidence vote. . . . I proposed instead of a debate that the parties make statements. It was so ruled. Begin did not keep his word, and instead of a statement made an obnoxious speech."[145]

2

Face to Face

SOME TIME AFTER the signing of the armistice agreements and the collapse of the Lausanne talks, the relations between Jews and Arabs ceased to be conducted as a confrontation between states. The armies no longer fought and the diplomats no longer talked. Now the Israeli–Arab conflict was limited to the contact between individuals, face to face, in one country, the triumphant and the defeated. It was a painful encounter, a blend of cruelty and compassion, arbitrariness and righteousness, greed, suspicion and fear. But there was also goodwill as well as some shame.

At the first session of the first Knesset there were three Arab members out of the 120: the Arabs of Israel had been allowed to vote and be elected. One of the Arab MKs appeared in the assembly wearing a *tarboosh*, another wore a traditional *keffieh* and *aqqal* (all traditional Arabic headdresses). Yosef Weitz, of the Jewish National Fund, who was among the guests, saw this as a bitter insult. "It chilled the heart and angered the soul," he noted later in his diary. He asked himself what those Arab MKs felt when they swore allegiance to the state. "Isn't it filled with lies and deceit? No. Nevertheless, I do not want there to be many of them. Perhaps they will integrate into society. But it

43

will take several generations before they become loyal to the state."[1] Many shared that opinion: "The Arab minority is a danger to the state," said Yigael Yadin to Ben-Gurion, "in time of peace just as much as in time of war."[2] Ben-Gurion imposed martial rule which limited the Arabs' rights and freedom. Tewfik Toubi, MK, a Haifa-born Arab and a Communist, warned, "The denial of democracy and freedom to a national minority leads to the denial of democracy and freedom to all citizens."[3] Toubi maintained that "democracy and freedom are indivisible"; he was wrong.

As soon as the United Nations General Assembly resolved, on November 29, 1947, to partition Palestine into two states, one Jewish and one Arab, the Labor party, MAPAI, began to prepare the ground for the practical problems brought about by everyday living in the Jewish State. The party instituted a number of committees, including one whose major concern was to clarify Jewish-Arab labor relations.[4] The committee began its work within days of the UN Resolution, working on the assumption that the country would be divided in accordance with that Resolution and the two states, Jewish and Arab, would live side by side in peace, with fully integrated economies. The committee pointed out several problems, but on the whole tended to be optimistic. It was to be expected that the first few months would be difficult: "It could well take a year for the two of us to give up all that has accumulated inside of us during the last few decades," said Pinhas Lavon, General Secretary of the *Histadrut*, the national labor union. However, it was assumed the Arabs would eventually accept the situation.

In the meantime it was proposed to print pamphlets and leaflets to persuade them that their lives would improve with the creation of the Jewish state. The status of the working class was the main concern at those meetings much more than Zionist ideology. The idea was that Arabs would become integrated in the Histadrut, and would therefore lend additional strength to the working class in the country. Once the state was established, they said, there would be hundreds of thousands of Jewish immigrants, who would all work, so that in any case the labor market would be overwhelmingly Jewish, and there would be no reason to refrain from opening jobs to Arabs, too.* Lavon:

---

*Lavon did assume that the minimum wage of the Arab laborer would be "somewhat" less than the existing Jewish wage, but he stated that it would have to "come very close to it."

"Let us assume that during the interim period we are going to succeed in integrating the Arab workers into the social services of the Jewish state. In creating a single organization of all the workers in the government and municipal services, as well as taking over the entire business of work distribution, via the labor exchange, we will have created three central areas for continuous positive contact between Arab and Jewish workers. Those three areas will be the basis of daily communication, of common interests, progressing and evolving, and in time will provide the foundation for a joint organization of Arab and Jewish workers."

The participants in this debate also thought about the political aspect of the relations with the Arabs. They hoped to draw them from both the extreme right and left anti-Zionist camps, to a social-democratic center which would cooperate with the state, the Histadrut and MAPAI. To bring this about, they decided to revive the Arab workers' organization which had operated for over twenty years under the auspices of the Histadrut, the "Palestine Labor Alliance."

All this expressed the tendency to integrate the Arabs into all aspects of life in the Jewish state including the army. Lavon posited,

> There is no question that the state will have an army, and obviously we shall not put up with having two separate armies, one Jewish and one Arab. There will be a single army. I believe that the army should not only be a good employer, but also should be a major influence in accelerating positive revolutionary development—if the army will just realize what every army does, that it is not merely a device for the technical training of soldiers, but also . . . understand its political function in national and social education.*

Lavon considered the integration of Arabs into the life of the state a test of the Zionist idea and of Jewish morality: "For the first time we shall be the majority living with a minority, and we shall be called upon to provide an example and prove how

---

*Another committee set up by MAPAI for the preparation of independent statehood dealt with the educational system. Its members insisted that the Arab minority had the right to educate their children in their own language, but warned against the proposal which had been put forward by Ben-Gurion, among others, that the Arabs would enjoy cultural autonomy. Such autonomy, said the education committee, would lead to irredentism. The committee recommended that the Arab educational system be integrated into the general system. The Minister of Education would have three deputy ministers, one of whom would be an Arab.[5]

Jews live with a minority," he said. He also considered the
state's image in the eyes of the world:

> This state will in some ways be a glass house, and every time we
> yawn, and anything that we do, big or small, will be photographed
> by the entire world. Whatever we do or fail to do, for that matter,
> will make news throughout the world.

He believed that it was possible to integrate the Arabs as equal
citizens, but warned:

> The twenty years that we have been educating our public, and espe-
> cially the last ten years, have not been conducive to promoting
> Jewish–Arab co-existence. The reason has to do with the circum-
> stances in which the Jew and the world find themselves. The
> Israeli-born generation, with its crude and primitive nationalism;
> the Oriental communities, with their historical and natural urge to
> avenge the years of humiliation and repression they suffered in
> Arab countries, which could easily be aroused when they suddenly
> discover that now we are the masters, the rulers. . . . All these add
> up to a picture of very real dangers. . . ."[6]

In the following months the war raged in the country, and
while it was at its height, the independent State of Israel was created. Hundreds of thousands of Arabs fled or were driven out of
their homes. The Israeli army suffered heavy losses; many were
killed or injured by Arab guns. Almost every family was affected. In view of all this the desire for the integration of the remaining Arabs as equal citizens of the state had diminished.
Considering their small number, it no longer seemed necessary
to integrate them, and the tendency grew to regard them as a
"fifth column." The state's policy vis-à-vis the Arab minority
vacillated between the desire for them to be integrated and the
urge for them to be isolated. The swing from one tendency to the
other was not always rational. It did reflect security considerations, economic interests and clearcut political aims, but it was
also affected by vindictiveness and fear. From time to time, the
policy changed directions, expressing the internal conflict between "soft-hearted" and "hard-hearted" policies, the former optimistic, the latter pessimistic. The 600,000 Arabs who had vacated the country gave rise to hope; the 100,000 or more that
remained, caused worry. "There are too many Arabs in the country," said Itzhak Ben-Tsvi, voicing the sentiments of many.*

---

*From the minutes of that meeting of the MAPAI secretariat:

Shlomo Lavi, MK: ". . .The large number of Arabs in the country worries me. The
time may come when we will be the minority in the State of Israel. There are

In the provisional government, which served until the first general elections, there was a Ministry for the Minorities, headed by Behor Shalom Shitrit. While serving in this capacity, Shitrit stated that his ministry was responsible "for guarding the interests of the Arabs."[8]

Tiberias-born Shitrit, formerly a policeman and justice of the peace, was included in the Cabinet because the leaders of MAPAI felt they should include a Sephardic Minister. As such, they assumed that he was the most appropriate person to deal with the Arabs, a position that, at first, seemed unimportant to them. But they soon realized the true significance of this post, and concluded that it could not be left in the hands of a minor minister, who was not of the Ashkenazi "inner circle." Shitrit's inclination to "guard the interests of the Arabs" made the "inner circle" suspicious.* A few months later, the Ministry was closed down and Shitrit had to be satisfied with the Ministry of Police. Jurisdiction over Arab affairs became a bone of contention between various authorities and officials, because it represented considerable power. The Foreign Ministry, the army and the General Security Services all wanted it. There were several ministerial committees which dealt with Arab affairs, but the policy was determined by Ben-Gurion himself, with the assistance of a limited number of advisors and aides, from the staff of

---

now 170,000 Arabs in the country, including 22,000 school-age children. The natural increase among Arabs is high and keeps growing, especially if we give them all the economic advantages which we are intending to give: health, education and big profits. There is no such rate of natural increase anywhere in the world, and we have to give careful thought to this imminent danger. Such an increase could match our immigration. . . . We may reach the point when the interests of the Arabs rather than of the Jews will determine the character of the country. . . ."

Eliyahu Carmeli, MK: "I'm not willing to accept a single Arab, and not only an Arab but any gentile. I want the State of Israel to be entirely Jewish, the descendents of Abraham, Isaac and Jacob. . . ."

Yehiel Duvdevany, MK: "If there was any way of solving the problem by way of a transfer of the remaining 170,000 Arabs we would do so. . . ."

David Hakohen, MK: "We didn't plan the departure of the Arabs. It was a miracle. . . ."

Z. Onn: "The landscape is also more beautiful—I enjoy it, especially when traveling between Haifa and Tel Aviv, and there is not a single Arab to be seen."[7]

*The Israeli elite was composed mostly of Jews born in Central Europe and of their descendents; they were commonly referred to as *Ashkenazim*. Sephardic Jews, also commonly referred to in English as Oriental Jews, came mostly from Arabic countries. Most of them were not immediately accepted in the Ashkenazic elite of Israel. The files of the short-lived Ministry and Shitrit's statements in the Cabinet do indeed reflect a tendency to treat the Arabs as fairly as possible.[9]

the Prime Minister's Office, the Security Services and the army. Moshe Sharett and the Foreign Ministry staff were expected to make the policy look better than it actually was; Eliezer Kaplan, the Minister of Finance, and his office, were placed in charge of abandoned property.

A few days before the Declaration of Independence, Ben-Gurion wrote:

> It's now necessary to lay down the law for an occupied town or village. Who governs: the local commander or an appointed governor? On whose behalf? What are his rights vis-à-vis the army—the population—their property? What may the army confiscate? . . . Should it be declared military territory? By what law? How do we deal with looters? Should there be compensation for looted property? Should Arabs be expelled? What about captives? What of remaining Arabs? . . . Who looks after the Arab needy? With whose budget?[10]

A few days after the atrocities committed during the seizure of Ramlah and Lydda, and before the conquest of Nazareth, which was expected to attract the attention of the international press, Ben-Gurion summoned Elimelih Zelikowitz, "Zelig" Avner, and ordered him to impose martial rule in all the occupied territories.

Major General Avner, a Russian-born immigrant, was then 52; he had served in the Turkish army in the First World War and in one of the Hebrew regiments in the British army in the Second. He had been one of the first commanders of the *Haganah*, Israel's pre-state army. His colleagues did not admire his gifts as a general. "He may be a little backward in that capacity," Ben-Gurion conceded.[11] The army did not cooperate with Avner: he was not given the personnel he needed nor the vehicles, and at times it happened that he was prevented from joining the occupation forces and restraining their soldiers. "In Beersheba he was deliberately pushed aside, and the army failed to control its men," noted Ben-Gurion.[12] The Civil authorities also sought at first to evade the martial rule and its restrictions, and Avner frequently complained about it to Ben-Gurion.[13] But within a few months the military government became institutionalized and expanded. By the end of 1949 it employed over 1,000 people. Ben-Gurion explicitly defined the Military Governor's responsibilities:

> The governor takes care of the registration of the population, the supervision of its movements, protection of life and property (the

prevention of robbery and looting and the investigation of complaints against the army), and fights against infiltration by combing the area and checking identities. . . . The village heads have been ordered to report infiltrators . . . to seize weapons . . . evacuate semi-abandoned villages . . . distribute arms for the security of villages (by the English system: swear in a few men and give them army rifles); general care of the population; provision of food and fuel. . . . Health administration: clinics have been opened; Education: some 45 schools have been opened, teaching 6,900 children, with 163 teachers (up to age ten, boys and girls study together); water supply, employment . . . social aid . . . municipal services. . . .[14]

Some of this was done on a temporary basis, following the occupation, but within three months Ben-Gurion ordered that the Military Governor be the sole representative for all the government ministries among the Arab population.[15] Some of the ministries objected, and the government appointed a committee to investigate the objections. The committee concluded that "for reasons of security and the social conditions of the Arabs" it was desirable to maintain martial rule and to empower it to "coordinate, direct and supervise" the work of the various ministries, "from the political, security and various other aspects."[16] The controversy reflected both an administrative and a political struggle for the exclusive control over the lives of tens of thousands of people. The politicians believed that whoever ruled the Arabs would also be in control of their votes. It was assumed that martial rule would prevail for many years to come. And so it did.

The legal basis for the establishment of martial rule was derived by Israel from the British mandatory government, in the form of some 150 Emergency Defense Regulations promulgated in 1945. In the 1930s such regulations were used to put down the Arab revolt; in the 1940s they served the authorities in putting down the Jewish revolt. At that time they were bitterly protested by Jewish jurists. Dr. Menahem Dunkelmann, later Justice of the Israeli Supreme Court, stated: "While these regulations are a menace to the entire community, we, as lawyers, have a special interest in them, as they constitute a violation of elementary concepts of law and justice. They amount to sanctioning a purely arbitrary power in the hands of the administrative and military authorities. Such arbitrariness, if approved by a legislature, makes for anarchy. . . ." Dr. Bernard Joseph—later Dov Yosef, Minister of Justice—said:

The question is, shall we all be subjected to terrorism under official seal. . . . There is no certainty that a citizen may not be imprisoned for the rest of his life without trial, there is no guarantee of personal freedom, no appealing the acts of the commander, no petitioning the High Court of Justice. . . . The license of the administration to exile a citizen at any moment is truly boundless. Moreover, it is not necessary for the person to have even committed an offense—it is enough that a decision is made in some office, and the person's fate is sealed. . . .

Yaakov Shimshon Shapira, future Attorney General and Minister of Justice, stated:

The regime created by the Emergency Regulations is without precedent in a civilized country. Even Nazi Germany had no such laws, and what happened in [the extermination camps of] Majdanek and other places was a violation of the law. Only one kind of system resembles these conditions—that of a country under occupation. We are being reassured that the Regulations will be used only against criminals, not against the entire population, but so did the Nazi ruler in Oslo, Norway, reassure the population that no harm would come to any citizen who minded his own business. . . . We must declare before the entire world—the Defense Regulations of the [British] Palestine Government mean the destruction of the rule of law in this country.

A conference of the Jewish lawyers in the country held in 1946 declared that the extension of the authority given to the government by the Emergency Defense Regulations deprived the Palestinian citizen of the basic rights of man, and that moreover the regulations subverted law and justice, constituted a grave danger to personal freedom and imposed arbitrary rule free of all legal supervision.[17]

With the creation of the State of Israel the Knesset adopted the British Defense Regulations, except those which had been used to limit Jewish immigration. Within a few months the Knesset supplemented those regulations with Israeli ones.*

*Menahem Begin, leader of the right-wing Herut party, feared that these regulations might one day be used against his movement as they had been by the British authorities. He denounced the emergency regulations saying:

I hereby declare that if the Knesset does not throw out these new emergency regulations proposed for approval by the Defense Minister, then the Knesset is not worthy of its name and function. We, the men of the *Irgun*, declare that these Nazi laws will neither be passed nor recognized. We shall violate these statutes day and night and we shall incite the entire nation against them, even if we have to go to prison.[18]

The Emergency Regulations enabled the military authorities to close off the Arab areas and to restrict entry and exit only to those with permits. This meant that every Arab inhabitant had to apply to the military government office or to the police in his district to obtain a permit to leave his village, whenever he wanted to do so and for whatever reason, be it work or business, a doctor's appointment or to visit relatives. The soldiers could issue the permit or refuse to do so, without giving any reason other than "security considerations." The permit noted the purpose of the trip, sometimes its exact route, the day, and sometimes the exact time. The military government was very meticulous in issuing permits. Buses were frequently stopped on the roads and the Arab passengers taken off to verify their permits. Regulation 109 empowered the military government to deport people from their towns or villages; Regulation 110 empowered it to summon any person to present himself at a police station at any designated time and place, or to remain confined to his house; Regulation 111 made it possible to place a person under administrative arrest for an unlimited time, without explanation and without trial. Violators of military government orders were tried by military courts and if convicted, could not appeal. Officers of the military government had extensive authority to impose fines and other penalties even without trial.

A few months after the creation of the state, a District Court Justice in Tel Aviv, Shalom Kassan, refused to pass sentence in accordance with the Emergency Regulations. "I cannot be expected to rule against my conscience," he wrote.[19] But he remained in the minority. The Supreme Court tended to believe the representatives of the army when they argued before it that the orders issued by the military government had been founded on security considerations, and as a rule was disinclined to investigate any further.[20]

Among the soldiers and officers who were sent to rule over the Arabs were ones who had either been found unfit for active service because of age, or low military profile or who were recently injured in battle. Some of them were vengeful, after a war which had shown no mercy to civilians.[21] Most of them had no experience in the kind of work that the martial rule would expect of them, and they knew little about proper administration. The martial rule was, therefore, marked from the start by its arbitrary nature. Minister Shitrit told the Ministerial Committee

for Abandoned Property about a military governor who had imposed a curfew on a certain Arab village, thus preventing the inhabitants from going to work. When their Jewish employers protested, he proposed to lift the curfew for a fee—850 *mil* per Arab
worker a day, of which the worker would receive 350 *mil* and
the military government 500.[22] The supply of food, at a time
when there was rationing and shortages, and the marketing of
Arab agricultural produce under military supervision, without
any other official control, led to irregularities and corruption.
"There is corruption." Elimelih Avner reported to Ben-Gurion.[23]
There were many reports about thousands of people taken from
their homes for inspection and identification. Representatives of
the military government would gather them in an open field,
keeping them there for many hours in the sun, without food,
drink, or toilet facilities—men, women and children. When they
left their homes they were ordered to leave the doors unlocked.
The houses stood unguarded. When they returned they often
found that the soldiers had stolen household effects, jewelry and
cash.[24] These things occurred repeatedly. Along with the cur-
fews and the demand for permits, such acts served to scare, hu-
miliate and harass the Arab population. Tens of thousands of Arabs, living under martial rule, experienced arbitrary intrusions
into their private everyday lives—soldier versus peasant, face to
face. Most of them were villagers, who were still dazed by the
defeat. They were a frightened, leaderless people; they caused no
danger to state security.

Martial rule was initially instituted to prevent the return of
refugees, or "infiltrators," as they were called, and to prevent
those who had succeeded in crossing the border from returning
to their homes.[25] In the process, other Arabs who had not infiltrated the country were sometimes driven out as well. The second role assigned to martial rule was to evacuate semi-
abandoned neighborhoods and villages as well as some which
had not been abandoned—and to transfer their inhabitants to
other parts of the country. Some were evacuated from a "security cordon" along the borders, and others were removed in order
to make room for Jews. The third function of martial rule was to
impose political supervision over the Arab population. In the
process, the Arabs were isolated from the Jewish population.

On the evening of July 1, 1948, representatives of the Arab
population of Haifa were sent for by Rehavam Amir, the com-

mander of the conquered city, to discuss the removal of the Arabs from the Carmel ridge. It was a meeting of high tension, opening as something of an historical confrontation between the triumphant Zionists and the defeated Palestinians, and ending with a very matter-of-fact, technical discussion of the ways of carrying out the order, which was listed as Number 2699/Operation/4b. From the minutes of that meeting:

> Rehavam Amir apologized (in Hebrew): "I'm sorry I can't speak Arabic, nor do I understand it. Would Mr. Yaeli explain to the visitors why they have been called here."
>
> Avraham Yaeli interprets into Arabic the Haganah commander's order to remove the Arabs from the Carmel ridge and the "German Colony" area, etc., down to Wadi Nisnas, where abandoned houses have been prepared for them. The order states that the operation must be carried out by July 5. He asks the Arab representatives to help carry out the transfer, in order to make it easier and simpler for the people. . . .
>
> Tewfik Toubi: "I don't understand—is it a military order? Look at the condition of these people. I can't see any reason, even a military one, which calls for such a step. The intention is obviously to create an Arab ghetto in Haifa. This is not what the people expected who remained here and undertook to live [in the State of Israel]. We expected different treatment. . . . There are some who say that if these are our rights in Israel, it would have been better if the British had remained. If there are suspicious persons whom you regard as dangerous, we won't object if you take steps against them. But as for the people living in the 'German Colony,' I don't believe they are any danger to the army. We are asking that these people remain where they are."
>
> Bulus Farah: "It's described as a military action, but in fact it's a political one. It's racism! . . . We thought that when the British, who were the cause of all that's happened here, left the country, the relations between the two peoples would improve and the situation would settle down. Now we see it's the reverse. We can hardly see it as an improvement if we have to move into a ghetto. If there are elements who worry you—take steps to gather them together, but not all the people."
>
> Amir: "You are sitting here and giving me advice, when you've been brought here to hear the order of the Haganah command and to help! I do not meddle in politics and I don't deal in it. I'm only carrying out the orders. . . . Since I've been responsible for these areas I've done my best to ensure that even under conditions of war people will be comfortable. We've seen to sanita-

tion, water, etc. I have not hesitated to shoot at Jews if I thought they were going to damage property. I want life to return to normal as soon as possible. Wherever there was a possibility that workers could open a co-operative store, I did it. I am constantly pressuring the authorities to open a school. Whenever people came to me and asked for help, I gave it to them, as long as it did not interfere with the war effort. . . . This is a war and conditions can't be changed in time of war. I must carry out the orders! I have to see to it that it's carried out by the 5th. I've asked the Arab representatives to come here so as to carry it out with the minimum distress to the people concerned, and so as to help you as best I can. . . . I want the work to be done by persons whom you will appoint, and I will help them. This doesn't mean that if it isn't done I won't do it myself. But though I'm a soldier, I also have a heart, and it pains me if a person is hurt unnecessarily. I can understand and my heart aches when a person must leave a place he has lived in for decades. But what can I do? I don't want to enter into arguments, because it's not up to me. And I firmly reject the words which were uttered here, about a ghetto, because it isn't true! I don't intend to enclose the area or surround it with barbed wire. I don't intend to close the shops. No! People will go on with their normal lives, only they will be concentrated in one area. The people will leave the military zones at once, and (concerning this order) there's no room for argument. That means Stella Maris, Wadi Jamal, Abbas Street and the 'German Colony' . . . In Stella Maris there are some 90 families, in the 'Colony' 180, in Wadi Jamal 47, in Abbas Street 50. I inspected all of Wadi Nisnas and the place has good, well-constructed houses ready to be moved into. Above all, the orders must be carried out properly. . . ."

Shehadeh Shalah: "If a man owns his house, does he have to leave it too?"

Amir: "Everybody must leave."

Shehadeh: "And if he lives on Yohanan Street?"

Amir: "Tomorrow morning I'll go with you and show you the streets and the boundaries and you'll immediately mark the houses and to whom they should be given."

Tewfik Toubi: "I understand that the decision stands and can't be altered. We'll forgo the argument. Now, has the commander considered that there are families who cannot afford the costs of the removal?"

Amir: "Tomorrow morning we'll take care of the technical details. I'll see to vehicles and gas, but the people will bear the costs themselves. . . ."

Victor Hyatt (in English): "Today is the first of July, tomorrow is the second, and there are many people who haven't heard of the order at all. It's easier for people who have little furniture, but for those who live in apartments and have a lot of heavy furniture it will be harder to make the move, especially as there are no people to do it. These should be taken care of first."

Amir: "We'll discuss all these details. We've taken that into consideration, too. Four days is a very long time and it was given so that it can be carried out properly. . . . It'll be better for you to finish quickly, while it's still in my hands. . . ."

Shehadeh: "There are Moslems, too."

Amir: "The Moslems will readily gather in Wadi Nisnas. There are only 140 Moslem families."

Yaeli: "Later they will come to appreciate it, and realize that the fact that their being concentrated in one area is a blessing. When the schools are opened and life returns to normal, they'll discover it was all for their benefit. Now it looks like a sudden blow. When they are concentrated they will also be protected from thefts and so on."

Arab representatives: "But the time is short!"

Amir: "I can't change it. . . ."

Bulus Farah: "And when the war is over, will the people be able to return to their homes in Wadi Jamal, etc.?"

Amir: "I haven't thought about it and I don't know what will happen later. I receive orders and carry them out. . . ."[26]

At this time the Haifa municipality had instituted a committee for Arab affairs and another one for the "normalization of day-to-day living." The members of the two committees complained that the Ministry for the Minorities, the Foreign Ministry, the Ministry of Defense and the Prime Minister's Office all ignored their existence and their advice. Some of them had qualms above moving the Christian Arabs from their homes on the Carmel into the abandoned houses of the Moslem Arabs in Wadi Nisnas. "You can't gather 3,000 human beings as if you were gathering eggs," said one of them. "For decades there have been personal relations between the Arab and the Jewish population here. . . ." Amir reminded them that the subject "had been discussed more than once," and maps had even been drawn of the areas under discussion. The inhabitants of Stella Maris threatened to appeal to the Vatican. Only if the Pope ordered them to leave their homes, they said, would they do so. Tewfik Toubi volunteered to go up and talk them into it. The minutes

of the meeting record that afterwards they all went out to Wadi
Nisnas "and the Arab representatives saw that the place was
spacious and good and that they would manage comfortably."27

Thirty-five years later, retired Ambassador Amir recalled,
"The people refused to leave their homes until they saw the
trucks and the soldiers. We told them that if they did not load
their things then we would do it for them, and then, of course, I
wouldn't be responsible for any damages. Someone broke down
and began to load, and it had a psychological effect on the others.
I am still proud that the order was carried out in a humane
way."28

Tewfik Toubi, Communist MK, 35 years later recalled: "I
was only 26 at the time. When they told us to go to the military
governor of the occupied city we didn't hesitate: 'The National
Liberation League,' which I represented, and which later became
a part of the Israeli Communist party, recognized the State of Israel, as a natural consequence of its support for the Partition
Resolution of November 29. Obviously, the evacuation caused
great suffering to the residents. As I recall, however, there was
no violence. All the same, it was a very cruel thing to do. The
aim was—as I said at the time—to concentrate the Arabs in a
ghetto."29*

In the first half of November 1948, Emanuel (Manu) Friedmann arrived in the Arab village of Jish in Upper Galilee and ordered its inhabitants to leave their homes. Friedmann, of Rosh

---

*Ben-Gurion used to claim that reports about the expulsion of Arabs were
fabrications designed to defame the state. He called on the Knesset Committee
to seek ways of combatting "such disgraceful allegations."30 He was referring
to the appearances of Tewfik Toubi. The Arab Communist irritated him intensely. Once Ben-Gurion asked the military governor whether there was any
truth in Toubi's accusations. The governor denied them, and Ben-Gurion
noted his reply in a tone of "I thought as much," as if the expulsions had never
taken place.31 As an articulate, educated and elected Arab Communist MK,
Tewfik Toubi was a novel and provocative phenomenon, to which the first Israelis found it difficult to adjust. He was often reprimanded for not appreciat-
ing the privilege he had been given to sit in the Knesset and talk like an equal.
However, Nathan Alterman, the poet, wrote a poem in his honor:

   He's a member of the Knesset
   He's an Arab Communist in parliament
   By right and not by favor . . .
   Perhaps it's time to remember this, comrades.32

In April 1949 the US consulate in Jerusalem predicted that the influence of
the Communists over the Arabs in Israel would increase, and that Toubi would
become their leader.33

Pinah, was the liaison officer between the army and the Arab population. He told the villagers that the army was asking them to leave their homes, for their own safety, and that they would be able to return two weeks later. The news spread rapidly through the village, and within minutes there was a crowd. One of the people present was a young boy who had just returned from Lebanon: he had fled from Jish while the fighting was still going on. "I can still clearly remember the argument between the big, blond Jewish officer and my teacher of religion, Shamas Atnas Akal," he later recalled. "Friedmann said the army was asking us to do this and Akal asked what would happen if we didn't. Friedmann said we had to, and Akal asked as a personal favor if Friedmann would let him speak on the telephone to his good friend, Itzhak Ben-Tsvi, a leader of MAPAI and later President of the State. The two of them went in a jeep to Safed. The rest of the villagers went to the church, to pray for the success of the mission. An hour later—it seemed like eternity—the two came back with the news that the order had been cancelled. Ben-Tsvi had gotten in touch with Behor Shitrit and the two of them persuaded the army to give up. In the meantime, we heard that a similar order was given to the inhabitants of Bir'em, our neighbors. They began to pack and move to Rami, their neighbor to the west. Shamas Atnas Akal said that his friend Ben-Tsvi told him the people of Bir'em could move in with us until they were allowed to return to their village. And indeed, the next day they began to come over and settle in the houses which the Moslem villagers had abandoned."[34]

Attorney Anis Shakur of Haifa remembered: "I was then a boy of ten. The rumor spread in Bir'em that the authorities had ordered us to vacate the village within 24 hours and move to Lebanon. There was a great panic. With the long trek before us, we all, children and adults, went to seek camels and donkeys to carry the baggage. I remember that some people went down to the nearby vineyards and streams to bury valuables. My father went to Rosh Pinah, to see Emanuel (Manu) Friedmann, who was in touch with us, and from there to the Military Governor, Elisha Soults. Then he went to see the Minister for the Minorities, Behor Shitrit. These efforts helped—the order of expulsion to Lebanon was changed for a two-week removal to Jish. Manu Friedmann came to the village and said, 'Don't take many things. You'll be back in a few days.' My father believed him. Instead of moving to Jish, we went to stay with my married sister in Horfeish. Only a year later we moved to Jish. There my father paid six pounds for the abandoned room of a Moslem. In Bir'em my father was a farmer—here he became a cobbler. There was only the one room—it served the entire family, as well as the donkey and the cobblery business. Water had to be carried from the stream. We used the vineyards as a toilet. The Bir'em children did not mix with the local Jish children. They regarded us as outsiders and looked down on us. There we learned to be refugees."35

Some days later Ben-Gurion noted in his diary, "I questioned Chief of Staff Yaakov Dori and Moshe Carmel (the commander of the northern front) on the situation in Galilee. Moshe said that for military reasons he had to impose a curfew along the border and drive the villagers of the frontier southwards. Bir'em, Nebi Roubin, Tarbihah, Ikrit. . . . He's ready to freeze the situation, stop expelling them and not let any return. . . ." Ben-Gurion ordered him to inform the villagers that the authorities would consider their return to their homes "once the border was secured." He agreed to the "freeze" and ordered a stop to expelling people.36 Two months later, the military governor, Rehavam Amir, wrote: "Unfortunately, I cannot set a date when the [Ikrit] refugees can return to their homes. Moreover, it's unlikely that the day is near."37

Some time before this, a local intelligence officer in Haifa reported on the situation of the refugees in the northern villages:

Arbat Betoul—More than 200, from Hattin, some in tents, some in the olive groves out in the open, some inside the houses.

Bouq'ia [Peki'in]—Nearly 4,500 refugees. Most of them living under the olive trees around the village, mainly on both sides of the road east of the village.

El Mougar—About 500. All inside the village. They come from Haddah, Rena and Tiberias.

Soukhmata—About 600. Half live among the olive trees, and rest in the village. Make a living harvesting the olives for the village.

Deir el Kassi—About 200. Most of them from Sefforieh. Living at their own expense, in the village. . . .

Rama—1,000. Some of them employed in agriculture and the olive harvest of the village. Living among the trees of Nadi Salameh, not far from Rama, are another 2,200 persons, refugees, in great distress. Mostly from the villages of Mi'ar, Damoun, Birweh, Manshieh and Samarieh.38

Early in May, Ben-Gurion noted: "There are about 17,000 Israeli–Arab refugees and infiltrators. How many of these are refugees and how many infiltrators?—Unclear." The Prime Minister issued an order forbidding refugees to return to their villages.[39]*

The people of Ikrit and Bir'em were never allowed to return. They were not the only ones, but they were exceptionally stubborn and were particularly good in public relations. They never gave up—they wrote letters, roused Knesset members, journalists and clerics from all over the world. Time after time they petitioned the High Court of Justice. On Christmas Eve, 1951, ten days before the Court was to hear the second petition of the Ikrit villagers, the army entered the abandoned village and blew up its houses. Only the church remained standing. On September 16, 1953, while the Bir'em petition was awaiting the decision of the High Court of Justice, airforce planes flew over the abandoned village and bombed it down to the ground. The villagers of Ikrit and Bir'em continued to fight for their right to return to their villages. After a time they were allowed to bury their dead there.

The transferring of Arabs from place to place, whether at the request of the army or to make room for Jewish settlement, was discussed occasionally by the Ministerial Committee for Abandoned Property. Some of the minutes of the sessions of this committee describe it as the "Committee for Arab Affairs." Ben-Gurion in his diary referred to it as a Committee "for Removal and Expulsion."† Ben-Gurion listed its members—the Foreign Minister for Minorities, the Finance Minister, the Ministers of Agriculture and Justice and himself. There was also a committee "for population transfer" and for several months a "refugee resettlement committee."

Previously, the Minister of Finance had stated that at first only places empty of Arabs would be settled. Nonetheless, the possibility was raised that at a later stage Arabs might be removed from their villages for "strategic or economic" reasons.[42]

Speaking to the Ministerial Committee for Abandoned Prop-

---

*A few weeks earlier the commander of the Haifa zone wrote: "Acting in accordance with the opinion of all the bodies responsible for security, the military government has decided that under no circumstances are the Arab inhabitants to be returned to the villages lying near the vital communication roads of the country."[40]

†The editors of the Prime Minister's diary saw fit to correct his wording. According to them, the committee dealt with "evacuation and repopulation."[41]

erty the Minister of Agriculture demanded that Arab villagers who are living in Israel not be evacuated unless their new location and source of income is determined at the same time. "This is essential from the point of view of justice, as well as the security of the country," he stated.[43]

One day in the fall of that year journalist Gavriel Stern, correspondent of *Al Hamishmar*, took a walk in the mountains around Jerusalem. Suddenly, amid the ruins of the abandoned village of Walaja, on the as yet undefined border with Jordan, he ran into an infiltrator. "I used to know that village well before the deluge," Stern recalled years later. Walking through the abandoned houses he said he felt as if he were on an archeological tour. Everything looked neglected, but in some of the houses the whitewash still gleamed on the walls, though the floral decorations which had been painted on them had faded. There were torn mattresses and rags on the floor, a shred of a receipt for cement which had been paid for in 1947, and a British food card. Stern recognized the name on it. He climbed up to the roof. Somewhere out there was the border. While gazing at the enchanting landscape and thinking about the fate of man in war, he suddenly noticed two figures moving slowly, one behind the other. Pacing confidently, they vanished from sight below the village and then reappeared. "A few minutes passed and then I saw them climbing up among the houses," recounted Stern. "One was a man, a middle-aged Arab, carrying a hoe, and a few steps behind him a woman. I called out to them, '*Sah bedeneb*' (health to your body), the Arab countryman's greeting. The man stopped still, perfectly immobile, as if paralyzed. The woman vanished among the houses. Then very slowly we approached each other, embarrassed. When he realized that I was nothing more than a citizen strolling through the hills he calmed down somewhat and we sat on the ground and exchanged cigarettes. Then he asked, stammering slightly: 'What nationality are you?' He searched for a point of departure for opening a conversation with someone who plainly belonged to the enemy. 'I've heard that things are not well with you either,' he said at last, as if discussing the weather or the prospects of the coming harvest. . . . Then we discovered some mutual acquaintances, at which point he called to his wife: 'Hagar! Hagar!' (yes, like Ishmael's mother!), but she had already fled. . . . He used to live in this abandoned village, and escaped with the others when the Israelis stormed the front lines. 'Do you see those houses over there?' he asked. 'There are some caves nearby and most of the refugees from the village live in them.' He talked about the unemployment and poverty over there. 'Everything is very cheap and plentiful—only we have no money. They say the money is on your side, but there is nothing to buy.' 'What's the point of coming here?' I asked. He looked at me gravely and replied in a subdued tone: 'A home is always dear.' He has no doubt that one day they will return to their land."[44]

Early in January 1949 Ben-Gurion noted in his diary: "Infiltration is increasing. It's reached 3,000 to 4,000. The infiltrators must be expelled and the Ministry of the Interior forbidden to issue permits to infiltrators. . . . But the main problem is prevention. No Arab should be expelled if there is any doubt whether he infiltrated or has been here all along. When it is certain—he must be expelled."[45] A week later he noted, "Recently there have been mass searches and some one thousand infiltrators have been expelled. . . ."[46] In the latter half of January, the Greek-Catholic archbishop of Transjordan, Michail Asaf, announced that scores of people from the villages of Shfaram, M'ilya and Tarshiha (inside Israel) had arrived in Amman. They were men, women and children, both Moslem and Christian. When the war broke out they fled to Lebanon. Then they tried to go home, but once inside Israel they were detained, loaded on trucks and driven to the border, which they were forced to cross. Before being expelled, the archbishop reported, they had their passports confiscated; their money and the women's jewelry was stolen from them.[47]

A few days later some 500 people were forced to leave the villages of Faradiyeh and Einan, on the Acre-Safed road. About a half were sent across the border to Jordan; the other half were moved to other villages. About two weeks later, some 700 people were expelled from Kfar Yassif. They had moved there during the war, having abandoned their homes in adjoining villages. Most of them were taken by trucks to the Jordanian border and ordered to cross it.[48]

In mid-April 1949, the US consul in Jerusalem reported that "several hundred" Galilee Arabs—all Israeli citizens—had been expelled together with some infiltrators. The consul gathered that the expulsion had been carried out by order of local army officers, against the government's policy. Documents in the Israeli

State Archives bear out this supposition. The Arabs of the town
of Majdal—later to become the city of Ashkelon—were also expelled by the army, but in that case it was with the Prime Minister's approval.[49]*

On August 21, about ten o'clock at night, the Jaffa police arrested two women and five children, aged between ten months
and ten years, took them in their pyjamas and drove them to the
border near Qalqiliya which they forced them to cross. According to the police, they had no permit to reside in Jaffa. They had
left the city during the war and returned one night to join their
husbands who had stayed behind.[51]

Several months later the weekly *Haolam Hazeh* published a
picture story entitled "How Infiltrators are Expelled." A half-
page photograph showed infiltrators standing in a single file,
their backs to the camera. Most of them wore traditional peasant dress; one wore a European suit that had seen better days,
his posture seeming to express submission and defiance, fatal-
ism and resilience, all at the same time. Standing before them
were two Israeli soldiers in shabby uniforms and peaked caps,
their rifles pointed at the captives. The contrast between the
Arab civilians, who were standing in a rigidly straight line, and
the sloppy Israeli soldiers, who looked like highwaymen, gave
the picture a grotesque quality, as if it had been staged. "There
may be many who believe that intimidating the infiltrators is
the only way to prevent future infiltrations," wrote the weekly
magazine, "but experience shows that even from the point of
view of efficiency this is the wrong method. . . . Ruthless treatment will not deter them." Overleaf there was a series of other
photographs: a truck fully loaded with peasants, while others,
seated on the ground, awaited the next vehicle; soldiers supervising them, their weapons cocked; one of these was wearing

---

*On December 31, 1948, the Ministerial Committee for Abandoned Prop-
erty discussed the future of Majdal. According to Elimelih Avner, "An investigation of the situation by the Ministry of Defense showed that there are 1,600
Arabs there, concentrated together and fenced in. . . . The Ministry has no objection to populating Majdal with Jews and it is in fact desirable from the security viewpoint." The Committee approved the project of populating the town,
"while ensuring that the Arabs are not expelled from their homes without
other arrangements." A few months later, Weitz concluded that the Arab population of Majdal was "not viable" and that it was a burden on the government.
"Best transfer them to Jaffa," he decided. Eventually, they were expelled to
Egypt.[50]

British-style wide shorts; another soldier, hands in pockets, head tilted, seemed to be listening to a peasant who was standing before him, pleading, his hand outstretched. "I'd rather be shot than die of hunger," ran the caption, naming the speaker—Halim Hamdan. One of the picture captions read, "Note the number tattooed on the guarding soldier's arm. Many of the immigrants who have been through the hell of the European concentration camps lack the proper attitude toward the Arab captives of the State." A week later the journal published a reader's letter, saying: "It seems as if the correspondent did not write all that he had to say, and there seem to be gaps in the picture sequence. If you know the whole truth, why don't you tell it?" The editors replied: "There are some things which are better left unpublished."[52] Meanwhile, all along the border an eight-meter strip was marked and declared a military zone. An outsider found in the zone would be shot without warning. As a result, the number of infiltrators diminished. "The searches scared them off," wrote Ben-Gurion.[53]

In utter secrecy, for fear of publicity and speculation, Arabs were urged to sell their lands and emigrate. Yosef Weitz, of the Jewish National Fund, was actively engaged in this effort and was occasionally successful. Thus, for example, in the village of Ar'ara, "So far 2,500 *dunams* [625 acres] have been purchased, complete with trees, houses and belongings," Weitz noted in his diary. "The belongings are sold at once and the houses are sealed. The Arabs who sell them receive their money in Transjordanian currency. They are taken with their luggage to the border facing Barat'a. There they are met by buses from Tul Karem and taken all the way to Transjordan. So far 200 Arabs have crossed over. Reports coming from there are satisfactory: some have gone into business in Amman and others went in for agriculture. This movement of leaving Israel continues, in spite of propaganda spread by Arabs militating against it."[54]

Toward the end of the year Weitz proposed an extensive project of aiding Christian Arabs to emigrate to South America. He wanted to purchase land for them, in the province of Mendoza, Argentina, as well as other places. He revealed the project to the Israeli ambassador in Argentina, Yaacov Tsur, and at some point brought it before Ben-Gurion. The prime minister sent him to Argentina to see what could be done. Weitz went there, inspected the land, calculated everything down to the finest detail—number of people, acreage, dollars—and even gave the project a code-name, "Operation Yohanan." However, nothing at all came of it, according to Weitz because the government was unable to make up its mind.[55]

The Arab population of Israel was thus divided into several categories. The majority had fled, or had been driven out, before and during the war—a total of some 600,000. Of those who remained, a few thousand were expelled from their homes; but most of them were permitted to remain in the country and become Israeli citizens. They numbered between 150,000 and 160,000. Some crossed the borders in secret and tried to return to their homes—these were the infiltrators, whom Ben-Gurion ordered expelled. However, thousands of them were allowed to remain, and a few thousand more were allowed to return under the family reunification plan.*

One night some soldiers broke into a café in the Ajjami quarter of Jaffa and tried to drag out a young woman who was sitting there with her boyfriend. The woman was Jewish, the man Arab. The incident turned into a violent row between Jews and Arabs. The daily *Haaretz* wrote in its editorial:

> As long as the Jewish citizen supposes that it is wrong to be seen in the company of an Arab, or to employ an Arab, the Arab citizen will be considered a stranger in our state. And a man who considers himself a stranger in the country in time of peace, will readily become an enemy in time of war. . . . The Arab who assimilates among us, who learns the Hebrew language and culture, would be a natural bridge between us and the rest of the Arab minority as well as the neighboring Arab countries.[57]

There were not many incidents of this kind. Most Jews did not mix with Arabs and most Arabs did not "assimilate" in Israeli society. They lived side by side, almost without contact. It wasn't enmity alone that kept them apart, nor the differences in

---

*In the State Archives there are scores of files with information concerning the government's policy regarding the minorities, including what is known in bureaucratese as "population transfers." A portion of these files are closed to researchers, and another portion is "yet to be opened." Something of their contents, however, may be learned from the Archives' index listing those files of the Ministry for the Minorities: Expulsion of Inhabitants; Transfer of Inhabitants; Concentration of Arab Residents; Complaints about Police Treatment; Demolition of Arab Houses; and (Tiberias, Jaffa) Acts against Civilians. Further information about the expulsion of several hundred families from three Galilean villages may also be found in the *Knesset Record* and in several verdicts of the Supreme Court.[56]

the way of life and culture; the authorities also segregated the two peoples. Arabs were not only confined to certain parts of the country; they were also prevented from direct contact with civil and administrative officials. In February 1950 Moshe Sharett warned his fellow ministers:

> There is a growing number of cases of Arab citizens of Israel applying to members of the government and to central offices not via the authorized officials, i.e., the military governor or the local officers in charge of Arab affairs. . . . All these applicants share the desire to circumvent the local government and wish to avoid having to deal with it in the particular case, because that authority is seen as unamenable to them. . . .
>
> . . . When there is a direct application by Arabs who are residents of Israel, your offices should first verify the details of the cases in question with the appropriate local military authorities and not respond to the applicants until the matter has been clarified, and then do it in full cooperation with the authorized local government. Also, it would be preferable if the answer would not be given to the applicants directly, but that the final decision should be transmitted via the local military governor or the regional officer for Arab affairs.[58]

The isolation of the Arab population from the political, administrative and social system was part of the intention to guarantee the political supervision over it. The political aims of the martial rule in the early years of its existence were summed up in the following words, contained in a top secret memorandum: "The government's policy . . . has sought to divide the Arab population into diverse communities and regions. . . . The municipal status of the Arab villages, and the competitive spirit of local elections, deepened the divisions inside the villages themselves. The communal policy and the clan divisions in the villages prevented Arab unity. . . . Martial law has ruled all this time with complete and total authority."

In the eyes of the dazed, divided and frightened population, the memorandum went on to explain, martial rule represented the "new triumphant power," whose nature the Arabs had not yet understood. As far as that population was concerned, it represented the military power which had set up this government. It served as the sole and central channel for all the extensions of the state authority which functioned in the Arab sector, "so that each and every Arab felt his daily dependence upon the military governor who was in charge of his area." At this time Arab society was led by a number of *mukhtars*, sheiks and heads of clans, and they represented the Arabs in their dealings with the military government, "thereby enabling the latter to rule over a whole community through a handful of people." During those years the work of the various government departments in the Arab sector was "irregular and inconsistent, both on account of the severe security restrictions which had been imposed on the Arab-occupied zones, and the government ministries' lack of efficiency in dealing with Arabs." Thus, in effect, the military government bore the responsibility for most of the government's dealings with the Arab populace, and served as a kind of liaison between the two.

The system of permits and closed zones also produced a complete dependence of every Arab citizen in the affected areas upon the military government. MAPAI, being the ruling party responsible for the security of the state, created Arab lists for the general elections, placing at their heads individuals from the traditional Arab leadership, whose main business it was to mediate between the authorities and the Arab populace: "In this way," the memo went on to explain, "the party could avoid having to form a particular ideology for its Arab voters, and also ensured that those lists would not consolidate into an independent Arab bloc. . . . The policy of communal division bore fruit, and . . . succeeded in creating barriers, albeit sometimes artificial ones, between certain parts of the Arab community, as in the case of the mistrust between the Druze and the other Arab communities. This policy enabled the state to prevent the formation of a unified Arab bloc and left considerable leeway for the leaders of the respective communities to concern themselves with their communal affairs, instead of general Arab ones. This document, which bears the date September 1959, was entitled 'Recommendations for Dealing with the Arab Minority in Israel.' Its author is not named. The main recommendation made by this report is that every effort should be made to integrate the Arab minority into the life of the country, in contrast to the former policy, and in accordance with the recommendations of the committee, set up by MAPAI following the Partition Resolution of 1947."[59]

The leaders of MAPAI were concerned with the interests of state and security, as defined by them, but MAPAI also had the interests of the party in mind. "The Arab voters were secured through the military government," stated one of Ben-Gurion's aides years later.[60] Another aide was Yehoshua (Josh) Felmann, later Palmon, born 1913, one of the Jewish Agency's "Arabists," like Eliyahu Sasson and Reuven Shiloah, but unlike them, a self-proclaimed field worker. After the creation of the state he became an aide of Behor Shitrit, the Minister for the Minorities, and was one of those who instigated the dissolution of that Ministry. He then became the Prime Minister's advisor on Arab affairs. He was put in charge of liaison between the Military Governor and the government Ministries, as well as the coordination of martial rule, which gave him considerable power. Years later he said in an interview:

> The 1929 anti-Jewish riots in Palestine taught me that we had only two alternatives before us: surrender or the sword. I chose the sword. I was not surprised that the Arabs fled. It was a natural reaction. It was the best of them who fled—the leaders, the intelligentsia, the economic elite. Only the "small fry" remained. I behaved toward them as a wolf in sheep's clothing—harsh, but outwardly decent. I opposed the integration of Arabs into Israeli society. I preferred separate development. True, this prevented the Arabs from integrating into the Israeli democracy. Yet they had never had democracy before. Since they never had it, they never missed it. The separation made it possible to maintain a democratic regime within the Jewish population alone. I was not a member of MAPAI, but I thought that if Ben-Gurion did not remain in power it would be a catastrophe for the state. My policy . . . was not designed to provide votes for MAPAI, but instead for Ben-Gurion's rule. At least, that was how I saw it at the time. . . . The main problem was that of the infiltrators. We expelled a few thousand, but we failed to expel tens of thousands. In that sense we failed—the number of Arabs in the country continued to rise steadily.[61]

3

Dividing the Spoils

IN THE EVENING of February 28, 1949, a soldier of the 169th Regiment entered an abandoned Arab building not far from the boundary line dividing Jerusalem. On the ground floor he discovered a dry goods store with a large quantity of glassware. Some ten days later the police arrested two of the regiment's soldiers in Jerusalem's Mahaneh Yehuda market carrying items from that store. The affair was the cause of an extensive investigation, which uncovered a written agreement between a low-ranking army commander and some private contractors. The contractors agreed to remove the goods to the warehouses of the Custodian of Abandoned Property, as required by law. In return, they were entitled to claim 30 percent of the value of the goods as a reward for handing in abandoned property. In this particular case, they also undertook to donate 10 percent of the value to the soldiers' fund. The company commander explained later that his experience in the occupied neighborhoods had taught him that in such cases it is impossible to control the men. He stated that he had to promise them some sort of reward, if only in the form of added income for the soldiers' fund; otherwise they might have suspected him of receiving a personal reward from the Custodian. The Chief of Military Police in Jerusalem noted, "There is good reason to meet the soldiers' demand for 10 percent of the value, in view of the fact that private contractors were going to be making such large profits so easily."[1]

During the war and afterwards plundering and looting were very common. "The only thing that surprised me," said David Ben-Gurion at a Cabinet meeting, "and surprised me bitterly, was the discovery of such moral failings among us, which I had never suspected. I mean the mass robbery in which all parts of the population participated."[2] Soldiers who entered abandoned houses in the towns and villages they occupied grabbed whatever they could. Some took the stuff for themselves, others "for the boys" or for the kibbutz. They stole household effects, cash, heavy equipment, trucks and whole flocks of cattle. Behor Shitrit told his colleagues of the Ministerial Committee for Abandoned Property that he had visited some of the occupied areas and saw the looting with his own eyes. "From Lydda alone," he said, "the army took out 1,800 truck-loads of property." Minister of Finance Kaplan admitted: "As a matter of fact, neither the Ministry of Finance nor the Custodian of Abandoned Property is in control of the situation, and the army does what it wants." The Custodian, Dov Shafrir, told the ministers that the regional commanders and their adjutants wanted to stop the looting, "but not the storekeepers of the various companies and squads."[3]

Shafrir, a native of a small village in the Ukraine, was about 50 when he took on the post of Custodian, two days after the conquest of Ramlah and Lydda. Earlier he had been active in a public housing project. As Custodian he was subordinate to the Minister of Finance. "It was obvious to me that the nature of the work entrusted to me called for fast and firm action, if we were to take control over the territory and the vast amount of property spread over hundreds of towns and villages," he wrote in years to come.[4] To do this, he had to dispatch men to go from house to house, from shop to shop, from warehouse to warehouse, from plant to plant, from quarry to quarry, from field to field, from orchard to orchard, and also from bank to bank and safe to safe—to count, measure, evaluate, estimate, replace locks on doors and transfer all moveable property to well-guarded warehouses, while maintaining a correct inventory of the property and its location. It included a total of 45,000 homes and apartments, about 7,000 shops and other places of business, some 500 workshops and industrial plants, and more than 1,000 warehouses. At the same time, it was necessary to continue harvesting the crops and picking the olives, gathering the tobacco and the fruit in the orchards—a total of over 800,000 acres. It was also necessary to take care of livestock—goats, sheep, hens—as well as market the produce, collect the profits and deposit them in the Treasury. This would have been an impossible undertaking even if the Custodian had had at his disposal battalions of skilled and honest workers. In fact, the staff assigned to do the work was very small, most of the personnel was inexperienced and knew nothing of administration, and some were dishonest. Ben-Gurion himself noted that there were thieves and crooks among them.[5] The Custodian would have had his task cut out for him even if the army had cooperated with his staff in order to prevent the plunder, but very often the army did not help. Hours, and sometimes days, passed before the Custodian and his staff were permitted to enter the occupied villages and towns, and by then all they could do, in some cases, was to note the destruction and the looting. In Haifa, Jaffa and Jerusalem there were many civilians among the looters. "The urge to grab has seized everyone," noted writer Moshe Smilansky. "Individuals, groups and communities, men, women and children, all fell on the spoils. Doors, windows, lintels, bricks, roof-tiles, floor-tiles, junk and machine parts. . . ."[6] He could have also added to the list toilet bowls, sinks, faucets and light bulbs.

The Military Governor of Jerusalem, Dov Yosef, wrote Ben-Gurion: "The looting is spreading once again. . . . I cannot verify all the reports which reach me, but I get the distinct impression that the commanders are not over-eager to catch and punish the thieves. . . . I receive complaints every day. By way of example, I enclose a copy of a letter I received from the manager of the Notre Dame de France (a monastery). Behavior like this in a monastery can cause quite serious harm to us. I've done my best to put a stop to the thefts there, which are all done by soldiers, since civilians are not permitted to enter the place. But as you can see from this letter, these acts are continuing. I am powerless."[7] Ben-Gurion promised he would discuss with Moshe Dayan the possible measures to be adopted in order to put an end to the robbery.[8] The subject troubled him greatly. Prior to the occupation of Nazareth he ordered Yadin to "use submachine guns on the soldiers if he saw any attempt at robbery."[9]

A secret report, written by the Custodian of Abandoned Prop-

erty, tried to explain how people "succumb to the grave temptation of looting," and why. First there was the massive flight of
panic-stricken Arabs who abandoned thousands of apartments,
stores and workshops as well as crops and orchards. Second, the
property concerned was in the midst of the front-line combat
area during the transition from mandatory to Israeli rule. This
meant there was no stable authority with which to be reckoned.
" . . . The moral sense of the few who were attacked by the many
and managed to survive, justified the looting of the enemy's
property," reported the Custodian. "Passions of revenge and
temptation overcame great numbers of people. Under those conditions only an extremely firm action by the military, administra-
trative, civil and judiciary authorities might have saved, not
only the property, but also many people, from moral bankruptcy. Such firm action did not take place, and perhaps could
not, given the circumstances, and so things continued to go
downhill without restraint."[10] Years later the Custodian removed the veil of secrecy: "The inspectors found most of the
houses broken into, and rarely was there any furniture left," he
wrote in his memoirs. "Clothes, household effects, jewelry,
bedding—other than mattresses—never reached the warehouses
of the Custodial authority. . . ."[11] More than 50,000 Arab homes
had been abandoned, but only 509 carpets reached the Custodian's warehouses. The Custodian attributed it all to the "weakness and greed of many Israelis, who in normal circumstances
would never have permitted themselves to act thus with regard
to other people's property." He indulged in some philosophical
speculation about it: "Indeed, history repeats itself in all that
concerns human nature. In our own chronicles it is stated simply and plainly without any circumlocutions: 'But the Children
of Israel committed a trespass in the accursed thing, for Achan,
the son of Carmi, the son of Zerah, of the tribe of Judah, took of
the accursed thing' (sacred loot) (*Joshua* 7:1). As you travel
through the country today, through the towns and in places settled by new immigrants and demobilized soldiers, as you observe the teeming life . . . your joy is mingled with sadness, the
sadness of the shadow of Achan, who took of the accursed
thing."[12]

In Cabinet sessions too the problem of looting was often discussed. Minister Shitrit reported thefts in Jaffa and Haifa, Minister Mordehai Bentov asked about a convoy of spoils which left
Jerusalem and Minister Cizling said: ". . . It's been said that

there were cases of rape in Ramlah. I can forgive rape, but I will not forgive other acts which seem to me much worse. When they enter a town and forcibly remove rings from the fingers and jewelry from someone's neck, that's a very grave matter. . . . Many are guilty of it."[13]

Amin Jarjouria, MK of the (Arabic) Nazareth Democratic List, which was associated with MAPAI, reported: "Two days after the seizure of Jish, in the Safed district, the army surrounded the village and carried out searches. In the course of the search soldiers robbed several of the houses and stole 605 pounds, jewelry and other valuables. When the people who were robbed insisted on being given receipts for their property, they were taken to a remote place and shot dead. The villagers protested to the local commander, Manu Friedmann, who had the bodies brought back to the village. The finger of one of the dead had been cut off to remove a ring. . . ."[14] In the State Archives there are many files containing information about the plundering and looting, including the acts of Arab robber gangs. Some of these files are still closed to researchers. However, something may be learned from the index titles: Plunder of Abandoned Arab Property; Looting; Possession without Permit; Robbery. Yosef Lamm, MK (MAPAI) stated, "None of us behaved during the war in a way we might have expected the Jewish people to behave, either with regard to property or human life, and we should all be ashamed."[15]

After a while the Custodian himself began to distribute the confiscated property. To begin with, Shafrir later reported, goods, materials and equipment were turned over to the army, directly from the stores in the occupied towns. Merchandise which the army did not require was put up for sale. The sale was conducted by special departments instituted for the purpose, staffed, as much as war conditions allowed, by personnel trained in the principal branches of commerce. Other merchandise was sold through negotiation with merchants or industrialists, depending on the type of materials. "The army had the first choice of any goods and materials it might require," Shafrir said. "Next were the government offices, the war disabled, the Jewish Agency, the local authorities and public bodies, such as Hadassah." The army also needed most of the workshop equipment such as cabinet-making shops, locksmiths-works, turneries, iron-works, tin-works and the like. Industrial plants which could be operated on their existing sites were leased out by contract, "whenever possible," according to Shafrir. Plants which no one wanted to lease were sold to the highest bidder.

The sale of furniture, Shafrir said, "was an especially complex and difficult business and took a long time." The army had removed from the houses and obtained from the warehouses furniture worth tens of thousands of pounds for its offices, homes and clubs. A ministerial committee resolved to have the remaining furniture, which was mostly from warehouses, evaluated by professionals and furniture dealers, and sold to a variety of buyers at this valuation price. If any furniture was left after the general sale, the Custodian would determine the method of selling it. The priority list for buyers was as follows: the families of the war disabled, soldiers' families, government employees who had been transferred from Jerusalem, civilians who had been injured in the war, and last of all, ordinary civilians. "In reality," the Custodian later remembered, "the last category never got to purchase any of the furniture, because the higher categories bought practically all of it."[16]

Yosef Yaakobson—an orange grower, and later an advisor to the Ministry of Defense—suggested to Ben-Gurion that he expropriate a shoe-making plant from its Jaffa owner and turn it over to the shoe-making enterprise Min'al of kibbutz Givat Hashloshah. Ben-Gurion consulted the Minister of Finance and Kaplan expressed the opinion that the private property of Arabs who remained in Jaffa should not be expropriated. Ben-Gurion disagreed; in his opinion only the property found inside private residences should not be expropriated. Yaakobson told him that the army was removing goods from Jaffa property estimated at 30,000 pounds daily. Attorney Naftaly Lifshitz of Haifa informed him that in the banks of that city there were 1,500,000,000 pounds in deposits belonging to Arabs. "The banks are willing to turn this property over," noted Ben-Gurion, and so the government, too, took a hand in the division of the spoils.[17]

Minister of Agriculture Aharon Cizling wrote to Ben-Gurion:

Again and again in our meetings we discuss the issue of the abandoned property. Everyone expresses shock, bitterness and shame, but we have yet to find a solution . . . up to now we have dealt with individual looters, both soldiers and civilians. Now, however, there are more and more reports about acts which, judging by their nature and extent, could only have been carried out by (government) order. I ask . . . on what basis was the order given (I hear it has been held back to dismantle all the water pumps in the Arab orange groves). . . . If there is any foundation to the reports which have reached me, the responsibility rests with a government agency. . . . Meanwhile, private plundering still goes on, too.[18]*

Cizling himself represented certain well-defined interests. Minister of Justice Rozen suggested that he address himself to the kibbutzim, including those of his own movement, and ask them to cooperate with the Custodian of Abandoned Property in accordance with the regulations, stipulating that anyone in possession of abandoned property must inform the authorities within two weeks. The Minister of Agriculture, a member of kibbutz Ein Harod, replied that it was "awkward" for him to approach the kibbutzim in this matter. At a meeting of the Ministerial Committee for Abandoned Property, Cizling recommended that no steps be taken against those kibbutzim which were "tardy" in reporting their possession of abandoned property. His recommendation was adopted. His colleagues decided that he would consult with the national secretariats of the kibbutz movements, together with the Minister of Finance, "to discuss the issue."[20]†

Some time later, Ben-Gurion ordered an inspection of all the kibbutzim and *moshavim* (villages) of Lower and Upper Galilee for an inventory of "flocks [cattle, abandoned sheep], and other property 'taken' from the Arab villages during the war and after; crops, furniture and all other objects, were to be presented to the Minister of Defense."[22]

A few days after the capture of Jaffa, Giora Yoseftal, Chief

---

*In the Custodian's report it was stated that "a widespread operation of dismantling the (water pump) engines had been carried out throughout the country. This had to be done in order to collect all the motors in the abandoned orange groves because of the many robberies, and so they could be put to use when they would be needed." Cizling raised the issue of the plundering of the orange groves in the Cabinet, too.[19]

†By the time Shafrir reached Beersheba, two days after it was captured, the army had already removed several tractors from the town, but had left a few others where they were. The Custodian's staff removed the remaining ones and placed them in surrounding kibbutzim for "storage." Shafrir wrote to the Ministerial Committee: "Presumably the Ministry of Agriculture will not wish to remove them from the Negev, and it will be necessary to distribute them among the kibbutzim."[21] In his report he stated that heavy and agricultural equipment were sold at the recommendation of the Ministry of Agriculture.

of the Jewish Agency's Department of Immigrant Absorption, went to see how many new immigrants could be settled in the town. Many of the streets were empty when he arrived, the houses abandoned and the shops boarded up. The smell of war was still in the air as well as the residual odors of life that had existed there earlier.[23] Yoseftal, a tall *yekkeh* (German Jew), proper and very thorough, took care to obtain the documentation showing that he was acting in accordance with official policy. The documents included one from the Custodian and one from Ben-Gurion himself, confirming that Jaffa was intended for the settlement of new immigrants. "Jaffa will be a Jewish city," wrote Ben-Gurion in his diary, "War is war."[24] Yoseftal set up a "housing committee" in his department, and assigned it the task of distributing the houses among the immigrants, in accordance with qualifications and criteria which he himself determined.[25] But the time was inauspicious for committees and criteria—the houses in Jaffa fell to whoever grabbed them first.

Shafrir wrote:

With the intensification of immigration in the summer of 1948, the institutions which looked after the immigrants themselves began to demand that parts of the city which were still under occupation be made available to them. The property included warehouses and shops from which the merchandise had yet to be removed, as well as fully equipped workshops and plants. In Haifa the inspector's office began to issue apartments to the Absorption Department as early as July. The intention was to proceed through the city, quarter by quarter, allocating the apartments and business premises, after the goods had already been taken out of them. But the order was not followed. Hundreds of immigrant families were sent to take possession of apartments, and this caused confusion both in the collecting of goods and in the distribution of apartments. In Jaffa the situation was considerably worse. A certain part of the city was scheduled to be opened on September 10, and a particular allocation of houses was actually agreed upon—to be given to the Absorption Department, the army, the government officials who had been transferred from Jerusalem, and for the children of the settlements who had been evacuated during the war and who had been living in Tel Aviv schools, as well as to the soldiers' families. The Tel Aviv Absorption Department ignored this agreement and went ahead and organized a mass invasion of hundreds of families . . . before the date that was originally agreed upon for the opening of the city to civilians. The government appointed a committee to handle the distribution of apartments in Jaffa. The committee met and reached authoritative conclusions. But once again no heed was paid to the proper agreement. This time the social welfare officers sent hundreds of soldiers' families. Thus the populating of Jaffa was achieved by continuous invasions and counter-invasions [of unauthorized immigrants]."[26]*

By established custom, whoever succeeded in placing a bed in a room and spending the night in it, acquired the right of possession. One day Avraham Amsalem, age 19, entered the house of Mohammed Abu Sirah in the Ajjami quarter, and, threatening the Arab with his submachine gun, invaded and occupied the hallway of his house. The man was brought to trial and in court he explained that he was about to get married and had nowhere to live. He was sentenced to five days in prison.[28] A few weeks previously, a few score soldiers, some of them disabled, invaded Arab houses in Wadi Nisnas and Abbas Street in Haifa. Carrying arms, they appeared at six o'clock in the morning, and forcibly ejected the residents. Then they threw out their belongings and brought in their own. The police came and removed them, but by evening they had invaded other people's homes. They, too, had nowhere to live.[29]

Not only Arabs were subjected to such violence. Moshe Yupiter, an Israeli immigrant, got his apartment from the Custodian, but he was constantly harassed by people who would present themselves, in twos and threes, as Jewish Agency officials, demand to inspect his rooms, check the lease agreement and ask other questions pertaining to the apartment. Yupiter sensed that they were not Jewish Agency officials, and more than once these "visits" ended in threats and curses. He was fearful. "There was no one to go to," he complained. "There is no civil police and the military police is far away from here."[30] Custodian Shafrir confirmed that "the police help little and the military police not at all." After receiving permission from the Ministry of Police, Shafrir managed to recruit a few policemen of his own to work for his office.[31]

Altogether, between 140,000 and 160,000 immigrants were settled in abandoned homes: in Jaffa some 45,000, in downtown Haifa about 40,000, and in Acre about 5,000.[32] The man who

---

*The Absorption Department strenuously denied these charges. According to its spokesman, it was the Ministry of Defense which attempted to seize houses designated for immigrants.[27]

was put in charge of resettling Acre was Mordehai Sarid. "We consulted a map," he later recalled. "I knew which houses I was getting and I worked with engineers to determine what we would do with each apartment. One place needed sinks installed, another required a coat of paint, while other places needed flooring and sewage."[33] The expenses were covered by the Jewish Agency.[34] One day Sarid asked about some immigrants and was told that they were "getting organized." "Splendid," he said, "let them get organized." One of his aides explained what the phrase meant. "They are stealing tables and wardrobes from abandoned houses." As Sarid put it, he was "terribly disturbed"; he summoned the most influential persons among the immigrants and demanded that they all return the stolen property. According to him, "almost everything" was restored.[35]

Mordehai Elkayam was placed in charge of settling immigrants in Ramlah. His first step was to tour the town, accompanied by two social workers. Then he planned the repopulation of the town, quarter by quarter, in conjunction with the military governor. "We decided to start with one particular quarter," he related later. "There was no electricity, but there was running water. The houses were in fair shape. Not much work needed to be done." Three days later the first immigrants arrived—36 families from Bulgaria. Elkayam went to Ramlah with only two aides. He recruited his staff from among the immigrants themselves. Their job was to inspect the empty houses and determine how many families would occupy them. When the immigrants arrived Elkayam's staff would take them to the apartments, and divide the rooms and the use of the facilities among them. Elkayam recalled, "They would paste on the front doors the names of the families and the number of rooms they were entitled to, so that they would not 'squat' in any more rooms (than they were given)." He said that the immigrants bought furniture from the Custodian, and some had brought a few items with them from abroad. But when asked whether they stole furniture from the Arab property, he replied: "Well, of course, there was a good deal of confusion. They bought, they took, in any case, they managed. The early arrivals still found a few pieces of furniture here and there. The later arrivals found nothing."[36] In some cases, immigrants squatted in rooms which had not been assigned to them and had to be forcibly removed by the army.

By the end of the year some 600 shops in Ramlah had been distributed to immigrants. Elkayam had no idea what a city might need, so he went to Tel Aviv. "I went through the streets and made a list of all types of shops," he related later. "I estimated more or less how many groceries were needed, how many butcher shops, how many barber shops and how many cafés." The shops were then distributed, as he described it, by a special committee, giving first consideration to the disabled. But some of the shops were leased to people who could pay for them.[37] By May 1949 some 8,000 people had been settled in Ramlah. In Lydda, too, some 8,000 were settled. At that time there was still no electricity in Lydda, and there was a water shortage. However, most of the political parties had already opened offices and clubs in the town. Of the abandoned properties turned over to immigrants those already operative were: a button manufactory; a carbonated-drinks plant; sausage, ice, textile and macaroni factories.[38]

In Jerusalem the situation was the same. In April it was decided to allocate 400 apartments to government officials who would move to Jerusalem. They had a choice of homes in the better neighborhoods of Baq'a, the "German Colony" and the "Greek Colony." The Absorption Department got the poorer houses of Musrara and Lifta. Shaul Avigur, one of Ben-Gurion's closest advisors, was to be the absolute arbitrator in any disputes.[39] The document detailing this division of property does not mention the elegant quarter of Talbieh. The houses there were given to senior officials, associates and people with important connections—government officials, judges, professors at the Hebrew University, etc. In Jerusalem, too, people were sent to take possession of empty houses. The immigrants' center in Baq'a sent them to occupy apartments assigned to government officials.[40]

Hundreds of people moved in on their own initiative. In the files of the Absorption Department there are lists of such squatters together with recommendations to let them remain in the apartments they had seized, as if they had obtained them legally:

Klein, Moshe. Date of Immigration: 7.22.49. Country of origin: Hungary. Number of persons: four. Squatted on 12.1.49 in Bloc #160, Section #302, number of rooms: 2. Date of recommendation: 1.25.50. *Masud, Amram.* Date of immigration: 3.1.49. Country of origin: Algeria. Number of persons: 8. Squatted on 8:23.49 in Bloc

#112, Section #13, number of rooms: 2. Date of recommendation: 1.24.50.

It seems that the recommendation was a mere formality.[41] Itzhak Ben-Tsvi warned:

> If we go to the leaders of the Jewish communities abroad they too will ask how the vacant Arab residences were occupied. With more than 400,000 people evacuated and only 70,000 settled, it could be interpreted as negligence on our part. The proper utilization of the abandoned residences is imperative![42]

And so tens of thousands of Israelis, soldiers and civilians, helped themselves to the spoils. One took an armchair, another a rug, a third took a sewing machine and a fourth—a combine; one took an apartment and another took a vineyard. Very quickly and easily a whole class—albeit a small one—of newly prosperous people appeared on the scene: merchants, speculators, contractors, agents of all sorts, industrialists and farmers. Some stole what property they could, others received theirs legally. A good many of the transactions fell into that grey area between what the law permitted and what was considered illegal, between outright robbery and official expropriation.

Before the appointment of the Custodian there was a Committee for Arab Property, established by Israel's pre-state army, the *Haganah*. After the capture of the Arab quarters of Haifa, Tiberias, Safed, Acre and Jerusalem, local attorneys were appointed to supervise the abandoned property. The decision to centralize and formalize the procedures for handling the property came as a result of the growing amount of property and the increased incidence of looting. Under British rule there had also been a Custodian—for German and other alien property. At first the Custodian was seen as a temporary trustee of property left behind by the refugees, which would have to be maintained until their return. The Emergency Regulations, which served as the legal framework for the Custodian's functions, limited his prerogatives: he could not sell the properties he had in his charge, but only lease them for a period not exceeding five years. Most of the refugees were not allowed to return, and with few exceptions, Israel did not return their properties to them, although it did not expropriate them formally. The government did declare its willingness to compensate the refugees, but only as part of a general peace settlement.[43] The question of what would be done

with enemy property had preoccupied Ben-Gurion even before
the Declaration of Independence. "The property belongs to the
government," he resolved.[44] The Prime Minister was deeply interested in the methods of expropriating the ownership of the
abandoned property.[45]

Starting in the latter half of 1948, the Ministry of Justice
worked on the drafing of an Absentees' Property Law, giving the
Custodian a share in the ownership of the property he had hith-
erto controlled as a trustee, and authorizing him to transfer it to
a newly established "Development Authority." The Ministry's
draft proposed a literal definition of the term "absentee,"
namely, one who was no longer present in the territory of the
state. When the draft was brought before the Ministerial Committee, Moshe Sharett demanded that the definition be changed
to designate anyone who had left his home after a certain date
(November 29, 1947), regardless of where he might have lived
thereafter. He drew attention to thousands of refugees who had
left their villages and settled in Nazareth. If they were not defined as absentees, it would be necessary to let them return to
their homes. Sharett also raised the possibility that Israel might
one day seize Nablus on the West Bank, which was a "reasonable likelihood," he thought. In that case thousands of refugees
would come within Israel's jurisdiction and they would demand
to return to their homes and take back the properties they had
abandoned. Sharett's reservation was accepted. Consequently,
the definition in the law was changed to embrace all who had
abandoned their "usual place of residence," even if they were
still living in Israel. Some time after, the Custodian was authorized to sell the abandoned property to the development authority, and the Government of Israel authorized the latter to sell it
to the Jewish National Fund. More than half a million acres
were thus expropriated from their owners. A few thousand of
these owners were actually living in Israel, yet the law defined
them as absentees, even if they had only left their homes for a
few days and stayed with relatives in a nearby village or town,
waiting for the fighting to end. Later they came to be referred to
as "present absentees." The majority of them were not allowed
to return to their homes. Those refugees who were permitted to
return to Israel after the war were also formally absentees and
their property was not restored to them.

In one of the Prime Minister's Office files there is a correspondence between several government Ministers, arising from the application of a Haifa Arab lawyer, Elias Koussa, to David Hakohen, MK. The attorney wished to know what was the ruling in the case of an absentee who had been allowed to return to Israel under the family reunification agreement, and after his return received properties which had not belonged to him before leaving, whether by way of purchase, inheritance or any other means. The Minister of Justice expressed the view that an absentee remains an absentee forever, even when allowed back and so long as he is an absentee his property belongs to the Custodian, regardless of when or how he acquired the property. Police Minister Shitrit disagreed. Eventually the law was changed to make it possible for "present absentees" to acquire new property.[46]

The law had other bizarre aspects. Yohanan Bader, MK (Herut) stated, "According to this law, the Israeli army is full of absentees. . . . Every man who went to war on or after November 29, that is to say, left his city—is an absentee, unless he has a certificate to prove that he is not an absentee."[47]

The authority of the military governors was also utilized to expropriate lands. The military governor would issue an order to expel villagers from their homes, or forbid them entrance to their fields and thereby prevent them from cultivating them. Then the Minister of Agriculture would declare the lands to be uncultivated and use his authority to hand them over to others to cultivate. In this way Arab farmers lost their lands without actually losing their title to them. Other laws which served the same purpose were later passed. The properties of the *Waqf* (the Moslem religious authority) were also frozen as if they belonged to absentees. According to the Moslem religion, the *Waqf* properties belong to God. "God has become an absentee!" wrote poet Rashid Husein in one of his protest songs.[48]*

---

*When the Minister of Finance brought the Absentees' Properties Law before the Knesset he warned the members not to talk carelessly: "We are a small country," he said, "but the interest of the world in all that happens and is said here is immense. It's as if the eyes of the world are constantly on us, watching, exploring, analyzing every step, every act, every word." To put Israel's actions in a better light before the eyes of the world, Kaplan was careful to point out, apologetically that in India and Pakistan, too, the governments had expropriated the properties that the refugees left behind.[49] An internal report, which was not published, noted other precedents: Turkey had expropriated the property of the Greeks and Armenians; Bulgaria expropriated the property of the Greeks; Iraq of the Assyrians; Czechoslovakia, Rumania and Yugoslavia expropriated the properties of the German minorities.[50]

In September 1951 the Custodian M. Porat—who had succeeded Shafrir—sent a secret report to the Minister of Finance.
He wrote, "The fact that we are holding the property of legal residents of the country, who otherwise enjoy all the normal rights
of citizenship, is a source of great bitterness and constant agitation among the Arabs who are affected by it. Most of the complaints made by Arabs against our department are made by 'absentees' who see their property in the hands of others and can't
bear it. These absentees try by every means to get their lands
back, and offer to lease them even at exorbitant rents. In accordance with the general rule originally established . . . our office
does not lease the lands expropriated by the government to the
present absentees, so as not to weaken our control over the properties in our charge, and this gives rise to complaints and bitterness. Clearly, this policy does not enhance a spirit of good citizenship among the Arabs who returned, and the question arises
whether the state, having allowed certain Arabs to come back,
or approved their infiltration *de facto*, should provoke their extreme resentment and expose them to the inordinate incitement
of certain political elements. In my opinion, it should not. That
is to say—the government policy should make the legal definition of 'absentee' match the normal connotation of the word's
meaning, i.e., a person who is absent. That should be the policy.
The question remains, how would the policy be applied. It
seems to me that at present there is no practical way of carrying
out the policy I have suggested, at least with regard to real estate. The number of 'present absentees' runs into the thousands,
most of them owners of real estate. There are already new people
living on some of these properties, particularly in the border settlements. Any attempt to return the properties to these absentees would, therefore, adversely affect thousands, or tens of
thousands, of settlers, not to mention army camps and installations."[51]

To relieve the resentment of the "present absentees," the
Custodian proposed that their bank accounts be released to
them, and that a way be found to compensate them for their
properties. Attorney General Shapira had made the same recommendation long before, though without any illusions: "In the
end we shall both pay compensation and still be considered
thieves," he predicted in August 1949.[52] And so it was. The gov-

ernment offered to compensate only a few of the property owners and its offers were hardly tempting. Only a few accepted
them, and the compensation was generally viewed as unfair.[53]*

In the Knesset debate about the work of the Custodian,
Yaakov Gil, MK, of the centrist General Zionists, claimed that
90 percent of the abandoned property was being given to members of MAPAI. "Other parties, and ordinary Jews who belong to
no party," he said, "are left out and have received no benefit
from this property. The Custodian handles the property as he
pleases, to suit himself and the party to which he belongs, his
friends and associates. . . . The entire country has become a single *Politbureau!*"[56] But some property was also allocated to various other parties and political organizations.[57]

The abandoned property in the villages was divided in much
the same way as in the towns and cities.[58] While the war was
still going on, Levi Shkolnik (Eshkol), Head of the Settlement
Department of the Jewish Agency, went on a tour of the Arab
villages which had recently been abandoned and captured. As he
put it, he saw "the traces of what had been and was no longer"—
the houses broken into, plundered and burned. "The sight sank
through my eyes and nostrils into my head, brain, blood, and
heart. . . ."[59] One day, in the latter half of 1948, Eshkol drove up
to Jerusalem. With him were his driver and Raanan Weitz, his
aide. They passed near Birieh, a little village perched on top of a
rocky hill southeast of Ramlah, overlooking the road to Latrun.
"I didn't know the details, yet" he related later, "but I believed
that the desolate and abandoned place might help solve the problem of settling the nation." He stopped the car and he and Weitz
went for a walk through the village. As they proceeded to Jerusalem they drew up a plan. Eshkol related, "That evening I . . . sent
for the engineers, asked the Engineer Corps for assistance and
began to turn the great wheel which enabled us that very winter

---

*In one Foreign Ministry file there is a record of correspondence which
links the possibility that Israel would pay compensation to the Arab refugees
with the possibility that West Germany would compensate the Jews for the
Nazi crimes.[54] At some stage the idea was also raised that the property of Arabs
in Israel would be held as security against Jewish property in the Arab countries. This was Behor Shitrit's proposal. The Legal Advisor to the Foreign Ministry rejected it. When the sale of abandoned Arab property was finally allowed,
Israeli undercover immigration agents in Iraq telegraphed in horror: "What's
going to happen to Jewish properties here?!"[55]

to transform more than 45 abandoned villages into lively new settlements."[60]*

In the latter half of 1948, the settlement department of the Jewish Agency prepared a list of several dozen Arab villages which it proposed to repopulate with new immigrants. Most of the villages had been abandoned, but a few were not quite empty. Some were meant to be demolished and their lands to be used for new settlements. Some of the Cabinet ministers criticized the army for demolishing some of the villages it occupied. The subject was brought up time after time by Ministers Shitrit, Bentov and Cizling. "As I travel about I hear rumors about the destruction of property and I should like to know who gave the order to do this," said Cizling at one meeting. "I was in Beit Shean and was told by people I trust that the army commander had received an order to destroy the place. . . . These are facts about villages which I have seen destroyed. In the Hefer Valley I saw Arab villages which had been abandoned by their inhabitants and were not destroyed during the campaign. Now they are in ruins and whoever did it should be called upon to explain. . . ." Ben-Gurion replied: "When you say Beit Shean, that is a particular place. But when you mention generally 'ruined villages'—I can't send people to look for ruined villages." Cizling asked: "Who destroyed the village of Cherkass in the Hefer Valley? At an earlier meeting I mentioned Moussa Goldenberg who reported an order to destroy 40 villages and named you, as the source of that order. I stated then that I did not believe it was really done in your name. I am not speaking now about the political aspect, but about things which seem to be happening by themselves, without control. Even if I agreed with a certain act—I wouldn't accept it being done by itself."[62]

Not everything happened "by itself": in September Ben-Gurion informed the Ministerial Committee for Abandoned Property that the commander of the central front, Tsvi Ayalon, considered it necessary "to demolish partially" 14 Arab villages, for reasons of security. "As it is extremely difficult to convene

---

*But at the end of November he said to his Jewish Agency colleagues that he was aware that the Arabs might yet return to the occupied zones. "Since our own agriculture is intensive," he said, "we may be able to give them some of the lands for cultivation." He expressed the view that he did not care to house the immigrants permanently in Arab houses, but meant to build them new ones.[61]

the committees," Ben-Gurion wrote his ministers, "would you please let me have your opinion [on the destruction of Arab villages] in writing. I shall await your answer within three days. . . . Lack of response will be viewed as consent." The ministers demanded further information.[63] In September 1949 the Cabinet debated the destruction of the old city of Tiberias. Yigael Yadin was quoted as recommending that the entire city, except for the holy places, be destroyed, in order to prevent the Arab residents from returning.[64]

The authorities also included in their plans lands owned by Jews. They were inclined to emphasize that most of the Arab lands they proposed to expropriate were not cultivated, and that even after the expropriations the Arab villages would still have enough lands to sustain them. The planning was done in close cooperation with the army. The army recommended certain locations and often demanded that they be settled. The assumption was that the new settlements would serve to fortify the country's borders and prevent the return of the villagers who had fled and been driven out in the course of the war and its aftermath.[65]

Yosef Weitz, of the Jewish National Fund, saw the new plans as the direct sequel to the efforts made by the Zionist movement over the past years, through the Jewish National Fund, to "redeem" the land. Hundreds of thousands of acres had been purchased from their Arab owners over the years, bit by bit. The process continued after the Declaration of Independence. "I marked on my map land areas of one village after another," noted Weitz in his diary, "and I should like to swallow it all."[66] Weitz spent most of his time traveling around the country. The abandoned villages set his imagination alight. At night, standing empty and dark, he wrote the villages "terrified" him. By day, when he saw them looking so picturesque and blooming, but still empty, he "felt ashamed" that they had not yet been settled by Jews: "This is a wide country," he wrote, "the sense of its breadth makes one feel so secure."[67] Ben-Gurion thought that purchasing land was a waste of money. He preferred to expropriate the land and thought that the Jewish National Fund's willingness to pay only made land more expensive.[68] Weitz continued to purchase, among other reasons, because he feared that the Fund and all its staff would become superfluous and be closed down. "Ben-Gurion's way of thinking is that the state is above everything, and that the Zionist Federation is only there to serve it, and should exist only as long as it is needed," he noted bitterly.[69]

Before long, the government decided to promote the settlement of immigrants in the abandoned villages of Galilee. In August 1948, the Ministerial Committee discussed the creation of 61 new settlements. The settling authorities recommended that only 32 of them, on some 30,000 acres, be built for the time being. Of those lands some 14,500 acres belonged to Arabs, 5,000 to the government, 5,000 to other owners, chiefly German, and in one case to the *Waqf*; about 5,000 acres belonged to Jews. The Ministers considered the future of the Arab inhabitants and made suggestions for transferring them legally.[70] The Minister of Agriculture described the legal arrangements as "a fiction."[71]

A few days later officials of the Department of Health went out to inspect an abandoned Arab village on the outskirts of Jerusalem. They were accompanied by representatives of the military government and of the Absorption Department of the Jewish Agency. The health inspectors found Anopheles—malaria—mosquitoes in the village, and stated that before it could be re-inhabited the houses would have to be fumigated with DDT and the water wells purified. This was a budgetary problem, and the Health Department proposed using volunteer labor. It was easy work, the Department promised, offering the volunteers protective gloves for the purpose. The Jerusalem District Officer informed the Department that there was as yet no plan for resettling the village, but in the meantime the staff of the Jewish Agency's settlement section had already gone there to inspect the place. On their return they reported:

". . . We have no data concerning the size of the lands, as there are no accurate maps of the village and environs, but as far as we could tell from examining the site, the cultivable lands are considerable, extending over a few hundred acres. These lands have been cultivated for many years by the former inhabitants of the village. Around the houses there are orchards, fruit trees and olive groves, which would be suitable for sustaining future settlers. In view of the above, we recommend that the village be settled in two different ways. 1) Houses with home farms, each on a total of 1.25 acres, the land to be used for growing vegetables and fruit trees. In addition, each settler would raise between 500 and 1,000 head of poultry. 2) The village center would serve to settle artisans, who would have their workshops and quarries there, serving both the local population and that of Jerusalem. The two groups can amount to a total of 150 to 200 families—i.e., 50 units of houses with home farms, and the rest housing only. The buildings are generally well constructed and do not require much repair. There is a water well beside each house, and the proximity of the central water pipe that supplies Jerusalem makes additional water supply a possible alternative. There are no modern toilets, but they could be provided. There are community buildings in the village, such as a school, a central building for public institutions, etc. . . ."[72]

A slight misunderstanding ensued in the next few weeks between two departments of the Jewish Agency, each of which wanted to be put in charge of the village. In January it was decided that the village would be handed over to the Absorption Department, which would establish an immigrant camp on the site. The decision was made at a meeting which was also attended by Shaul Avigur, one of Ben-Gurion's top aides. In the minutes of that meeting it is stated that approval by Avigur was tantamount to approval by Ben-Gurion himself. Therefore, an immigrant camp was established in the village. In the following weeks they looked for a contractor whose offer would be lower than that of *Solel Boneh* (the *Histadrut* construction corporation); they also persuaded the *Hamekasher* transport company to open a bus route to the village, and the post office to connect it to the telephone network. Jerusalem Mayor, Daniel Oster, was called upon to make a contribution—he offered a four-inch water pipe. Simultaneously, they settled the village with immigrants from Poland, Rumania and Slovakia, members of an association which was linked with the orthodox movement *Poalei Agudat Israel*. A cooperative store, a medical clinic and a synagogue were opened. The Ministry of Education inquired if it was necessary to open classes in the village. By the summer of 1949, 5 acres of olive groves had already been ploughed over and 300 crates of plums had been marketed from the village orchards. The grape harvest began and a new settlement was well under way. The village was now given the name Givat Shaul Bet. In the past it had been known as Deir Yassin.[73]

There is a file at the Prime Minister's Office, dealing with the rural settlement of immigrants, which contains a letter signed by Martin Buber and three other noted scholars, Ernst Simon,

Werner Senator and Cecil Roth. They asked Ben-Gurion that Deir Yassin be left uninhabited, or at least that its settlement be postponed until the wounds had had a chance to heal. "We are well aware of the hardships suffered by our brothers, the new immigrants, who have reached their homeland after many years of wandering and being confined in concentration camps, and here too are still without a proper roof over their heads," wrote the scholars. "Moreover, we fully realize that the Government of Israel must provide for their housing to the best of its ability. However, we do feel that Deir Yassin is not a suitable place, or, at any rate, that the time has not yet come to decide on establishing a Jewish settlement in that village. The name of that village has become infamous throughout the Jewish world, the Arab world and the whole world. In Deir Yassin hundreds of innocent men, women and children were massacred. The Deir Yassin affair is a black stain on the honor of the Jewish nation. The Zionist movement, the army and our government of the time (the Jewish Agency Executive), all felt this acutely and most unequivocally condemned the deed at the time.

"There are certain symbolic acts in the life of a nation that must be avoided, and there are certain educational values that must be preserved. In the case of this great and ancient nation, and this state, so small and so young, this is even more imperative. We hope that time and constructive acts of friendship will heal even this sore wound, which is far too fresh—just as fresh as our own memory of the tragedy of April 13th, when the medical convoy to Hadassah on Mount Scopus was massacred (24 hours after the massacre in Deir Yassin). The time will come when it will be possible to conceive of some act in Deir Yassin, an act which will symbolize our people's desire for justice and brotherhood with the Arab people. We are already now proposing such an act. But in the meantime, it would be better to let the lands of Deir Yassin lie fallow and the houses of Deir Yassin stand uninhabited, than to carry out an act whose negative symbolic impact is infinitely greater than the practical resolution it can offer. Resettling Deir Yassin within a year of the crime, and within the framework of ordinary settlement, would amount to an endorsement of, or at least an acquiescence with, the massacre. Let the village of Deir Yassin remain uninhabited for the time being, and let its desolation be a terrible and tragic symbol of war, and a warning to our people that no practical or military needs may ever justify such acts of murder and that the nation does not wish to profit from them."[74]*

A few months later the village was mentioned again. This was in the course of a Knesset debate on the government's decision to permit the return of 100,000 Arab refugees to Israel.

> Yaakov Meridor (Herut): "Soviet Russia knew how to solve the problem of the Volga Germans during the war. There were 800,000 Germans in that region. . . . They transferred them to the east, beyond the Urals. If there should be a second round of fighting, where shall we transfer this fifth column? With the coastal region being only 10 miles wide, how shall we do it? Or perhaps we'll have to evacuate Tel Aviv so as to settle them there and keep an eye on them."
>
> Tewfik Toubi (Communist): "You're preparing another Deir Yassin!"
>
> Meridor: "Thanks to Deir Yassin we won the war, sir!"
>
> A. Ben-Eliezer (Herut): "Don't be so sad."
>
> A. Cizling (MAPAM): "Don't boast about Deir Yassin."
>
> E. Raziel-Naor (Herut): "There's nothing to be ashamed of . . .!"[75]
>
> Zalman Aran (MAPAI): "As a member of the Knesset I must comment on one interjection that was heard here yesterday from the Herut benches. The interjection was, We are not ashamed of Deir Yassin."
>
> A. Ben-Eliezer: "How many Deir Yassins have you been responsible for?"
>
> Aran: "For your sakes, I should like to say that I don't believe you're not ashamed of Deir Yassin."
>
> Ben-Eliezer: "You don't have to bring up something that you yourselves performed."
>
> Aran: "I don't know that we performed any Deir Yassins."
>
> Ben-Eliezer: "If you don't know, you can ask the Minister of Defense!"
>
> Aran: ". . . If I thought that the State of Israel would be capable of Deir Yassins, I would not only not wish to be an Arab here—I wouldn't want to be a Jew here!"[76]

In the Central Zionist Archives and in the State Archives there are many files dealing with the resettlement of Givat Shaul Bet. The former name of the village is given in brackets, evidently without any indication of embarrassment. The press, too, re-

---

*Ben-Gurion did not answer this letter. Buber and his associates sent him a copy, and then another copy, until the Prime Minister's secretaries wrote back that he was presently too busy to read their letter.

ported the resettlement as if it had been an ordinary village, like any other. Several hundred guests came to the opening ceremony, including the Ministers Kaplan and Shapira, as well as the Chief Rabbis and the Mayor of Jerusalem. President Haim Weizmann sent written congratulations. The band of the school for the blind played and refreshments were served.*

Amid the diaries, letters, telegrams, memoranda, reports, minutes, essays, poetry, prose, newspaper articles and speeches written during those months, a few lines recorded from a speech made in the Knesset by Dr. Zerah Warhaftig, in the course of a debate about the absentees' property, stand out:

> . . . Who better than us, a people without land, who for so many generations could not call even a few feet of land its own, can know and must know how to appreciate land. The word for man in Hebrew (Adam) is derived from the Hebrew word for land (Adamah). Our Sages said, "A man without land is not a man." Only now that we have a state and a land of our own, can we be called both a nation and men.[80]

With the mass immigration of Jews, especially from Arab countries, the newspapers tended to portray Arab emigration as part of a general exchange of population and property between the incoming Jews and the outgoing Arabs: Jewish immigrants

---

*The press expressed no qualms in reporting the resettlement of other abandoned villages, a total of 350. The reports reflect a solid belief in the right and justification of the resettlement. *Davar:* " . . . At the sound of the Israeli soldiers marching, the Arabs were seized with a great terror and left their homes, with their heavily loaded camels and donkeys, en route for the border. . . . And now in Jamsin—renamed Givat Amal—live new residents, recently arrived via Cyprus, survivors of the camps of Europe. . . . They sit around a long table, with one remnant of the abandoned furniture, and tell their tales. . . ."[77] *Haaretz:* " . . . Patches of brilliant green are now surrounding the houses in the abandoned villages, thanks to the activities of the Ministry of Agriculture that helps the new immigrants develop their home farms. . . ."[78] *Dvar Hashavua:* " . . . You will not recognize Aqir! More than a thousand immigrants have settled in the abandoned village. . . ."[79] Similar descriptions were published about Deir Yassin. The immigrant camp was later turned over to the Ministry of Health, which converted it to a sanitorium for the mentally ill. Parts of the village became one of the neighborhoods of the new city of Jerusalem, other parts remained deserted.

from Arab lands had left their homes behind, just as the Arabs in Israel had, the papers contended.

The daily *Haaretz* worried more about whether the abandoned villages would provide enough housing. "We are on the verge of a serious crisis with regard to immigrant absorption," warned the respected paper. "In another month the abandoned lands will hold no more room for new immigrants."[81]

PART II

Between Veterans and Newcomers

4

The First Million

ITHIN 48 HOURS after the Declaration of Independence, two ships sailed into Tel Aviv harbor. One was called *'Medinat Israel' (The State of Israel)* and the other, *'Lanitsahon' (To Victory)*. On board the two were several hundred immigrants.

The Law of Return, giving every Jew who settled in Israel the automatic right to become a citizen, was actually enacted more than two years later, in July 1950. However, the Provisional Council of State had abolished the British regulations restricting Jewish immigration within days of the creation of the state, opening the gates wide to all Jews. They came like a tidal wave: in the first six months of Independence 100,000 immigrants arrived. In 1949, over 250,000. As a result, the population of Israel increased by 50 percent during that period, or, in other words, by the end of 18 months a third Israeli was added for every two Israelis who had lived in the country before Independence. One out of three Israelis was therefore a newcomer and a stranger. They were also strangers to each other, having come from almost every country in the world and speaking any number of different languages. In those days the wanted ads in the newspapers generally listed "Hebrew-speaking" as one of the required qualifications for employment. Toward the end of the year the immigrant who made the Jewish population of Israel one million arrived. The poet Nathan Alterman wrote exuberantly, praising statistics:

> "It's good to be a million
> You look at them and your eye grows moist
> Tears twinkle. And why?
> For we've said it, brother—statistics
> Is not always something dry. . . ."[1]

The figures were, in fact, quite dramatic.*

A few weeks before the Declaration of Independence MAPAI began to draft the state's policy of immigration and absorption. The committee set up for the purpose drafted a budget for the absorption of 150,000 immigrants within the next two years, though some of its members thought the number might reach 250,000. No one imagined that the figure would come to 400,000 people.[3] The government intended to adopt a four-year development plan whose aim would be the doubling of the Jewish population. This, then, was the national goal—to absorb 600,000 immigrants within the first four years after Independence. It was achieved, but the number of immigrants who arrived in the first year, 1949, was ten times the number that came in the fourth.[4] It was generally agreed that the rate of immigration should be speeded up, since the Jews might not remain so eager to come later on, or might be unable to do so. The state and the Zionist movement organized mass departures of Jews from their countries of origin and transported them to Israel, by air and by sea, generally at public expense; it was extremely expensive. In certain countries Jewish emigration entailed breaking local laws. In others, Jewish lives were in jeopardy, so the secret

---

*The largest group of immigrants to arrive in 1949 was from Poland (47,000); next, from North Africa (39,000); Yemen (35,000); Turkey (26,000); and Bulgaria (20,000).[2]

Land of origin	1949	From creation of state till 3.31.51
Eastern Europe	109,262	271,188
Asia	71,271	164,787
North Africa, with Egypt and Libya	39,442	77,083
Western Europe, America and unlisted	19,166	46,617
Totals:	239,141	559,675

services of the Zionist movement and the state were called upon to help. The State of Israel needed them. "Many see them as cannon fodder," observed one newspaper.[5]

The right of the Jewish people to be like any other nation, with a sovereign state of its own, was defined in the Declaration of Independence as a natural right. The declaration referred to the Holocaust: the State of Israel was created to provide the Jews with a safe haven. It was described as the state of all the Jews and whose main goal was the ingathering of the exiles.[6] "The people who live in the state," wrote David Ben-Gurion, "are but the seed of the people for whom it was created."[7] From time to time he also spoke about saving the Jews in the Diaspora. "*Aliyah* (immigration to Israel) saves Jews from destruction. . . . We must do everything to save them," he said to senior officials of the Foreign Ministry in April 1949. But this was said in passing. On the whole, the notion of "saving Jews" was not what drove Ben-Gurion to absorb so many immigrants in 1949. Immigration obviously enhanced the political, social, economic, ideological and psychological image of the new state, but, for Ben-Gurion, the most vital reason for promoting immigration was for the sake of the state's national security and military might, and it was that which mattered most.

When the Foreign Ministry staff asked to be briefed before the Lausanne conference, Ben-Gurion defined for them the interests of the state: "The main thing is the absorption of immigrants," he said. "This embodies all the historical needs of the state." He then explained why immigration would strengthen the country's security better than anything else. "We might have captured the West Bank, the Golan, the entire Galilee, but those conquests would not have reinforced our security as much as immigration. Doubling and tripling the number of immigrants gives us more and more strength. . . . That is the most important thing, above all else." He spoke in a similar vein about settlement: "We have conquered territories, but without settlements they have no decisive value, not in the Negev, nor in Galilee, nor in Jerusalem. Settlement—that is the real conquest." And since for settlement you need immigrants, said Ben-Gurion, "the future of the state depends on immigration." He expressed the same ideas before the institutions of his party. Here, too, he emphasized the defensive importance of immigration and rarely referred to the need to save Jews.[8]

Consequently, Israel's foreign policy set immigration as one of its main targets. Israel's diplomatic representatives and friends in Washington, Paris and London worked to facilitate the departure of Jews from North Africa, Libya, Egypt, Iraq, Iran and Yemen. Israeli representatives in Eastern Europe brought up the issue directly. "With unceasing, and at times nagging, pressure, we argued, explained and knocked on the door of every heart," wrote Israel Barzilai, Israel's Ambassador in Warsaw, to Foreign Minister Moshe Sharett.[9] Sharett himself had a lengthy meeting with the Soviet Deputy Foreign Minister, Andrei Vishinsky, to explain Israel's immigration needs.[10] The young state, which has just fought for its existence in the War of Independence, the few against the many, was treated with sympathy and goodwill in almost all capitals. It was seen as a democratic, well-intentioned state, a home for the survivors of the Holocaust and a safe haven for refugees and the persecuted from all over the world. The Israeli representatives noted also some sudden, unforeseen changes, though some of their projections were soon shown to have been mistaken. The Israeli Ambassador to the Soviet Union, Golda Meir, tried, as she put it, not to ask for exit permits for Jews in her official meetings in Moscow, fearing that a negative response there would also affect the rest of the Soviet bloc. "Golda reported that they listen to everything willingly," Itzhak Refael, Head of the Jewish Agency's immigration department, reported to his colleagues, "but they show little sympathy for immigration to Israel. They say, 'Let them come from America; there, there is danger of anti-Semitism, not in the USSR, where there are equal rights.'"[11] In December 1948 Ambassador Meir wrote to the Jewish Agency Executive that it was her distinct impression that "we are reaching the end of the exodus from Eastern Europe."[12] In fact, the mass immigration from there was about to begin again.

Some of the efforts made by Israel to open the gates for Jewish migration also served to enhance commercial relations between the state and the countries of Eastern Europe. Thus in the latter half of May 1949, a trade agreement was concluded between Israel and Poland. Israel promised to purchase within a year 16 million dollars' worth of Polish goods, chiefly food products, iron, timber, textiles, chemicals, machinery and paper. For their part, the Poles were to buy from Israel goods totalling only

3.2 million dollars—razor blades, dental drills, oils, scrap iron, etc.[13]

At the opening of the negotiations which led to the agreement, Israel's Ambassador to Poland, Barzilai, pointedly mentioned the connection between the agreement and the prospect of Jewish emigration from Poland. At this time the question was being debated by the Polish government, and Barzilai thought that the decision might be influenced by economic considerations. He, therefore, favored an agreement which would give preference to Poland's economic interests. Two months after the agreement was signed, the Jews of Poland were allowed to leave. The Polish government agreed to Israel's demand to allow each emigrant to take out a sum equivalent to 150–200 dollars—albeit at the official rate of exchange, which was about a third of the black-market rate. The Poles also promised eventually to release the money Jews would leave behind, and announced their willingness to negotiate the question of compensation for confiscated Jewish property, as part of the economic transaction between the two countries. Israel found it difficult to meet its obligations—in the first eight months after the agreement Israel bought only six million dollars' worth of goods, and the Israeli Embassy in Warsaw warned that if the agreement was not kept, the emigration of Jews might be halted.[14]*

A memorandum on the trade agreement with Poland stated, "Ambassador Barzilai judged it most appropriate to include certain economic advantages in a commercial agreement, but under no circumstances was it to be in the form of head tax, as is customary in certain countries of the Eastern bloc."[16] Barzilai settled with the Polish authorities not only the legal and financial ar-

---

*In August 1949 it was assumed in the Foreign Ministry that the Polish government's motives in permitting Jewish emigration were based chiefly on internal considerations:

> ... The desire to put a stop to the emigrational restlessness, to put an end to the multiplicity of parties among the Jews, to integrate the remaining Jews in the economic structure, and to instill in them a single patriotism. These reasons coupled with the activities of the Ambassador and the Embassy who consistently emphasized that it is not possible to eliminate Jewish communal distinctiveness in Poland ... before giving those who wish it the right to make their home in Israel.

The same was true of other countries. In Poland, of course, the Holocaust carried added weight: "The best Polish literature treats it as an open wound, a sin which must be atoned for."[15]

rangements entailed in the departure of the Jews, but also the technical details involved, down to the issuance of passports, railroad timetables and so forth.[17] The Israeli representatives in other capitals functioned in a similar manner—half diplomats, half travel agents. Almost every one of them acted as businessmen at one stage or another. Israel and various Jewish philanthropic organizations, mainly in the United States, paid large sums of money for the exit permits of the Jews from Eastern Europe.

The arrangements varied from time to time and from place to place. In Bulgaria every person who left was paid for. Efraim Shilo was one of the Israeli undercover agents who first established diplomatic relations with the Bulgarians, even before the Declaration of Independence. "It began in Belgrade, Yugoslavia," he recalled later. "The connections were built up gradually, leading from one person to another, by way of the leaders of the Jewish communities, first in Belgrade, and then in Sofia, Bulgaria. Someone knew an official in one of the Ministries, he knew another official, and that official introduced me to a second or third secretary in one of the embassies, and so on slowly, until we reached the right person. I was there as a journalist."[18] The "right people" were the secret servicemen and the Ministry for External Trade. The first transaction permitted only the use of Bulgarian ports for the embarkation of Jews from Rumania. Shilo proposed leasing Bulgarian ships and port services. He also purchased from the Bulgarians the supplies needed for the ships, and he paid in dollars. The Bulgarians also demanded $50 for each Jew they let out and Shilo agreed. Payment was made by check, in Prague, Czechoslovakia, or care of the Bulgarian Consulate in Zurich, Switzerland. The money came from the American Joint Distribution Committee, the great Jewish welfare organization, generally known as the Joint. Everything was quite official, only secret. Shilo later offered to pay $100 for every young Jew who would be allowed to leave Bulgaria, and later still offered $300 for every Zionist prisoner released and allowed to leave for Israel. Shilo stated, "There was lots of goodwill and sympathy. There's no doubt about it. But they also made some money out of it. I handled it only at the beginning, and as I recall, during that period we paid the Bulgarians some three million dollars. Later others took my place and they also paid." Some of the migration transactions were tied to arms purchases Israel later made in Eastern Europe, mainly in Czechoslovakia.

Shilo explained: "Things were very complicated. Some of the people involved dealt both in arms and in emigrants, both on our side and on those of the governments with which we dealt. There was also, of course, a political angle—much depended on our ability to arouse sympathy for our cause, and there was the financial interest to sell us arms as well as Jews." Permission to let the Jews depart for Israel was viewed by the Eastern bloc as a form of military aid, reinforcements for the Israeli army in its struggle against British imperialism.

In some cases payment for the exit permits was made in the form of goods, machinery and farm equipment, or in the form of hospitals and old-people's homes built by the Joint. Some of the agreements were signed only after months of hard haggling. Such were the negotiations which took place in 1949 with the government of Hungary. The Hungarians demanded two million dollars for 25,000 Jews—$80 a head. This asking price was lower than the Rumanian one, which was then demanding five million dollars for 50,000 Jews—$100 a head. But after a while the Hungarians also raised their price, until in the end they demanded a million dollars per 1,000 Jews, i.e., $1,000 a head. They proposed to release only men over 50 and women over 40. Negotiations proceeded in a business-like way, as if they were not discussing human beings at all. "1. Too expensive; 2. Not enough; 3. Inadequate quality," was the response to one of the Hungarian proposals. The negotiations went on for months. Ehud Avriel, Israel's Ambassador in Prague, recommended concluding the agreement. "I have been troubled by great misgivings throughout these past months in which I negotiated with the Hungarians," he wrote. "But I felt obliged to bring this unfortunate affair to a positive conclusion, on the terms which have been the same for the last three months. . . . We came to the conclusion that a refusal of these terms on our part would allow the Hungarians to renege on their commitment and cause a prolonged deadlock."[19]

Avriel hoped that this transaction would lead to other, more favorable ones. The Israeli government hestitated, fearing, among other reasons, that the high price would set a precedent, but in the end it was agreed that the Joint would pay the Hungarians a million dollars for 3,000 exit permits—$300 a head. The Hungarians reserved the right to select the emigrants, but added a bonus—40 special permits for leaders of the Jewish community, to be chosen by the Israeli Embassy. The arguments that ensued in the Zionist movement raged for weeks—everbody wanted to choose their own activists.[20] All parties to the transaction felt its sordidness even though all could point to the achievement of worthy goals. The Hungarians could say that they had sold them to strengthen their economy; the Joint could say that they had bought them for humanitarian reasons; the Israelis could say that the Jews were purchased as one traditionally pays ransom for hostages. But the Hungarian government had difficulties explaining to its citizens why only Jews were allowed to emigrate; the Joint would find it awkward to explain to its contributors, mostly in the United States, why it was sending such vast sums behind the Iron Curtain, at the height of the cold war. In Israel, the government wished to avoid a debate over whether it was justified in spending a million dollars to bring in additional immigrants, instead of investing the money in improving the lot of those who had already arrived and were living in camps. All parties therefore agreed to keep the details of the agreement secret. The ninth clause in the twelve-clause Israeli–Hungarian protocol stipulated that not only its details, but the very existence of the entire transaction would remain confidential.[21]

During the first few months of Independence, in the course of the war, the importance of the Jewish Agency Executive, also known as the Zionist Executive, diminished despite the protests of its members. "This state is not only the State of Israel," said one of them. "It's the state of the entire Jewish people and belongs to the Zionist movement as a whole. Members of the Zionist Executive have a right to voice their opinions, and the Zionists in the Israeli government must obey their instructions."[22] Another member demanded that those of the Jewish Agency Executive who had become Cabinet Ministers resign their membership in the Executive, for "surely it's unthinkable that the Zionist Federation should receive orders from the Government of Israel. It would make it a Zionist *Comintern.* . . ."[23]

Three months after the creation of the state, immigration policy was not being made clear to everyone. S.Z. Shragai related the case of a French Jewish tourist who had been asked to deposit a sum of money as a guarantee that he would not settle in the country. Shragai: "It should be stated explicitly whether there is free immigration. . . ."[24] The Chairman of the Executive, Berl Locker, raised the question whether it was permissible for one country to organize the emigration of people from another country.[25] In a similar vein, they debated the question of who would organize the immigration to Israel and who would finance it. After a time it was agreed that the Jewish Agency would be in charge of bringing the immigrants to Israel, at its own expense, through the United Jewish Appeal (UJA) and the Joint. It also underwrote the expenses for the immigrants' accommodation in the camps. Then they argued about the question of who would subsidize the absorption of the immigrants once they left the camps. The Minister of Finance told the Executive that the government would be unable to pay for immigrant absorption, because of the high cost of the war—"seven million pounds a month."[26] Levi Eshkol, too, warned that "the government was suffering [financial] difficulties."[27] Eshkol was a senior government official and member of the Executive, both at the same time. Some days later he informed the Executive that the government would be prepared to deploy its organizational resources to take care of the immigrants, but that it had no funds.[28] The dispute went on for a long time—nobody wanted to pay.* The Jewish Agency was only supposed to deliver the immigrants, but its past function as the "government" of the Jewish community in pre-state Palestine and its new function as the "government" of the Jewish people, plus its ability actually to finance the immigration, gave the Agency considerable say in forming immigration policy as well. Matters of political and international importance, such as the negotiations with Hungary and the like, were left to the government, but the numbers of immigrants to be brought from each country were determined by the Jewish Agency. In February 1949 the Agency resolved that the immigration quota for that year would be 250,000, and the government approved its resolution.

Following the Declaration of Independence, the Jewish Agency's Immigration Department was placed under the direction of Itzhak Werfel (later Refael), of the religious *Hapoel Hamizrahi* party. He had taken part in the Jerusalem Committee, which ran

---

*In March, when the immigration was at its height, Dr. Israel Goldstein, a Member of the Zionist Executive, proposed leaving the immigrants on board their ships in the harbor for several days, in order to pressure the government into doing more for their reception. When it was pointed out to him that this would entail much suffering, Goldstein replied, "I see no harm in that. . . . It will rouse the government and the UJA contributors to do more. . . ."[29]

the city during the war. Refael regarded his new post as a promotion, and proposed to run his department as an absolute ruler. As he put it, he considered himself to be his party's representative.[30] He was then 34 years old, the son-in-law of Rabbi I.L. Maimon (formerly Fishmann), one of his party's leaders and a minister in the government. Refael ran the immigration business with boundless energy and considerable organizational skills. He was an ambitious man—"I very much wanted to succeed," he wrote years later.[31] Members of the Executive charged him with political intrigue, and some said he was not to be trusted.[32] Among other things, they discovered that the number of immigrants who arrived each month was almost always higher than the figure he had submitted for their approval. He had earlier proposed to the Executive that 330,000 immigrants should be brought in that year, and had reluctantly accepted the limitation of a quarter million agreed by the Agency and government.[33] Refael wanted them to be received in unlimited numbers, and was inclined to disregard their hardships after arrival. "In my opinion there is nothing terrible about their living in tents for a while," he once said.[34] The main thing was to bring them in. So eager was he to "finish off the Diaspora" as he put it that he opposed the building of new synagogues outside of Israel. "As a religious man, I tell you, it's a crime to build synagogues abroad, when tomorrow we shall have to close them down."[35]

The files of the Immigration Department depict a worldwide enterprise—from Uruguay to Burma, from South Africa to Canada, from Afghanistan to Albania. Documents in these files are written in a dozen languages, all expressing a passionate desire to get to Israel. Intense pressure was applied by Jews everywhere on the Jewish Agency to speed up their immigration. Some sent the Agency desperate pleas for help, to save them from economic hardships and from persecution. The Jewish Agency established offices in many countries, called the *Eretz Israel* (Land of Israel) Offices. Their directors registered candidates for immigration, placed them in different categories, organized their passage and arranged for their baggage to be shipped. It entailed an intense and complicated administrative effort. Everywhere there were endless difficulties to be overcome—some legal and political, others bureaucratic and technical. The Zionist representatives dealt with innumerable human problems and at times they also had to deal with personal tragedies, each immigrant having his or her own special story. The undertaking demanded resourcefulness and courage. The picture that emerges from these files is one of dedication in the face of dangerous risks, even death at various clandestine operations in an effort to bring Jews to safety. It also reflects much confusion and overlapping authorities, as well as quarrels and disputes among the various agents—some representing the Jewish Agency, some the political parties, and some belonging to the Immigration Department, under the leadership of Hapoel Hamizrahi—others to the absorption agencies controlled by MAPAI; in addition there were the Israeli embassies, the immigration officers and the leaders of the local Jewish communities. Now and then there were cases of corruption. Efraim Shilo stated, "It was a mad operation at a mad time. There is no point in looking for rational considerations or rational actions."[36]

Within a few months after becoming Head of the Immigration Department, Refael sought to define his relationship with the *Mossad le-aliyah bet* (the Organization for Illegal Immigration). During the British Mandate in Palestine, the Mossad was responsible for smuggling Jews out of countries where they were endangered and bringing them into Israel in defiance of the British restrictions on Jewish immigration. After the creation of the state, the Organization continued to operate as part of the Jewish Agency. Its principal office was in Paris, headed by Yosef Barpal of kibbutz Ramat David, who had been a central figure in organizing illegal immigration during the British Mandate; it was he who had organized the first illegal immigration ship, the *Vellos*, and subsequently, many others.[37]

As far as Refael was concerned, the Mossad's function was to be his "travel agency."[38] In fact, it took care of the immigrants' transportation, whether by railroad, by sea or by air, and its representatives had to submit to the Jewish Agency's authority.[39] In addition, they continued, as they had before the creation of the state, to plot clandestine operations, in the Arab and Eastern blocs as well as other countries. Some Mossad agents were officially legal residents in those countries, others were not totally legal, some used false identities and others worked undercover, sometimes with and sometimes without collaboration with the local Zionist communities. They also worked in conjunction with the local Zionist movement. In some places they had no connections at all, and worked entirely on their own, totally devoted to their mission.

Where governments did not allow Jews to emigrate, these Mossad agents contrived to smuggle them out by night, through the mountains and forests, by camel caravans or rickety boats: from Morocco to Algeria, from Libya to Malta, from Yemen to Aden, from Iraq to Iran, from Hungary to Austria, from the Soviet sector of Vienna to the American sector.

The agent in Austria suspected that there were many spies among those would-be immigrants.[40] The Mossad's agents in Iraq wired home: "The broadcasting code of the US Consulate has been stolen by the British. From now on, all information on Jewish emigration sent out by the Americans is being reported by the British to the local secret police."[41] At the beginning of March 1949, small groups of Syrian and Lebanese Jews began to escape to Israel. From Damascus they would go to Beirut, and from there, by car, to the Israeli border. They would cross it near Metullah, after walking for an hour or so. A top secret report of the Israeli police describes a meeting which took place, at the request of the Mossad, between an Israeli Deputy Chief Commissioner and the Lebanese Chief of Police. The Israeli proposed to his Lebanese counterpart, first, to put an end to the private organizations that smuggled out Jews for a high fee, and, secondly, to set up a refugee commission which would receive semi-official recognition from the Lebanese government, and which would conduct its business in total secrecy, under the supervision of the Lebanese government. The commission would charge each would-be Jewish immigrant a "head tax" of 25 to 30 Lebanese pounds, or whatever sum the Beirut authorities would determine. The refugees would be brought over at the rate of 150 to 200 a week. An agent of the Mossad, holding a foreign passport, would stay in Lebanon and arrange things.[42] In some countries, the Mossad organized the Jews in self-defense groups and trained them in the use of arms.[43]

Acting as a secret service, the Mossad used code names in all its operations: the agent in "Goshen"—i.e., Egypt—signed his reports "Maxie"; Iraq was "Berman"; Iran—"Goldman"; Bulgaria—"Baruh," etc. The agents communicated by wireless, and at times they received their instructions, in code, by means of a Hebrew songs request program on the Israeli radio. They also made use of a network of helpers and informers, including customs and border officials, secret and regular police agents, local governors, army officers, foreign consuls and even government Ministers and Heads of State. One agent of the Mossad met with the Hungarian Prime Minister, Mátyás Rákosi; another met with Nuri Said, the Iraqi ruler; still another with the Shah of Iran, etc., all with the aim of obtaining exit permits for Jews. Almost everywhere they offered bribes, and almost everywhere the bribes were accepted. Shlomo Zalman Shragai: "We opened Swiss bank accounts for the Moroccan cabinet ministers. The Sultans of Yemen preferred dollars in cash. The Rumanians, too, wanted cash."[44] Ben-Gurion noted in his diary that "in Rumania you can't do anything without money. From top to bottom. Even the Party wants money."[45] The Swiss government allowed the Egyptian Jews to stop over in Switzerland en route to Israel, thanks to pressure exerted by *Swissair*, which flew them from Cairo. Itzhak Refael noted: "Preliminary contacts indicate that the Chief of Police in Transjordan would be willing, in collaboration with Abdullah's black wife—who holds shares in the *Transjordan-Iraq Carrier Company*—to help transfer the Jews of Baghdad via the Bnot-Yaacov bridge to Israel."[46] The Iraqi Premier, Tewfik Sueidi, was connected with *Iraq Tours*.[47] The shipping companies of Eastern Europe also favored Jewish emigration to Israel. A letter from a Bulgarian shipping line stated that the company was eager to keep up its business association with the Jewish Agency, "out of sincere desire to do our share in building up your country."[48] The modes of operation were extremely varied. Thus for a time, access to Rumania's Jewish Foreign Minister, Anna Pauker, was gained through her good personal friend who lived in Brussels. An old personal friend of the US Ambassador to Iran was asked to approach him and get him to influence the Shah not to turn back the Iraqi Jews who had crossed the border into Iran on their way to Israel. When Itzhak Refael visited Warsaw, he ran into an old school friend who had in the meantime become an influential person in Poland's security services.[49]

But the emissaries from Israel were not only there to save or to liberate Jews. They were also there to promote the Zionist cause. "The awakening of the Jews of Poland will not happen by itself," wrote the Israeli Consul in Warsaw. "They must be motivated and organized."[50] This was equally true in other places:

"Of late, thanks to the intensified activities of our people, many Jews have begun to apply for foreign passports, using either money or proofs of having had a foreign parent," wrote Efraim Shilo in his report about the situation of Jews in Egypt. "Our men are encouraging the masses to emigrate."[51] The encouragement involved social and communal activities, courses in Hebrew, occupational training and so forth. The immigration agent in Bucharest sent a secret report to Tel Aviv: "Working through the local leadership and every reliable Jew we have met, we are urging the Jews to make applications for emigration and for passports. In September 1949, the Joint allocated $30,000 per month for helping the Jews of Rumania. The help is organized by the Israeli embassy. It is directed to youth movements, Zionist activists, Jewish communal leaders who can be aided without risk to the enterprise, rabbis, ritual slaughterers, Rabbinical students. . . . For our movement (*Hapoel Hamizrahi* and its religious *Bnei Akiva* youth movement) I receive between 1,300 and 1,500 dollars every month. Moreover, I have ordered another 5,000 dollars a month to be distributed, for the religious needs of the community. . . ."[52] The propaganda methods employed by these agents combined scare tactics with inducements. They warned the Jews that if they did not leave at once they would not be allowed to leave later. They told them that the Mossad's help in arranging their passage, and the aid given by the Zionist movement, would only remain available for a short while, and then no one would be left to help them. Efraim Shilo explained, "It's true that we encouraged the Jews to leave. It's true that we urged them. We believed that if they did not leave at once it would be too late. We really believed it. Some of us had been at this work since the Holocaust, so it's obvious why we urged them to leave. Also the State needed them." At times they were promised eternal happiness in Israel. "People were simply cheated," stated Jewish Agency Executive Giora Yoseftal.[53]

To keep them from hearing about the difficulties of settling in Israel, it was proposed by Itzhak Refael that immigrants' letters back to their families should be censored. This was, in fact, done. "They lied to me," wrote an immigrant from South Africa to his mother. "I want to return at once. If I don't leave in a week I shall starve. Please, dear, beg, borrow, steal, pawn whatever you have, only send me the money, or I shall not hold out another week. . . . This is a Godless country." The mother never received this letter. It was confiscated and put away by the Mossad, where it remained in its files, bearing the stamp "Detained by Censorship."[54] When Refael heard that the Government of Czechoslovakia was considering letting the Jews take some of their property with them, he gave an order to keep it quiet—"or it would have lessened the Jews' willingness to leave" until it became known what they could take with them.[55]

A Zionist agent in Vienna objected to the order to help Jews escape from the Soviet sector of the city even if they did not intend to go to Israel. "If the political situation causes them distress and makes them want to leave Vienna, then it is our business to make use of this distress to get them to go to Israel, and not to alleviate it by helping them to move to the refugee camps in the American sector."[56] Others agreed. Foreign Minister Sharett gave his Cabinet colleagues part of a letter he received from Dr. Shmuel Eliashiv, Israeli Ambassador to Czechoslovakia, which said: "It turns out that a good many of the people who have been taken out of here across the border by a variety of means have remained in Vienna and do not intend to proceed to Israel. This has been the cause of much embarrassment and has resulted in difficulties to our people in Vienna and we've been asked to stop the operation we have been carrying on so far. We do not intend to follow this advice, but the situation calls for some thought. Of course, if we could obtain mass emigration, we would be able to send the people directly to the port, so they would not be able to stop en route. That is what has been done and is being done in Poland. But [here] the question arises, Is our great expenditure of energy and nerve in recent times worth it, for people who only wish to make use of us for their personal interests, and who can only be brought to Israel by force? Obviously I am not ready to reach negative conclusions now, but we find little encouragement in our work under these circumstances."[57] It appears that this Israeli diplomat did not feel that Israel had a human, Jewish Zionist duty to save Jews in distress irrespective of their final destination, but only insofar as the operation promoted the interests of Israel and served its purposes. At the same time, there were some who thought that steps should be taken to worsen the situation of Jews in their various countries. Itzhak Ben-Menahem, nicknamed "Gulliver,"

in years to come, a hero of various military operations inside
Arab states wrote:

> Mass immigration will pour in only as a result of distress. This is a
> bitter truth, whether we like it or not. We must consider the possi-
> bility of initiating the distress, of bringing it about in the Diaspora.
> . . . For Jews have to be made to leave their places of residence. As
> the poet said, He will not waken unless roused by the whip, he will
> not rise unless forced by plunder.[58]*

Such ideas were not alien to the people entrusted with the
immigration. Itzhak Refael reported: "Conditions in Libya today
are not bad. There is a danger that this source of immigration
will come to an end."[59] The Chairman of the Zionist Executive
said at one of its meetings: "Even Jews who don't wish to leave
[their homes] must be forced to come. . . ."[60]

The Mossad was the most radical in this respect. Its demand
to speed up and intensify the rate of immigration no doubt derived to a large extent from its agents' direct contact with Jews
in distress. The Mossad's files and those of the Immigration Department are full of hair-raising descriptions of what the emissaries saw in many countries. They wrote:

> The situation of the Jews in the Moroccan Atlas Mountains is be-
> yond description. Mere reading or hearing about it cannot convey
> the reality that such conditions exist in our times. Whoever has not
> seen a family of eighteen huddled in one room, five meters long,
> which serves for living-quarters, kitchen and workshop; whoever
> has not visited rooms in which hundreds of children, all half-naked
> and with eye diseases which will never be treated, are taught to-
> gether; whoever has not met the "teacher," whose only method of
> teaching is the whip; whoever has not smelled the peculiar smell of
> the entire quarter—would never believe that such wretchedness
> can exist, and that fellow human beings be allowed to live like this.
> . . . The rate of infant mortality here is one of the highest in the
> world. . . .[61]

Similar reports came in from other countries. The Mossad's
demand to step up the immigration was a sincere call for rescue;
the organization felt responsible.

---

*This was written upon Ben-Menahem's return from the United States,
where, together with other army officers, he had visited Jewish communities
as an emissary from Israel. In his preface to Ben-Menahem's book published after Gulliver was killed in action, David Ben-Gurion wrote: "I have not read
many books which are as gripping and moving, provoking pride, sadness and
respect, as this one."

The Mossad's agents often encouraged the Jews to leave without taking into account the conditions for their reception, and once they were on the move, pressured the Zionist Executive to increase the quotas. "We can by no means hold up the departure of those who already have visas. They've sold everything and are sitting on their luggage. . . ."[62] Itzhak Refael used to swamp the Executive with letters from every country desperately crying for help. So did the Mossad's Yosef Barpal. "I could talk to you for hours and tell you frightful things," he said to the Executive.[63] It was not always true, however, that the Jews needed rescuing. On occasion, their distress resulted from the arrangements they had made for departure, upon the encouragement and advice of the Israeli emissaries. Thus the Executive had no way of knowing when there was a real need to rescue Jews and when, on the contrary, the need had been created in order to put pressure on the Jewish Agency to increase the immigration quotas. This imposed a heavy burden on the Executive.

Barpal's demand to step up the immigration also reflected the Mossad's organizational and economic interest; it sought to grow. Before being taken over by Itzhak Refael it had been, as Refael put it, MAPAI's "private estate." "I believe I would not be far wrong in assuming that the great, unsupervised budget of the Mossad benefited not just a few party funds," he wrote years later.[64] It is a reasonable assumption, which can be neither proved nor disproved. The fact is that the Mossad handled millions of dollars without any outside control. The Controller of the Jewish Agency examined the records of the Mossad in the years prior to the creation of the state. Though he said that he found great willingness to help him in his work, the books he was shown did not, in his opinion, reflect the true financial situation. He ascribed this to the clandestine nature of the Mossad's activities. Two years after Itzhak Refael took over the Immigration Department, the Controller once again asked to inspect the books, and this time, he said, he ran into delaying tactics designed to evade his supervision, so that in the end he gave up. So it would seem that under Itzhak Refael of the Hapoel Hamizrahi the Mossad had as much to hide as in the days of MAPAI.[65]*

*The Controller's report includes an interesting comment on the smuggling of Jews out of Europe prior to the creation of the state. The books, he found, were kept in good order. "On the basis of the Jewish Agency's accounts for 1945–1946 and those of the escape operations for 1947–1948, we have ob-

However, the Controller did succeed in uncovering at least one dubious financial matter. During the period of illegal immigration, before independence, the Mossad had purchased several ships, and at the beginning of 1948 created a company called "*Oniyot Usfinot* (Ships and Boats) *Ltd*," to serve as the legal possessor of the vessels. The company's stock was owned entirely by the Mossad. With the beginning of mass immigration, in the latter half of 1948, these vessels carried tens of thousands of immigrants. The Jewish Agency Controller assumed that the company showed considerable profits, and his report reveals that the Mossad operated on quasi-commercial principles. The Joint paid the Mossad for the passage of every immigrant it carried, some 40 pounds sterling per passenger. The sums ran into millions, and the Jewish Agency wielded no control over this money. The minutes of the Executive's meetings reflect this fact. "Sometimes immigration is speeded up simply because the Mossad wants to make sure the ships are full," objected Member of the Executive Tsvi Hermon.[67] The Controller charged the Mossad with "exploiting" the immigrants and making excessive profits. He also accused it of overcrowding the ships. "The *Negbah* can carry 600 to 700 passengers, yet it is loaded with 1,200, and they travel in subhuman conditions. This is very profitable."[68] The Mossad's files abound with documents disclosing the unbearable conditions which prevailed on its ships. "It could be said that it is a shame and a disgrace to transport immigrants in such conditions," one report stated. "If a non-Jewish company were to do this, we would have raised a great outcry, and rightly so. My own conscience is far from clear. I feel as if I am taking part in an inhuman and immoral enterprise."[69]

Indeed, the documents depict the Mossad as a type of travel agency. There are tens of thousands of telegrams dealing with timetables of sailing and arrival, with passenger quotas and fares. In June 1949, the Mossad purchased shares in *El Al*, the national airline, and the Jewish Agency's Finance Department wondered in whose name they were registered.[70] The Zionist Executive viewed the Mossad with profound suspicion. Member of the Executive Israel Goldstein demanded that the Mossad be

tained the sum of $2,775,000, representing the total expenses of the entire operation from the beginning until it came to an end as an autonomous operation."[66]

shut down altogether. He protested that it was spending vast sums of money without any supervision. Other members of the Executive also believed that, despite his claims to the contrary, Itzhak Refael was unable to control it. "I do not believe that Refael has a decisive influence in this headquarters," said Moshe Kol.[71] Columnist Moshe Kramer of *Haaretz* also suspected the Mossad: "The men in Europe do not submit to the central authority here. One way or another, they have got hold of considerable funds and they are acting on their own initiative. . . . As they see it, the organization of immigration is something like a parcel service, and the more business it does, the better. . . . They have established a sovereign kingdom of their own. . . ."[72]

The Mossad did not last much longer. Its official demise came in March 1952, in a memorandum signed by Itzhak Refael and two officials of the "Organization for Special Assignments," Israel's Secret Service, also commonly known as the "Mossad." The Organization for Special Assignments was entrusted with investigating the possibilities of Jewish immigration from the Arab countries, as well as its preparation and execution. It was empowered to carry out "undercover operations to establish contacts with Jews and bring them out" [of their countries]. The Jewish Agency undertook to finance these operations; the immigration policy remained its prerogative.[73] Efraim Shilo related, "1949 was not a good year for the Mossad. The great enterprises of the days of illegal immigration were over. In fact, all that was left to be done was to arrange the transportation. It was very frustrating."*

They came for all kinds of reasons, varying from time to time, from country to country, from community to community and from person to person. There were as many good reasons to stay on, or to emigrate to other countries. Not all the immi-

---

*The Mossad resisted the plan to close it down. At one point it looked as if it would cause a political crisis. Dr. Nahum Goldmann talked about it with Ben-Gurion, but in vain.[74] There was no more need for the Jewish Agency's secret service. Representatives of the Ministry of Defense in Paris wanted to control the Mossad's property there, but they were too late. Before it was closed down, the Mossad's properties had been transferred to *Zim*, the national shipping line. The Jewish Agency's Controller determined that the vessels had been sold to *Zim* for far less than their actual value, a difference of thousands, possibly millions, of dollars. Previously, the Mossad paid *Zim* excessive fares, and when the Controller questioned them, he was told that it was meant to help develop Israeli shipping. Subsequently, some of the Mossad's senior officials became directors of *Zim*.[75]

grants to Israel came because they wanted to live there; many came because they had no other choice. Some came because they were Zionists and believed that, being Jews, their place was in the State of Israel. Some had been brought up in Zionist homes or had been members of Zionist youth movements. Others became Zionists—or more confirmed Zionists—as a result of the Holocaust, or the creation of the State of Israel, or both. Some were drawn to the Zionist idea, or to the decision to go to Israel, by the propaganda efforts of the Zionist movement in their countries. Israel's diplomatic representatives and the Jewish Agency's emissaries in Europe reported from almost all capitals that thousands of Jews wished to immigrate and that many of them were already packed and ready to go. Some of the Israeli Embassies were besieged by masses of Jews, and in some places they even dared to demonstrate openly, demanding exit as, for example, in front of the Soviet Embassy in Bucharest.[76] A report from Warsaw describes long lines in front of the registered-mail counters in the post offices, of people sending the Israeli Embassy requests for visas; the embassy staff worked day and night.[77] For some, going to Israel was a religious act, stemming from profound messianic yearnings. Others simply followed their family and friends: the movement was infectious. Some left because they feared to remain on their own, when the rest had departed, and yet others went because there were no longer any communal institutions left to give them a sense of belonging and security. After their arrival in Israel, some of them could not explain why they had left their countries beyond saying, "I did what everybody did."[78] Some left hastily, fearful that later it would become impossible to get out. In Eastern Europe the Stalinist regime was spreading and the Jewish businessman feared for his livelihood. Some opposed the regime for ideological reasons, and knew they would be subjected to persecution and repression. Many Jews wished to retain their contacts with relatives abroad, and this, too, the Communist regimes did not approve of.

In the Arab countries, too, some of the Jews wished to go to Israel, and others left merely because they were persecuted or suffered hardships, even hunger. Both in Europe and in the Arab countries there were Jews who wanted to emigrate, but not necessarily to Israel—if they could, they would have gone elsewhere. "This is an element remote from any Zionist ideals and their only concern is making money," reported the Israeli Consul in Munich, disgustedly.[79] The Israeli Ambassador in Warsaw described the fears of the Jews of Poland who had heard of the unemployment and housing shortage awaiting them in Israel. "Fear and bewilderment are causing many of them to delay their departure," he wrote.[80] Similar reports arrived from North Africa and the Arab countries.

A national myth cultivated in Israel regarded the immigration as part of "the great struggle to realize the age-old dream of the liberation of Israel." As expressed in the Declaration of Independence: "From the time that the people was forcibly driven from its homeland, it remained faithful to it in all the countries of the Diaspora, and never ceased to pray and hope to return to the Homeland and restore its sovereignty." This may have been true of a small percentage of Jews in the world. Most others remained where they were, and most did so of their own free will. The Zionist movement evidently failed to prove its case to the vast majority of Jews. This was a source of great ideological embarrassment; the Zionist ideology therefore had to be reinforced with dire predictions about the future of world Jewry and the danger of yet another Holocaust. "New catastrophes, no less dreadful, may yet happen," said Ben-Gurion.[81] And the writer S. Shalom warned: "This is an age of annihilation, of utter peril. We are facing the question whether we will or will not exist as a people."[82] Yaakov Zrubavel, a MAPAM leader and member of the Jewish Agency Executive insisted, "The Zionist Executive must hasten to help the millions of our brothers who are subject to persecution and in peril of their lives, to extricate them from the inferno and bring them to their safe national haven, to the State of Israel. This is an imperative of rescue." Zrubavel was speaking about the Arab countries, whose Jews were in no danger of annihilation. The "imperative of rescue" was to do what had not been done during the Holocaust. "We were too late in Europe," Zrubavel said, as though confessing a sin. "We were just not fast enough to come to the aid of the millions of Jews and save them when it was still possible to do so."[83] David Ben-Gurion, however, was more concerned about the future of Israel, commenting, "For thousands of years we were a nation without a state. Now there is a danger that Israel will be a state without a nation."[84] Upon arrival the new immigrants were often looked down on as an uprooted mass of refugees with no pride and no

dignity. They were commonly described as "human debris"—
Avak Adam in Hebrew. Many of them, however, were ground
into debris only after their arrival, as part of the process of migration and the hardship of resettlement. That happened both to
Oriental immigrants from Arab countries and to Ashkenazi
newcomers from Europe.

5

Working and Fighting Hands

SHORTLY AFTER THE immigration wave had crested, Giora Yoseftal was credited with a saying, often repeated in the months and years to come: "Israel wants immigration, but the Israelis don't want the immigrants."[1] His words contained at least a grain of truth, as many immigrants were indeed unwanted. "Israel is a small country and cannot take in all the crazy Jews in the world," said Levi Eshkol. He was referring to the mentally ill,[2] but the physically weak or ill, and the aged, were also less than enthusiastically welcomed. "We need workers and fighters," stated Eliezer Kaplan, the Minister of Finance.[3]

There were some who did not want immigrants who belonged to certain political parties, or who came from certain countries; some welcomed only immigrants who came as ideologically driven "pioneers," while those who came as mere "refugees" were despised. There was something un-Zionist about all this, and occasionally an anti-Jewish note was struck. The attitude of the first Israelis toward the newcomers was complex and self-contradictory, charged with emotions and infused with prejudices, reflecting their self-images as Jews and as Israelis. The key to their attitudes toward the immigrants lies in their contemptuous attitude toward the Diaspora. Most tended to regard themselves as Israelis first and Jews second. Israel was above all. They often talked about the "elimination of the Diaspora," and the head of the Jewish Agency's Organization for Immigration once made a significant slip of the tongue, when he referred to the "elimination of the Jews."[4] They discarded ancient Jewish cultures, and they did so without compunction, for they believe that they were making the only relevant history; the State of Israel meant more to them than the preservation of Jewish culture abroad.

When new immigrants reached Israel's port, they were first taken to a camp called *Shaar Haaliyah* (The Gate of Immigration). Before Independence it had been a British army camp, known as St. Luke's. The authorities tended to treat it as a detention center. The local Chief of Police thought that the camp should be barred to non-residents except for the regular staff.[5] In the Knesset, Yaakov Meridor, MK, protested against the barbed-wire fence which surrounded the camp, "like a British or other detention camp."[6] After a while they replaced the fence with a wall and reinforced the watch. Nevertheless, people who wanted to get inside or out were able to do so without difficulty. There were breaches in the wall and the watch was careless. Among the people who made their way in were relatives of the immigrants, contractors, factory-owners and orange-growers looking for cheap labor which in the camp was unmediated and unprotected by the Labor Exchange; also money-changers and black-marketeers, thieves who stole the immigrants' belongings and the Jewish Agency's property, prostitutes who offered themselves to the male inmates and men looking for a good time among the female ones. Entering the camp, they found themselves in the midst of a vast and immensely colorful crowd: some dressed in tailored, Central European suits, some in long white robes, North African style, some in peaked caps ("refugee hats," as they were called by the Israelis), some in flowered kerchiefs and black turbans. It was a confused mass of people of all ages, from all countries, bewildered, helpless, rushing about, carrying suitcases and baskets, crates, bundles and babies, with countless children who screamed in every language under the sun. There were European Ashkenazis as well as immigrants from Arab countries; for all it was a time of trial and tribulation.

The camp enabled the authorities to carry out the formal process of immigration: the Border Control examined the immi-

grant's papers, customs officials examined his luggage, Jewish
Agency representatives registered personal data, medical inspectors examined their bodies—a general check-up for internal diseases, as well as eye and skin examinations, lung X-rays and
blood tests for venereal diseases. A journalist who was invited to
observe the medical process described it as an immense assembly line: "The immigrant becomes a number," he wrote.[7] One
thousand people underwent these examinations every day. The
young ones were inoculated against tuberculosis, and everyone
was disinfected—they had to take off their clothes and be de-
loused with DDT powder. Many of them, both Ashkenazi and
Oriental immigrants, would later remember the DDT as the
symbol of humiliation. The "Gate of Immigration" was originally meant to serve as a way-station for three days to a week,
but as the number of arrivals grew, their stay became more and
more protracted. From here they were taken to other camps,
where they sometimes remained for many months.

One day a young man turned up in one of the camps and introduced himself as an immigrant from Germany. He handed
the Jewish Agency official an immigrant's document identifying
him as Haim Klopstock, bachelor, age 28. The official copied
the details from the blue document to a white cardboard card,
took the blue document and gave him the white one, together
with 3 coupons—for dinner and supper that day, and breakfast
the next. "Tomorrow," the official informed him in Yiddish,
"you must come back here and stand in line for the coupons.
Without coupons you won't get any food." Then he sent him to
the quartermaster store, where the white card was taken away
and the immigrant was made to sign his name in a book, ac-
knowledging receipt of the following equipment: two grey wool-
len blankets, a sheet and a bar of soap. The blankets had yellow-
ish stains on them, and had obviously been used and not
washed. The soap was hard and ill-smelling. Then the store-
keeper sent him to look for a vacant bed.

"Haim Klopstock" was in reality Arye Gelblum, a correspondent for the daily *Haaretz*. The head of the Jewish Agency's
Absorption Department, Giora Yoseftal, had enabled him to
go through the immigration absorption process under a false
name.[8]

The quartermaster did not know where to direct Gelblum, as
the camp was full almost to overflowing. Gelblum took his suit-

case in one hand and the things he had been given in the other, and set forth. He saw before him a row of hall-like structures, roofed with tin. They had served the British forces for storage. There were also some tents to one side. He opened door after door and everywhere he saw the same sight—scores of beds, one next to the other, all along the walls, and in the middle bundles, crates and suitcases piled up. Clothing and eating utensils were everywhere. Many people were lolling on the beds, their clothes undone, eating, playing cards or lying idly. Gelblum estimated that there must have been at least a hundred in each hall, both men and women. A rotten smell hung in the air. Here and there were diapers hanging on strings, and scores of children ran playfully among the beds. In each hall he was told that there was no more room. Later he found they had lied to him—they did not want to crowd the place any more. A pregnant woman told him to force his way in. Gelblum related:

> I passed by her tent, and saw her trying to light some faggots which she had gathered on the surrounding dunes in order to cook something for her baby, who was lying on some rags on the ground, yelling with all its might.
>
> The tiny tent, originally intended for two or three people, was packed full of beds, leaving no room to move. "We came here on Friday, two days ago," the woman told him. "There were four hundred of us and the camp was full. There was no room for any of us. We stood here in the open, in the pouring rain . . . until after nightfall, while they set up the tents for us. The tent leaks and the rain gets into the beds. . . ."

The younger immigrants had forced their way into the meeting halls. Gelblum, too, managed to grab hold of a vacant bed near the door in one of them.

> People kept going in and out, and not one of them remembered to close the door. Being the one nearest to it, I became the self-appointed doorkeeper. Most of the people who came in did not live in my hall, but had to pass through to get to the adjoining hall.

Many of the immigrants took their meals to their halls, and some actually cooked for themselves. Gelblum went to the dining hall. The tables were strewn with sticky food remnants, the walls were bare, except for some notices of MAPAI, MAPAM and Hapoel Hamizrahi pasted up around the serving hutch. The notices called upon the immigrants to register with the parties' representatives who would be visiting the camp on certain days. He waited 35 minutes for dinner before his turn came. He handed over his coupon and received a tin bowl with vegetable soup, a tin plate with a ball of gefilte fish, some cereal and two slices of bread. There were no knives, forks or spoons to be had. He asked why this was so but got no answer. Being hungry, he had to eat with his fingers. Later he was told that the reason no cutlery was issued was that the immigrants stole the utensils. Gelblum then asked why were they not made to sign a receipt for the utensils, as they did for the blankets and sheet. He later found out the real reason probably was that the supervisors of religious dietary laws in the camps feared that the immigrants would not take care to separate the utensils for dairy and meat dishes. Supper consisted of five green olives, a slice of cheese and some bread.[9]

That evening the people in Gelblum's hall recalled the great pogrom in a city in Yugoslavia. It had lasted for three whole days: more than 3,500 people, about 1,000 of them Jews, were slaughtered by Hungarian troops. This was in winter. Whole families were taken out of their homes and led through the streets to the Danube. Here they were made to strip naked. The river was frozen and the Hungarians broke holes in the ice, led the victims to the edge of the holes and shot them in the back, so their bodies fell through the ice. Babies were not shot—they were flung up and smashed against the ice. This was what they talked about that night, while in another corner some people told each other about their experiences in Auschwitz. But they also talked about their future in Israel. Where they would live; where they would work; how they would manage. . . . They passed on advice they had received in the course of the day— how to evade the regulations, how to hoodwink the officials. Night came. Gelblum observed:

> . . . By now almost all of them have taken off their shoes and socks and the hall stinks and will stay stinking through the night. I don't know why, but for some reason they are always afraid to open a window and let in a little air. Perhaps out of exaggerated fear for the children, perhaps to avoid endless arguments, because there is always someone who objects to an open window. . . . The small children are put on their chamber pots, in the midst of everybody, and then to bed. The older children are partly undressed and also put to bed. Here and there old men and women are already trying to sleep.

They groan and clear their throats, unable to fall asleep, and then moan some more, whether it is from old age or ill health. But the majority are still talking from bed to bed. A group of Moroccans have dug up a bottle of arrack (an anise liquor) from somewhere and have started to drink. Many people smoke, and the smoke fills the hall, mingling with the general stench and the odor of sweaty bodies in a hall whose windows are all shut tight and whose roof is hot tin. The faces are fiery red. It's eleven o'clock, but the lights can't be turned off, because the switch for all three adjoining halls is on the other side of the partition, in a hall where most of the inhabitants are North Africans, and they are still making lively noise. So when darkness finally falls depends on them. Already there are loud snores and whistles and groans from different corners of the hall, and they never cease, not even momentarily.

Men and women take off their clothes in public, walk around in slips and undershorts. Someone plants himself directly in front of me, strips down to the skin and begins to scratch. Almost all of them remove only their outer clothes and sleep night after night in the underwear they have worn all day. One rarely sees anyone in nightwear, except some young girls who had a technique of changing under the bedclothes. And still the electric light is on. Already at the beginning of the evening there were some young men sitting along the wall to my right, talking to the young women. Some of them are soldiers—at least, they are clearly not camp inmates. They remove their clothes and embrace the girls. Nearby a woman breast-feeding her baby looks on indifferently, and a man snores peacefully. . . . The Turkish family beside me is already asleep. I have been talking with the Bulgarian family on my left. Husband and wife and their 13-year-old son sleep in two beds here. Finally, the man said good night, took the boy, who woke up, and moved him aside, and then joined his wife. A few moments later he came out from under the blanket, picked up the boy—who had watched it all closely—put him back and went to sleep. . . .

At long last, after a good deal of shouting back and forth, the light is turned off. I try to go to sleep. There is a crunching sound from the crates and bundles all around—mice. I turn over to the other side and turn back quickly again, because my face all but touched my neighbor's smelly feet. Suddenly I hear a sound like rain, but the idea is absurd. The weather outside is summery. But surely no one could be urinating in the hall. I dozed off again, but the sound re-awakened me. . . . When I turned my eyes I saw my neighbor, the Turkish woman, squatting between her bed and mine and urinating. In fact, most of these people, and especially the women, do not go out at night to the outdoor toilet, which is quite far from the hall. Not only the children and the old, but men and women of all ages get up incessantly during the night, to urinate or to evacuate, right there in the hall, among the beds, into tin cans left here for the purpose, and the sounds never cease. . . . The air grows thicker and thicker, the stink of the bodies more acrid. And all the while people break wind, loudly and triumphantly. . . . Yet despite it all my belly rumbles, dissatisfied with the meager supper. I doze on and off. On the other side of the partition a baby keeps crying, "Mama!" Her mother evidently tries to nurse her, but after a while she groans, in Yiddish, "I can't any more," and the baby screams. . . .

About five o'clock some start to get up, and of course whoever is up makes as much noise as if no one was still asleep. . . . Nobody washes. In some camps there are hot showers, but in others there is no installation for hot water at all, so that all through the winter it is impossible to bathe, even if they want to. There are entire camps with thousands of men, women and children, where there is not a single shower room, not even for cold water. And when there is a wretched little bathroom, it is occupied by inmates who have nowhere else to stay. . . . The regular washrooms, with a few taps for washing one's hands and face, are utterly filthy, and needless to say do not boast such luxuries as a shaving mirror. . . . Wherever an attempt was made to install normal toilets, they became so filthy within a few hours that it was impossible to use them, and they have generally been closed down. . . . In many camps, therefore, the toilets are nothing more than holes in the ground, lined with sheets of tin, without any sewage or running water. These holes soon fill up and stink up the atmosphere, but in the absence of any other facility, people keep using them, though they overflow with excrement. Most of the toilets are enclosed, but sometimes they are only enclosed back and sides, and open to the corridor, so that as you go in you pass by people of your sex sitting side by side—and sometimes even of both sexes. . . . Even when they are quite enclosed, they cannot be locked. In at least one camp the toilets are not in the form of cubicles, but fairly large rooms with several holes in them, where people all do their business together, and it is not unusual to see a whole family going there together. . . .

In the morning Gelblum went to get his breakfast. "They gave us bread and jam," he noted. "People were already crowding the front of the office, waiting to get their daily food coupons."

The records of the Jewish Agency, which were made available only a generation later, confirm the journalist's description.[10] When the Jewish Agency took over the former British army camps they were nearly in ruins. Before leaving, British soldiers had smashed the windows and doors, sinks and toilet bowls, and even some of the buildings' walls and foundations. The Jewish Agency repaired as much as it could, but the pace of immigration grew much faster than had been expected, so new camps had to be created hastily. At the beginning of January 1949, there were about 28,000 people living in the immigrant camps, one out of every four immigrants who had already arrived. The rest had managed to find housing. Each immigrant stayed between four and six weeks in the camp. Toward the end of the year the camp population numbered more than 90,000, that is, two out of three immigrants, or one tenth of the population, and they remained in the camps for many months. Tsvi Hermon, of the Absorption Department, told the Zionist Executive that conditions in the camps were unacceptable: "It is not an exaggeration to say that conditions were better in the refugee camps in Germany, after the war."[11] In August another official of the Absorption Department, Yehuda Braginsky, warned that food supplies were running out: "Ten percent of the population here will be going hungry."[12] Indeed, before long there were acute food shortages. In the first three days of September the camps received only bread and milk for the children. The quantity of vegetables was reduced by two-thirds. In the immigrant camp at Pardes Hannah the immigrants staged a hunger demonstration that week.[13]

The physical conditions in the camps, the crowding, the inadequate sanitary arrangements and the poor nutrition, which did not suit the eating habits of many of the immigrants, all caused their health to deteriorate rapidly. Many had arrived in poor health, and now more fell ill. Epidemics were not uncommon. Some people died, including children. Dr. Moshe Sne, MK, a physician by training, reported to the Knesset that 200 out of the 370 children in the Raananah immigrant camp were sick. In the Pardes Hannah and Lydda camps, he stated, there were not enough doctors who could even examine all the children who were being brought to the clinics, and the hospitals admitted only one out of four children who were sent to them by the doctors. This meant that 75 percent of the children referred by doctors for hospitalization were not admitted.[14] "I have seen new settlements where hundreds of immigrant families live without a regular doctor on the spot and without a proper clinic," reported Yaakov Gil, MK (General Zionists) to the Knesset.[15] "In the abandoned villages and towns I have seen hundreds of people suffering from infectious diseases living at home and endangering the health of their families, because there are no rooms available in the hospitals. . . . In a village, near Hadera, I saw two families of five persons each in one wooden hut, with a consumptive child lying in the same bed with all the others."[16]

A day in the life of one of the immigrant camps was given in a newspaper story:

> An immigrant camp. A bright day. A mother hangs washing on the line. Beside her, her three-year-old daughter picks flowers, running back and forth. Suddenly the child trips and falls into a deep pond. There are three such ponds in the camp, originally part of the British army camp. In the British army there were no three-year-old children, whereas in the immigrant camps there are many and the ponds are wide open. The mother begins to look for her child. A few minutes later she is fished out of the pond, lifeless. There are two thousand people in the camp, and they all shout for first aid. Two hours pass before it arrives. The baby, too, waited for it, in the sun, beside the pond, lifeless.

This happened in the Netanyah camp.[17] The children in the camps did not go to school, as there were neither schools nor kindergartens there. Also, most of the camp inmates did not work.

In the Prime Minister's Office there are some files with reports about those camps, including some which were written by foreign charity and philanthropic organizations. One of them observes: "Historically speaking, the camps in Israel reflect one of the most ironic failures in the world—Jews keeping other Jews in camps. It seems they have not learned anything from their own tragedy."[18]

None of the camp inhabitants knew how long they would remain there, completely idle. They felt depressed, aggrieved and frustrated. In the meantime, Israel remained an unknown country to them—they did not see its landscapes, meet its people, or learn its ways. Their first encounter with the country was with the intricate bureaucracy and indifferent officials, political manipulators and the black-marketeers. They experienced months of humiliation, repression, and doubts, to the point of losing their faith both in themselves and in the future. While living in the camps they also came across well-meaning officials who were devoted to their work, but most of them were unable to help. Giora Yoseftal warned: "We are ruining these people and making them degenerate."[19] But he, too, was helpless: "There is nothing to be done," he said, "but quietly cry."[20]

As the head of the Jewish Agency's Absorption Department, Yoseftal was responsible for the camps. At this time he was still called Josefsthal, the name of his ancestors who had resided in Ansbach, in southern Germany, for the previous five hundred years. He had come to Israel shortly before the outbreak of the Second World War and, together with his wife Senta, had been among the founding members of a kibbutz. In 1943 he joined the British army and in 1945 was appointed head of the Jewish Agency's Absorption Section, as it was then called. Thereafter, he directed the reception of immigrants, whether legal or illegal. He had worked among the immigrants who were held by the British authorities in the detention camps, and in the Displaced Persons camps of Europe. He was a devoted and competent man.

Then came the mass immigration, and the country was not ready to receive it. Yoseftal knew this, and he hoped that the pace of immigration would slow, but he did not dare fight for it. One of his associates, Israel Kessar, recalls him as a bulky man, always vacillating between his professional career as a jurist and expert in social welfare, and his political career in MAPAI. "We often talked about it," Kessar said. "He had a hard time in the party, whose leadership was composed mainly of men from Eastern Europe. Because he had come from Germany, they did not promote him."[21] Nevertheless, in time he was appointed the party's General Secretary and later Minister of Labor. But he remained something of an outsider in the political establishment. He tried unsuccessfully to learn Yiddish, and in fact never even managed to learn Hebrew properly. While spending day and night at the task of absorbing immigrants, he endeavored to instill in his staff something of his own humanitarianism, a genuine concern for the individual. But the rate of immigration was too fast and furious. Yoseftal felt each immigrant's pain and suffering. At one point, he revealed to members of the Zionist Executive, he had almost suffered a nervous breakdown.[22]*

---

*Yoseftal had realized very early what was going to happen. He spoke of the "coming catastrophe" even before the creation of the state. He maintained that it was inevitable because the "prominent men," who should lend a hand with the immigration absorption, were not doing so. They want immigration,

Levi Eshkol, head of the Settlement Department of the Jewish Agency, continued, in the meantime, to travel through the abandoned Arab villages. A few score he earmarked as potential immigrant settlements. He threw himself into the task with that enthusiastic energy which was easily recognized in all of the "founding fathers," a blend of strict allegiance to an ideology combined with an urge to get things done at all costs. Eshkol was addicted to the doing, and was less concerned with theory, thereby foreshadowing the pragmatic tendency which would eventually affect his entire party. He said that his great love was for land and water, and indeed he had taken part in the founding of kibbutz Deganiah Bet, and of the national water corporation, *Mekorot*. However, like the rest of Ben-Gurion's immediate entourage, he took part in almost every other sphere of national affairs, whether it be financial, military, political or international. Division of labor, assigning each person his own special field of endeavor, was foreign to the "founding fathers'" spirit; everyone was involved in whatever had to be done. Eshkol was considered a rising power. His acquaintances remember him as a shrewd, though not sophisticated, man, exuding warm, rough-hewn *yiddischkeit*, the heritage of his Hassidic rabbinic ancestors in the Ukraine. Describing his first visit to that first abandoned village he had discovered on the road to Jerusaleum, he wrote: "I felt that if 'out of distress I called the Lord' we would find the wisdom and the resourcefulness to guide and direct the tidal-wave of immigration to the fields, which were crying for workers. . . ."[24] As Itzhak Koren, a MAPAI leader, saw it, it was a moment of grace. "It looked as if Providence itself joined these people with this land," he wrote.[25] According to him, the immigrants "responded *en masse*" to the call for settlement on the land, "testifying to the profound yearning for renewal and roots in the Land of Israel."[26] This was not completely true; many of the new immigrants did not wish to become farmers. There were those who were practically forced to settle on the land.

One morning in mid-October three new immigrants from Morocco, residents of the former Arab quarter of Baq'a in Jerusa-

---

he charged, and don't care about absorption. He was referring to Ben-Gurion, among others. "When Ben-Gurion proposes that I go to the United States, and does not even know what I am doing, it shows what we're up against," he told his colleagues. Ben-Gurion's diaries do, however, record a few meetings in which he dealt with the problems of the immigrants.[23]

lem, stood waiting for a bus in the central bus station. Moshe Sabag, Shimon Atias and Shlomo Avihatseira brought along sandwiches, as they were proposing to travel around the country in search of an abandoned village or free land, to start a village. With them was a representative of the Jewish Agency's Settlement Department, by the name of Agamy. He recorded the events of that day, hour by hour: ". . . 7.50—We leave Jerusalem. 9.50—We reach Tel Aviv. . . ." At 12.30 they left Tel Aviv and at 3.30 they reached Ein Hod—"This is the new name of Ein Khood," noted Agamy—formerly an Arab village, on a hill about fifteen minutes' walk from the road. Having scattered among the houses and talked to the inhabitants, the visitors from Jerusalem were disappointed. Agamy stated, "They didn't like the place because of its steepness. Water has to be brought uphill from the wells. The land is more cinders than soil, and the Arab buildings are old and dilapidated."

At five they left Ein Hod for Athlit, hitchhiking to get there. This was a village in the process of being built. Most of its residents were from North Africa, and the majority were still living in tents, though nearby houses were being built for them. The soil was being tilled by bulldozers and heavy farm machinery. Agamy noted that "those who are trying to persuade people to live on the land, had better emphasize that here most of the hard work is done by machinery, and not as the *fellahin* [farmers] of North Africa do it." The village residents had gone to a celebration in the abandoned village of Igzim (in time to be, Kerem Maharal), but the visitors from Jerusalem met some of the women and talked to them. Most of them had arrived five or six months before. They seemed contented. Athlit also looked attractive to the visitors from Jerusalem. "If you make the necessary arrangements," they told Agamy, "we'll be ready to move in this week." "They have a very practical attitude," Agamy noted in his report. "The land is level and fertile. Mr. Sabag, who had done some farming in his youth, examined it. There is plenty of water and it's near the shore. It's not far from the main road or from the city. The new buildings are modern. Also, the place is in the heart of the country, far from the border. As for the hot climate—it's no worse than their native country." However, there was one thing that bothered them, and Agami scrupulously noted that, too: "For some reason the grocery store is run by a Polish Jew." They would have preferred him to be North African, like themselves.[27]

Yosef Freund, from the village of Herut, who helped train the immigrants, described the lottery for the first houses and plots in Yavneh, which was to be settled by immigrants from Bulgaria: "They were filled with excitement! When the time came to draw the lots the atmosphere was positively festive! I, too, felt tremulous, as if first in love again. I remembered the same tension, the same excitement, when we drew lots for the first farms in my village. . . ."[28] Yet someone from the Ministry of Defense, who happened to visit Yavneh a few weeks after the lottery had brought tears to its settlers' eyes, reported to Ben-Gurion: "I saw a frightful scene of hundreds of women and children standing in the middle of the village waiting for the tank truck which would bring water, for drinking and washing. Yavneh has plenty of water and there are many wells, but no adequate water system. I don't know how long this state of affairs has been going on, but it's been more than a few days. The people told me that vegetable plots which they had cultivated with great difficulty were perishing for lack of water. . . ."[29] The Settlement Department continued to file optimistic reports about Yavneh, describing the first mules, the hen-houses and vegetable gardens, but in fact the farming community failed. The first settlers abandoned the place and it became a slum.[30] A year later the Prime Minister received a report about the critical condition of many new immigrant villages. In 27 there was severe unemployment. "In these villages there is actual hunger," the report stated. "Men, women and children are literally starving." The author of this report, Ami Asaf, of the Cooperative Settlement Movement stated that the settlers could not even afford the price of the food rations due to them, so they remained in the stores. Nor did they have money to purchase the clothes which were sent to them for a nominal fee. "I am fearful that these hungry men, people who can't bear to see their children go hungry, will resort to desperate acts," he wrote. Ben-Gurion passed his letter on to Eshkol, asking for his comments, and Eshkol consulted with the Minister of Labor, Golda Meir. Eshkol then wrote a reply in Ben-Gurion's name:

a) There will be no hunger in our midst. . . b) It would seem that the immigrant villages are unable to sustain themselves from their

farms in the initial stages of their existence since their prosperity
depends chiefly on the development of the economy. These villages
need, and are entitled, to receive a share in the outside and public
works in order to supplement their income. . . .[31]

But that had not been the purpose of settling them: they had
been meant to be self-sufficient farmers.

One of the problems was the varied level of experience and
motivation among those settling on the land. Some of the immigrants settled on the land willingly. Some had previously engaged in agriculture, and others were willing to try a new way of
life. Some had been urged by the Jewish Agency to join farming
communities, and a few were compelled to do so against their
will.

Aryeh (Lova) Eliav, who was then one of Eshkol's aides, recalled scenes of immigrants refusing to get off the trucks that
brought them to the settlements, and having to be made to do so
by tilting the vehicles' platforms, so that they slid off.[32] The
story of the new immigrant settlements was not, then, a tale of
untarnished success. For many of the settlers it was a tale of ag-
ony and failure. Some of the abandoned villages were unfit for
human habitation. There were adobe houses which were all but
ruins. Most of them had neither electricity, running water nor
proper sewage. Some were remote from any road. The renova-
tions were not always sufficient, and they were often late. Material help, in the form of money, mechanical equipment and livestock, was sometimes inadequate. The marketing system was
not always efficiently organized and many of the settlers found
it difficult to adapt to it, partly because they could not understand why they had to market their produce through *Tenuvah*—
the Histadrut union produce cooperative—rather than directly
through the city markets and on the black market, where they
could receive a much better return. Also, many of the immigrants did not adjust to the cooperative methods and mutual
help which prevailed in the cooperative villages. In some places
there were no health and educational services. The Jewish
Agency and the Cooperative Settlements Movement sent them
instructors to help them in the early stages, but some of these
people had never given instruction before and did not know
what to do. A few quit and told ghastly tales about the backwardness and strangeness of the new settlers. Most of the immigrants had no idea how to cultivate the land they had been given,

or what to do with the cattle and poultry they had received. In fact, most of them were sent to their villages without any advance preparation. David Ben-Gurion explained why this happened:

In the past, we used to bring in an immigrant after years of training. We had set up pioneer farms all over the world and we would keep the pioneers there for several years, to prepare themselves for life here, for the work, to learn the language and the country before they even came here. Now we shall bring in Jews as they are, without any advance preparation . . . because we haven't the time and they haven't the time.[33]

Only a few thousand immigrants were absorbed by the kibbutzim, and just a few hundred immigrants created their new kibbutzim on their own. All the farming communities together, cooperative and communal, old and new, absorbed only two out of every ten immigrants.[34] The rest settled in the cities and towns, and they, too, faced great hardship.

In the last week of April 1949, some 300 immigrants came from Ramlah to Tel Aviv, to demonstrate in its streets, demanding bread and work. They tried to break into the former Kessem cinema, which was now the seat of the Knesset. A large police force barred their way. Then they marched into government offices, and there, they were promised jobs in public works.[35] Two weeks later hundreds of new immigrants forced their way into the Jewish Agency's building in Haifa. They broke into the offices of the Absorption Department and destroyed its furniture. They were demanding work and housing. Two of the officials present promised to convey their demands to their superiors. Then the police dispersed the demonstrators by force. A few of them subsequently needed medical treatment and some were detained by the police.[36] Ten weeks later dozens of demonstrators from Jaffa stormed the Knesset. They broke through the gates and entered the courtyard. A few of them were armed with sticks. At the last moment the police managed to stop them from forcing their way into the assembly hall, where a debate on the compulsory education law was then taking place. Before they broke through the gates the Speaker, Yosef Shprintsak, had agreed to see a delegation of the demonstrators, but then he changed his mind. "One cannot negotiate with gate-crashers," he announced.[37] The Jewish Agency held closed meetings in which the "catastrophic situation" in the towns abandoned by the Arabs was discussed, in view of the reports that in some of them people were actually starving.[38] Three months later a member of the Knesset disclosed that she had seen a report describing how children on their way to school were assaulted by other children who robbed them of their packed lunches.[39]

In the meantime, thousands of housing units were being built in all the towns and cities—two-story buildings with minute, one- and two-room apartments, as well as small prefabricated and wooden structures. The standard of construction was poor and there was not enough of it. Public housing came under the jurisdiction of the Ministry of Labor, headed by Golda Meir. The former school teacher from Milwaukee, where she had been brought from Kiev as a child, had served in many public roles since her arrival in Israel in 1921. She had been a leading figure in the Working Women's Council, the Histadrut Executive, MAPAI and the Jewish Agency, and for many years she was a member of Ben-Gurion's immediate circle. Like the others, she had taken part in all spheres of public activity. Generally known as Golda, she was especially gifted in raising funds for the Zionist cause, and was particularly effective with American Jewish donors. She was an impressive, even formidable person, physically rather unattractive, yet with a distinct charm of her own, marked by a unique blend of very Jewish optimism and with a very Israeli kind of grimness. She used to say that things could be worse and that everything will be alright because it has to be alright. And she believed that Israel was all alone with the whole world against it and had only itself to rely on. She had an important advantage over the rest of the "founding fathers," in that she could speak English properly. For this reason she was often entrusted with diplomatic missions including the negotiations with King Abdullah. After Independence, she was sent as Israel's Ambassador to the Soviet Union. Following the first general elections, however, she was recalled and included in the Cabinet. A hard yet sentimental person, wise at times yet simplistic, she tended to be both self-righteous, sarcastic and intensely zealous about whatever she believed in, at times on the basis of false information. All this emerges vividly from her speeches in the first Knesset, which, at the age of 51, she addressed as Minister of Labor. Her job dealt with the availability of building materials and production technology, their quantities and costs, but she chose to speak about terror and joy, courage and delight, bravery, sin and shame, always in her own distinctive emotional manner. When unemployed immigrants demonstrated in the streets she reacted as if they were intentionally trying to annoy her, and the press, according to her, was deliberately distorting what she had said in order to provoke her.[40] "We have no alternative!" she would often declare, when justifying the government's housing policy, because that was how she saw things: either black or white.[41] When Members of the Opposition questioned her decision to house several thousand new immigrants in wooden huts, instead of houses, she replied that she had approved the act because she did not have the courage to oppose it: "I am no hero, and I can't bring myself to say, let there be five, six, eight families in every room until we can build each a one- or two-room apartment. I knew it was an illusion—we are not going to be able to build them houses in the near future."[42] So she put them in wooden huts.

When Yosef Serlin, MK and Israel Rokah, MK (General Zionists) criticized the rate and standard of construction, she responded with her usual sarcasm:

> How I envy Mr. Serlin, who can calmly and generously review different forms of housing. Wooden huts should never have been built for the immigrants. Prefabs are no good. No one can live in them. Only one kind of house will do for Mr. Serlin, and his aesthetic sense: a nice, big, solid house. . . . Moreover, Mr. Serlin has a rival in his own party, Mr. Rokah. Mr. Rokah's aesthetic sense is even more highly developed. . . . Mr. Rokah says that one room is not enough for a family. I won't argue. I am just as aware as he that two rooms are a minimal requirement for a family. . . .[43]

But she did not hesitate to justify housing a family in a single room:

> . . . There is no harm if a family of three, or even of four, lived in one single room. . . . We intend to provide a roof. Not a ceiling—a roof. No plaster—only whitewash. The immigrant himself will in time plaster the walls and add a ceiling. A few months later he will add a room and a porch. There's no harm in this. . . .[44]

Her spartan-puritan manner was her trademark. It stemmed from the genuine shortage of money and materials, as well as from her character and world view. The prefabs she referred to in her speech were small concrete structures, containing a single room, a kitchenette and a lavatory. They were produced by a then novel method, using a casting machine which had a long barrel; they came to be known as Golda's cannons. A *Haaretz* correspondent who observed the process compared it to the way children build sandcastles on the sea shore: "They raise a bucket over a barrel of sand—and lo and behold, another house has been added."[45]

In the early half of the year, the Minister of Labor announced to the Knesset that by the end of the year there would be 30,000 housing units ready.[46] Three months later she "rejoiced" in being able to state that the plan was being fully carried out—by the end of September the first 15,000 units would be ready, and the rest would be completed by the end of the year. This, she said, would provide housing for "the great majority" of the immigrants who were presently living in the camps.[47] Before the year ended, she received a report stating that not 30,000, but just over 27,000 units had been ordered, approximately only 18,000 of which were completed; more than half of them were wooden huts. In the meantime, the number of immigrants in the camps kept growing.[48]

In the latter half of April the leaders of MAPAI began to fear that the entire scheme of immigrant absorption was about to collapse, largely because of the housing shortage. Giora Yoseftal reported to his party's Secretariat that the camps in his charge could have held 40,000 people, "in more or less humane conditions," yet in reality they housed 56,000, half of them in tents. Zalman Aran, MAPAI's Secretary General, warned that the situation in the camps was "catastrophic," reflecting "almost criminal neglect" and threatened the future of the state and of world Jewry. Pinhas Lavon, MK, who was Secretary General of the Histadrut labor union, predicted "a major explosion," and Eliyahu Dobkin of the Jewish Agency described the situation as "an utter horror." Members of the Secretariat demanded an immediate evacuation of some of the army camps, to provide accommodation for the immigrants, while the wooden huts were being constructed for their housing. Ben-Gurion ruled that the immigrants would have to make do with tents. He promised that the possibility of using some army camps would be looked into, yet he warned, "We won't evict the army. . . . The army could bring down the government if we evict it." He felt that the projected wooden huts were too expensive. He agreed that the situation in the camps was grim and very difficult, and supported Lavon's proposal to impose a special immigration-absorption tax, yet at the same time maintained that the "overall situation was not as dreadful as people said," and that there was no reason to panic. Construction companies would be consulted, he promised, and the Histadrut general council would discuss the situation and draw its own conclusion. "There is no need to put pressure on any one of us," he stated. Lavon, in a rare outburst, reproached him, "What you are saying is so far removed from reality that I am surprised at you!" But Ben-Gurion remained adamant: "I don't understand this delicate attitude—that people must not live in tents. . . . We are pampering them. People can live in tents for years. Whoever doesn't want to—should not come here."[49]*

On March 27, the Chairman of the Jewish Agency Executive, Berl Locker, announced that Levi Eshkol was about to make a "revolutionary proposal." When called upon to speak, Eshkol stated that the present system of immigrant camps was a damnable invention. "Somebody devised it to destroy us."[53] He suggested that instead of wasting away in the camps, the immigrants be sent to work. Whatever prompted the Jewish Agency Executive to eliminate the camps and make the immigrants self-supporting required no "revolutionary" brilliance. Providing food and services to tens of thousands of people in the camps was extremely costly, and the Jewish Agency was unable to meet the expense. In addition, it had become evident that life in the camps was having a deleterious effect on the immigrants' morale. Yoseftal wrote the Minister of Finance, Eliezer Kaplan, that there was an atmosphere of apathy in the camps, which "destroyed their initiative and accustomed them to being depen-

---

*Yoseftal ascribed the slow rate and poor standard of construction to "a thousand reasons," including limited funds, as well as a scarcity of building materials and labor, but he also attributed it in part to the "dictatorship of the major construction companies."[50] There were also disputes between the government and the Jewish Agency—the latter fearing that the government would banish them from the entire enterprise. "They'll take all our responsibilities away, one by one. . . . First absorption, then housing, then the settlement. . . . And since there is no other functional reason for us to exist, we will have nothing to do. I see this as a great danger."[51] The Jewish Agency was supposed to build 2,000 of the projected 30,000 units, and failed to do so. A memorandum to Golda Meir stated that their failure to do so was because they were short of funds. Hermon predicted, "There is no alternative. We are going to have slums, poverty-stricken neighborhoods and oppressive overcrowding."[52]

dent on others." He warned that some of the immigrants hated the Establishment and some were trying to find work outside the channels of the official Labor Exchange, which could eventually lead to the Labor Exchange's demise, and cause great damage to the ruling MAPAI.[54] The mood of the immigrants also worried the politicians. Pinhas Lavon described the camp dwellers as "carriers of the counter-revolution." As he put it, "One day a hundred thousand such people, cooped up in the camps, without any other outlet—could get together and rise up against us, and cause an explosion that would blow away both the government and the Knesset."[55] In other words, the camp-dwellers were endangering the stability of the regime.*

So, within two years after the state was established, they began to transfer immigrants to working villages. But now, when the Jewish Agency started to evacuate the camps, they learned that some of the immigrants preferred to remain there, under the umbrella of its protection and at its expense, rather than have to face the difficulties of settling down outside. At one point the Jewish Agency actually worsened the conditions in the camps, in order to encourage their inhabitants to leave. Among other things, they closed down the kitchens and stopped distributing food. "We, in the absorption department, are using the pressure method," said one of its officials, Yehuda Braginsky. It was a ruthless kind of pressure, he stated: "The man must leave the camp, and so we try to push him as hard as we can."[57] The 10,000 or so who were settled in the working villages were employed in forestation projects or in cultivating the abandoned olive groves. Some of these villages eventually became permanent habitations, while others became new immigrant installations called *Maabaroth* (transit camps). Most of them were established on the outskirts of cities. Within two years they accommodated 250,000, constantly increasing in numbers as the other camps were emptied. Life in the Maabaroth was somewhat more bearable than in the immigrant camps. People began to work and the children attended school. But before long new arrivals were taken straight from the ports to the Maabaroth. For these people, who had not experienced the immigrant camps, the real-

---

*Zerah Warhaftig, MK, of the religious Hapoel Hamizrahi party, also feared the camp-dwellers, as though they were a gang of savages, penned up in enclosures. "Imagine what would happen if one hundred thousand Jews were to emerge from the camps and ask, 'What's this? You live in apartments, you have jobs—and we have to live here in tents, in internment camps?'"[56]

ity there was grim enough. They lived in great poverty, on the fringes of society, dependent on a bureaucratic, political and economic establishment, which did not always act in their best interests. At first they lived in tents, generally one tent per family, though sometimes two families had to share a tent. Later a better type of canvas hut was introduced, which was to be followed by quonset and wooden huts. These structures were not connected to the water and electrical systems, the water being supplied by only a few taps out in the open. These few outlets had to suffice for a whole population. The water was of poor quality and had to be boiled before consumption. There were public showers and public toilets, usually no cleaner and of no better quality than those in the old camps. Kerosene lamps and burners for light, cooking and heating were used. The schools lacked desks and chairs, blackboards, chalk and textbooks. A few experienced teachers volunteered to teach in these schools, as a national-educational mission. Some of them were sent by the army. Most of the teachers, however, were themselves new immigrants, and some of them could not speak Hebrew. Moreover, the Histadrut clinics in these camps suffered from a chronic shortage of doctors and nurses, equipment and medicines.

Since only a few of the Maabaroth were included in the municipal jurisdiction of the major cities, the standard of services they received was very low. Some camps were created far from centers of population and the residents were unable to find employment. The men were employed as construction workers for the government or the Histadrut, or they were employed in forestry, either in the orange groves or in agriculture, for the Jewish National Fund, the Custodian of Abandoned Property or the kibbutzim. The Histadrut construction company *Solel Boneh*, the orange growers and some of the kibbutzim, greatly benefited as a result of the abundance of labor. The wages were low and partly subsidized by the government; and there was not enough work to go around. Consequently, the power of the Labor Exchange increased greatly, and with it the power and highhandedness of MAPAI. The residents were wholly dependent on them, and it became part of a daily routine to have to line up in front of the Labor Exchanges. Quarrels would often break out, which would require police intervention.

In the more than one hundred Maabaroth there was always intense activity on the part of the political parties, who, as part of the coalition arrangements, handed out the key posts to their supporters. Giora Yoseftal reflected, "At election time we did a great deal of harm in the Maabaroth and the new settlements by making promises that could not be kept and by achieving our ends through the despicable means of buying votes."[58] Life in the camps and the Maabaroth became part of the absorption process experienced by all immigrants, from European and Arab countries alike. In years to come, they would remember the humiliation more than the material distress; "My old man wept," recalled novelist Sami Mihael.[59]

Within three years of the creation of the state, there were as many new immigrants as there were residents who had lived in the country before Independence. And they continued to come. The accepted view was that they ought to forgo their cultural distinctions and adopt a new identity. Novelist Aharon Appelfeld wrote about a boy from Poland who was mistreated and even severely beaten by his native comrades because he had not become suntanned like them. He assured them that he was trying hard to darken his skin, but they said that if he really wanted to, he would have changed long before.[60] The ability to change was later defined as a condition of becoming a part of the country.[61] This was also the general view expressed in the discussion between David Ben-Gurion and the writers. "This people is ugly, impoverished, morally unstable and hard to love," said poetess Leah Goldberg. As she saw it, the Israeli writer had to learn from Dostoyevsky and Gorky—who were not deterred by ugliness, stench and degradation. What one had to reveal in the new immigrant, the Holocaust survivor, was the true image of Man, which was hidden deep inside the man with the black-market dollars in his belt. Yet, she added, it required "tremendous effort."[62] Ben-Gurion stated: "Among the survivors of the German concentration camps there were people who would not have survived if they had not been what they were—hard, evil and selfish people, and what they underwent there served to destroy what good qualities they had left."[63]*

---

*The rejection of the Diaspora did not infrequently produce descriptions sounding like anti-Semitic caricatures. Journalist Arye Gelblum described the "typical new immigrant" as "A short little Polish Jew with prominent jaws, accompanied by his little fat wife."[64] Poet Nathan Alterman wrote about the Boston Jew who, after a visit by Ben-Gurion to his city, straightened his back; the Jew was described as a tailor, of course, a ladies' tailor.[65] Yosef Barpal, of the Mossad, wrote about the Jews who preferred to remain in Europe: "We took 2,100 Jews out [of Hungary]. They are now in Austria. In Austria these people opened their eyes wide—here they can do business. Just give him a chance, and

As soon as the first immigrants started to arrive, a continuing discussion developed in Israel about "regulating" the flow of immigration and applying a "selective" policy. The debate did not refer much to the problems of Jews in the Diaspora, nor to the hardships of absorption in Israel. The issues discussed were the needs of the country, its manpower requirements and the financial difficulties in providing for the immigrants. Ben-Gurion, who opposed any restriction on immigration, used to speak about the "state's absorption throes." He calculated that for the United States to make a similar effort, it would have to take in thirty million immigrants a year.[68] He tended to ignore the hardships suffered by the immigrants. The debate was heated, and seemed to test the Zionist patriotism of the participants. Israel Goldstein, Member of the Jewish Agency Executive, stated: "The overall situation of immigration absorption is very worrying, and while we cannot cope with all of the immigration, we might be able to reduce it somewhat and regulate it with regard to countries where Jews are not in danger."[69] S.Z. Shragai, another Member of the Executive declared, "None of us will agree to reducing the rate of immigration!"[70] This was not strictly true, but those who voiced the idea risked being called defeatists, unpatriotic or skeptics. Moshe Kol said, "When we first went to war with the Arabs the financial situation of our defense was worse than our present financial situation with regard to immigration. Nevertheless, we made tremendous efforts and succeeded. Now I should like to see us making the tremendous efforts needed to overcome the problem of immigration."[71] In those days planning was considered a useless effort and improvisation was the order of the day. "If we had worked with a plan," said Berl Locker, "we would never have dared to think of absorbing 150,000 immigrants (the number at that time)."[72] Itzhak Refael demanded that everybody's views on the matter be made public, "I don't want to be known as the one who sought to reduce immigration," he exclaimed. But Berl Locker replied that if their real positions were made public, the press would use it to attack certain Members of the Executive.[73] Thus the people who

---

the Jew will soon strike root."[66] The same note was struck by several emissaries. The Mossad's agent in Libya reported: "There's about 3,500 Jews here who are not thinking of emigrating to Israel in the near future. They are attached to the fleshpots. . . . They will continue to play roulette, do business, eat meat and make money."[67]

recognized the need to slow down the rate of immigration did not dare make their opinions known, for fear of being attacked by the media.

Dr. Goldstein was bold enough to persevere, "I can understand why we couldn't discuss this question before the elections, but I don't see why we can't do so now. . . ."[74] Gradually, as the flow of immigration continued to swell, others came to share his opinion, among them Levi Eshkol: "If we don't regulate immigration we'll fall," he stated: "It will destroy our social and economic independence. . . ."[75] Some time later he warned, "We must not become beggars. It will destroy Zionism."[76] And again, "Immigration such as you propose . . . is suicide."[77] Some days later Eshkol said:

> In the past three months death stared us in the face. . . . I ask myself, how a public body can be so irresponsible? . . . If there had been more serious public control, the people responsible would have had to stand trial. How could we bring Jews and settle them in tents? But here everything passes quietly. The fact is that the right hand does not know what the left hand is doing. I regret to say—and I know that many good people here will not agree—we haven't got the means to carry out our decisions. . . . We are facing a catastrophe, the people in the camps will starve . . . because there is no money. If only we could repress our inclinations and decide to conduct the immigration according to some sort of plan. There is a given number of potential immigrants in the world. Let us prepare a plan for 24 or 30 months, during which time we will bring in a certain number, satisfying both the needs of the immigrants and the needs of the country. Let us not invest all the money in supplying the immigrant camps' kitchens, so that we'll have some left for housing. But we're not doing this. What we're doing is putting them in camps and having them eat up the money. . . .[78]

Dr. Israel Goldstein did not view it as a matter of "inclination" but of politics. "The government decided on encouraging this vast and unrestricted immigration before the elections, because it did not dare to restrict it at that time. Now, after the elections, no one is willing to take on the responsibility for absorbing the immigrants."[79]

Those in charge of immigrant absorption, Tsvi Hermon and Giora Yoseftal, based their demand to slow the rate of immigration on the hardships of the new arrivals. Yoseftal was almost in despair. "The tap has been turned on and nobody will dare turn it off, and they say that this is the great Zionist enterprise. They say that if only we, who are in charge of absorption, would try harder—everything would be all right. . . . We see immigrants, not Immigration, and we say that there must be some kind of gradual slowdown, based on joint consultation. We must take political aspects into consideration, . . . but not the fear that someone might go off to America. The person who does not wish to come here, of his own free will, and yet comes here anyway, is a tragedy, because we're making him into a tragedy here."[80] But all these things were said in closed sessions, in the greatest secrecy. Outwardly, they all pretended that things were going as well as they should.

Somewhat belatedly, and gradually, the daily *Haaretz* also dared to demand a slowdown in immigration. To begin with, the paper only called for a "better psychological preparation of the immigrants before arrival." "They should be told in advance that the State of Israel is not a paradise," it declared, "where roast geese are handed out on the streets."[81] Two months later it became more explicit. "There is no way to avoid reducing the dimensions of immigration."[82] Between the former and the latter editorial, a member of the Jewish Agency Executive, Meir Grossmann, published an article in the right-wing opposition newspaper, *Hamashkif,* saying:

> The hasty transportation of immigrants, without knowing where we shall house them and what will happen to them, derived largely from the purely military needs of a nation at war. There was urgent need for manpower, both for the armed forces and for development. . . . We must convert the spontaneous immigration into a planned, orderly and systematic process, coordinated in time and space. To begin with, we must bring in the young pioneers. Next, we should speed up the immigration of people who can support themselves since they will not be a burden on the community. Third, immigration must be tailored to match our capacity for absorption.[83]

Other newspapers rejected this view. The pro-government *Dvar Hashavua* wrote:

> All the well-meant advice about slowing down immigration is senseless. It is not in our power to slow down the immigration, because it is a spontaneous phenomenon. But even if we had the means to slow it down, we would not have the right to do so. No one knows how much time we have to bring over masses of Jews

from countries where they face monstrous dangers whenever there is a crisis in the world, nor does anyone know how much time we have to build up the state and strengthen it so that it can stand another test, if it should come.[84]

"The population must be greatly increased in the very near future," wrote the religious *Hatzofeh*, which represented the views of Itzhak Refael; "without sufficient population the state will collapse. . . ."[85] Refael himself told the Members of the Jewish Agency Executive: "We are at the end of the phase of mass immigration. The problem of immigration will continue to trouble us greatly in the future, but in a different way—the question will be—how shall we get more immigrants and where from?"[86] He explained that the prospects for immigration depended on the rate of emigration, the first Jews to leave draw others after them. "Immigration hinges on its pace," he stated. "The faster it goes, the larger the numbers. Otherwise they will go elsewhere."[87] Ben-Gurion said in the Knesset, "To the best of my knowledge, there were neither houses nor jobs awaiting the six hundred thousand Children of Israel when they started the Exodus from Egypt, yet Moses did not hesitate a moment and delivered them from there."[88] *Haaretz*, however, wrote in an editorial, "It is not the purpose of our struggle to create a problem of Jewish refugees resembling that of the Arab refugees in the neighboring countries."[89]

Concurrently with the debate on "regulating" the immigration, there was also an argument about "selecting" the immigrants: the first Israelis were troubled by the quality of the "human material" coming into the country. "It is no secret that there is some quite undesirable material among the immigrants," wrote one newspaper.[90] Similar expressions were heard in the Jewish Agency Executive. Dr. Nahum Goldmann: "A state and a nation are entitled to exercise a certain ruthlessness. If we bring in aged people and invalids, other organizations must bear the burden. I see no harm in it if Jewish organizations look after these sick people abroad. A more efficient selection is good for the immigration and there can be no ideological objection to it."[91] Even Itzhak Refael was less than decided on this question: "I am in favor of selecting immigrants," he assured the Members of the Executive, and told them of his efforts to avoid undesired immigration:[92] "I held up 2,000 visas in Tunis, which had been issued to old people and invalids, and gave an order not to bring them over. I held up 800 visas in France, which were issued to sick and aged people . . . also invalids in Germany, 5,000 people. . . ."[93] The problem preoccupied them repeatedly; some of the things they said were cruel. When Moshe Kol explained how Jewish children were delivered from Christian hands and brought over through Youth Immigration, Eshkol asked: "Are we interested in delivering every child, at any age?"[94] "I am bitterly grieved by the number of old, sick and disabled people coming here . . . they amount to 18 percent," complained Tsvi Hermon.[95] In December 1948 it was decided to prepare a list of diseases, sufferers of which would not be allowed to come. "In the meantime, the order has been given to hold up the immigration of the chronically ill," said the resolution.[96] Eliyahu Dobkin complained, "When immigration is spontaneous, those who should not come, do, and those who should, don't. Was it really necessary to bring over the entire old-people's home of Pavlovdov? We have not been sufficiently selective with regard to the immigrants."[97] Dobkin was referring to an old-people's home in Bulgaria. The correspondence concerning it, between the agent of the Mossad, Shaike Dann, and his superiors, has been preserved. In one of his letters the agent wrote:

Don't try to upset me with the death of two old people and with diseases. Between the medical inspection which they undergo here and their departure, 4,500 people could fall ill several times, and two young people could die on land, not only two old people at sea. . . . The authorities don't agree to let the old folk stay here. . . . And if the old people remain behind, their sons and daughters will stay with them, and we'll condemn these Jews to remain here forever. . . . Of course we are doing everything possible to reduce the number of old people.[98]

Nahum Waxmann, the Immigration Department's representative in Rome, wrote to the *Eretz Israel* Office in Paris: "Recently problematic elements, from a social and medical viewpoint, have begun to come from Egypt. Altogether, there are few people coming out, and we hardly see the good and healthy elements that used to come out in the past. It looks as if this is no accident, but that someone is doing it deliberately, sending us the mentally-ill, lonely souls whose families would like to get rid of them, extremely old people without families, etc."[99] Minister of Immigration Shapira wrote to the immigration officers abroad that while the state's policy was to keep the gates open to any Jew who wished and could come to Israel, it was necessary to point out that it was their job to promote the immigration of Jews who could contribute to the development of the country and prevent the immigration of those who might "hold up our war effort."[100] In June Tsvi Hermon proposed to the Executive that it should make it public and official that the Jewish Agency could not be responsible for the welfare cases, and that it was therefore going to stop bringing them to Israel.[101] It was at that meeting that Levi Eshkol said that Israel could not take in all the crazy Jews in the world. He proposed informing the *Eretz Israel* Office in Germany that until further notice no invalids and no potential welfare cases were to be brought over.[102]*

Following months of continued negotiations, the American Joint Distribution Committee assumed responsibility for those immigrants who, according to the Jewish Agency, were unfit to take part in the development of the country, the old, the disabled, the mentally ill, etc. According to the Zionist Executive, "Israel cannot be expected to act as sole philanthropist for the entire Jewish people."[104] This reflected an Israeli, rather than Jewish or even purely Zionist point of view.

Other categories were also considered undesirable. For example, the decision to permit the immigration of the Karaite community of Egypt came only after lengthy vacillation and disputes among rabbis and scholars. "Heaven forfend that we should bring this deadly plague into Israel's vineyard," ruled the Chief Ashkenazi Rabbi of Jerusalem, Tsvi Pesah Frank. Sephardic Chief Rabbi Uziel recommended that they be allowed in, as did Itzhak Ben-Tsvi, later President of Israel. The decision to let them in was eventually made by Ben-Gurion himself.[105]† Dr. Y. Meir, General Director of the Ministry of Health, said he had been "horrified" to read in the newspapers that there was an intention to bring in the Falashas of Ethiopia. "I hope that this report is unfounded," he wrote to Giora Yoseftal.[106] Eighteen

---

*On the other hand, Yosef Barpal, head of the Mossad, said: "We must bring in even the village idiots," but added that they must be brought last.[103]

†The Karaites are members of a stream of Judaism established in Baghdad in the middle of the 8th century. The basis for their belief is that they do not recognize any of the rabbinical interpretations of the Bible and rely only on the laws of the scriptures. Other differences exist between them and the traditional Jews. As a result the orthodox establishment in Israel refused to recognize them as Jews.

months later the Jewish Agency's representative in Aden, Shlomo Schmidt, reported: "My investigation shows that the problem of the Falashas is not at all simple, because these people's ways are not much different from those of the Abyssinians, and that intermarriage is natural among them. There is also among them a large number of people with venereal diseases. . . ."[107] Dr. S. Bernstein, representative of the Jewish Agency's Immigration Department in New York, sent Itzhak Refael a list of 370 American Jews who wished to go to Israel. Between them, they stated, they had about three and a half million dollars, namely a little under ten thousand dollars per person. The representative estimated that their total capital was actually greater than they had declared, but in Jerusalem the attitude was to do everything possible to dissuade them from coming. "Many of them are not young," wrote Yaakov Weinstein, of the Immigration Department, "and the sums at their disposal are rather limited. We must generally beware of people over 50 who are not skilled workers, and of this type of capital, or they might become a burden on the Israeli public. . . ." The representative in New York would not give up, so Weinstein wrote him again: "The absence of young people and pioneer youth in your list worries me a good deal. I think it is superfluous to emphasize our state's urgent need for young and pioneering forces, and extensive activities should be undertaken to promote immigration from those circles."[108]*

Arye Gelblum divided the immigrants into three groups: the elite, the second-rate and "African Arabs." As for the Bulgarians, he wrote, they are indeed praiseworthy. The Turks, too, are good quality, only less intelligent.[117] This was the usual way of discussing them, in generalized, collective terms. Ruth Klieger

---

*Even after the Law of Return had been enacted, in 1951 the Ministry of the Interior refused to permit the entry of a group of old women from Bulgaria. The Attorney General had to intervene and rule that the Law of Return made their admission unexceptionable.[109] Other undesirable immigrants were communists,[110] members of Lehi (the "Stern Gang"),[111] uncircumcised children,[112] intermarried couples,[113] and journalists.[114] On the other hand, certain people were more welcome than others: Zionist leaders were given priority and various kinds of assistance after arrival, including housing.[115] There was an ideological debate on the question of whether non-pioneering, older capitalists were desirable immigrants. Some argued that they were not brought over because they would not vote for MAPAI. On the other hand, it was claimed that the reason the religious parties pressed for stepped-up immigration was that many of the immigrants were religious. Every party accused the others of exploiting immigration to promote their political ends; quite often this was true.[116]

(Aliav), who used to work for the Mossad was sent to inspect the immigrant camps, after which she sent the Prime Minister's Office a report about the immigrants and their dispositions according to their lands of origin:

Those from Europe, including Rumania and Hungary, have no pioneering spirit at all. They expect a life of luxury and will live only in the city. Do not learn the language. Most of them brought something with them. Many of them have brought substantial amounts. They are not disposed to collective absorption, but tend to disperse independently. They view the Jewish Agency with contempt. They are noisy, full of complaints about having been brought here. They don't see Israel as their final destination. There are professionals among them and all kinds of skilled workers. Those from Shanghai (who had gone there from Central Europe) are cultured. Few of them are professionals. There are a few doctors and other members of the liberal professions. They will settle for nothing but life in a city and lack all desire to become absorbed as a productive element within an organized economic framework such as a kibbutz. The Yugoslavs, Bulgarians and Czechs are of a high cultural level. Productive and healthy. They will settle readily in farming communities, but not in kibbutzim, which they view as another form of the kolkhoz (Russian collective farms). Most of them are communist-oriented, and have organizations of their own. There is among them a high percentage of trained people, including intellectuals and members of the liberal professions. Among both Yugoslavs and Czechs there are many mixed marriages, both men and women. Immigrants from India: a low cultural level. Most of them have worked in factories. Will be absorbed as laborers or farmers. Syrians, Iraqis, Iranians and Tripolitanians: Most of them speak Hebrew, having belonged to pioneering, Zionist movements (especially the Iraqis and Iranians). Their ambition is to live on the land, in some cases even in kibbutzim. They are generally healthy. Turks: Good human material. A fairly high cultural level. Will settle anywhere and accept any kind of work. Will be easily absorbed. Clean and fairly healthy. A strong family structure. About 25% of them are children. North Africans: Mostly destitute, hot-tempered, unorganized and nationalistic. A large percentage are inclined to live on the land. Few have any skills. Have difficulties learning. . . . Easily influenced. Of low cultural and social level. 25% to 30% are children. Yemenites: Mostly destitute, 60% have no relatives in the country, suffer from trachoma and skin diseases. . . . Most of them very eager to live on the land. Work is their main purpose in life. Quick-witted and unorganized.[118]

Eventually all were brought in, without anyone ever being "regulated" or "selected." Even those politicians who said that the rate must be reduced and that only "positive human material" should be brought over in the first phase, dared not stand up for their views in public, for fear of being branded as skeptics, who lacked Zionist and patriotic fervor. They were trapped in the dilemma of fearing unlimited immigration and fearing to limit it. It was not easy—the need for workers and fighting men was real and pressing. There was also the memory of the failure to save some Jews who might have been saved during the Holocaust, and so many people feared to take the decision to leave any Jews where they were, where their lives could be in jeopardy. There was also the fear that if they were not brought over at once, they would later be either unable or unwilling to come.

Time showed that they were mistaken: the mass immigration was a heavy burden on the state. It brought to Israel people who either did not wish to come in the first place, or were disappointed after their arrival, among other reasons because of the difficulties they encountered trying to settle in. Most of the immigrants had not been in danger in their native lands, and most of the countries were willing to let the Jews leave years later. Members of the government and the Zionist Executive who would not openly dare to advocate an immigration slowdown also erred in evaluating the public mood: already at the beginning of 1949 eight out of ten Israelis felt that some sort of "planning" must govern immigration. They believed that priority should be given to the members of pioneer youth movements, young farmers and skilled workers.[119]

For most Israelis, the immigrants were *terra incognita*, as one newspaper put it. They lived in their camps, their villages, the abandoned towns, without any immediate contact with the existing population.[120] "In the past, every wave of immigration became absorbed by the older population," wrote another newspaper. "The present immigration exists beside the established population."[121] Some people spoke about "two camps," others about "two nations" or "two worlds."[122] Martin Buber feared the mass immigration. He foresaw that the poor communication between the communities contained frightful dangers. "I keep looking for a common heritage," he said, "but I don't see it. All I see is broken tablets."[123] Ruth Gruber, an American journalist, wrote Ben-Gurion to say that most Israelis seemed horribly indifferent toward the new immigrants. "The old population fought for the immigration and won, but now nobody takes any interest in the camp dwellers for whom they had fought. The few who do feel guilty about conditions in the camps say, 'We suffered when we arrived—let them suffer, too.'"[124]*

The indifference of the public reflected that of the national institutions, including the army. The Jewish Agency had great difficulty getting the army to give up camp space for the immigrants.[127] The army sent soldiers and officers to help in the camps, but it was in response to orders, not out of sympathy. Yehuda Braginsky, of the Absorption Department, reported:

> During the floods in Lydda, when 16 inches of water fell, we negotiated with the Prime Minister, asking him to provide us with some means of rescue. We asked for the use of the airfield in Kfar Sirkin. We were told that it was out of the question—"someone" needed it, and it was forbidden even to talk about it. They offered us Tel Nof, which was surrounded by paratroopers on one side. . . . The paratroopers who were near the camps warned us that they were going to plant land mines along our side, so that the people in the tents would not venture near. So we had to give up the idea.[128]

At times the public indifference was reflected in the behavior of kibbutz members. Four Jews who had been smuggled across the Lebanese border reached the gates of kibbutz Misgav Am, after a long and exhausting trek on foot. The kibbutz turned them away. They walked on for two more hours and reached kibbutz Manarah. There they were allowed in, but, as the emissary who accompanied them reported, the kibbutz warned that if their accommodation was not paid for, no more immigrants would be allowed in.[129]

Almost everywhere there were complaints by farmers that immigrants from the camps were raiding their orchards, picking fruit for themselves. One orange grower wrote a series of letters—including one to the Prime Minister—demanding that the authorities protect him from the immigrants, whom he de-

---

*The youth movements did send their members to the camps. Their written impressions reveal deep shock, a feeling of strangeness, but also much good will. "Often you stand there completely helpless. . . . You are pierced by the question, Can a nation be moulded out of all this?"[125] Various voluntary organizations also worked in the camps, and when a project was announced to offer homes to immigrant children during the winter, there were more volunteers than there were children who needed them.[126] In the course of the year a special immigration-absorption tax was also imposed.

scribed as something between a gang of gypsies and a swarm of locusts. Unable to protect his property, he said, he was contemplating frightening them off with smoke grenades.[130] But he was not alone in this problem: "Things have become so out of hand," wrote the Farmers' Association to the Minister of Justice, "that this year many farmers have abandoned those of their fields which adjoin the immigrant camps, feeling that there was no point in investing money and efforts in cultivating lands whose harvests they will not reap."[131]

In January 1949 the local council in Raanana wrote to the Jewish Agency, demanding that no more immigrants be sent into the town. B. Ostrowsky, who headed that local council, wrote Giora Yoseftal,

> Following our meeting and the promises made on your side that the Raanana immigrant camp will be converted into a children's home, you continue to send more and more new immigrants into the camp, moving them over here from the camp in Beit Lidd and others. Yesterday and today more families arrived. It is very very difficult for us to understand why you are so eager to ruin Raanana—what has Raanana done to deserve this, and why are you so obstinate? The town council offices are filled each day with hundreds of people shouting "Bread and Work!" and every single day we hand out what is virtually welfare to hundreds of families. Whatever happens, we shall have to close down the local welfare office, the schools and all the other institutions, and some say that the local council should collectively resign and hand the management of the town over to you. We insist that you stop sending any more immigrants here! Not one more immigrant! . . . You must fulfill your promise and save this town.[132]

Most of the camps did in fact become a burden on the small local councils, including some whose total populations were equal to or less than those of the immigrant camps. The powerful mayors, who wielded considerable influence in government, such as Tel Aviv's Israel Rokah, Ramat Gan's Avraham Krinitsi and Haifa's Abba Houshi, knew how to keep the number of such camps in their jurisdiction down to a minimum.

The Zionist Executive noted with concern that immigrants were much too heavily concentrated in the cities and their respective suburbs, and demanded that more efforts be made to direct them to the country.[133] The daily *Haaretz* maintained that the authorities were not doing enough to ensure that the immigrants settle as farmers.[134] This was a widespread view. In those days there was a shortage of manpower in the farming community, and except for certain associations of demobilized soldiers and a few youth movement groups, few Israelis wanted to go and live on the land. Nevertheless, eight out of ten Israelis were disturbed by the flow of immigrants into the major cities, regarding it as a threat to the country's social and economic foundation. Almost all Israelis who were asked, said that the immigrants should be directed to agriculture. About half of them thought the immigrants should be forced to do so.[135] An official publication of the Jewish Agency contained a proposal that the immigrants be compelled to undergo a period of agricultural training in one of the agricultural communities, or in "a special institution," for a period of no less than one year.[136] The immigrants' refusal to do what many native Israelis would not do, was interpreted as an impertinent rejection of the agricultural ideology which was still widespread; it was as if they were deliberately defying the country's ethics and ignoring its needs. One newspaper stated that the food shortages were a direct result of the fact that so few immigrants were opting for agriculture.[137] A Jewish Agency public relations publication warned that the concentration of immigrants in the cities was creating slums, "quarters in which poverty, idleness, crime and violence breed—a new Carthage."[138]

Also during those months tens of thousands of soldiers were released from the army.[139] Some of them were immigrants. Many of these veterans could not get used to the indifference and callousness of the public. They, too, like the immigrants, altered the human landscape in the streets. Every now and then they demonstrated to protest against unemployment and lack of housing. Their distress became a political football, to be exploited in the general elections and in the Knesset. "A new subculture arose from the front lines [of battle]," wrote recent veteran Uri Avneri in his war diary. "These men have evolved their own style, their own world-view and leadership."[140] This description fitted Weimar Germany better than Israel, but it is true that there were men who had just been released from the terrors of war, and were still dazed, confused, seized by inward conflicts, scarcely able to get back on their feet, searching for their proper place in the world. A study of soldiers about to be released showed that they were inclined to break away from what they had been doing before being drafted, and to begin new lives. Eight out of ten said they would rather not return to their former jobs. Four out of ten said they planned to move away from their former residences.[141] In Tel Aviv they, like the immigrants, were offered psychological assistance to relieve them of "fears, stammering, inferiority complexes as well as marital and sexual disturbances."[142] "Accept him as he is," was a newspaper's advice to a woman whose husband had returned home from the war and was finding readjustment difficult.[143] The immigrant who had been described upon arrival as human dust, a refugee, a creature of the Diaspora, inferior human material resistant to change, evader of agricultural work, with illegal dollars hidden in his belt—had now become a competitor on the labor market, too. Seven out of ten Israelis held that veterans should be given priority over the immigrant, in employment and housing.[144] But the authorities were not quick to assist the veterans. They were sent back and forth from office to office, entangled in a frustrating bureaucratic maze. The lines in front of those offices were so long that the men had to get there at four o'clock in the morning if they wanted to be admitted, and some slept overnight in front of the offices to ensure their admission.[145] In the summer the MAPAI Secretariat was informed that half the unemployed men were veterans.[146] The result was that there were repeated clashes between the veterans and the immigrants. "I came here with my family on board an immigrant ship," wrote one new arrival.

We lived in an immigrant hostel until the Jewish Agency arranged a two-room apartment for us in Jaffa. I found a job and after the wanderings and torments we had known we were happy and grateful to be here, free citizens of the State of Israel, which was created by the efforts and the blood of pioneers, the Israel army and the whole population. And then one evening a group of soldiers broke into our house, smashed down the front door, and started to take out our belongings, saying that they were going to occupy one of the rooms, although they had no license to do so. When my mother and my wife, who is in the seventh month of pregnancy, argued with the soldiers, they were beaten up. I produced and showed them the Jewish Agency's permit for the apartment, and the contract I had signed with the Custodian of Abandoned Property, but they said they did not recognize the authority of the Jewish Agency or the government, and that the army had the right to act in these matters as it saw fit, without permission from the said authorities. ... Such acts of anarchy are frequent enough in our neighborhood. . . .[147]

Ben-Gurion tended to do more for the soldiers' housing than for the immigrants.[148]

In one of the government offices in 1949 there was an official who used to send the leaders of the country all kinds of suggestions for improving things. When the number of people in the immigrant camps reached 100,000, the man wrote Levi Eshkol that the camps had become "nests of idle and lazy people," swindlers who took advantage of "the public courtesy" and the "hospitality" with which they had been welcomed. They do not want to become useful citizens of the state, the official declared, but only "to eat and drink at Ben-Gurion's expense." Ben-Gurion was sent a copy of this letter and it was passed from hand to hand in the Prime Minister's Office. Ben-Gurion's secretary, Nehemiah Argov, wrote to Zeev Sherf, the Cabinet Secretary, that "it is worth reading."[149] Ben-Gurion himself did not see the letter, but he expressed himself in much the same spirit when he charged that "one hundred thousand people are living in the immigrant camps, eating the bread of charity," in a speech he made before the eighth convention of the Cooperative Settlements Movement.[150] In his view there was no justification for it. A few weeks later Ben-Gurion commissioned an investigation into the possibility of recruiting the immigrants in "labor brigades" and "companies," who would carry out public works, including construction "for the public good." This was a distinctly Bolshevik idea, though not the first of its kind. Toward the end of the War of Independence, there was a "military works brigade" in Haifa, which recruited men to work in the ports. There was also a proposal to establish a "labor brigade" to revive the Negev.

Ben-Gurion thought of mobilizing immigrants between 18 and 45, who would be employed "without private profit" in a quasi-military system. Thus, he hoped, "the nation's money" would not go to waste maintaining idle immigrants, and "national works" would be carried out without needless expenditure. In addition, Ben-Gurion believed that the labor brigades would provide the immigrants with skills and work experience, a knowledge of Hebrew and "national discipline." He figured that the recruited men would receive "all the basic necessities for themselves (and their families) as well as a small wage, just like the soldiers in the regular army."

A commission was appointed which obediently studied the proposal with great care—none of its members rejected it out of hand. In their final report they did note that the proposal would be strenuously objected to, both in the Opposition and the Coalition. Yosef Almogi of Haifa told his colleagues about the intense political opposition that was aroused by the "military works brigade." At that time, MAPAM members protested against the creation of a labor system which was not subject to the authority of the unions nor entitled to their protection.[151]

In the end, the commission proposed that to start with, only men and women who could be conscripted in accordance with the National Service Law would be recruited. This would save "unnecessary debates" in the Knesset. At the prompting of the Jewish Agency's Absorption Department the commission referred to particular immigrants, some 7,000 in all, who were described as "a demoralizing element, whose influence on the population in the camps has led to restlessness, agitation and riots." The Absorption Department stated that they were "anti-social human material." The commission recommended that these people be sent to the Negev, because "the material is easily transportable," as though they were discussing baggage. When the commission found that the army would be unable to provide the men who would maintain "strict military order" in the camps, it came to the conclusion that the best thing would be to impose "a semi-military order ... while promoting an atmosphere of study, work-competitiveness, occupational training and the possibility of forming groups for future settlement or free cooperatives." In fact, what it contemplated was something between a penal colony and a re-education camp. But no sooner did the commission complete its plan for the first camp, to be set up near Beersheba and to hold 3,000 recruited immigrants, than the anticipated "strenuous objection" arose. Shalom Cohen, who represented the Ministry of Labor, wrote the commission that the proposal was "a great idea," but that his Ministry would be unable to include the cost in its budget, nor could it turn jobs over to the immigrants in the Negev, either on the roads, or anywhere else.[152] One way or the other, the proposal died. It is worth recalling, though, as an indication of the general mood of the time.

By the year's end, the Jewish Agency had organized a mass rally in Tel Aviv to welcome the unknown immigrant who had brought the population up to one million. The rally was widely publicized on radio, and a special poster was printed for the occasion. The "masses" were unimpressed; not more than fifteen people showed up for the rally. Jewish Agency Executive member, Yehuda Braginsky summed it up in the following words, "What a shame!"[153]

6

Nameless People

ITZHAK REFAEL ONCE WARNED his colleagues on the Jewish Agency Executive that if they insisted on "regulating" the immigration quotas only the immigration from North Africa would remain for it could not be reduced; "everyone agrees that we do not want this to be our only source," he said.[1] He had earlier visited a transit camp in Marseilles where the immigrants from North Africa stayed awaiting their passage to Israel. "The North African human material is not particularly good," he told his colleagues.[2] On his way back he also stopped in the Displaced Persons camps in Germany. He viewed their inmates as also being bad "human material," who were given to a "Diaspora mentality." However, he said he was relieved by the visit: "I must say that the human material (in Germany) is better than I had thought, especially after having visited the North Africans in Marseilles."[3] One of the Mossad's agents in Casablanca reported: "The Moroccans are a very wild people."[4] A few months later the Foreign Ministry prepared a circular for all Israeli representatives overseas, drawing their attention to the fact that at this point most of the immigration was coming from Middle Eastern countries. The percentage of the population that does not belong to the "Ashkenazi community" is steadily growing,

and will eventually constitute one third of the Jewish population of Israel. "This will affect all aspects of life in the country,"
the Foreign Office warned its diplomats. Its conclusion was that
the "preservation of the country's cultural level demands a flow
of immigration from the West, and not only from the backward
Levantine countries."⁵ Israel, which had absorbed with difficulty the waves of immigration from Europe, was even more reluctant to take in newcomers from the Arab countries. They
were met with dismay and hostility. "You are familiar with the
immigrants from those places," said Shoshana Persits, MK.
"You know that we do not have a common language with them.
Our cultural level is not theirs. Their way of life is medieval. . . ."⁶ Yosef Weitz stated, "While I was talking with Yosef
Shprintsak, he expressed anxiety about preserving our cultural
standards given the massive immigration from the Orient.
There are indeed grounds for anxiety, but what's the use? Can
we stop it?"⁷ Yaakov Zrubavel, head of the Middle East Department of the Jewish Agency, concurred. "Perhaps these are not
the Jews we would like to see coming here, but we can hardly
tell them not to come. . . ."⁸

At a meeting with writers and intellectuals David Ben-
Gurion predicted that the immigrants from the Arab countries
would yet produce a new Berl Katsenelson (the Labor movement's leading ideologist). As he put it, "Even the immigrant
from North Africa, who looks like a savage, who has never read a
book in his life, not even a religious one, and doesn't even know
how to say his prayers, either wittingly or unwittingly has behind him a spiritual heritage of thousands of years. . . ."⁹ Yet
some time later he published an article in which he said: "The
ancient spirit left the Jews of the East and their role in the Jewish
nation receded or disappeared entirely. In the past few hundred
years the Jews of Europe have led the nation, in both quantity
and quality." When Ben-Gurion spoke of Europe, he was referring "especially" to Eastern Europe. Published in the Government's Annual, Ben-Gurion's article gave a virtually official
stamp to the view that the house of a Jewish rag-merchant in
Plonsk, Poland, for instance, was endowed with the "ancient
spirit," while that of, say, a Sorbonne-trained Jewish physician
in Algeria was not.¹⁰ Europe's Jewry, wrote Ben-Gurion, shaped
the entire Jewish people throughout the world,¹¹ whereas "the
Islamic countries have, in the past few hundred years, played a

passive role in the history of the nation."[12] He stated that Zionism was largely a movement of Western Jews, specifically those of Europe and America.[13] He illustrated his point by comparing the income from the Zionist fundraising in the United States and Europe with that in the Arab countries. The Jews of Europe, in his words, were "the leading candidates for citizenship in the State of Israel."[14] This, to him, was the true significance of the Holocaust: "Hitler, more than he hurt the Jewish people, whom he knew and detested, hurt the Jewish State, whose coming he did not foresee. He destroyed the substance, the main and essential building force of the state. The state arose and did not find the nation which had waited for it."[15] In the absence of that (European) "nation," the State of Israel had to bring in Jews from Arab countries. Ben-Gurion compared them with the Africans who were brought in as slaves to America.[16]*

Some time after the number of immigrants from the Arab countries began to exceed that from Europe, the quarterly *Megamot* approached five prominent scholars of the Hebrew University in Jerusalem, Ernst Simon, Nathan Rotenstreich, Meshulam Groll, Yosef Ben-David (Gross) and Karl Frankenstein, all of Central or East European origin, and asked them to consider this new problem. They approached it with appropriate academic rigor, their articles bearing titles such as "Absolute Criteria" and "The Dignity of Man." Karl Frankenstein's article ended with the sentence: "We must recognize the primitive mentality of many of the immigrants from the backward countries." The others were of the same opinion. Frankenstein proposed that in order to understand the mentality of the immigrants it should be compared, among others, to the primitive expression of children, the retarded, or the mentally disturbed. Yosef Gross was of the opinion that the new immigrants from the Arab countries

---

*At one of the sessions of the Knesset Constitution, Law and Justice Committee, Ben-Gurion referred to the Jews of Morocco as "savages," but hastily added that they were no different from the others. "They tell me that there are thieves among them. I am a Polish Jew, and I doubt if there is any Jewish community which has more thieves in it than the Polish ones."[17] Following a meeting with the Chief of Police, Yehezkel Sahar, Ben-Gurion noted some of the reasons for the increase in crime: the transition from war to peace, the problems of veteran soldiers and immigration, "especially the Moroccans."[18] A few years later Ben-Gurion wrote to Justice Moshe Etzioni: "An Ashkenazi gangster, thief, pimp or murderer will not gain the sympathy of the Ashkenazi community (if there is such a thing), nor will he expect it. But in such a primitive community as the Moroccans'—such a thing is possible. . . ."[19]

were suffering from "mental regression" and "a faulty development of the ego." His colleagues discussed "the nature of primitiveness" at great length. As a whole these articles project an
Ashkenazi consensus, which was partly paternalistic and benev-
olent as well as being supercilious and contemptuous. The notion that European culture was endangered in Israel was already
discernible here and there. All the participants in the *Megamot*
symposium considered the absorption of the immigrants from
the Arab countries to be a cultural mission, believing that if only
these immigrants would acquire the values of European culture,
the distinctions between the newcomers and the older population would be erased and the various communities blended into
one. Karl Frankenstein did, however, demand "respect for the
other as he is," and Ernst Simon warned that "as long as we asso-
ciate primitiveness exclusively with its negative aspects, the
country which now faces the absorption of hundreds of thousands of immigrants with a primitive mentality might split into
two camps, one of which will manifest a sense of superiority and
the other a sense of inferiority. . . ." Among the positive aspects
of primitiveness, Simon noted religious faith and prayer, the "intense emotional reaction to manifestations of kindness, beauty
and holiness," as well as a "true cordiality in inter-personal relations," which he attributed to the immigrants from the Arab
countries, as distinct from those of Europe. He believed that the
Oriental immigrants must not be subjected to an artificially-
imposed alien culture, and certainly not all at once, for fear that
they might find themselves in "a vacuum of values," which
could lead to "spiritual impoverishment and social and moral
deviations, that would endanger not only them, but the entire
country."

None of the participants in the symposium thought about
the distribution of resources in the new state, nor about the en-
croachment of poverty with an Oriental origin. When they
spoke of "community problems" they meant the "primitiveness" of the Oriental communities. They all came to the same
conclusion—the immigrants from the Arab countries had to be
uplifted from their backward state. They assumed that the immigrants were of the same mind—since they wished to become
absorbed in the country, they would also naturally wish to be
uplifted from their backwardness. They all agreed that this
should also be the policy of the government.[20]

Most of the Press's references to the immigrants at the time were negative and less than 20 percent of the papers' references presented them in a positive light.[21] The overwhelming majority of publications that took an unfavorable view were referring to the immigrants from the Arab countries. At the beginning of the mass immigration the newspapers employed a negative tone when writing about the immigrants from Europe, survivors of the Holocaust too: "They are lazy," wrote one newspaper. "They have grown accustomed to living at public expense. . . . They have already stolen 20,000 plates and 18,000 forks, and now they are stealing sacks of food, so that armed guards have had to be stationed outside the stores."[22] The same newspaper wrote a while later: "Most of the new settlers, who are almost without exception survivors of the concentration camps, and as a result of their experience abroad, have removed fixtures from the houses, such as door frames, pipes and faucets, and sold them in Tel Aviv."[23]

Such descriptions grew less frequent with the passage of time. In their place came derogatory descriptions of the Oriental immigrants. The newspapers described them as unfamiliar with modern sanitation and toilet paper, as growing vegetables under their beds and hiding their babies in crates to save them from the doctors and their medicines. In March 1951 *Haaretz* described the condition of the Iraqi immigrants in one of the camps: "Many of the parents send their children to steal, and the teachers are helpless to prevent this. 'If I don't do as my parents tell me,' said one little girl, 'they give me less food and double the beatings. . . .' The children sometimes drink 'arrack and are trained to lie. . . ."[24]

Even before the immigrants from Arab countries began to arrive in large numbers, *Haaretz* published the following commentary by Arye Gelblum, one of the most provocative articles ever to be published in Israel:

    . . . This is a race unlike any we have seen before. They say there are differences between people from Tripolitania, Morocco, Tunisia and Algeria, but I can't say I have learned what those differences are, if they do, in fact, exist. They say, for example, that the Tripolitanians and Tunisians are "better" than the Moroccans and Algerians, but it's the same problem with them all. (Incidentally, none of these immigrants will admit that he is (North) African—"*Je suis français!"*—They are all Frenchmen from Paris and almost all were captains in the *Maquis*.)

The primitiveness of these people is unsurpassable. They have almost no education at all, and what is worse is their inability to comprehend anything intellectual. As a rule, they are only slightly more advanced than the Arabs, Negroes and Berbers in their countries. It is certainly an even lower level than that of the former Palestinian Arabs. Unlike the Yemenites, they lack roots in Judaism. On the other hand, they are entirely dominated by savage and primitive instincts. How many incidents does it take, for example, to train them to stand in line for the food in the dining hall without creating a riot. A Bulgarian Jew who stood ahead of them in the line and would not give way, promptly had his nose slashed by a [North] African. And more than once they fell on the Jewish Agency staff and beat them up. The camp staff is in constant danger of such attacks.

In the [North] African corners of the camps you find filth, gambling, drunkenness and prostitution. Many of them suffer from serious eye diseases, as well as skin and venereal diseases. I have yet to mention robbery and theft. Nothing is safe from this anti-social element, no lock is strong enough. Not only other immigrants' property, but the equipment of the camp itself, is constantly being stolen. In one camp in which I stayed they broke into the general store and cleaned it out. In another camp, for instance, a person died and was laid out in the hospital morgue. When the burial staff returned to the morgue after the funeral, they found their tools had been stolen.

The [North] Africans bring their ways with them wherever they settle. It is not surprising that the crime rate in the country is rising. In certain parts of Jerusalem it is no longer safe for a young girl, or even a young man, to go out after dark. And this is before the young [North] Africans have been released from the army. Incidentally, they had often assured me that as soon as they had finished fighting the Arabs, they would go to war against the Ashkenazis. In one camp they planned a revolt, which entailed seizing the guards' rifles and murdering the local Jewish Agency functionaries. When the police arrive there are often violent fights. But above all there is one equally grave fact and that is their total inability to adjust to the life in this country, and primarily their chronic laziness and hatred for any kind of work. Almost without exception, they are both unskilled and destitute. They all say that in [North] Africa they were "merchants." What they really mean is they were peddlars. And they all want to settle in the city. What can be done with them? How are they to be absorbed? . . . Have we given sufficient thought to the question of what will happen to this state if this should be its population?—And then, in addition, [other] Oriental Jews will eventually join them, too! What will happen to the State of Israel and its standards with this type of population?

Obviously all these Jews are entitled to come here no less than others, and they should be brought over and absorbed, but if it is carried out without consideration for our limited capacities and if it is not done gradually, they will "absorb" us rather than we them. The peculiar tragedy with these immigrants, in contrast to the bad human material from Europe, is that there is nothing to hope for from their children, either. To raise their general standards from their communal depths would take generations! Perhaps it is not surprising that Mr. Begin and Herut are so eager to bring all these hundreds of thousands at once—they know that ignorant, primitive and poverty-stricken masses are the best raw material for them, and could eventually put them in power. . . ."[25]*

Deciding to emigrate to Israel from one of the Arab countries was often a very personal decision, as it was in Europe. It was based on the particular circumstances of the individual's life. They were not all poor, or "dwellers in dark caves and smoking pits," as poet Nathan Alterman put it.[29] Nor were they always subjected to persecution, repression or discrimination in their native lands. They emigrated for a variety of reasons just as the ones who had emigrated from Europe, depending on the country, the time, the community and the person.

There is an unsigned report in English in one of the Jewish Agency files about the situation of the Jews in Libya. The report describes a considerable variety of conditions. "Almost all of them are religious," it stated, "but culturally there are major differences between those who speak Arabic (often writing it in the Hebrew alphabet), and those who speak Italian. The majority belong to the first category. There is also a third group, who speak Hebrew. . . ."[30] Most of them lived in Tripoli, but

---

*A few months later the Chairman of the Association of Immigrants from North Africa reported: "In Morocco and Algeria Herut is taking over. Slowly but surely it is making headway and running very deep."[26] An agent in Algiers reported: "It should be remembered that Jabotinsky once visited Algeria and many still remember his visit."[27] David Horowitz, then General Director of the Ministry of Finance and subsequently President of the Bank of Israel, said during a political consultation with Ben-Gurion: "The population in the camps is becoming a sort of second nation, a rebellious nation which views us as plutocrats. This is incendiary material, eminently useful to Herut and the Communists. It's dynamite. . . . The immigrants are in some ways taking the place of the Arabs. There is also a special attitude emerging on our part toward them; we are beginning to harbor an attitude of superiority."[28]

some lived in the provincial towns and in the villages. Most were tradesmen and merchants, but some were farmers. Not all were affected by the economic crisis which Libya was then experiencing, and those who were, did not all suffer to the same degree.[31]

In February 1949 the Jewish Agency in Jerusalem received a report about the situation of Jews in French North Africa. The author of the report, Yaakov Kraus, had visited Casablanca, among other places, and he wrote:

> There are eighty thousand Jews in this city, fifty thousand of which live in the ghetto. The crowding in these quarters is atrocious, and the hygienic conditions frightful. Congenital syphilis is widespread, and so are trachoma and a scalp disease. In one town at the foot of the Atlas Mountains we found an entire community that was blind. Whoever was still able to see would soon go blind, because of the ubiquitous trachoma. There is no helping them, because there are no doctors and no one who treats the disease.

On the other hand, Kraus wrote about the Jews of Algeria that "for the most part they engage in commerce. As merchants they used to hold important positions in the economic life of the country, and still do. ... There are many physicians among them, as well as lawyers and teachers. Some of the professors at the University of Algiers have international reputations. . . ."[32]

Efraim Shilo also visited North Africa as an agent of the Mossad, and he also wrote a report. He placed the Jews into two categories: the first who lived as a small minority in the midst of a hostile Arab environment, in constant danger and in a state of slow degeneration—"a slow death," the report described it. They were impoverished, lacked education and "the most elementary human amenity." For them, immigration to Israel was a real liberation. But there were others, whose situation was "relatively normal," and for them the question of going to Israel was "much the same as it was for any dense Jewish population in Europe before the last world war." According to this report, "the composition of the population and the human material were roughly the same as had come from Poland before the war." Shilo estimated that only 30 percent of the Jews of Tunisia and Algeria had to be saved. The remaining 70 percent were in no danger. In Morocco conditions were worse—there, he estimated, some 60 percent of the Jews had to be saved, but the remainder he described as living a "relatively normal" life.[33]

The files of the Mossad are packed with reports about the situation of the Jews in those countries. Some of them are horrifying:

> The situation of the Jews further inland, is particularly bad especially in Cyrenaica (Libya), where the Arabs are openly threatening to massacre them when Sheikh el-Senoussi comes to power. In small towns and villages Jewish girls are often forced to convert to Islam. A typical case happened just two weeks ago: a local Jewish girl whom an Arab wanted to marry got on one of our ships. When the Arabs in her town discovered this, they demanded that the Jewish community supply them with fifty Jewish virgins within a week. That night more than fifty Jewish families fled that town and came with their daughters to Tripoli.[34]

Similar reports came from other Arab countries, from Yemen, Iraq, Syria, Lebanon and Egypt. But there are also reports about Jewish communities who lived in those countries in comfort and in relative security, on good terms with their Arab neighbors, even after the creation of the State of Israel and the War of Independence. Some reports note that local government circles sought to encourage Jewish emigration, to overstrain the Israeli economy,[35] while others sought to stop Jews from going to Israel to avoid strengthening the country with the additional manpower.[36] Economic motives led some countries to encourage Jewish emigration and others to oppose it. Sometimes the authorities wanted to hasten the departure of the Jews to avoid unrest and pogroms; sometimes they needed the Jews as a popular diversion for the masses, to keep them from reacting to other problems.[37]

Some of the Jews emigrated spontaneously, whether as a result of distress or persecution, or for Zionist or religious reasons. Others came in response to the Zionist propaganda disseminated by the Zionist emissaries in their countries. Some drifted with the emigrating mass, and some actually found themselves in Israel against their will. Hedda Grossmann of kibbutz Ein Hamifrats was sent to France to train North African youth prior to their immigration. Among them was a group of boys from Morocco. She wrote:

> All of them were filled with an intense desire to go to *Eretz Israel*, as were all members of their community, and they had prepared themselves for it. But most of them had no idea what it was all for.

They were simply carried on the crest of the wave of Jewish emigration from their town, unaware of the causes, motives and aim of the movement. Their supreme ambition, nurtured by activities with the right-wing *Betar* youth movement, the sole Zionist factor in their lives, was to join the Israel army, be a Jewish soldier and wage a ruthless vengeful war against the Arabs.[38]

The mass exodus from Morocco began after the pogrom in Oujda, shortly after the creation of the State of Israel. Many Jews sold their belongings or left them behind and fled to Algeria. The French police tried to stop them from crossing the border, mobilizing thousands of gendarmes to guard it and to stop every vehicle and train for inspection. Jews who were caught trying to cross the border were detained, beaten and then driven back.

At the beginning of 1949 the Mossad generally distinguished between private, individual escape and organized escape led by Jewish groups, either from the underworld or from the Zionist leadership. Individual escape was usually arranged from Casablanca where lower-level officials sold Jewish exit visas and passports. One Mossad report concerning the organized escape referred to a certain Jew by name of Tourjman,

> who betrayed to the police those Jews who failed to pay him the price he demanded. A leader of the Fez community told me that gangsters in his city demand that young women who wish to go to Israel give themselves to them as well as to Arab and French policemen. . . . The escape which is organized by the political parties, notably (the religious) Hamizrahi, is also channeled through the same corrupt channels in Casablanca. . . . There are all over Morocco scores of wealthy and intelligent Jews who regard themselves as unofficial consuls of Israel, and who intervene on behalf of particular individuals to obtain exit visas for them. They also provide their protégés with money for the journey and notes to the headquarters of the leftist *Hehaluts* youth movement in Marseilles. Needless to say, all this produces endless confusion and dreadful anarchy in all the procedures which accompany the escape. . . .[39]

At this time the agent Yany Avidov was in Algeria. He demanded that everything be done to hasten the immigration of the refugees who were pouring into Algeria from Morocco and Tunisia. "We have sent people into Morocco," he wrote, "to stop the flow at the source. We are even providing railroad fares for the destitute to take them back from the border to their

points of departure." Nevertheless, they continued to swarm in
by the thousands. Avidov warned that the Moroccan Jews' presence in Algeria was increasing the danger of an Arab pogrom,
"whether big or small."[40] In July 1949, after prolonged and tedi-
ous negotiations, the Jewish Agency's man in Rabat, Jack
Gershuni, concluded a four-part agreement with the French
Governor of Morocco, providing for Jewish emigration to Marseilles, to be carried out discreetly, but no longer illegally.[41]
"This agreement is an important achievement," boasted Yosef
Barpal. "In the midst of all the difficulties, the Mossad can be
proud of the political work it has done and which has brought us
this far."[42] The Absorption Department of the Jewish Agency
was not so enthusiastic. "The stepping up of the immigration
was quite irresponsible," they charged. "An artificially-created
wave of unstoppable migration is bringing in very poor human
material in terms of absorption."[43] A few months later Tsvi Hermon, of the Absorption Department, said: "I've spoken to the
Jewish leaders there and I know that there was no messianic
movement in Tunis. The messianic movement was organized!"[44]

There were agents in North Africa who encouraged emigration to Israel. In some places the Zionist awakening actually
worsened the situation of the Jews, and as things grew worse,
their anxious desire to leave increased. Something of this sort
happened in several countries. The most characteristic is the
case of Iraq. The official version—which many years later was
given the legal validity of an Israeli court decision—was that the
Jewish immigration from Iraq to Israel, known as "Operation
Ezra and Nehemiah," was the outcome of "the longings of Iraq's
Jewry for the Holy Land, and the intolerable persecutions of the
Iraq authorities, which hunted, imprisoned and hanged Jews."[45]

The exodus from Iraq began during a limited period beginning in the first half of 1950, when the Iraqi parliament resolved
to let them leave. In effect, it amounted to an expulsion. Most of
the Jews were forced to leave and their property was confiscated.
Various sources, including reports of the Mossad for Immigration, indicate that the move of the Iraqi parliament came partly
in response to the activities of the Zionist movement there,
aided by the agents of the Mossad who smuggled Jews across the
border to Iran. The Mossad's files abound with telegrams report-

ing the persecution of Jews in Iraq, but almost all of them refer
to Jews who had been involved in the activities of the Zionist
underground, or who were suspected of belonging to it. There
was little harassment of other Jews.[46] In March 1949 the Israeli
public was appalled to hear that seven Jews had been hanged in
Iraq on charges of Zionist activity. The report was given considerable coverage; there were editorials and public protests, including in the Knesset. But the Mossad's agents in "Berman,"
i.e., Iraq, telegraphed: "There is no truth in the report about the
hanging of Jews on charges of Zionism. A few have been sentenced to death, but they are already out of the country. Many
have been tried, but mostly because of letters they received from
Israel."[47] However, the heads of the Mossad for Immigration had
intentionally fomented worldwide furor against Iraq, in order to
hasten the legislation permitting the emigration of Jews.
Toward this end they formulated a series of proposed actions, including a statement by the Israeli Foreign Minister in a special
meeting with foreign correspondents, agitation in the international press, attempts to block a loan Iraq was seeking to obtain
from the World Bank, the incitement of pressure and disturbances around Iraq's Ambassador to the UN, including demonstrations and booing as he entered and left the UN building, as
well as an attempt to arrange a face to face meeting with him, an
appeal to the UN, an appeal to Mrs. Eleanor Roosevelt, an "unof-
ficial hint" that Israel might set up an underground movement
against the Iraqi ruler, Nuri Said, and an official communication
to the US, British and French Embassies in Israel that Iraqi Jews
in Israel might vent their fury on Israeli Arabs. "It should be emphasized that the Government of Israel is taking steps to ensure
the safety of its Arab citizens," the document added, "but it
should be hinted that in practice it might not be possible to
avoid Arab casualties." It was also proposed to send delegations
of Israeli Arabs to the major embassies in Tel Aviv to warn them
of the danger they were in as a result of the persecution of Jews
in Iraq. All this was meant to force the Iraqi government to expel
the Jews, some of whom were Zionists who wanted to go to Israel and some of whom would have preferred to remain in Iraq.
Shortly before the Iraqi parliament resolved to let the Jews leave,
the Mossad office in Tel Aviv received a telegram from Baghdad,
saying: "We are carrying on our usual activity in order to push

the law through faster and find out how the Iraqi government proposes to carry it out."[48]*

When, after the Declaration of Independence, Israel's gates were opened, the first to be brought over were the thousands of illegal immigrants who had been deported by the British authorities to Cyprus, many of whom were survivors of the Holocaust who, since the war, had been kept in the DP camps in Europe. Their distress was plain to see. The Jews of Morocco, on the other hand, were far away and their distress was not as visible. In October 1948 Itzhak Refael told the Jewish Agency Executive that priority must "of course" be given to the Jews of Eastern Europe, because they might not always be allowed to leave. The Jews of North Africa and "to some extent" those of the Arab countries, would come second and third.[51] The General Director of the Ministry of Immigration, Y. N. Bahar, thought that the Jews in the Arab countries should be given priority, but his Ministry had little influence on the order of immigration, which was determined by the Jewish Agency, whose members agreed with Refael.[52]

At that time there was still enough room in the abandoned Arab houses, most of which were given to the first arrivals,

---

*On January 14, 1951, at about seven p.m., a bomb—or perhaps a handgrenade—was thrown into the courtyard of the Mas'oudah Shemtov synagogue in Baghdad. This was the meeting place for the Jews about to leave for the airport. At the time there were hundreds of Jews in the place. Four people, including a boy of 12, were killed and some 20 wounded. This was not the first attack on Jewish centers in Iraq, but it was the most notorious, in part because of the persistent rumor that it was the work of Israeli agents bent on scaring the Jews and prompting them to go to Israel. The rumor named one particular agent of the Mossad, Mordehai Ben-Porat, who many years later served as a Cabinet Minister in Israel. It is significant that the rumor arose at all, and that it was persistently repeated, even by Iraqi Jews. Obviously, the idea was not unthinkable. In 1981, Ben-Porat sued a reporter, Barah Nadel, who referred to the rumor, and after prolonged negotiations they settled the dispute out of court. Nadel stated that he had been influenced by the malicious reports of the Iraqi government, and apologized for what he had written. "The Israeli agents who worked in Iraq—both those sent out from Israel and the local activists—carried out their mission irreproachably while risking their own lives," the verdict stated.[49] Nevertheless, the affair remains a mystery—no one knows who attacked the Iraqi Jews or why. When the files of the Mossad were opened to researchers, they were shown to include a correspondence between the Mossad's agents in Baghdad and their superiors in Tel Aviv on the subject of the synagogue attack. The exchange of telegrams seems to confirm that neither side knew who was behind the attack.[50]

namely, the Jews from Europe. By the time the Jews from the Arab countries arrived most of those houses were occupied. Thus the priority given to the immigration from Europe intensified the communal inequalities which had existed even under the British Mandate. When Ruth Klieger toured the transit camps on behalf of the Prime Minister, she encountered a group of immigrants from North Africa. This was in the first half of 1949, and though the country and its people were still strange to them, they were already, as Klieger reported, depressed, "seized with a sense of inferiority and of being discriminated against."[53] Many of them brought this feeling with them, and indeed, the discrimination against them had begun even before their arrival.

Most of the immigrants from North Africa received no advance preparation before coming to Israel. The Arab countries remained somehow outside the Zionist movement's sphere of activity, whether on account of the dangers involved, or because its leaders regarded those communities as a primitive fringe. The few Jewish Agency emissaries in North Africa were aware of the dangers of such an attitude and warned against it, but they were ignored. "The work in North Africa may fail for lack of regular agents to deal with escape from there," charged Yosef Barpal.[54] Agent Misha Rabinowitz wrote that "the present immigration, given its makeup and conditions, with its lack of preparation and organization, will place the State of Israel in an intolerable situation. In time to come, we may witness a Moroccan ghetto" in Israel.[55] Another agent wrote, "There is gross discrimination now, and it begins in North Africa." He was referring to the paucity of emissaries and the tiny budget which had been allocated for advance training and preparation in those countries. "This is an Israeli problem," he wrote. "It might result one day in the creation of two racial groups in a single country. . . ."[56] Ben-Gurion tended to blame the leaders of those communities themselves: "For years I have been asking the Sephardis to send gifted young people to the Oriental countries, to work among the Sephardic communities there, especially among the youth, to prepare it for immigration and to look after the immigrants here, and I got no response. . . ."[57] In the Jewish Agency many believed that only Ashkenazi agents should be sent to North Africa. "Three young Sephardic men have just gone there," wrote Ben-Gurion. "Dobkin thinks it's a mistake—they respect only the Ashkenazis."[58]

The travel arrangements were often inefficient and many times the conditions that prevailed were inhumane. Iris Levis, who was sent out by the Jewish Agency to North Africa in February 1949, described the transit camp in Algiers:

In the *Alliance Israelite* building and the little alley behind it live masses of people, crowded like animals. From top to bottom, and even on the stairs, you see people sitting with their belongings. They live, cook, fall ill, give birth and die, men and women, young and old, all of them together. More than fifty people live in one room of four or five square meters.[59]

A physician who worked in one of the transit camps in Marseilles reported to the Immigration Department in Israel:

The immigrants from North Africa arrive here utterly destitute, and almost without clothing. During the passage to Marseilles, which lasts three days, they receive no food. Conditions on board are very bad. The people sleep on the floors without any blankets and are not adequately dressed for the weather. On December 23, 1948, a child died on a ship en route from North Africa, and the French authorities in Marseilles determined the cause of death was exposure and hunger. I am asking you to get in touch at once with the responsible bodies, to improve the situation. . . . In two of the camps there is a great shortage of blankets. People sleep in concrete barracks, on army campbeds, without mattresses, and only a single blanket each. As a result of the bad housing conditions and the recent decline in nutrition, twelve children have died in these camps. . . . There is a shortage of soap and clothing. . . . I can't understand why in all the European countries the immigrants are provided with clothes while the North African immigrants get nothing. . . .[60]

Hedda Grossmann described the process of moving and migrating from a psychological perspective:

The boys were all from large families and leaving from their native lands either disrupted or broke family ties. Homesickness and disquiet concerning the rest of the family were continually affecting our people and in the beginning caused outbreaks of hysteria, wild behavior, tears and outcries in the night. Some of the boys were generally quieter and more restrained, but their suffering and tension were considerable. . . . In time the boys found various compensations. Casual friends were called brother and sister, and the instructors—parents. There were expressions of physical affection very close to homosexuality, whose origins are easily understood in the context of the relationship between the sexes in this community. . . . This will no doubt cause trouble when they arrive, in view of the fact that there are very few girls and the sexual ratio being so unequal among the Oriental immigrants. In our group, for example, there was not a single girl.[61]

Some parts of Grossmann's report read like an anthropological survey of a remote tribe. It reflects much sympathy and a sincere desire to help, but also a strong sense of alienation. The Jewish Agency emissary in Libya, H. Tsvieli, described the Jews he met there as if he were trading in horses: "They are handsome as far as their physique and outward appearance are concerned, but I found it very difficult to tell them apart from the good quality Arab type."[62]

The poor conditions under which the Jews departed, voyaged to Marseilles and stayed there, led the leaders of the Zionist Federation in Morocco to instruct the Mossad's agents to desist from encouraging the Jews to leave North Africa by all means and all routes. They demanded that the agents devote themselves instead to preparing the immigrants for life in Israel. A year later it was reported that there was a sharp decline in the number of immigrants from North Africa, as a result of the information that reached them concerning the hardships of settling in Israel. "The first thing one notices now is the obvious reluctance to go to Israel," wrote one of the Jewish Agency emissaries after visiting the transit camps in Marseilles. According to him, it had become a widespread attitude: "The people virtually have to be taken aboard the ships by force."[63]

Among the immigrants from North Africa and other Arab countries there were many who did not possess the necessary qualifications which would enable them to have equal status in Israel. Thousands were relegated to the fringes of society even before arrival. In the cities of Morocco there were entire communities which had migrated there from the villages, in order to take economic advantage of the US armed forces landing in Morocco during World War II. Some engaged in peddling, and others in prostitution and crime, and they occupied entire slum quarters. Among the youngsters in her charge, Hedda Grossmann found boys who had grown up in miserable orphanages. There were gangs of thieves and drunks among them. "These will pose a considerable problem for the social services in Israel," she noted.[64] Many of the immigrants came to Israel because they were prompted by relatives, or by the initiative of community leaders, who wished to get rid of them—many were old, sick or welfare cases. The closer they were to French culture, had an education, a profession, or were less religious and traditional in their way, the less they were inclined to go to Israel, preferring instead to settle in France. But even for those who were not sick, aged or destitute, even if they coped well with the process of migration and resettlement, their culture was not the European one which Israel sought to adopt. Many could not read or write in any language. Many had received minimal education, often only a religious one. Almost none had any useful connections in Israel—they found neither relatives nor acquaintances in the Israeli establishment. They knew no Hebrew and were unfamiliar with the bureaucratic system. They brought with them a communal-patriarchal tradition which left little room for individual initiative. Their strangeness reinforced their image as primitives, and their image intensified their alienation.[65] Soon after their arrival they adopted the sense of deprivation felt by those who had come before them. Many of the immigrants from Europe, on the other hand, were helped by relatives and friends who had been in Israel for some time, as well as by families overseas; many would later receive reparations from Germany, which also served to widen the gulf between them and the immigrants from Arab countries.

The North Africans' feeling of deprivation was very intense and painful from the start. "I seem to be a stepson to the Israeli people," wrote Yosef Amoyal, a cobbler from Jaffa, to Prime Minister Ben-Gurion.[66] In years to come it would be argued that it had all been planned that way, that there was an "Ashkenazi conspiracy" to keep them in a state of deprivation and inferiority. There is a remarkable document in the files of the Immigration Department, written in minute capital letters on a sheet of cardboard, whose anonymous author states that he was a doctor who had worked for six months in the North African transit camps in Marseilles. He describes the history of the Jews of North Africa and their present situation, and goes on to provide a highly literary description of the everyday routine in the Marseilles camps. He concludes by stating that the North African immigrants would supply Israel with cheap labor—"coolie labor," as he put it—to replace the Arab workers who did this type of work before Independence. The standard of living of the North African Jew was no higher than that of the Arab farmer, he remarked, and in Israel it would be higher than it was before. The North African immigrants will, therefore, readily adjust to their status, even though it will remain lower than the European standard of Ashkenazi Jews. . . .

The document was not ignored by the Immigration Department—someone ordered it typed and retyped, two and three times over, in many copies. It was subsequently edited, perhaps for publication. The editor polished the text and changed a few words. The passage about the coolie, the Arab farmer and the Moroccan was omitted. Perhaps the editor thought it was non-sensical, or perhaps he feared that it was too offensive to have in print.[67] But the idea was not a new one. There is a record, marked secret, of some remarks made by Berl Locker, Chairman of the Jewish Agency Executive, to the American-Jewish politician, Henry Morgenthau, in October 1948: "In our opinion the Sephardi and Yemenite Jews will play a considerable part in building our country. We have to bring them over in order to save them, but also to obtain the human material needed for building the country."[68]*

They were assigned the worst and least profitable part of the country's agriculture—in the mountains, in Galilee and Judea. The rich, easily cultivated, soil in the coastal region and the south was given mainly to immigrants from Europe. There were exceptions, such as the village of Tsrufah on the Carmel coast, which was settled with immigrants from Tunisia, Morocco and Algeria, or Rinthia, near Petah Tikvah, in the center of the country, which was built for Moroccan immigrants, and others. On the other hand, immigrants from Europe were sometimes settled in the mountains of Galilee and in the Negev. The best locations, however, were not allocated to immigrants from the Arab countries. Former immigration official Arye Eliav explained: "This was not an Ashkenazi conspiracy. It happened because the people in charge of the settlement projects, such as Shmuel Dayan, Yaakov Ory, Tsvi Yehuda and others, looked for people who most resembled them, in their general mentality and world-view, and so, inevitably, in their background. They did not have a common language with the others, which is natural enough, as the others were strange to them. They were, of course, well aware of the difference in the quality of various locations, and they fought for the best ones. This was primarily a political

---

*This had been done before, when Jews were brought from Yemen to replace the Arabs in the struggle for "Hebrew labor," long before the creation of Israel.[69]

Celebration of the passage of the UN resolution partitioning
Palestine and creating the Jewish state, November 29, 1947.
*"Their dream was the fuel that powered their action, the cement which
bound them together, the myth and the consensus."*

The expulsion of Arab infiltrators, June 1950.

Homes for new immigrants.
"For the U.S. to make a similar effort, it would have to take in 30 million immigrants in a year."

In an immigrant camp.
"Thousands of people with no showers."

In an immigrant camp.
"People can live in tents for years. Whoever does not want to should not come here."

At the Shaar Haaliya (Gate of the Immigration) camp for new immigrants.
"We destroy these people."

At the Shaar Haaliya camp for new immigrants.
"There is nothing to do but quietly cry."

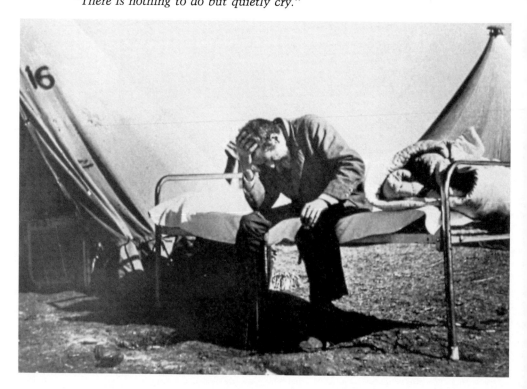

In the deserts of Yemen, on the way to the airfield.
"The sick will die on the way over."

Inside a "Magic Carpet" plane.
"Frozen with horror."

New immigrants from Yemen arriving at the airport near Tel Aviv. *"The most poetic of the tribes of Israel."*

David and Paula Ben Gurion on an official visit to Tel Aviv (1951). *"The source of all authority, creator of precedents and values, unique in his generation."*

Menahem Begin delivering an election speech.

US Ambassador James McDonald distributing food to Israeli children.

Above left: Government poster "Kill the Black Market or it will kill you."
Above right: Austerity in Tel Aviv.
Below: An official from the Office of Supplies and Rationing searches for forbidden food.
"They wanted meat."

struggle, and often a very tough one. The best sites fell, on the whole, to the kibbutzim and the Cooperative Settlement Movement. The religious Hapoel Hamizrahi and other movements which had their own settlements ended up with the remainder. When a good location was available they naturally wanted to settle it with good people, as they understood the term. They sought among the immigrants for people with the best potential for success. They also took into account the possibility that the settlers would then vote for MAPAI. This is how it happened, never with bad intentions."[70]*

Yosef Weitz predicted:

> The mountain regions will be served best by settling them densely with simple Jewish peasants. The harder they cultivate the land, the more they will discover its economic value. This they will be able to do with plain work in every corner, around every rock. Our modern farmers who worship the machine will not do for this purpose. This will be the great revolution in our settlement. The kibbutz and the cooperative village have ceased to account for our dense development, except in the sphere of field crops. But in this area, too, the ordinary worker will do well. The conquest of the wilderness and the recovery of the soil will probably be carried out by Jews from Yemen, Iraq and Morocco."[71]

According to Weitz it was difficult to find kibbutz people who were willing to settle in the mountains. When, some time later, he talked with Yosef Shprintsak, who expressed the concern that the immigration from the Arab countries would cause a cultural decline in Israel, Weitz noted: "There is indeed cause for worry, but . . . the Yemenites work!"[72]†

---

*At the beginning they attempted to create mixed cooperative villages, with immigrants from Europe and the Arab countries together. Later they gave up the attempt.

†Moshe Sharett, in speaking with the Soviet Deputy Foreign Minister Vishinsky, put it differently:

> There are countries—and I was referring to North Africa—from which not all the Jews need to emigrate. It is not so much a question of quantity as of quality. Our role in Israel is a pioneering one, and we need people with a certain strength of fiber. We are very anxious to bring the Jews of Morocco over and we are doing all we can to achieve this. But we cannot count on the Jews of Morocco alone to build the country, because they have not been educated for this. We don't know what may yet happen to us, what military and political defeats we may yet have to face. So we need people who will remain steadfast in any hardship and who have a high degree of resistance. For the purpose of building up our country, I would say that the Jews of Eastern Europe are the salt of the earth. . . .[73]

The leaders of MAPAI were conscious of their Ashkenazi exclusivity. "We have no common language with them," lamented Ben-Gurion: "Neither Hebrew nor Yiddish!"[74] They looked for ways to extend their influence to the "others," and set up a special department to deal with the Oriental communities. But they were so far removed that they had no idea whom they ought to include in the new department's jurisdiction: should it be only the "Sephardis," or ought the Jews of Bulgaria to be included, too? Should all immigrants from the Arab countries, including the Yemenites, be under its purview, or should the Yemenites be handled by a special department? "I am afraid to speak of the Oriental communities these days," quipped Party Secretary Zalman Aran, half-humorously, half-worriedly. "Before long, with the growing immigration, we may have to speak of the Ashkenazi communities."[75] When they debated the makeup of the first Cabinet it was assumed that all its members would be Ashkenazi. Zeev Sherf stated, "Eleven ministers in the government—that is the ideal number. If there must be a Sephardi, there will be twelve ministers." In considering what to do with an elected representative from the Sephardi party David Remez noted, "We'll have to find a proper post for the Sephardi minister, and it won't be easy. . . . The Sephardi minister cannot have any grandiose pretensions. . . ." Zalman Aran thought that the interests of the country required that there be a Sephardi minister in the Cabinet, but not everyone agreed. "If we bring a Sephardi into the government," said one member of MAPAI's Center, "we shall be consolidating that ethnic gang for decades to come. We don't need this sort of thing!"[76] Zalman Aran knew better. "The Moroccans will go to Herut," he warned. "The Oriental communities are the mainstay of Herut."[77] As early as January 1949 he also knew why: "In the poorer quarters of Tel Aviv they voted for Herut to revenge themselves on our party, for the sins of a whole generation."[78]*

In the fall of 1949, the Polish government permitted the Jews of Poland to emigrate to Israel during a period of one year, starting in September. It was variously estimated by the Israelis that between 15,000 and 25,000 would emigrate. At this time the number of people in immigrant camps in Israel was approaching

---

*Aran maintained that the government should undertake a massive economic and educational rehabilitation effort to improve the situation of the Oriental Jews, "to atone for the many sins of the Ashkenazi community."[79]

100,000, more than half of whom were from Arab countries.* Toward the end of the year, the Jewish Agency Executive had come to the conclusion that the Polish Jews deserved a better reception than their predecessors. "There are respectable people among them," it was said, by way of explanation. To spare them the hardships of the camps, it was proposed to house them in hotels, or, alternatively, to evacuate one entire camp and make it comfortable for them. At the same time the Jewish Agency hastened to make arrangements for their permanent housing which were, in part, in houses that had already been earmarked for the immigrants from Arab countries. They also sought to obtain special budgets to facilitate their acquisition of the apartments, and even considered a special fund for that purpose to be raised abroad. Members of the Executive talked openly about giving preference to the Polish immigrants, and some said they should have special privileges. "A good many of us are of the same tribe," noted one of them.[81] There was debate on the subject, however, with some dissension among the Executive. Among those who pressed hardest for the Polish privilege were Itzhak Greenbaum (Independent List) and Itzhak Refael (Hapoel Hamizrahi); Levi Eshkol (MAPAI) and Tsvi Hermon (MAPAM) strongly objected to it. S. Z. Shragai (Hapoel Hamizrahi) and Moshe Kol (Progressives) too, did not feel comfortable about it. They were all aware that giving preference to the Polish immigrants was wrong and so they resolved to keep it secret.

E. Dobkin: " . . . We must give this immigration special privileges and I am not afraid to say this. . . ."

L. Eshkol: "If you have one hundred thousand people in camps, including many from Poland, and all of a sudden you give the Ashkenazi ones privileges, you can imagine the outcry: 'The Ashkenazis get everything!' "

T. Hermon: "If it's a question of privileged absorption, I'm afraid none of us will stay alive. . . . Can you imagine twenty thousand people getting special treatment?"

*In February 1950, 70 percent of the residents in the camps were from Arab countries, i.e., a little more than their percentage in the total immigration. By the end of that year there were already more than 50 Maabaroth transit camps and work villages in the country. Eighty percent of their inhabitants were immigrants from the Arab countries. The other 20 percent came from Europe.[80] The rest of the immigrants, mostly from Europe also, had found, or had been provided with, permanent accommodations.

It was decided to appoint a committee to study the matter.[82] The
Executive reconvened two months later:

> I. Greenbaum: "We have to prepare a hotel for 800 people, in order
> to receive the immigrants who will be coming from Poland at
> the end of November. We have to hurry so that we're not
> caught unawares and respectable people won't have to go to the
> camps. There are people among them who have held high posi-
> tions and it will be a scandal if we have to send them to the
> camps."
>
> E. Dobkin: " . . . An exceptional effort must be made to facilitate
> the absorption of these people. There is nothing wrong about a
> public committee hiring a hotel to house these immigrants. . . .
> The whole immigration from Poland depends on the absorption
> of the first arrivals. If we fail, they will cease to come. . . . It
> would be a terrible blow to the entire Zionist movement."
>
> M. Grossman: "I believe that we must do all we can to help absorb
> these immigrants, but I object to the initiative coming formally
> from the Executive. No one abroad will understand it. With all
> due respect to the Jews of Poland, it will not be understood.
> Why should we suddenly be giving special attention to these
> Jews more than all the others? It will have to become known
> that a special member of the Executive is dealing with the Pol-
> ish immigration. What about the Jews from Germany, Mo-
> rocco, Tunisia, Tripoli and all the others? I agree that we shall
> decide whatever we want to decide, but Mr. Greenbaum should
> not be appointed by the Executive. He is a known and respected
> personality among the Polish Jews and will do whatever he has
> to do. We shall all help him. But I don't want the whole world
> to know that we've undertaken to look after this matter. . . . A
> public committee for the Polish Jews could be established, but
> Mr. Greenbaum should not be the representative of the Execu-
> tive on that committee. I can already see the newspaper head-
> lines. I agree that we set aside funds for this purpose, but with-
> out publicity, because that would damage us and there is no
> need. . . ."
>
> B. Locker: "We are all in favor of this operation, then. The question
> is, do we do it officially, on behalf of the Executive, or not."
>
> I. Greenbaum: "You can count on me that there won't be any pub-
> licity."

It was resolved "that a public committee should be created to
help absorb the immigrants from Poland. Mr. Greenbaum will
be a member of the committee, with the consent of the Execu-

tive, and will periodically report to it about the committee's work. Outwardly, however, Mr. Greenbaum will officiate in this operation as one of the leaders of the Polish Jewish community."[83]

A week later the Executive discussed the allocation of a special camp to the Polish immigrants, where each family would have a separate room—unlike the vast dormitories in the usual immigrant camps described by Arye Gelblum in his reports. The Absorption Department undertook to provide such accommodation for 2,000 immigrants from Poland. Itzhak Greenbaum demanded that the same conditions be provided for all the Polish immigrants. The Absorption Department said it was impossible.

> I. Greenbaum: "This means that by February we'll have to put the Polish immigrants into wooden barracks holding 20 to 30 beds, one beside the other, families all sleeping together, one beside the other. . . . The reports they will send back home will make a very bad impression. . . ."
>
> I. Refael: "The immigrants from Poland are not like the others. The others, who are now making all sorts of demands, did not want to come and kept putting it off. So we haven't the same obligations toward them, whereas the Polish Jews didn't come because they couldn't. . . . If we spare them the camps and give them priority in housing, they will manage better in Israel than most of the Oriental inhabitants in the camps because many of them have the skills that are needed for the economy. It will be a blessing to the country. That's why I suggest we give them a priority in housing. The Polish Jews have been living well. For them, the camps are much harder than for the Yemenites, for whom even the conditions of the camp mean liberation. So I see good reasons for giving the Polish Jews priority. The preference must be in two ways: (a) the Polish Jews must be given priority in getting whatever housing is available; (b) I support Mr. Greenbaum's suggestion insofar as it is possible, to give them better conditions in the camps. . . . A special fund could be set up for housing loans, which would come from either relatives or the money brought by the immigrants themselves. These are not like the immigrants from Yemen, whose names you can hardly figure out. When a Polish Jew gets a loan he knows he has to return it. . . ."
>
> Y. Braginsky: " . . . There is a possibility that we may obtain one more camp, the one in Athlit, which is now occupied by Yemenites. We'll take them out, shove them wherever we can, and then we'll have a camp for three to four thousand people, but

it will be crowded, and it will be in the same condition as the other camps. . . . We've tried to keep a reserve of 200 to 300 apartments at 200 *liroth* apiece. We'll take those houses which we have already allocated to the North Africans and the Yemenites and give them to the Poles. We'll need 200 times 300 *liroth* for this. The question is how to put this sum together. . . ."

E. Dobkin: "We've decided to give preference to the Polish Jews and I think we have done the right thing. . . . But the idea is to give preference to only the first batch. I can't guarantee to do this for those who will come after. We wanted the first arrivals to write back to Poland and say that things are not so bad here. . . . I don't have to do this for every ten thousand who get here. . . . Those who come later can put up with the same conditions as all the other immigrants. . . ."

I. Greenbaum: " . . . Instead of putting the Polish Jews in this situation, it would be best to do it with the Jews of Turkey and Libya. That won't be hard for them. You should know that these people (from Poland) are coming from Upper Silesia, where each family had a 3- to 4-room apartment, German apartments, German furniture, all the comforts of a German city. . . . There are doctors among them. . . . Will you put a doctor into a camp like Beit Lidd, or Pardes Hannah—how do you think he will feel, what will he think?"

It was resolved to instruct Levi Eshkol, Itzhak Gruenbaum and an official of the Immigration Department to "seek ways and means" of accommodating the Polish Jews in keeping with the proposals which had been made at the meeting.[84]*

The scoop of the year could be claimed by the American journalist Ruth Gruber. In Israel many people knew about it, but—as often happened—the military censorship forbade publication of the story until after it had appeared abroad. On November 8,

*Dobkin and Locker belonged to MAPAI; Braginsky to MAPAM; Meir Grossman to the right-wing "Revisionists." The Israeli Ambassador in Warsaw, Israel Barzilai, also urged giving the Polish immigrants special terms. His proposals were brought up in the Cabinet and rejected.[85] At first Ben-Gurion supported Greenbaum's position but later he changed his mind. "There must be no discrimination between immigrants," he wrote. "There is no justification for giving the Polish immigrants special advantages. Whoever doesn't want to come can stay away. The immigrant is not doing the people of Israel any favors. . . ."[86] But the Committee for Polish Jewish Immigrants did obtain special terms for the immigrants from Poland in the camps, in housing, in loans and grants, partially at state expense, in keeping with the resolutions of the Jewish Agency Executive.[87]

1949, it became public knowledge: "Tens of thousands of Jews were taken in a dramatic operation from Yemen to Aden, and from there flown to Israel."[88] It was called "Operation Magic Carpet," though the immigrants themselves preferred to describe it with the biblical reference "On the Wings of Eagles."*

The Jews of Yemen had lived in that country for thousands of years, since biblical times. Before "Operation Magic Carpet" there were tens of thousands of Yemenite Jews living in Israel; Itzhak Ben-Tsvi estimated their number at 35,000.[91] The first group arrived in the early 1880s, about the time that the first Zionist immigrants came from Eastern Europe.[92] A few thousand more arrived during World War II and after. During the Israeli War of Independence the British authorities in Aden forbade Jewish males of military age to leave the crown colony, just as they did in Cyprus, where the illegal immigrants were held in detention camps. The negotiations to allow immigration from Aden were among the first diplomatic efforts of the State of Israel, and indeed the ban was lifted before long. However, aside from the British authorities, permission also had to be obtained from the Imam of Yemen and from a whole string of sultans, provincial rulers in the British protectorate. A representative of the World Jewish Congress, Leon Kubovitzky, met with the Imam's delegate in Aden, Ahmad Gibli. The latter explained that the ban on Jewish emigration had been imposed at the request of the Arab League. He did, however, take a great interest in the armistice talks in Rhodes, and finally promised to go and see the Imam about the matter. Shortly after the armistice agreement of February 1949 between Israel and Egypt, the Imam permitted the Jews to leave.[93] His consent came as a surprise to the Israelis, who concluded that the reason for it was the famine which was then affecting Yemen. The Imam may have preferred to have the

---

*Ruth Gruber was invited by the Joint to accompany one of the flights from Yemen to Israel. Later there was some dispute as to whether it was meant for publication or as background briefing. She published her story in the *New York Herald Tribune*. At any rate it was impossible, of course, to keep the masses of immigrants from Yemen invisible. When they arrived the Jewish Agency published big advertisements in the press, asking the public to donate clothing, "winter garments for immigrants from the Middle East," and everyone knew who they were meant for. Ben-Gurion hinted that there was immigration from Yemen in a speech he made on November 7, and continued the following day, after the story had been published. He seemed surprised by it.[89] He praised the newspapers which had kept the secret. *Haaretz* protested that publication had been banned.[90]

Jews leave the country and their property behind them. Another possible cause was the king's fears that anti-Jewish riots would place his rule in jeopardy. According to certain sources, the Imam's brother was opposed to the exodus for political reasons, in order not to strengthen the newly established State of Israel; concurrently some Palestinian refugees were beginning to reach Yemen.[94] The Yemenite Jews were going to join the Israeli army and the Zionist cause. But then, the emigration of the Jews brought a considerable profit to the Yemenite government. In addition to the property, they also extracted various fees, described as "protection fees," "passage fees," "head fees," etc., not to mention straightforward bribes.

Sultan Audli permitted the use of the Mokiris airfield on condition that some Jews leave by motorcars through the territory of Sultan Faudli and with the latter's consent, fearing that otherwise he would incite the other sultans against him for permitting the Jews to leave for Israel. Jewish Agency representative Yosef Tsadok described the Sultan Audli as an intelligent young man. "I gave him presents, including blankets and rugs, which made a great impression on him," he wrote.[95] The ruler of Bahrein asked that 2,000 Jews be left in his territory, in order to keep the Islamic commandment of acting as protector to the Jews. He was told that going to the Land of Israel was also a commandment, but he insisted that at least a few old Jews be left behind. In some places the Jews were not allowed to leave until they had taught some young Moslems their art of silver and gold smithing.

Yosef Tsadok, himself of Yemenite origin, was a member of MAPAM, who was sent to Yemen by the Jewish Agency's department for the Jews of the Middle East. He was an adventurer and a gifted storyteller: He wrote:

> Near the border two buses, filled with escapees, caught up with us. One of their drivers, who was known to me, said that the police were after them. I immediately instructed the driver to turn off the "road" to a wooded hill. The jeep was covered with branches, the driver and his helper lay down at a little distance from it and I crawled into a cave. Despite my fears, and the weird shapes I imagined in my mind, I managed to hold out for four hours, almost without moving. . . . Unfortunately the jeep blew a tire just as we were approaching the Yemenite border. After attempting in vain to keep it going as it was, I had to continue at a dead run to the Alhaboushi

border. There I found Sheikh Assayef and asked for his protection. Once that was promised me, I stayed with him until the mended jeep arrived and I could continue on my way to the camp, which I reached late last night. This time I managed to smuggle only 33 gold pounds belonging to the Jews. . . .[96]

Following the establishment of the State of Israel, the messianic fervor of the Yemenite Jews was once again revived, as it repeatedly had in earlier centuries. The fact that the Israeli government was headed by David Ben-Gurion suggested to many of them that this was the kingdom of David. Some of them were desperately poor, subjected to oppression and discrimination, and for them the passage to Israel was a liberation. But there were others who lived peacefully and at ease, as farmers, goldsmiths, craftsmen of all kinds, and merchants. There, too, the Jews had to be encouraged to go to Israel, and there, too, the messianic longings had to be organized. Using local messengers, Yosef Tsadok distributed "missives of redemption" to the Jewish communities, calling upon them to leave their homes and instructing them how to reach Aden. In one of his letters to Jerusalem he urged his superiors to send out more emissaries "to awaken the sleepers and rescue the laggards."[97] In the early stages of the Yemenite exodus, Itzhak Refael reported to the Jewish Agency Executive that it was very difficult to cope with the swelling stream of immigration, and that two agents had been smuggled in at great risk to prevail upon the Jews not to come out in large groups, as there was no way of bringing them over all at once.[98] However, a year later, when the flow subsided, Refael reported that Arabs had been hired to "urge" the last Jews to depart.[99] He did not say how the "urging" was done. The Jewish Agency emissary in Aden, Shlomo Schmidt, asked permission to propose to the Yemenite authorities that they expel the remaining Jews from their country.[100]

Years later Yosef Tsadok wrote:

The sight of the gleaming white Skymaster gladdened the hearts of the Jews. "They looked at it from afar, their eyes glowing with happiness; they will mount the Messiah's flying white donkey and fly for eight hours all the way to Israel! They were overwhelmed with joy and enthusiasm. For two thousand years they had waited and prayed for this hour to come. It was their great privilege to live through it, when their parents and forefathers had died in exile, longing for redemption."[101]

The newsreels showed them alighting from the airplanes, lying down on the landing strips and kissing the ground of the Holy Land. "They are all overjoyed to be in Israel," wrote Ruth Klieger to the Prime Minister.[102]

An Israeli physician, Dr. Yosef Meir, who was sent to Aden with two other doctors, wrote a memorandum describing the arrival of the immigrants at the Geula (redemption) transit camp in Aden:

> ... Fifteen luggage buses arrived, packed with 313 nude, or half-naked individuals—whether on account of the heat, or from habit, or from lack of clothes. Crowded, filthy, full of sores, their faces stare blankly, silently. Even after greeting them it is hard to get them to say a word, whether from exhaustion, they say they have been en route for 15 days, or from apathy and fatalism, or fear of the future. Some asked us if we were English, despite the fact that we spoke Hebrew and had attempted to befriend them. They start to come down one by one, slowly and quietly, in perfect silence. There is hardly even the sound of a baby crying. They resemble a flock of sheep returning from the meadow in the evening, moving slowly one by one, until they reach their pen. In this case, it is a dark shed where they all crowd together. The first night they receive bread, water and dates. This is the first night that this ancient Jewish race meets with the Jewish races of Europe and the Middle East. There is no joy in their faces, no sign of excitement, nothing to suggest a sense of relief and an end to trouble. I would go so far as to suggest that their expression is a bestial one, though we know that their intelligence and intellectual capacities are fairly high. . . .[103]

The Aden transit camp was built for 500 people. The Israeli doctors found 12,000 there, lying on the sand, without so much as a tent. Dr. Meir wrote:

> The day after their arrival they are washed in the scanty water available, given straw mats and made into full-fledged camp members. During the day they crowd around the registry office, the clinic and the places where supplies and clothing are issued. The rest of them huddle around small fires on which they cook their food. Later in the evening they all, young and old, sprawl on the sands and sleep. . . .

Dr. Meir noted that the more civilized among them, those of Aden, owned primus stoves; he placed civilized in quotation marks. There was no kitchen in the camp, nor a dining hall nor toilets. "They relieve themselves inside the camp or nearby,"

wrote Dr. Meir. He assumed that if there had been toilets the
people would not have used them. Sometimes there were sand-
storms and sometimes heavy rains fell, "and all the refugees and
their belongings were soaked through."[104] Dr. Meir reported that
no one could say how many in the camp were sick, or who they
were. "Some of them make it to the clinic, to get a bandage, or a
shot of quinine, or penicillin. Others give up the ghost where
they lie, especially old men and women." The women gave birth
on the sand. "The nurse gets there just in time to cut the umbili-
cal cord." When they are brought to the clinic or the sick-room,
the women lie there exhausted, indifferent, their newborn babies beside them, "showing neither joy nor resentment." Between 50 to 80 percent of the babies born in Yemen died at birth
or soon after, Meir said, and commented, "Is it any wonder that
death is so natural and common for them? And this is a serious
danger, because among them it is not enough to see the sick and
treat them—one must seek them out among the thousands of
people." The dead were buried in the sands—"and no wailing is
heard," noted the doctor.*

The shock of the uprooting and migration hit them with tremendous force. When they arrived at the Geula transit camp in
Aden they were often required to take off their clothes and hand
them over to be burned, for fear of diseases and vermin. In their
place, they were given new, alien clothing, some of which had
been sent from Israel, a Western style of dress which they had
never worn. The women felt nude in the dresses they received,
since they had been accustomed to wear tight leggings under
their dresses. Some of them did not get new trousers or leggings
to replace the ones that had been burned. Whenever a stranger
approached them in the camp they would crouch, hiding their
legs in the sand, deeply ashamed. As soon as the immigrants arrived at the camp they were warned that from here on they

---

*Dr. Yosef Meir was the general director of the Ministry of Health. He
came to the conclusion that the Yemenite immigrants should be brought to Israel as soon as possible, preferably all at once, in one hundred planes. In the
course of that year other people visited the camp in Aden. The Foreign Minister, Moshe Sharett, celebrated Passover Eve there. Several journalists were allowed to visit the camp, including the radio correspondent Shlomo Barer, who
subsequently wrote a fascinating book about it, describing the way in which
the flights from Aden were carried out by a small, adventurous American airline.[105] In the files of the Jewish Agency there are some bitter complaints about
the attitude of some of the camp supervisors to the immigrants.[106]

would no longer be allowed to marry child-brides or have more than one wife, as they had been used to do. The law in Yemen stipulated that girl orphans were to be given to the Imam or the sultan, and so the leaders of the Jewish community would marry them off at once, to save them from being converted to Islam. In Aden, too, the Israelis tried to instill in them, all at once, the idea that the status of women was equal to that of men. Some of the people who were supposed to record their names were unable to understand them, and so they gave them new names that were easier to pronounce.[107]

Before they boarded the airplanes their luggage was taken from them and set aside. It included ancient Torah scrolls, religious objects, jewelry and embroidered garments, exquisite gold and silver workmanship. When they were urged to leave Yemen they were encouraged to bring with them "their dearest spiritual and historical belongings, books of all sorts, especially the ancient ones and manuscripts, as well as clothing and jewelry, whether private or communal property." They were told that their property would be sent after them by ship. Some of that baggage disappeared en route, some jewelry and religious articles made their way to antique and souvenir shops in Israel. When Itzhak Ben-Tsvi visited Aden he went into the baggage stores, opened a few of the crates and rummaged in them. "I intended to check carefully and see if there were any valuable material there which could be purchased for the Institute for the Study of Jewish Communities in the Middle East, which I intend to establish under the aegis of the Hebrew University," he explained later.[108] Some of the sacred books were no longer recognizable after arrival. Some were declared communal property and sent to the synagogues in the new Yemenite settlements.* Photographs taken inside the planes on the eight-hour, world-to-world voyage, show the immigrants looking frozen with horror. A visitor who saw them in one of their camps in Israel wrote: "Even if

---

*There was a considerable degree of corruption involved in the immigration procedures. Some of it was discovered by the controllers, and some in the course of investigations of thefts of immigrants' property[109] The Jewish Agency emissaries in Aden conducted bitter rivalries among themselves and conspired against each other. They promoted their political parties among people who had no idea what they were talking about.[110] In one of the files there is a note written by Dr. Yaakov Weinstein to Shlomo Schmidt—both of the religious *Mizrahi*—asking him to "pay the (Yemenite) Rabbi Badihi a small sum, pocket money, every month."[111]

their teeth were pulled out of their mouths they would not put up any resistance."[112]

In the 18 months between May 1948 and December 1949 about 35,000 immigrants from Yemen arrived in Israel, and in the following years another 14,000. Three flights daily, a total of 450 flights, brought them all over.[113] The planes flew over the Red Sea and the Negev. The entire operation cost nearly $4,000,000 dollars.* Ben-Gurion saw it as the latter-day Exodus: "No economic consideration or financial difficulty will hold up their immigration," he wrote in his diary.[115] In the Knesset he said, "We cannot wait with the immigration from Yemen until Mr. Begin becomes Prime Minister." The *Knesset Record* notes in brackets, "Laughter."[116] In the inner chambers, however, there was no laughter. There was a debate whether these people should be brought over at all. Itzhak Greenbaum asked: "Why do we have to put an end to the Yemen Diaspora and bring over people who are more harm than use? By bringing Yemenites, 70% of whom are sick, we are doing no good to anybody. We are harming them by bringing them into an alien environment where they will degenerate. Can we withstand an immigration of which 70% are sick?"[117]

A few months earlier Levi Eshkol said that he had no fears of the Yemenite immigration, because it was a "hardworking element."[118] But in September he consulted with Giora Yoseftal about the question of "what to do with the Yemenites." He said he had no idea how to employ them.[119] A short while later Eshkol told his colleagues that he was willing to "postpone" the immigration from Aden.[120] That was when conditions in the camps there were described as "sheer horror." Yehuda Braginsky, of the Absorption Department, told the Executive: "We haven't prepared any camps or houses [for the Yemenite immigrants]. So what should I do? I put up barbed wire and keep them penned in like animals in a state of illusion."[121] Some members of the Executive did not believe that the Jews of Yemen needed to be saved, as the reports had it. "I see no harm in these people

*In May 1949 Itzhak Refael suggested to Ben-Gurion that the Yemenite immigrants could be brought over by sea to Eilat. Flying them over, he said, cost 87 dollars per person. By ship it would come to only 30 dollars. Moreover, their landing in Eilat would justify the construction of a road from Beersheba to the southern port. Refael thought the Joint would agree to share in the cost of construction. Ben-Gurion approved the suggestion, but nothing came of it.[114]

staying in Aden," said Eliyahu Dobkin, and Moshe Kol voiced
the suspicion that the British authorities were promoting the
Yemenite immigration "in order to destroy us."[122] In this debate Itzhak Refael, too, was among those who opposed "regulating" the immigration. Not many sick people among the Yemenites would reach Israel, he assured his colleagues, hinting that
the sick would die on the way over.[123]

Dvar Hashavua described them as "a fabulous tribe, the
most poetic of the tribes of Israel. Their features bear the ancient
Hebrew grace, and their hearts are filled with innocent faith and
a fervent love for the Holy Land."[124] Their folklore was believed
to be biblical. Ben-Gurion wanted the immigrants from Yemen
for the same reason he wanted all immigrants, to strengthen the
state and its army, but he was unusually receptive to their problems. "Children are dying like flies," he wrote. "We must save
them. Here too their mortality rate is high, but at least there is
better and more efficient medical care."[125] Some weeks later he
said that if they were doomed to die, let them at least die here.[126]
Following a visit at the Tel-Hashomer hospital, he said in an unusually emotional speech:

> This is one of the most horrific scenes I have ever witnessed. In the
> ward which the army has turned over to the sick Yemenite chil-
> dren, I saw little babies who looked more like skeletons than living
> human beings. They have not the strength to cry, and many don't
> have the strength to eat. Yet in their eyes there was still the glow of
> life, and their eyes are the eyes of Jewish children, precious chil-
> dren. And Jewish doctors and Jewish nurses look after them with
> devotion and love. At that moment I understood the phrase "joyous
> tremor." I was shaken and deeply moved by the great and terrible
> scene. Yes, these are indeed the pangs of the Messiah.[127]

But even Ben-Gurion was not free of ambivalence in his attitude toward the Yemenite immigrants. Though he felt warmly
disposed, he was also conscious of a sense of strangeness, which
made him recoil from them and wish to change them. He wrote
a long letter about it to the Chief of Staff, Yigael Yadin.

> This tribe is in some ways more easily absorbed, both culturally
> and economically, than any other. It is hardworking, it is not at-
> tracted by city life, it has—or at least, the male part has—a good
> grounding in Hebrew and the Jewish heritage. Yet in other ways it
> may be the most problematic of all. It is two thousand years behind

us, perhaps even more. It lacks the most basic and primary concepts of civilization (as distinct from culture). Its attitude toward women and children is primitive. Its physical condition poor. Its bodily strength is depleted and it does not have the minimal notions of hygiene. For thousands of years it lived in one of the most benighted and impoverished lands, under a rule even more backward than an ordinary feudal and theocratic regime. The passage from there to Israel has been a profound human revolution, not a superficial, political one. All its human values need to be changed from the ground up.[128]

Ben-Gurion wished to improve the general health and hygiene among the Yemenites, including the care of babies, "the use of toilets," better nutrition, "healthier clothing and footwear," and so forth. He sought to employ the army for this purpose. But he also wanted to change their customs and way of life. "The Yemenite father does not look after his children and family as do we," he wrote. "He is not accustomed to feed his child properly before eating himself." He visited a Yemenite rabbinical lesson and commented, "This is probably how they used to teach in India . . . before the discovery of the alphabet." He gained the impression that the Yemenite immigrant children were learning their lessons by rote, mechanically, without comprehension. "This cannot be done away with by order," he wrote Yadin. "We must understand the soul of the Yemenite and treat his customs with respect, but it must be changed by gentle means and by setting an example." He wrote in a similar vein about the "dreadful gulf" between the men and women. "It must be closed," he stated, yet without unnecessarily hurting their feelings and habits, "with patience and much love." Some time later Ben-Gurion said in the Knesset that it was the government's aim to accustom the Yemenite immigrant to the ways of Israel, until he forgets where he had come from, "as I have forgotten that I am Polish."[129] A leaflet published by the Jewish Agency's Absorption Department warned:

> We must not allow them to become the hewers of wood and drawers of water, the shoeshine boys of our society. It is incumbent upon us to enable them to live a creative life. . . . The Yemenite community is quick-witted, naturally intelligent and diligent. It can raise its standards and develop flourishing settlements with healthy populations, if we invest sufficient effort in it, if we guide it, if the settlers are accompanied by teachers, doctors, nurses and

instructors, who will love them and help them acquire a new culture.*

Yet one instructor wrote: "Let us come before the Yemenite immigrant just as we are, without embellishment and without giving up our identity. If our attitude seems strange and painful to him—so be it. Let him struggle with it. Such an inner struggle enriches man."[130]

Most of the immigrants from Yemen were housed at first in four camps: in Athlit, the oldest immigrant camp; in Rosh Haayin, which was built in 1949, and was made up of four smaller camps; in Ein Shemer, which was constructed in August 1949, and in Beit Lidd II, which was constructed for the Yemenite immigrants in September 1949, near the older camps which had already been there. These were tent encampments. In Rosh Haayin there were eight families in each tent, living on the ground, without a floor or drainage of any kind.[131] By the end of 1950, the Yemenites were the largest community in the Maabaroth, constituting 40 percent of their inhabitants.[132] Prior to the creation of the state, there had been three settlements built expressly for Yemenites: Eliashiv (built in 1933), Geulim (built in 1936, settled by Yemenites in 1945) and Geulei Teyman (1947). There were also some urban quarters populated by Yemenites, such as Shaarayim and Marmorek. In the first five years after the creation of the state the Yemenites accounted for 6.5 percent of the total immigration, yet they constituted 24 percent of the rural settlement.[133] Of the 49,000 Yemenite Jews who came on the "Operation Magic Carpet," 34,000—i.e., some 70 percent—made their living by farming. Some had been farmers before they came, and some saw in the cultivation of the land a fulfillment of the messianic vision. Some were made to settle on the land, for lack of other employment, and a few of these were reluctant to do so. They were known as good workers, who were willing to do any work, no matter how hard. Those of them who had been tradesmen or artisans in Yemen and were converted into agricultural laborers in Israel felt that they had come down in the world. Between May 1949 and August 1953, 57 rural set-

---

*Ironically enough, their ancient culture was preserved, among other ways, in the numerous petitions that they sent to the authorities, the welfare offices, etc. Some of them are written in superb calligraphy, partially in the medieval *Rashi* script, with exquisite grace, as befits communications in the Holy Tongue.

tlements were established for the immigrants from Yemen, but
only 39 of them survived.[134] A third of these settlements were in
the mountainous regions, and some of the others were in inhos-
pitable areas.[135] Some of these villages were established, to begin
with, as labor villages. Many Yemenites were employed as laborers: "The Yemenites are employed in preparing the soil and
planting tomatoes, because a kibbutz member's labor is worth
more," wrote one newspaper. And in another article, whose subject was Arab labor, it was said that "new immigrants from
Yemen were working in a kibbutz, where they were receiving
wages like Arabs and not like Jews."[136] Zeharia Glouska, MK—
himself of Yemenite origin—protested against this and many
other kinds of discrimination, in the areas of housing and religious amenities, as well as in employment in government offices and child allowances. At that time allowances were paid
only for the first three children. Glouska maintained that veteran Yemenite soldiers were also discriminated against, and he
protested, too, against the failure of the national radio station to
broadcast enough Yemenite music. The programs for Yemenite
listeners, he said, were prepared by so-called experts, who were
Ashkenazi, and were worse than ludicrous. As he put it, there
seemed to be two kinds of immigrants: "The first is privileged
and coddled, as if he has been snatched away from a palace, and
must be sheltered from the too harsh rays of sunlight, and the
second comes bearing a load of trouble and torment and there is
not a ray of hope that his condition will improve in the State of
Israel."[137]*

The papers did not persist with the warm praise they had
showered on the "Magic Carpet" immigrants. Nor did the authorities. When one of the papers referred to the "river of excrement" flowing through one of the camps, the Jewish Agency replied that there was "a certain type" of immigrant whom it was

*Glouska knew how to fight, although his Yemenite party was no longer a
factor in the absorption of Yemenite immigrants. The first Knesset Committee
added 15 *liroth* to the salaries of married MKs. In the course of the debate about
it the question arose what should be done about MKs who had two wives.
Glouska demanded that they be given a double allowance. When he was told
that bigamy was immoral, he replied that the Bible did not forbid polygamy,
and that the Yemenites did not acknowledge the medieval Jewish ban on polygamy. "I think it is immoral to have one wife at home while having others
outside," he said. He won. MKs with two wives got a double allowance. Some
time later bigamy was made illegal.[138]

hard to accustom to hygienic habits—a reference to the Yemenites. However, the Jewish Agency assured the public that it was making a point of building toilets near the residences, to accustom the people to use them.[139] In September 1949 the inhabitants of Even Yehuda protested against a plan to include the nearby Yemenite quarter under its jurisdiction. The Minister of the Interior promised to make an effort to talk them into it.[140]

In the latter half of 1953, Ben-Gurion instructed MKs Zalman Aran, Israel Yeshayahu and Kaddish Luz to study the situation in the Yemenite settlements, five years after they had been built. They reported that most of the places they visited looked as if "sooner or later" they would become viable as agricultural communities. They did not observe any "facts or appearances" suggesting discrimination against the community. "If the Ashkenazi settlers thrive more, it is due to their initiative, their skills and adaptability, all of which provide them with better opportunities for managing their affairs, internally and externally." The committee phrased its conclusions very carefully, and only at the end noted, as if in passing, the existence of "a state of despair, which affects the settlers' faith in the future." The minutes of the meetings between the committee and the settlers reveal poverty, scarcity and neglect verging on degeneration because—among other reasons—the authorities have given them no help. Hundreds of families were unemployed for long stretches, because there was no work, and because the Jewish Agency's Settlement Department claimed that the Ministry of Labor was supposed to provide employment, and the Ministry of Labor maintained that it was the Department of Settlement which should take charge of it. The agricultural development was not carried out according to plan. Houses which had been built a couple of years before were already showing cracks. There was no transportation and no arrangements had been made to carry the produce to the markets. The agricultural instructors who had been sent to help the settlers were not always good enough. Having no income, the settlers stopped paying taxes, and so medical services were discontinued. There was no cultural activity at all. Many of the younger people left the settlements, and the people that remained were old. Many settlers left out of fear of the Arab infiltrators from across the border, some of whom had lived in those villages before the war. "The burden of guarding the settlements," noted the committee, "is undermining the physical capacity and the moral fiber of the settlers. Eventually, the security was also jeopardized. A reasonable arrangement would have to include some assistance from the state's security forces." Evidently no one had thought of this before.[141] More than ten years later the Ministry of Welfare admitted that the immigrants from Yemen had been treated as "primitive, helpless defectives"—their ways were considered undesirable, partly because they seemed harmful, and partly because they were un-European. The instructors constantly urged them to change their way of life, and undermined the traditional authority of their fathers and teachers. Some of the instructors acted also on behalf of their political parties.* MAPAI had its own Yemenite activists, but it did not know how to attract the community to its ranks. "It is not easy to distinguish between the Arab Druzes and the Yemenites," commented David Hakohen, MK. But he saw no cause for worry: "To them Ben-Gurion is everything."[143] Ben-Gurion himself thought otherwise: "the Yemenites," he noted in his diary, "will vote for Herut."[144]†

In April 1950 the Yemenite Association appealed to the Minister of Police Behor Shitrit to intervene personally in what they described as "strange events." The Association related the story of one Refael Yahya, of the immigrant camp in Ein Shemer, and his five-month-old baby boy. "In September 1949 the baby fell ill and the doctor ordered it to be taken from the immigrant camp for treatment. Since then it has not been seen and its whereabouts are unknown." The letter went on to describe a second and similar case: A baby girl who had fallen ill four months previously was removed from the camp for treatment and vanished.

---

*A study of the immigrant camp in Rosh Haayin—which later became a township—stated: "The forced reduction of social and cultural activities, the undermining of traditional authority, the lack of economic opportunity and the dependence on outside officials, all led to . . . aggressive behavior and at the same time to disease and physical debility. The separation of children from their parents, because of illness or neglect, further weakened parental authority and intensified the state of dependence."[142]

†Israel Yeshayahu, a docile Yemenite activist in MAPAI, later to be a Minister of Government and Chairman of the Knesset, rejected this view. "I consider it my personal and public duty," he said, "to put an end once and for all to the myth that Yemenites are Herot and Herot is Yemenite. . . . For some reason, every person whose skin is swarthy and speaks with an Oriental accent is taken for a Herot man."[145] An analysis of the voting patterns after the Knesset elections showed that in the Yemenite rural settlements as well as in Rosh Haayin, MAPAI won a sizable amount of support.[146]

The Minister of Police was in no hurry to reply. A week later the Yemenites sent a memorandum which likewise remained unanswered, and after two weeks they wrote again: "Repeated investigations in the immigrant homes in Rosh Haayin confirm that sick people disappear, perhaps they die and are buried, and no one knows when or where. We are astounded by a situation which nobody attempts to explain."[147] A satisfactory explanation of this affair has never been given. It remains as mysterious and disturbing as it was at the beginning, the saddest chapter in the saga of mass immigration to Israel. The number of children who were taken from their parents and "vanished" was in the hundreds.

More than twenty years later the immigrants from Yemen were no longer considered to be people "whose names you can hardly figure out," as Itzhak Refael had once put it. Now both they and their children had names. The Ministry of Defense had their names, and in time sent them draft notices. Some hundreds of those called up were believed by their parents to have died in infancy; now, at last, it had become the subject of a major scandal.[148] The Knesset appointed a committee to investigate the affair, "which has since been haunting the country in the form of rumors," as the committee put it in its report.[149] The rumors were that the vanished children, or at least some of them, had been sold to adoptive parents, in Israel and abroad. In the preamble to its report, the committee stated that "it was not surprising" that many of the Yemenite immigrant children disappeared. The committee ascribed the fact to the poor conditions in the immigrant camps in Aden and Israel, to the widespread ill health among the children, which necessitated removing some of them from their parents, and to the general neglect, verging on chaos, which reigned in all matters concerning the reception of immigrants, including the proper registration of their names and whereabouts. The committee investigated 342 complaints by parents whose children had disappeared, most of them from Yemen, and the rest from other Arab countries. There was one complaint by parents from Bulgaria. They all related that their children had been taken away for treatment or care in infant homes, and that when they came to fetch them, they were told that they had been transferred. They searched for them in one institution after another, encountering bureaucratic indifference, until they gave up in despair and returned to their tents,

as helpless as they had been depicted. After a two-year long de-
tective search, in March 1968 the committee produced 316
death certificates and somewhat fewer burial certificates, and
four living children. Twenty-two cases had left no trace at all—
most of these had been kept in the Rosh Haayin infant home and
that institution's files were never found.

The committee's attitude toward the affair was ambivalent.
On the one hand, it stated that "it was not surprising" that the
children had vanished, yet it described the phenomenon as "as-
tounding." In the next page of its report, it stated that in view of
the fact that 70,000 immigrants in all had arrived from Yemen,
the number of vanished children was "not extraordinary." The
total number of immigrants was in fact considerably less. Dov
Levitan, of Bar-Ilan University, has pointed out a basic flaw in
the committee's work. On the one hand, it determined that the
disappearances were due to the procedural chaos which prevailed at the time, which is a reasonable assumption; yet, at the
same time, it based its conclusion that most of those children
had died on the death and burial certificates, which, given the
said chaos, might easily have been forged. The committee did
not have the graves opened for examination. In his study, Dov
Levitan referred to the case of the child Braha Davidowitz, who
died in 1951 and was buried without her parents being allowed
to see her. They insisted on the body being exhumed and examined by a pathologist, and it was in fact discovered to be the body
of another child. Thus the suspicion that the Yemenite babies
had indeed been given, or even sold, for adoption in Israel or
abroad has not been entirely dissipated. The committee also investigated the rumors that the children had been given to adoptive parents abroad, but, according to its report, "was unable to
produce any results." However, it noted that the information
"would seem" to justify further investigation abroad. The committee submitted its report to the Ministers of Justice and Police
and recommended that such an investigation be carried out. But
the affair was dropped before long and forgotten.

Some ten months after the "Magic Carpet" flights began, a
poster was pasted up in the streets of Tel Aviv, concluding with
the question, "Are our Yemenite brothers to be treated like savage natives?!" The poster related the story of a new immigrant
from Yemen, Salem Yaakov Gerafi, who was shot to death by security guards in the course of a fight in the Ein Shemer camp

dining hall. Rumor had it that the man had been killed because he demanded that the ritual observances be kept in the camp. The poster was signed "The Jewish Believers."[150] Thus the immigrants form Yemen, who had been in the center of the confrontation between the veterans and the newcomers and between the European and Oriental Israelis, found themselves the focus of the conflict between secular and religious Jews as well.

PART III

Between the Orthodox and the Secular

7

Each in the Name of His God

SHORTLY AFTER the first "Magic Carpet" plane landed in Israel a disturbing rumor spread in the country: the Yemenite immigrants, it was said, were required to cut off their ritual sidelocks as soon as they arrived at the immigrant camps. Those who refused—the rumor said—had them cut off against their will. Minister of Education Shazar (who had just changed his name from Rubashow, rushed to the immigrant camp in Beit Lidd to investigate the matter. He was told that about a dozen boys had been made to cut off their sidelocks and a few girls to cut off their hair, all for health reasons. The camp physician had expressly ordered the measure: "In every case where the nurse has discovered a skin infection or hair disease, the hair must be cut, regardless of religious conviction—including the side-locks—or the infection will spread."[1] In certain camps it was estimated that at least 60 percent of the children suffered from such diseases. Shazar accepted the explanation he was given and left. Later it was learned that he had been misled—the excision of sidelocks had in fact been instituted in some of the camps as a routine practice.

Most of the Yemenite immigrants demanded a religious education for their children, as they had never known any other. Nahum Levin, who was in charge of education in the camps, thought otherwise, "Of the Heavenly Jerusalem they have had quite enough," he noted in his diary. "It is time to introduce some earthly Jerusalem into their world."[2] He had, however, no intention of undermining their faith. "We need not explain to them that there is no God," he wrote. "Let them pray as much as they want to." Yet religion appeared to him to be a divisive element, and he was seeking national unity, on the basis of a secular, social-democratic ideology. In his outline of education for the Yemenite immigrants he set as his objective an introduction to "civilization and knowledge of the world." What he had in mind was the secular Israeli way of life. "There is also need for political education," he added, "or the immigrants might be attracted by the worst." Some of the elements of civilization that he had in mind were heretical in their eyes, but Levin, insensitive to their cultural heritage, failed to appreciate this. The political education he introduced into the camps provoked the leaders of the religious political parties. One of them, David Tsvi Pincas, attempted to make this into a national issue. "We shall fight, even if it means civil war," he warned and the press predicted an Israeli *Kulturkampf* between the religious and the secular.[3]

Ever since the 1920s, the Israeli educational system had been divided into four subsidiary systems, linked with political movements. Two of the systems were secular, and in 1949 they accounted for about 75 percent of the students; the two others were religious. The whole system reflected the special status of the political parties in the country, whose influence permeated every aspect of life with the ideological intensity that characterized the time. Before the creation of the state, the political parties provided many of the services which people either could not or would not receive from the British authorities. These services included employment obtained through the parties' labor exchanges, medical care provided by the parties' clinics and hospitals, housing constructed by the parties' construction companies, or through the various settlement movements. The parties had their own industries, daily newspapers, marketing and food store networks, publishing houses, transport cooperatives, food stores, theater companies, youth movements, clubs for the elderly, women's organizations and—until the creation of the state—military organizations. Education was one of the services that the political parties provided for their supporters. It was an important tool for keeping the party's membership under control and for promoting its doctrine to the younger generation. Thus many schools taught what the parties wanted them to teach, which made the educational system pluralistic and quite diversified. In addition, each subsystem was fairly diversified within itself. The General school system followed either the Liberal and General Zionist parties, or the right-wing "Revisionist" (later Herut) party. Formally, this system was under the jurisdiction of the Jewish Agency, which financed it. The Labor movement school system educated children in the spirit of MAPAI, MAPAM and sometimes, even, the Communist party. This system was under the jurisdiction of the Histadrut Labor Federation. There were two religious school systems, one associated with the Zionist *Mizrahi* movement and the other with the non-Zionist *Agudat Israel*.

The General school system was founded during the "language war" which raged in the country in 1913, and provided the basis for the new Hebrew education.[4] It fostered the spirit of liberal nationalism which had prevailed among the middle classes of Europe at the end of the nineteenth century. The General teachers claimed to be promoting the "sacred values of Zionism and general education," as opposed to the other systems, which promoted either a religious or a socialist vision. Forty-four percent of Israeli children in 1949 attended schools in the General system, as opposed to 50 percent the previous year. The educational trend varied from school to school, sometimes from class to class. Some of the parents and many of the teachers were members of the Histadrut, but generally the pupils were the children of clerks, teachers, merchants, craftsmen and farmers. The parents subscribed to the daily *Haaretz* or *Haboker*, and sometimes bought the children's *Haaretz Shelanu*. The youth movement to which these children belonged was usually the Scout movement. In high school these were the first to smoke cigarettes, wear "stylish" shirts and hold "bourgeois" parties, with dancing in couples. They were also the first youngsters to start dating.

The pupils at these schools addressed their teachers formally, sometimes by their surnames, with Mr. or Mrs. attached. The teachers heard about the more innovative methods being introduced in the Labor movement system, but were not inclined to use them. They demanded respect from their pupils and did not expect affection. The lessons were given as lectures, and there was little incentive for independent work on the pupils' part, other than the homework they were given. Lessons were to be learned verbatim, and critical questioning was discouraged. The teachers were supposed to inculcate the qualities of diligence and perseverance, self-restraint and economy, order and discipline, respect for parents and obedience to the law, as well as love of country; the teachers were usually quite patriotic.

In the Labor movement schools, by contrast, the teachers were addressed by their first names or even nicknames. The system was the most innovative in its pedagogical methods. It began in the 1920s, and reflected the aims of a new Jewish society based on labor without exploitation, social equality and mutual help. The teachers were inspired by the educational principles of the Soviet Union, combined with the latest educational experiments in the United States. Physical work, particularly agricultural work, was viewed as of moral, social and personal value, in the spirit of A.D. Gordon, the spiritual leader of the Labor and kibbutz movement. This idea prevailed also in the system's urban schools. In 1949 some 30 percent of the school children attended Labor movement schools, and their number was growing year by year. They were supposed to acquire a working class consciousness, and to view the "national unity," promoted by the General school system, as a deception, designed to impose the "bourgeois spirit" upon the workers to prevent them from struggling for their "liberation."

Under this system the center of gravity passed from the teacher to the pupil. Lessons were not confined to lectures by the teacher, but included lectures by the pupils themselves, "staged trials," "projects," study circles and the like, within the framework of an overall "theme." The school encouraged the children to organize their own "community." The kibbutzim and the system's boarding schools gave them considerable autonomy in determining their own daily activities. The pupils were encouraged to join the MAPAI and MAPAM youth movements, and the youth movements were encouraged to participate in the activities of the school. They discussed racial discrimination in the United States and sang Russian folk songs. Pop and dance music were considered decadent and immoral. First thing in the morning—when in the General schools children gathered in the school yard to salute the flag and in the religious schools the pupils said their morning prayers—the Labor movement school population would gather to sing the anthem of the Histadrut. On May 1 they flew red flags and sang the "International." (As late as 1953 this led the General Zionists to withdraw for some time from the coalition government.) The teachers in the Labor movement schools frequently discussed politics and current events with their pupils, often linking the lessons, including the Bible, to these subjects.

In 1920 the Zionist Federation, convening in London, resolved to entrust Hebrew religious education to the *Mizrahi* movement. The movement's schools devoted much of their curriculum to religious subjects and taught the children to observe the laws of the Torah. Boys and girls were taught separately, the boys wearing skullcaps. The methods of instruction were very conservative, emphasizing discipline, sometimes including physical punishment. Yaakov Hazan, one of the leaders of MAPAM, once quoted a religious textbook which boasted of the fact that it did not teach the descent of Man from the ape. A few of the *Mizrahi* schools were open to outside influences and gradually began to teach boys and girls together, responding to the attitude of the pupils' parents, who belonged to what would later be called "the modern religious," as distinct from the ultra-orthodox viewpoint. Socially speaking, they belonged to the same strata as the families served by the General school system, and sought to teach something of the latter's curriculum, though not without reservations. In time they grew to be entirely different from the *Agudat Israel* schools. The amount of secular education offered in the *Mizrahi* school system varied considerably from school to school. They all, however, taught in Hebrew and in the spirit of Zionism. In 1949 some 21 percent of the children attended *Mizrahi* schools; the percentage declined steadily thereafter.

The *Agudat Israel*, ultra-orthodox, schools were strictly closed to the outer world. They tried to preserve the way of life of the old Jewish community in Palestine, dating back to the first half of the nineteenth century, and to the mores of the Jews of Eastern Europe. There were some minor differences between the schools of the *Agudat Israel* and its affiliate, *Poalei Agudat Israel*, but all devoted the bulk of the curriculum to religious studies, leaving very little time for any secular subjects, mostly, spelling and arithmetic. The children dressed like their parents—boys in long black coats, girls in long frocks. The girls

were taught to pray and to sew. Teaching was conducted in Yiddish and the children were taught that Zionism was heresy. After the creation of the state these religious schools became one
of the recognized subsystems, accounting for some 5 percent of
the pupils. Their number grew and by 1953 nearly doubled,
largely at the expense of the *Mizrahi*.

Most of the students in the two major secular school systems
came from nonreligious families. The teachers in these schools
did not instill antireligious feelings, but the students were not
encouraged to observe religious laws either. The General school
system was more inclined to foster the Jewish national heritage,
but that was confined chiefly to the Bible, with *Talmud* study
reduced to a minimum. There were no prayers or other religious
studies at school. The Labor movement school system treated
the Jewish heritage mainly in historical terms, as a humanistic
tradition, whose true expression lay in the commandment
"Thou shall not kill" and the prophet Isaiah's messianic vision
of swords transformed into plowshares. The Sabbath was interpreted as the laborer's day of rest, Passover as the festival of liberty, Pentecost as a harvest festival, and so on. Under MAPAM's
and to some extent MAPAI's tutelage, students in the schools
and the kibbutzim were taught to oppose clericalism and religious coercion, but were no longer entreated to revolt against
the reactionary decadence with which religion had previously
been identified. MAPAI's Israel Gouri, MK, once said that he did
not fear a religious man, but he feared men of religion, referring
to the religious parties.[5] Such was the sentiment in the Labor
movement school system.

All four systems charged each other with "snatching" children from each other, and indeed they all did, through both coercion and inducement. The General system made use of the municipal councils that its parties controlled in some of the major
cities. The Labor movement made use of the Histadrut, and the
religious systems used the religious services and councils. They
all distributed food packages from the United States. After Independence they fought primarily over the immigrant children.
Representatives of the religious parties campaigned among the
immigrants and convinced them to sign petitions to establish religious schools for their children. Representatives of the secular
parties convinced them to sign petitions asking for the opposite.
They all obtained signatures from people who could not read the

petitions they were signing, and they often forged signatures, too.[6]

Zerah Warhaftig, MK, submitted two complaints to the Minister of Education:

A. There were about 40 boys and girls of the Yemenite community at the religious school in Ein Kerem. On Saturday . . . representatives of the Histadrut came to the Ein Kerem Yemenite synagogue and persuaded the parents to move their children to the Labor school. They explained that those who sent their children to the Labor school would be given priority in employment over those who sent their children to the school of Hamizrahi. As a result of this pressure the parents transferred their children to the Labor school.

B. A spokesman for the settlers in Tarshiha gave the representative of the Religious Labor movement a letter signed by most of the settlers, asking him to provide religious education for their children. When the agricultural instructor heard of this, he demanded that the spokesman retrieve the letter. The settlers refused to do this, but after hearing the instructor's threats they feared that they would be punished if they did not retract their request. The letter was returned and there is now a nonreligious school in the place.[7]

The religious daily *Hatzofeh* complained about what it called "the child hunt" by secular schools, but added: "All means are fair. The struggle for the child's soul must be pursued with vigor. . . . The children of Israel must not be abandoned to the soul-hunters of the secular school systems." The paper published a report of an event that allegedly took place in Beit Dagon: "A leftist teacher" and two representatives of the Jewish Agency promised half an acre of land and a loan to whoever sent their children to the Labor movement school. "Agents of the Left are starving Jews in order to force them to give their children a secular education," the newspaper stated, and claimed, furthermore, that Histadrut agents were threatening to send new immigrants to the Negev if they did not register their children in the Labor movement schools.[8] The Histadrut daily, *Davar*, published countercharges:

—Every morning cars belonging to the religious movements come to the immigrant camp in Rehovot to snatch the children and carry them to their own schools in Rehovot.

—Recently some cars belonging to the religious bloc came to the Histadrut school in the Raanana camp and forcibly removed 23 children who had been studying there and took them to another place.

—Representatives of the religious bloc have taken to visiting the immigrant housing projects, where they distribute books, notebooks, food and clothes, to entice the immigrants to join them. They tell the parents that in the Labor schools the children are fed nonkosher meat, though it is known that hot meals are not provided at all in the new immigrant settlement schools, as there are no dining halls.[9]

David Ben-Gurion had to intervene in a number of cases, having received complaints from both religious[10] and non-religious parents.[11]The compulsory education laws recognized all four systems, and parents were allowed to choose the one they wanted for their children. When, in the latter half of 1949, the Compulsory Education Law was being debated, there were some, including Ben-Gurion himself, who wanted to abolish the separate systems and establish a single, nationwide school system, which would be subject only to the state and not to the parties. As the ruling party, MAPAI had hoped that the educational and political philosophy of the Labor movement would be adopted by the entire educational system.

Israel Rokah, of the General Zionists, said: "Let us have state schools, in which all the children of Israel will receive the same education, without reference to their parents' class!"[12] "Will the Labor system not tell its pupils that there was once a great Jew by the name of Moses?" asked Izhar Harari (of the Progressive party), "and will the Mizrahi school not tell its pupils that there was once a great Jew by the name of Karl Marx?"[13] Eliyahu Eliashar, a leader of the Sephardi List, warned half-seriously, half-provocatively: "Tomorrow a group of thirty nudists will demand a nudist school system, and we'll have to provide it, because it is the Minister of Education's dream that every child should receive the education his parents wish him to have."[14] In effect, the spokesmen for each of the different systems agreed that they all be abolished, on the condition that the unified system be their own. MAPAM and the religious parties made this amply clear. Feige Ilanit of MAPAM said: "There is only one chance for the unified education system—for it to be a pioneering, socialist system for the children of the workers and the children of the entire nation."[15] Agudat Israel's I.M. Levin put it this way: "Ideally, this is obviously the hope of every single Jew, and we all long for the day when we shall be a single nation with unified education." He meant an education in the spirit of God, but, knowing that it had no chance, the rabbi warned the Knesset: *"Touch not mine annointed"* meaning the children.[16] It was an emotion-charged conflict which permitted no compromise. "We are ready literally to give our lives for our education," proclaimed the leader of Agudat Israel, while Dvora Netser, MK, said of MAPAI's educational system: "This is our religion: That is what we believe in!"[17] And so they continued to educate their children, each in the spirit of their god. It was both an ideological conflict and a power struggle for the future soul of the state, between different world views and opposing concepts, between the vision of national unity and the need for pluralism, between the secular majority and the religious minority.

A few days after the Knesset passed the Compulsory Education Law, in September 1949, the inspectors of the different systems demanded that the schools in the immigrant camps also be opened for their inspection.[18] Everyone agreed that not every camp was suitable for any particular system, and all agreed that the education of immigrants should be divided among them, yet no one knew how to go about it. The general assumption was that the Yemenites needed a religious education, and so it was agreed that the schools in the Yemenite immigrant camps should be religious. However, they could not agree who should supervise them and who should run them—the two religious systems, or one that was unified. Representatives of the two religious systems failed to reach an agreement between themselves, and the other two systems were not willing to leave the Yemenite camps to the exclusive influence of the religious parties. It was therefore proposed that a single religious bloc be created, made up of the two religious systems, which would be supervised jointly by all four systems. The two religious systems concurred, but demanded that the representatives of the two secular systems who would take part in the joint supervision be religious individuals. Here the question arose whether it would be sufficient for them to be "observant," or should they also be "God-fearing and strictly observant." At one point someone proposed that the Chief Rabbinate be asked to resolve the problem.

With regard to the nonYemenite camps there were disputes in which every conceivable course of action was proposed: a single religious bloc, as in the Yemenite camps, or two religious systems; a single secular bloc or two secular systems; a religious bloc plus two secular systems; a single secular bloc plus two religious systems. There was also a proposal to establish a single system which would include a separate religious course, or separate classes, in the same school building, or in different school buildings, or special hours set aside for religious studies. Then they argued about the number of hours to be set aside for the purpose, and could not agree.

An important question which remained unanswered was what the secular system would be called. "Under no circumstances will we agree to be called the nonreligious system," declared the chief supervisor of the Labor movement schools, and he was promptly echoed by the chief supervisor of the General school system. They searched for a suitable title under which their systems could be introduced to the immigrants, one which would not betray the fact that they were secular, for fear that the immigrants would reject them out of hand. They also argued about the teachers: Was it possible for a secular teacher to teach in a religious school, and what did he or she have to do to be accepted as a religious person. Whenever they were stymied they reverted to the letter of the law and proposed that all the systems should be available in all the camps, and then recalled that the immigrants would not know how to choose between them, and so they would try a different proposal. At one stage the situation grew even more complicated when the Religious Labor faction in the Histadrut created its own school system, independent of the others. Until then it had always been understood that the religious parties had the monopoly over religious education, and the sudden emergence of a new religious school system allied to MAPAI confused the issue. They began to argue whether this was a separate system or a subsystem, and whether it was actually religious or only "traditional." The old religious systems viewed the new one as an unfair rival and described it as a deception. All these debates were conducted with the gravest concern and in the finest detail, first in the Ministry of Education and later in the Cabinet. The minutes of the meetings at the Ministry reveal it to be a confederation of rival factions acting against each other. The chief supervisors of the different systems talked in pedagogical terms, but what they were really engaged in was party politics, and they failed because as politicians they were both petty and inexperienced, and the divisions among them ran very deep.

Nahum Levin, who was in charge of education in the camps, was a slight, rather severe man, with a shock of white hair, Ben-

Gurion style. His acquaintances remember him as a humorless person, given to pathos, who was part political functionary, part educator and part bohemian intellectual. Born into an Ashkenazi family in Bokhara, he came to Israel in 1922, at the age of 21, after having participated in some Zionist conferences. In Israel he worked at first as a construction worker and then attended the teachers' college in Jerusalem. In the early 1930s he studied in Berlin, where he created a Jewish cultural center. A few months after the Nazis came to power he returned to Tel Aviv and took charge of the cultural activities of the association of immigrants from Germany. His secretary, Bronya Bendek, remembers him travelling all over the country by bus, in an effort to expand the evening Hebrew courses which he, himself, had begun. Municipal and local council heads, as well as the secretaries of local labor councils, learned that he would give them no rest until they too opened such evening courses. He was likewise persistent in extracting contributions for a special cultural fund, to finance the activities of the cultural department of the Jewish Agency.[19] He wrote study programs and textbooks, and in 1949 was one of the moving spirits behind the "Etsion" school, the first *Ulpan*, Hebrew school for immigrants, which was named after him when he died.

Levin was an honest, well-intentioned man, yet he tended to identify the Zionist ideal with MAPAI's ideological platform. He was inspired by a dream in which "an Israeli mentality" reflected "the true spirit" of the State of Israel, namely, "the spirit of the glorious Labor movement." All this he put down in his diary. Once he proposed to voice these ideas in a public lecture, but in the end preferred to keep them to himself. His widow preserved the draft of that lecture in which Levin wrote and then crossed out the following:

> The very first thing that the new immigrant must be introduced to, as soon as he lands in Israel, is our common ground, which is—the spiritual force created here largely, or perhaps exclusively, by the Labor movement, and which is now shared by the population as a whole and by the state itself, as the first general elections to the Knesset have shown. This is the will of the people that dwelleth in Zion. . . . Whoever is not attracted by it or is unwilling to accept it, can wait for the next elections. . . .[20]

This was the basic premise of the education that Nahum Levin had conducted in the Displaced Persons camps in Europe. It served him likewise when he supervised the education of immigrant children, which he did almost exclusively for nearly two years.

The comprehensive study program which he introduced in the camps differed from the programs of the four established systems but combined elements of them. After rising, the children had physical exercises, then prayers and breakfast, after which they studied for four hours. They had lunch at midday and then worked in the flower garden, engaged in sports and other social activities, including "discussions with the community's spiritual leader." They had another hour for prayer in the evening. Six hours a week were devoted to Hebrew, five to math, four to Bible, three to "Homeland Studies"—a total of 18 hours a week. Another program, of 30 hours a week, added two hours to Bible studies, and one more each to "Homeland Studies" and math. The additional hours were devoted to Jewish history, general geography, singing, handicrafts and athletics. Other than Bible studies, Levin included no religious lessons of any kind. The Bible was to be taught "in the traditional manner to which they have been accustomed in the religious schools." However, apparently this was not really the intention, for the next line reads, "The Bible must be taught from the viewpoint of the Land of Israel, as it concerns us today. It is not enough to explain the text or offer a facile historical interpretation—the text must be taught so as to illustrate the life of the people in its country, emphasizing the local geographical and natural elements." The teachers were to make use of maps and pictorial material for the purpose.[21] In his diary Levin asked himself what was "the secret of the great power of our national revival." He then answered his own question.

> We have freed the biblical texts of their archaic quality and restored to them their concrete content: *Six days shalt thou labor—Thou shalt love thy neighbor as thyself—That which is altogether just shalt thou pursue—Proclaim liberty throughout all the land unto all her inhabitants—.* . . . These have become the foundations of the worldview which we have sought to achieve in the cooperative and communal settlements in particular, and in the Labor movement in general.

Levin instructed his subordinates to introduce the history of Zionism and the pioneer movement in the first years of school:

"The immigrant children must be inculcated with love of physical labor in general and agricultural work in particular," he declared, and this was to be implemented by means of work in the garden and at various handicrafts. The program also included regular Friday evening celebrations, as well as the celebration of Holy Days. But only in the "traditional classes," which were to be created in "certain camps, according to need," were the teachers to pay extra attention to prayers and the religious Law. Those classes, too, according to the program, were to be in all other ways subject to the general regulations of the school. Few "traditional classes" were actually opened.

Levin was conscious of a conflict between the need to instill in the new immigrants—particularly those from Yemen—what he called "the spirit of the state," on the one hand, and "ancient tradition" on the other. He stated:

> This is a unique problem. I had known this tribe before, but my work brought me closer to them still. It is a noble tribe, perhaps the noblest of the tribes of Israel. Its enthusiasm, warmth and innocence are all blended together. Yet the Yemenites are very primitive. I have never seen such primitiveness elsewhere. And I say it as plainly as I can: we must build a bridge between them and the State of Israel. The question is, what kind of bridge will enable us to reach the Yemenites and them to reach us. My experience tells me, that it has to be the attraction of the state itself. There is only one language which they understand and want and which attracts them, and that is the language of the state. They are happy to have come to the State of Israel. Whenever I stand before them—as I have done more than once—I speak for the state. Then I feel no barriers between them and me. I tell you, the bridge of the state is the only bridge, the unfailing bridge, which can make citizens of the Yemenites. . . . After all, it is our duty and the duty of the state not to leave a Diaspora community in its Diaspora condition, but to make it a true partner in the tremendous and wondrous Israeli revolution, whose expression is the state.[22]

From time to time Levin would consult his colleagues about how to prevent the "kidnapping" of children by the religious institutions. This problem worried him no less—perhaps even more, as it was more extensive—than the activities of the Communist party in the camps. The latter was not banned because it was, as he noted in his diary, "a legitimate party." The religious institutions, however, he saw as aiming at goals which "sometimes conflict with the interests of the state."[23] "Any attempt to introduce the different systems into the camps would lead to division and a cultural war," explained Levin later. "From the viewpoint of the nation and our movement, it is imperative to preserve the unity of the education in the camps." He always maintained that he had also prevented the Labor school system from being introduced into the camps. Although Levin admitted that he had fought to prevent the introduction of religious schools in the camps, nevertheless he maintained that he was always careful to provide religious services for anyone who asked for them.[24] When he told the youth leaders that they must let the immigrants pray as much as they wanted to, he had intended to add that he was only raising the issue "because otherwise it could create problems, and then the youngsters would be turned over to those whom we would prefer to keep out." But he deleted this sentence from his lecture draft.[25] He noted in his diary that it was best to remove the children from the traditional religious school and to separate them from their parents. There were at this time about 7,000 children in the Yemenite camps. This was the background for the creation of the special youth camps, which were opened alongside the immigrant camps. It is easier to influence young people, Levin explained, and bring about "a change of values" among them than among the older people. Eventually, he hoped, they would adopt the "Israeli mentality" and perhaps communicate it to their parents. And who knows, they might even be able to uproot some of the superstitions they had brought with them from the desert.

Some time later the story of how this was actually done in the Ein Shemer camp was told by an old and dignified Yemenite rabbi, Moshe Yehiel Itzhak Levi. One day the director of the camp's cultural activities, Yehiel Aharon Aldema, announced that it had been decided to open a youth camp. The rabbi recalled:

> And what is a youth camp, we asked. He said it was meant for children between 14 and 18. We told him it was out of the question to have boys and girls in it together. The sinful impulse would prevent them from studying. He said the separation of boys and girls would be arranged. He rounded up everybody in the camp and made a speech about the youth camp: they would pray in the morning, then eat, then study Hebrew and math for two hours, then work in the fields and exercise. Then they would say evening prayers and then eat. After supper they would sing songs.

The people agreed and placed the children in the camp. But it turned out that there was no separation between boys and girls. They were studying together, boys on one side and girls on the other. The parents protested before the rabbis that this went against the received Law, and that it would ruin their children. The other promises were not kept either—there was no study of the Torah nor any prayers. I went to see my nephew Meir, who had been in the country longer than I and was working in the camp, and reproved him. He said it was not true. I went to look and found the boys and girls in one room. So he took the girls out of there and said they would study separately in the afternoon. The children's parents said he took them out to dance, and they decided that they didn't want their children in the youth camp. The camp remained, but many parents removed their children. Only the orphans remained.

The rabbi did not object when they proposed to show films in the camp, because they told him the films would teach the people "how to fight." Then he realized that he had been misled, because the films showed "men and women embracing." The dancing and the films enraged the parents not only because of the "immorality" they saw in them. As Rabbi Untermann, then Tel Aviv's Chief Rabbi, put it, "They draw the children to the cinema, they take boys and girls to dance, and then they rebel against their parents." And this, indeed, was the intention, as Nahum Levin spelled it out in his diary. The camp authorities maintained that the films had been made by the Jewish National Fund. According to them, it all started when they arranged a meeting between the immigrant children and the children of Kfar Vitkin, a nearby village, who were "orderly, well brought-up Israeli youngsters," as the Ein Shemer camp supervisor put it. The Israeli children sang "Israeli folksongs, songs of labor and heroism." It was true that they came wearing shorts, both boys and girls, and taught the camp children their dances. "If dancing the *hora* [an Israeli folk dance] is immoral—then they were immoral," said the supervisor, Yaakov Trachtenberg. He was deeply hurt—"thanks to the *hora* [which was quite popular among the first Zionist settlers in Palestine] we got our State of Israel," he said.[26]

One day the youth instructor of the Beer Yaakov camp, Nathan Maimoni, entered the class of Gitta Landau and announced to the girls that that evening there would be folkdancing in the club. The teacher objected—she disapproved of the permissive atmosphere in the club and she forbade her pupils to go there. Maimoni persisted. He told her he represented the Cultural Department of the Jewish Agency not any political party or movement. But she remained adamant. The following Saturday two representatives of the orthodox Agudat Israel party came to the camp and warned the people in the synagogue against the club. They described Maimoni as a leftist extremist. The teacher, Gitta Landau, organized separate Friday evening celebrations for boys and girls. Maimoni regarded them as deliberate confrontations.

The affair has been preserved in the files because Maimoni later claimed that while he was arguing with Landau, in front of the pupils, she declared that admiration for Theodore Herzl, the father of Zionism, was "idol worship," for which statement she was called up before Nahum Levin, who recorded their conversation:

> Levin: "What you said about Herzl, as Maimoni reported, is a very serious charge against you. If you admit it, there can be no connection between us, and you cannot teach within our system. If you deny it, we shall appoint a committee to investigate it."
>
> Landau: "I said it and I do not retract my opinion, which is shared by many people in Israel. I did not mean to say that Herzl himself is 'idol worship,' but rather that bringing his bones over [from Austria for the burial in Israel] is an alien ritual."
>
> Levin: "The function of the state, as distinct from the function of the political parties, is to bring people together. . . . You must never forget that you are representing the state here in Beer Yaakov, and as such you must act according to the instructions and the spirit of the state. . . . The youth instructor may not work with your pupils without your consent, but I am sure you will not be able to isolate them and stop them from taking part in the general activities of the camp. . . ."

As it happened, Gitta Landau's father was the Chief Rabbi of Bnei Brak, a town near Tel Aviv, and he reported the story to Chief Rabbi Uziel, who sent Levin a letter of protest. The unfortunate Levin had to promise for the umpteenth time that the club in Beer Yaakov was not engaged in antireligious activity, but was only giving the young people a "non-partisan Zionist education."[27] It was not easy to find one's way between "the spirit of the state" and the "ancient tradition."

His son, Eviatar Levin, recalled that his father was "profoundly attached" to Jewish tradition. He did not observe its rules, but at home they did light candles on Friday and on the Day of Atonement he attended the synagogue.[28] Levin himself once stated, in a letter to Minister of Education Zalman Shazar, that he was not a religious man, but that his attitude toward religion and tradition was "respectful."[29] He claimed that the cultural activity in the Yemenite camps was of "a religious nature," and that half the teachers employed by his department were religious. The department did everything possible to ensure that the immigrants would be able to observe the Law—it had sent to the camps prayerbooks, Passover *Haggadahs* (prayer books), and many *Megilloth* (scrolls of Esther), etc.[30] However, in his opinion all this served to strengthen the divisive element and weaken the unifying force. As he saw it, the secret of unity lay in the secular national pioneering spirit. He bore the heavy responsibility as best he could, and only thanks to him and to the staff of his department did the children in the camps get any education at all. But Levin had failed to comprehend that many, though not all, were repelled by his national pioneering and clung to their traditions.

Many immigrants complained that they were compelled to violate their religion, referring to a series of actions—some of them perfectly innocent and others quite deliberate—which they viewed as a threat to their right and ability to maintain their orthodox ways. Most of the acts they protested were done with no evil intent at all—as, for example, the removal of some furniture from the hut that served as the camp synagogue to the youth camp. Or a study hour which had been devoted to prayers and was re-assigned to sports. Or an instructor who took his youngsters on a hike one Saturday morning and suggested that they pick oranges in a grove on their way. Or a youth instructor who had a disagreement with the local rabbi.

The rumor that Yemenite children were being forced to cut off their ritual sidelocks caused such a furor that the government, anxious to placate the ministers from religious parties, appointed a committee to investigate the matter. The Committee's Chairman Gad Frumkin was the son of one of the founders of the Yemenite quarter in the village of Silwan, near Jerusalem, which was created at the turn of the century. He had served as a Supreme Court Justice during the British Mandate, but having been accused of taking bribes he was not asked to remain in his post after the establishment of the state. Some of the Committee's findings were of doubtful worth, but when members of the

committee went to the camps they did hear some shocking stories. There was the boy who was sent to the barber as soon as he
reached the camp. "He told the barber to cut the hair on his head
but not his sidelocks," his uncle recalled. "The barber said, 'You
don't need the sidelocks,' and cut them off without permission,
and the boy cried." Another boy, who would not reveal his name
for fear of harassment, described how his sidelocks had been
forcibly removed: "One person held me down and another cut
them off." Shaul Sharabi, of the youth camp in Beit Lidd, testified: "The instructress went to Camp II, brought a barber and
told him to cut the children's hair. I said to leave the sidelocks,
but she said, You don't need sidelocks in Israel. They left us a little hair on the top of the head. I didn't see any lice or diseases.
. . . I said it was forbidden and she said it was allowed." Seadya
Yehuda Avraham was one of the children in that group, whose
instructress was called Tsipora Zahavi. "Tsipora brought a barber from Camp II and said, 'Whoever wants to go on a trip must
get a haircut.' Five children got haircuts. I didn't have any hair,
so they had nothing to cut, only the sidelocks. Tsipora told me
that if I didn't get them cut off I'd be thrown out. . . ."[31] Zahavi
admitted that she had brought the barber, but said she did it for
health reasons. In reply to a question she admitted that the children had not been examined by a doctor or a nurse. She denied
threatening or cajoling the children to get their hair cut. So did
other instructors, but the Committee heard many boys, all of
whom insisted that their sidelocks had been cut off against their
will. In one of the children's dormitories they heard the children
adding, after the blessing of the food, a plea that "the All Merci-
ful punish Tsipora." It would seem that their prayer was heard,
because when the Committee's findings were published, Zahavi
was dismissed from her post.

Even before the Frumkin Committee's findings were released, David Ben-Gurion appointed another investigative committee to look into complaints that had reached him from the
village of Ameka in Western Galilee, which had been built a few
months previously for immigrants from Yemen. The villagers
charged that religious teachers were prevented from coming to
the village and that those who were already there were under
threat of expulsion. They also claimed that religious studies in
the village were being deliberately sabotaged by army maneu-
vers, complete with explosions and the like. The affair was

brought up in the Knesset and discussed by the press. The chief supervisor of the Labor movement's educational system, Yaakov Halperin, justified all that had been done in the village, which was associated with the MAPAI Cooperative Settlement Movement. "Any deviation from the policy of the movement disrupts the life in the place and undermines the proper function of its general and cultural spirit," he wrote.[32]

A year later a third investigative committee was appointed, headed by Ministers I.M. Levin and Golda Meir. They heard testimonies about the conduct of certain army personnel who had been sent to help out in the Yemenite camp of Yessir: ". . . The first day after the arrival of the army, the doctor told me that he was going to order all beards and sidelocks cut off, on account of the lice. . . . Lt. Colonel Kuperstock came on the third day and said he would send a teacher. I told him that we belonged to the orthodox Agudat Israel system. He said he didn't recognize it, that the army was in charge here and the army did not recognize the different systems. . . . The soldiers summoned the women to the medical orderly's room. One of the orderlies stripped them by force and they were naked and crying. They dusted them [with DDT]. . . . The big officer asked, 'How many children do you have?' Everyone had four or five children. 'You don't need so many children,' he said. We said, 'What could we do?—We go to the women and they get pregnant.' He said, 'Spill the seed on the ground.' We said it was forbidden. He said, 'Ask for a rubber at the general store.' We said it was forbidden. He said, 'You have to do it that way.' We said the Patriarch Jacob had twelve sons, the twelve tribes. He said, 'Are you wealthy like the Patriarch Jacob? You have nothing to live on. You don't need many children.' We said that the flood was a punishment for the spilling of seed. . . ."*

In his testimony before the Frumkin Committee, Nahum Levin confirmed that there was "fraternal dissension" between the religious and the nonreligious in the camps, but he charged

---

*Golda Meir assured the witnesses who appeared before the committee that the government would protect their religious way of life. However, she could not resist saying to them that if they were clean there would be no need to cut off their beards and sidelocks. "The Torah Law also demands that you keep clean."[33] The inhabitants of Rosh Haayin complained that there was no ritual bath in their camp. The camp authorities proposed to send the women to the ritual bath in Petah Tikvah, but the women were ashamed to travel there together by bus. As a result, the men could not cohabit with their wives.[34]

that it stemmed from the "divisive poison" instilled among the immigrants by "antiZionist agitators and propagandists"— meaning, the Agudat Israel.[35] Agitation in the camps reached a climax when the camp police in Ein Shemer arrested two young rabbinical students from Bnei Brak who had distributed a leaflet among the immigrants, saying among other things, that there was a conspiracy to "turn your hearts from your faith and the Law, to subvert your pure and innocent children and cause them to violate the Sabbath, and eat nonkosher food." The leaflet called upon the camp residents to elect a watchdog committee to stand guard over the preservation of religious observance. It went on to promise them that "tens of thousands of faithful Jews will support you, so you need not sell your souls for bread."

To Colonel Hoter-Ishai, the jurist, and Lt. Colonel Nehemiah Argov, Ben-Gurion's military secretary, these words amounted to "a call to rebellion." The two were sent by Ben-Gurion to the Ein Shemer camp following a violent outbreak there on February 14, 1950. That day, about 3:30 p.m., the two rabbinical students from Bnei Brak turned up in the camp and circulated the leaflet among the immigrants. The camp supervisor asked them to identify themselves and they refused, at which point he summoned a policeman. In their report to Ben-Gurion, Hoter-Ishai and Argov reconstructed the subsequent events. While the policeman was interrogating the two men in the supervisor's office, an angry crowd gathered outside and shouted for the release of the "two rabbis." There were between 50 and 60 people outside the hut—according to Ben-Gurion's investigators. There were about 1,000 people—according to Behor Shitrit, Minister of Police, in his statement in the Knesset.[36] One way or the other, tempers were rising fast. All the efforts made by the policeman, the supervisor, one of the community elders, and even by one of the detained rabbinical students, to calm the crowd were in vain. The two rabbinical students, standing outside the supervisor's door, began to say the evening prayers, which stopped the uproar for a while, but as soon as the prayers were over, it began again. Stones began to fly at the supervisor's hut. Moshe Yehiel Itzhak Levi, the community's old spiritual leader, came out and tried to soothe his congregation, but he too was stoned, and was only saved by the supervisor who drew him inside. The supervisor himself was hit on the forehead by a stone. Three more camp policemen who arrived on the scene were stoned, and one of them was hit on the head. The riot went on for a long time. When the rioters began to pull up the iron stakes of the recently planted trees, police reinforcements arrived and succeeded in dispersing the crowd. They had to fire their shotguns over their heads in the process.

The two investigators whom Ben-Gurion had dispatched to the camp after the riot reported that they had informed the immigrants on his behalf that

> (a) Every person in Israel is free to choose his way of life and bring up his children accordingly; (b) The State of Israel will not tolerate acts of violence, and any attempt to solve social or other problems by violent outbreaks and disorders will be stopped at once.

The minutes of their meeting with the camp residents report the officials as saying,

> Ben-Gurion has a special feeling for you Yemenites. . . . He will not rest until he has brought every Yemenite Jew to Israel. . . . We are all Jews. . . . Let each one bring up his children as he wishes, in the ways of the Law and tradition. . . . It is forbidden to kill Jews. . . . Ben-Gurion said that whoever raises his hand to another would go to prison, and you, the elders, will be held responsible.

The elders of the community asked to send Ben-Gurion their blessings and good wishes, and promised to obey him.[37]*

But the unrest in the camp did not cease. Before long it spread to other camps and from there to the political arena. This was a battle over the politicization of the immigrants. MAPAI wanted them for itself, and so did the religious parties. Zalman Aran, Secretary General of MAPAI, stated: "When we say that the religious education, the Kosher laws, the Sabbath, must be preserved, that does not mean entrusting the educational system exclusively to religious people. As soon as this is done . . . it becomes a political monopoly."[40] Itzhak Refael, of Hapoel Hamizrahi, believed that the struggle would determine the future of the religious parties: "If, God forbid, we fail in this struggle, then nothing short of a miracle will save us."[41] The immi-

---

*On the basis of the report submitted by the two officers, Ben-Gurion hastened to write to Ministers Maimon and Levin that "the tales of beards and sidelocks being cut off are without foundation. . . ."[38] He also wrote to Braha Tidhar, an instructor at the Rosh Haayin camp, that the officers had described to him "with enthusiasm and admiration" all her good works in that camp. The Prime Minister wished to thank her for her "sacred endeavor."[39]

grants themselves were not called upon to participate in the dispute. It was generally assumed, of course, that they would not understand what was going on. Before long the affair became a major political crisis.

D.T. Pincas was a skillful parliamentarian, an economist and jurist. The parliamentary correspondents covering the first Knesset chose him as their Man of the Year. They attributed to him the considerable prestige of the Finance Committee, which he headed. Pincas had previously headed the "Committees' Committee," which laid the groundwork for the Knesset's rules, and before that was one of those who drafted the Law and Administration Ordinance, as well as the Declaration of Independence. James Yaakov Rosenthal, the doyen of Israeli parliamentary correspondents, recalls him as a well-dressed man, a typical *bon vivant* Tel Avivian, whose speech combined a certain didactic quality, Jewish wit, Viennese repartee and Prussian precision.[42] Pincas could be said to have been born into the religious Mizhrahi party. His father, who brought him from Hungary to Vienna at the age of eight, was one of the founders of the religious Mizrahi movement in Austria, and Pincas himself joined in its younger circles in his youth. Before long he served as a delegate at the movement's conferences and on the central committees of various organizations. He studied law at the University of Vienna and worked in his father's bank. When he arrived in Palestine in 1925, age 30, he was appointed director of the Mizrahi Bank in Tel Aviv. His party was the chief interest in his life. Within a year of his immigration he married an adopted daughter of Rabbi Yaakov Bermann of Jerusalem, one of the leaders of Mizrahi. Before he became a member of the first Knesset, he had already served in a dozen different posts, from the Rabbinical Burial Society to the Haifa Institute of Technology. His salary was paid by the Tel Aviv municipality, where for years he headed the education department. He would also serve one day as Tel Aviv's Deputy Mayor. When he was still a member of the pre-Independence Representative Assembly and of the National Council, it was plain to everyone that his ultimate ambition was to serve as a Cabinet Minister in the future Government of Israel. After the creation of the state, Pincas resolved to have Rabbi I.L. Fishmann (Maimon) removed from his position as Minister of Religious Affairs which was the Cabinet post that

was traditionally given to Mizrahi.* Pincas and Maimon loathed
each other for personal reasons, but they were also diametrically
opposed on issues concerning religion and state, on domestic
problems and on the Arab-Israeli conflict. Pincas' views were
more to the right than Maimon's, and also more hawkish.† Pincas, skillful at political intrigue, took advantage of the dispute
over the education in the immigrant camps to strengthen his
own political position. At a meeting of the Knesset Education
Committee Pincas charged as follows:

> The activity now taking place in the immigrant camps can be de-
> scribed, in the mildest terms, as oppression and coercion in the
> spirit of [the Spanish] Inquisition against the Jewish faith. . . . There
> has definitely been deliberate action aimed against the Jewish reli-
> gion [in the camps]. I say that never before have the Jewish people
> experienced such coercion and exploitation of the helpless immi-
> grants [now residing] in the camps. They are being forced to aban-
> don their faith and their reason. The day before yesterday the Knes-
> set debated the international antigenocide convention, and I hereby
> state, with full responsibility, that the actions of Mr. Nahum Levin
> and his aides are cultural and religious genocide.[44]

Others also expressed themselves in harsh terms, "They look
upon the Oriental communities as if they were cattle," said
Rabbi Betsalel Cohen of Mizrahi. "They are beaten and humiliated because the Establishment can't stand religious people."[45]
The religious daily *Hatzofeh* described the immigrant camps as
"MAPAI's occupied territory."[46] But D.T. Pincas went further
than all of them: "I have in my possession facts which will show
that the camps are concentration camps of the kind that were
called *Katset*," he said in the Knesset.[47] The *Katsets* (German:
K.Z. for *Konzentrationslager*) were the Nazi concentration
camps. Pincas initiated and promoted a number of public pro-

---

*Ben-Gurion had assumed that the religious bloc would choose Pincas to
represent it in the first government, after the first Knesset elections, but he
was mistaken. "Rabbi Meir Berlin (Bar-Ilan, leader of Mizrahi) came, and not
Pincas, as I expected. . . . Then came the religious bloc leaders. Pincas' face fell
when he heard Rabbi Berlin appointing Fishmann as [a] member of the Cabinet."[43]

†James Rosenthal recalled that Pincas used to be very friendly with opposition leader Menahem Begin, with whom he used to exchange learned quotes in
Latin, which Rosenthal would interpret for the bystanders in the Knesset dining room.

tests, in Israel and abroad, including mass rallies and rabbinical excommunications. He kept urging his comrades in the Mizrahi, with Maimon at their head, to fight relentlessly until David Ben-Gurion's coalition government fell. He believed that in the next government he would replace Maimon.

Pincas' Inquisition speech was widely echoed abroad, and forced Minister of Education Shazar to intervene, though he would have preferred his Ministry's supervisors to sort out their differences by themselves. Shazar was, of course, aware that the Compulsory Education Law required him to make all the school systems available in the immigrant camps, but he often tended to disregard the letter of the law. Widely known as *Reb* Zalman, Shazar was a follower of the *Habbad* Hassidic movement and a tireless speaker, who could "talk on any subject that comes to hand until he runs out of breath."* He tried to steer the dispute over the immigrants' education into calmer water, but failed. He reached a compromise with the religious bloc, but his colleagues in MAPAI felt he had gone too far in satisfying the demands of the religious, and voted against the agreed terms. This happened once, twice, three and four times—the Minister would hold talks, conclude terms of agreement, only to have his party send him back to renegotiate the whole deal. It was rather pathetic. The leaders of MAPAI grew very angry at Shazar's compromises. Israel Gouri warned against the "great extortion" which, he claimed, the Mizrahi was trying to bring off. Beba Idelson saw it this way. "We have to see the ramifications of our decisions, or we shall be abandoning the children to the Jesuits." Zalman Aran feared what he called "a compromise with madness."[49]

They were equally incensed about the composition of the Frumkin Committee which was to investigate religious education in the camps. Zalman Shazar told them that Ben-Gurion had chosen the committee without consulting the others, following Rabbi Maimon's statement in the Cabinet that children

---

Maariv's editor, Azriel Karlebach, wrote about him as follows:

Reb Zalman had no need for position, power or government ministries. All he needed was a band of faithful followers to accompany him everywhere he went, attentive to his every utterance, ready to catch the fragments of ideas that floated through his head, and provide him with the audience he needed to clothe the intangible sparks in his mind with words which would echo in their minds and return to fertilize his imagination, sailing into the great blue yonder and plunging into the abysses of oblivion and soaring to the firmanent of distant vision, to the great delectation of both rabbi and flock. . . .[48]

were being forced "to give up their religion."[50] Ben-Gurion had in fact stated, before he set up the committee, that if it turned out that the charges made by the religious bloc were true, he would immediately resign.[51] Aran complained, "Except for our comrade Itzhak Ben-Tsvi, the Frumkin Committee is made up entirely of bourgeois-religious elements." All the members of the committee had studied in rabbinical schools in their childhood. Two were rabbis—MKs Kalmann Kahana and Avraham Shaag-Tsvebner—both members of the religious bloc. Shazar felt that the conflict had little to do with the situation in the camps: "The religious bloc has found out that we intend to broaden the coalition, which would mean a general reorganization and redistribution of the Ministries, including the Interior. So then the [religious] bloc decided to launch a general crusade, in order to protect their positions."[52] Nahum Levin, however, who was present at that meeting, offered a broader context for the conflict. "The war which the religious bloc has launched on our educational endeavor in the immigrant camps is only the beginning of a general assault on the country's culture. This is not a war for religion, but for political influence over immigration and for determining the future character of the State of Israel."[53]

When the crisis intensified, Ben-Gurion took over control of the negotiations from Shazar and began to conduct direct talks with the three Ministers of the religious bloc, I.M. Levin, Maimon and Shapira. They approached the issue as pragmatically as they knew how, often overlooking ideological differences and widely disparate world views, in order to prevent a deepening gulf between the religious and the nonreligious populations, and to preserve the existing coalition. Rabbi Levin contributed to the joint effort by commenting that the sidelocks of the Yemenites were of little importance: "A religious Jew may be without sidelocks," he said, "and a nonreligious one may have sidelocks.[54] He himself grew his sidelocks, but he tucked them under his hat on weekdays, and let them hang down to his shoulders only on the Sabbath.

Ben-Gurion tried hard to show his understanding of, and even sympathy for, the religious demands, in complete contrast to the antireligious trend which prevailed in his party. His letters to the religious leaders express conciliation and respect, "Even for a free-thinking Jew like myself, our faith is still something that requires respect, and any Jew who does not revere Judaism in one way or another is alien to Jewish history," he once wrote to the "comrade rabbis" Maimon and Levin.[55] He had earlier written to Maimon concerning Pincas' threat to start a civil war: "I was horrified . . . to read such dreadful expressions in *Hatzofeh*." He said that he did not fear a civil war, but "what we had tried to prevent so far was a culture war—*Kulturkampf*, in German—I'm now afraid that it will break out and that would be a disaster to the state." He sought to convince Maimon that the religious would stand to gain nothing by such developments. It was a six-page letter in which Ben-Gurion tried, among other things, to force the religious bloc to decide whether to remain in the government coalition or to leave it. "If we are such a wicked and sinful community, as you describe us, then you should not remain in the government with us." However, he tried to make the letter as friendly as possible:

> It was my privilege to work with you at the creation of the state and I have come to respect you as a valuable, serious and devoted man, as well as a comrade and a friend. It will not be easy for me to part from you and your colleagues, and whatever happens in the political sphere, your image in my mind will not change, nor will my personal respect for you diminish.[56]

A week later Ben-Gurion wrote to the leaders of his own party:

> Any education that the state will provide (and I hope that before long all education will be in the hands of the state), will leave religious Jews the option of religious schooling. Plainly, a religious school is not one that I, or other nonreligious Jews, consider to be religious, but one which religious people will be satisfied with. Therefore . . . let the religious who want religious schools determine the criteria which make a school a religious one. No one should intervene in this—of course on condition that the State . . . will freely determine the obligatory studies, sanitary requirements, etc."[57]*

Negotiations with the religious ministers ran into the same difficulties as those which had faced the chief supervisors of the

*Ben-Gurion did, however, deny that the religious parties could have a monopoly on religious education. He encouraged the Histadrut to establish its own religious schools within the Labor movement system, and proposed that it appoint Yemenite principals, "If you can find any." At any rate, he stated, "It is better not to create a religious school than to do it hypocritically or dishonestly."[58]

school systems, including the question of what the secular system was to be called. In the meantime, agitation in the immigrant camps continued. In February 1950 the religious ministers
boycotted the Cabinet meetings. Moshe Shapira was unwilling
to do so, but he had to follow the example of his two colleagues,
and these were urged on by yet more extremist elements: I.M.
Levin had to placate the ultra-orthodox *Neturei Karta* movement and I.L. Maimon had to demonstrate to Pincas that he was
doing something. Ben-Gurion was unwell at the time and as
soon as he recovered he had a meeting with Minister Shapira and
informed him in no uncertain terms that the religious ministers
would either have to participate actively in the Cabinet meetings or withdraw from the Cabinet entirely. This was not quite
the end of the dispute, but within a few weeks the religious ministers returned to the Cabinet and an agreement was reached:
the Yemenite immigrant camps would have religious schools
only, supervised jointly by representatives of all four systems,
who would themselves be religious individuals. In the other
camps there would be two systems, one of which would be religious. It seems that they gave up the attempt to name the
"other" system. The two systems would have separate buildings, and any problem that could not be resolved at the local
level, would be brought before a special ministerial committee
of four, divided evenly between religious and non-religious ministers. In this way the camps were opened to the religious parties' educational system and the religious ministers won what
was in effect a veto power in solving disagreements. To make
the arrangement perfectly legal, they amended the Compulsory
Education Law, to the effect that the principle of registration according to school system of choice would not apply in the immigrant camps as if they were extra-territorial domains.

The arrangement did not last. When they began to transfer
immigrants from the immigrant camps to the Maabaroth the issue arose once more. MAPAI declared that the arrangement
agreed upon for the immigrant camps was not applicable to the
Maabaroth. The religious bloc maintained that it was. The dependence of the Maabaroth residents on the labor exchanges of
the Histadrut enabled MAPAI to influence them and even to
compel them to send their children to the Labor movement
schools. It therefore proposed that the Maabaroth be opened to
all the systems. The religious parties, of course, preferred the ar-

rangement which had prevailed in the immigrant camps and had
enabled them to gain some influence among the immigrants.
They were also well aware of the power of the camp administra-
tors. "The administration must be religious. Even the janitor
must be religious," stated Rabbi Betsalel Cohen. "Just as the
Histadrut is the body that workers turn to, so the religious parties must be the body that people turn to in matters of religion."[59]

The row went on and on and meanwhile the children were
not getting any education at all. Two religious educators, outstanding scholars, who would soon move on to the academic
world, found themselves in the thick of the battle. The first was
an inveterate rebel, original, brilliant, infuriating, a voice of conscience, who in his old age would become a political outcast—
Professor Yeshayahu Leibowitz. The other was a member of the
establishment—cautious, moderate and greatly respected—Professor Efraim Elimeleh Urbach. Leibowitz was a member of the
religious Labor movement. He resigned when MAPAI sought to
take over the movement's newly formed school system. "It was
a disgraceful affair," he said years later. "MAPAI fell on it and
fought over it with the religious parties. They acted like share-
holders trying to take over a bank."[60] Urbach, a member of the
Mizrahi, who ran its department for education in the immigrant
camps, resigned in protest when MAPAI proposed to introduce
all the systems into the Maabaroth. Years later he said:

> I saw that it was hopeless. There weren't any blackboards or chalk,
> not to mention benches and desks. The children sat on the sand.
> There weren't even any teachers. Today I don't blame them for not
> providing more, and they did have other things to worry about,
> aside from education, but it seemed to me that they were more pre-
> occupied with party politics than with any other matter and that
> made me feel disgusted with the whole thing.[61]

The problem remained unresolved; it grew even more acute
and four months later it led to the fall of Ben-Gurion's second
Cabinet and to general elections. Two years later, the State Education Law was passed, which was supposed to put an end to the
division of religious and secular schools into separate systems.
The Labor movement system had by this time become the biggest of the four, and its heads expected that it would set the tone
for the entire state education system. It did not: the Labor movement schools were in fact integrated into the general state sys-

tem, in effect bringing about the end of the leftist schools in the cities. In reality Labor's socialist school system had begun to decline before it was formally superseded. The vast numbers of religious immigrant children engulfed by the system remained alien to socialist ideology, faithful to their religious traditions. MAPAI did try to satisfy their religious needs through the Labor religious system as well as through other means, thereby blurring its own ideological direction. Also, as the Labor system grew larger, it had to recruit more and more teachers who were strangers to its principles. Thus the "working-class schools" lost their special distinction and became increasingly like the General schools. The State Education Law merged the two secular school systems into one and its tenor was set by the General system. Meanwhile the religious schools continued to teach in their own way, being only administratively affected by the change. Under the supervision of the Ministry of Education the religious school system remained in the hands of the Mizrahi and later the National Religious party.

And all this time, with the fight over the immigrants' education continuing to arouse passions, the Frumkin Committee continued its investigations. In May 1950 it determined that it had been "a fatal error" to entrust that education to Nahum Levin and his staff. The committee stated that it had not found that "a deliberate war on religion" had been waged in the camps, and thus there was "no justification" in comparing Nahum Levin's work with the persecutions of the Spanish Inquisition. What Levin and his staff had tried to do was to speed up the immigrants' adaptation to life in Israel.

Their basic error had been to "apply their own criteria, or the criteria applied to immigrants from Europe." In this context the committee specifically referred to the immigrants from Yemen, Tripoli and Morocco. It stated that Levin and his assistants systematically prevented people from praying, from teaching the Torah and observing the Sabbath, and that they tried to persuade them, and in many cases compelled them, to cut off their sidelocks, all this in an effort to speed up their integration into Israeli society. The committee's report quoted many witnesses who had repeated the statement which they had heard again and again: "In Israel there is no need for sidelocks." The committee's findings were not surprising. "We have no confidence in such a government committee," said MAPAM's Feige Ilanit, MK. "It was designed to placate the religious bloc, rather than to discover the truth."[62] One of the committee's members, Rabbi Kalmann Kahana, confirmed this many years later, saying, "They understood how we felt."[63] The committee always stopped its sessions in the afternoon, to enable its members to say the evening prayer. Kahana: "It was a pleasant and very objective committee."

Nahum Levin awaited the outcome of the investigation perfectly calmly. He had not a doubt in the world that the committee would exonerate him completely. He was a naive man who believed in what he was doing and could not imagine that MAPAI would do him an injustice. Then one morning, at breakfast, he heard over the radio that the Minister of Education had "accepted his resignation." He could not believe his own ears, and simply assumed that the broadcast was mistaken. Soon afterwards he heard that this was the way they meant to get rid of him. Eviatar Levin remembered:

> Father went to Ben-Gurion and Ben-Gurion told him that someone had to resign, but that it would be inconvenient to dismiss the Minister of Education. Father was such a loyal and docile MAPAI man, that he accepted the verdict without a struggle. Ben-Gurion suggested putting him in charge of education in the army, in place of Aharon Zeev, but Father and Zeev were friends, and he did not want his friend to lose his post on his account. So he gave it up. The report hurt him badly. What hurt most was that Ben-Tsvi had had a hand in it. I believe he never recovered from it.[64]

Other persons dismissed with Levin were the coordinator of cultural activities in the Ein Shemer camp, Y.A. Aldema, and Tsipora Zahavi of the Beit Lidd camp.

Some of their associates and party comrades tried to help them—they wrote letters expressing their solidarity, published favorable articles in the Histadrut's daily Davar and lobbied in the Knesset. The Cultural Department staff went on strike to protest the committee's report and express solidarity with Nahum Levin. They demanded a new investigation. One of them, Yosef Shaked, spoke with Ben-Gurion. He told the Prime Minister that an injustice had been done to Nahum Levin, and that he should be exonerated. Ben-Gurion listened, but all he asked was where he had previously met Shaked. "It took quite a long time," Shaked recalled years later. "We both tried to remember—was it at such-and-such a convention, or at another. At last we remembered that it had been at the nonpartisan convention in Haifa. Ben-Gurion said, 'Ah, that's it!' And that was all. As for Levin, he promised nothing."[65] Speaking in the Knesset, Ben-Gurion praised the "marvellous dedication of all the workers in the immigrant camps, especially the women" but said nothing about Levin: Levin's so-called resignation remained in force.[66]

Levin made some comments in his diary on the committee's report. Among other things he noted:

> The report does not even mention the affidavit signed by 14 of the Ein Shemer teachers, in which they categorically denied the story about the shorn sidelocks. . . . Has the committee considered the possibility that some of the Yemenite children had already become Ashkenazified through contacts with relatives who had been Ashkenazified for some time? . . . Was it proved beyond all reasonable doubt that the cultural workers had done those frightful things, or that even if one of them was involved, that it was a systematic thing?[67]

His widow, Dania Levin, recalled: "The Yemenite children would cut their own sidelocks off, because they wanted to look Ashkenazi. I myself once saw a Yemenite child cut off his sidelocks with a piece of broken glass."[68] Levin poured out his heart in his diary: "I don't know how many times in the past people have been treated as badly as I have. . . . Is mental murder less cruel than physical murder?" And in a small address book, almost furtively, Levin also wrote: "Precisely the man in whom I had had such faith, whom I believed to be not only the personification of this most glorious age, but the personification of conscience—this man has treated me so badly. . . ."

Pincas was a shrewd and ambitious man. He deliberately dramatized Levin's "sins," believing that the stronger he came out on the issue the better his chances to rise in his party and eventually become accepted as its leader. His main concern was politics. Nahum Levin's main concern was education. He honestly believed that the Yemenite children should be educated to become secular Israelis. His worst mistake was that he identified the future of Israel with David Ben-Gurion's MAPAI and the party's particular Social Democratic world view. The party was of course much more pragmatic than Levin had thought; it eventually forsook the good and faithful man, who would never come to appreciate the irony of this.

Levin was a rather narrow-minded man, unable and unwilling to accept the Yemenite immigrants as they were. He never appreciated their own values and their cultural heritage, which was inseparable from religion. For him, they were primitive people; he thought to make them in his own image, forcing them to adopt his Ashkenazi values and mentality. He meant no evil but did little good.

Ben-Gurion did not promise anything, but when he read the Frumkin report it made him uncomfortable, in part because it contradicted the findings of the two investigators he had earlier sent to the camps. Now he sent the document to Attorney Yaakov Shimshon Shapira, who had previously served as Attorney General. Ben-Gurion stated: "Mere reading of the report arouses many doubts. There is hearsay evidence that there is favorable bias toward a certain type of witness and an unfavorable bias toward another type. There is also a considerable distance between the report and its conclusions."[69]* In November 1950 Dania Levin wrote Ben-Gurion: "You promised to end this painful and unfair business upon Nahum's return from abroad. I beg you, please keep your promise. Nahum's health has been badly affected and he is also badly depressed. Please do everything to end this affair." She was asking for him to be cleared and given another appointment. Her appeal to the Prime Minister was supposed to be a secret—she said her husband did not know she had written to him. A few months later Nahum Levin himself wrote to Ben-Gurion and asked him to clear him officially in the Knesset.[71]

But Attorney General Haim Cohen—who was not then the liberal judge he would be in years to come—advised Ben-Gurion to let things stay as they were. Cohen's advice was convenient, and Ben-Gurion took it. Eviatar Levin remarked: "Had my father received a letter from Ben-Gurion clearing him, he would have died a happy man." He died in 1959, embittered and forgotten, and seems never to have known about the correspondence between Ben-Gurion, Shapira and Cohen. As Shapira put it 35 years later: "That was not a committee. It was a load of rubbish." Rabbi Kalmann Kahana: "Levin failed to understand that this movement of mass immigration was totally different from

---

*The same reservations caused the Cabinet to adopt the conclusions only "as a whole." It did not adopt them all, but dared not reject them publicly.[70]

the immigration movement which had brought him here. He wanted to force it to become something that it was not."*

In addition to its mandate "to investigate all the charges of [anti]religious coercion in the immigrant camps," the Frumkin committee was asked to inquire into "the accusations in the international press and who was behind them," as well as "the sources of overseas propaganda around the said accusations." Shazar said to the committee that "such a thing should never have been made known in the world, not even to Diaspora Jewry," as though it was a dreadful secret and could have been kept as such. The committee, wishing to make its own position perfectly plain, saw fit to assert: "None of these complaints is intended to be hostile to the State of Israel." Among other things, the committee looked into the origin of the protest demonstrations which had been staged by ultra-orthodox elements in New York. In order to verify that they had been initiated in Jerusalem, the committee had all copies of telegrams between the two cities made available to it. They were found to include one sent by Ben-Gurion himself—a reply to the "New York Religious Bloc," which had protested to the Prime Minister about the "immense scandal" purportedly taking place in the immigrant camps. In his reply, Ben-Gurion wrote:

> I received your telegram and made its contents known to the entire Cabinet. None of us would deny the right of any Jew to express an

---

*Looking back, the rabbi made another significant statement:

I blame Levin's education for trying to take away from the Oriental immigrants not only their religion, but also their communal and cultural identity. However, in this matter I blame us too. The religious education, too, failed to appreciate the culture which those people had brought with them from Yemen, Morocco and Turkey, and we did them harm by imposing our own religious education on them. There were Yemenite children who knew entire chapters of the Bible by heart, and I, a Hebrew teacher, taught them as if they didn't know any Hebrew, because their accent differed from mine. And what did I teach them?—The cat sat on the mat. I did them harm. Today I feel that it was a disaster, not only to the immigrants but to the whole country.[72]

On the other hand, Dr. Baruh Ben-Yehuda said, looking back:

Who harmed, what harmed?! Crisis?—there was no crisis! What we did have was to make sure that not a single child remained without an education. Nowhere in the world has there ever been such an educational enterprise, in such dimensions, with the number of children who arrived, and kept on arriving, and while they were pouring in, an entire educational system was created for them out of nothing, and that was done at a time of economic hardship, in the midst of an international struggle and a military threat against the very existence of the state. That's what there was![73]

opinion, or criticism, concerning events in Israel. However, it is surprising that you have taken a position in a grave matter of which you know nothing, and issued a verdict without giving the accused a chance to be heard, as the Law of Israel requires. No one in the Cabinet knows the source of the information which you quote. I am especially astonished by the strange threatening manner with which you address the Israeli Government. The State of Israel is a democratic republic, founded on liberty, freedom of conscience and religion, and all its affairs are decided by the majority of its citizens in accordance with their convictions. Rest assured that we shall do nothing under threat, if it is not just or necessary. If you wish to have a direct influence on the path taken by the State of Israel, and to strengthen a certain movement within it, the most effective way for you, and for those in whose names you speak, to do this, is to come here and settle in the country. I assure you that we shall one and all be glad to receive you.[74]

Thus, inadvertently, alongside the subject under discussion, the investigation extended to the relations between Israel and world Jewry—Zionist and non-Zionist—i.e., to one of the basic problems of Israeli sovereignty. The State of Israel as yet had no experience in dealing with such pressures, and did not know how to withstand them. The committee established a general rule in the matter: "The committee believes that it is the right of Diaspora Jewry to take an interest in what is happening in the State of Israel, in particular matters which concern all Jews, and insofar as it does not amount to intervention in the internal affairs of the state, to approach its government with appropriate suggestions and demands."[75] This, of course, was a very generalized statement which did little to clear up the problem. In any event, the protests from abroad worried the government, in part because it feared the adverse effects it would have on the United Jewish Appeal.

The committee dealt with the leaks to the press as if they thought someone had committed treason. Its members could not see why the debate about religious education in the immigrant camps would arouse foreign media interest, without a deliberate attempt to incite such interest. They were also doubtful that foreign correspondents had obtained the information legally. Altogether, exposure in the international press was a novel experience for the young state. The committee took pains to explain that the "source of the agitation abroad with regard to charges of [anti]religious coercion in the camps is to be found in the religious circles in Israel and in the Israeli press. The signal was given in a comment which was made in the Knesset Education Committee."[76] This was a reference to Pincas' Inquisition comment. Pincas never retracted his statement, but a year later he took great pains to explain it: "It was not necessary for me to use the word, *Inquisition*. Only the boundless anger, the pain and inconceivable outrage which I felt at hearing those stories about the camps, left me with no other means of expression. And if, in fact, a religious child was forced to receive a secular education, then I still maintain that that is Inquisition."[77]*

A few days after he had asked that question Pincas raised another issue which troubled him—transportation on the Sabbath. "If we were able to do so," he said in the Knesset, "we would stop it, and permit vehicles only . . . to transport the sick, for state security or to save a life."[79] He almost succeeded in this. The popularity he gained as a result of the education conflict did not succeed in making him Minister of Trade and Industry, as he had hoped when the government first had to resign as a result of its austerity program. But when he suddenly changed his attitude and began to support Ben-Gurion's "State Education," he was included in the Cabinet formed after the second general elections. He was appointed Minister of Transport, displacing the aged Minister of Religious Affairs, Rabbi Maimon, who had until then represented the Mizrahi in the government.

The following summer the government decided to restrict private transportation because of the cost of imported fuel. Private vehicles and taxis were to be immobilized for two days a week, and Minister of Transport Pincas determined that for private vehicles one of those days would be Saturday. The regulation provoked a furious reaction. Once again the phrases "culture war" and "civil war" were bandied about, and one day, as Pincas came home, a hand grenade was hurled at him from an ambush. The police subsequently arrested two men—a painter,

*Most of the charges voiced during the "Magic Carpet" Yemenite immigration period had also been made in various forms during the immigration at the end of World War II. They were alike in content, and were similarly connected with party politics. In 1944, too, the religious parties charged that immigrants were forced to cut off their sidelocks, and the man who discovered it was the same D.T. Pincas.[78]

Shaaltiel Ben-Yair and the journalist Amos Keynan, whose satir-
ical column in *Haaretz* was very popular in those days. The two
were tried for attempting to assassinate the Minister in protest
against his Sabbath regulation, but were acquitted for lack of evidence. By then Pincas was no longer alive. He had not been hurt
in the attempt on his life, and made skillful political capital
from a "thanksgiving" march organized to celebrate the "miracle." Two months later, a few hours after he had said to his personal aide that he had no intention of dying soon, he died of a
heart attack in his room at the King David Hotel in Jerusalem.

8

The Battle for the Sabbath

O N SATURDAY, MAY 28, 1949, the congregation of the Zihron Moshe quarter in Jerusalem gathered in a local synagogue to protest against the cinemas opening their box offices and starting the early show before the Sabbath was over. The problem had arisen just then as a result of daylight saving time. Chief Rabbi Uziel was there, Rabbi Avraham Haim Shaag, MK, and numerous other prominent rabbis. They rebuked and vilified the cinema owners, describing them as despicable cynics who cared more for their money than they did for the Sabbath. Apparently they did not intend to stage a demonstration, but that day the ultra-orthodox Neturei Karta movement distributed leaflets calling on the faithful "to do something" to stop the violation of the Sabbath by the cinemas. Now, none of the speakers in Zihron Moshe could afford to demand less of his flock than the Neturei Karta were demanding, lest the latter appear more devoted to the Sabbath than they. So they called for a demonstration and the crowd marched on the nearby Edison cinema. Zihron Moshe had once been an elegant bourgeois neighborhood, but now it was inhabited by the lower-middle class ultra-orthodox. The Edison cinema, too, had known better days— Arturo Toscanini himself had once conducted a concert on its stage; that Saturday a Gregory Peck film was to be shown there.

The police had been alerted in advance. "I was informed that the ultra-orthodox were going to make trouble that Saturday," as Yeshurun Shiff, the Jerusalem Chief of Police, would testify.[1] The riot began about 6:30 p.m. The Sabbath would come to an end at 8:04 p.m., and the early show was scheduled to begin at 7:15 p.m. A police officer who arrived on the scene with a few dozen men told the crowd that there was no law against the sale of tickets on the Sabbath, and he would therefore protect the box office. However, he volunteered to arrange a meeting among three of the demonstrators and the cinema owner. "They asked me to close the box office and not open the theater before eight," the man said later, "and I agreed, because I wanted no bloodshed. Yet while we were talking, the demonstrators ripped out the iron door of the box office." What happened during those moments is not clear. Rabbi Moshe Porush-Glickmann recalled:

> When the people reached the cinema and saw tickets being sold during the very Sabbath, they began a peaceful demonstration, shouting "Sabbath!" One young man climbed on the wall and began to read aloud from the Bible. At once he was pounced on by the police who dragged him down from the wall and beat him with sticks. I pleaded with the police, and promised that I would try to calm the crowd and make the people stand a distance away to voice their protest. But the police would not listen. They took out their sticks and beat people, and also beat them with their fists.

According to Chief Shiff, "the crowd rioted and provoked the policemen, cursing them, pushing them, throwing rocks and breaking windows, and at one point they tried to break into the theater."

When the demonstrators were satisfied that the early show at the Edison would not start until after the Sabbath they proceeded to the Eden cinema, where a Yiddish musical comedy, entitled *The Jewish Melody*, was about to be shown. By then it was nearly 7 p.m. and the box office was open. There was a line of people in front of it. The demonstrators attacked them. "One of the orthodox grabbed me by the throat and tried to strangle me, while another one pushed me," said one of the victims, Gustav Lindner. "I fell down and my hand was injured by the wheel of a passing car, breaking my arm." When the demonstrators broke into the lobby and tried to enter the hall, the policemen beat them back with truncheons and also drove their vehicles at them, on the sidewalk in order to drive them away. "They beat people right and left," Avraham Stubb testified later, "mercilessly, brutally, viciously and cruelly. The place looked like a battlefield. People were beaten unconscious. . . ." Rabbi Porush: ". . . No one would have believed that Jewish policemen in Israel could behave so brutally with an orthodox crowd. I again pleaded with the policemen to let me pacify the crowd, and then one of them began to shoot." It was traffic patrolman Yehoshua Dabash. He had been touring around on his motorcycle and came across the riot. He drove straight into the crowd but managed to advance only a few yards, because people blocked his way, surrounded him and began to beat him on the head. Dabash feared for his life. He pulled out his gun and fired; no one was hit.

The local Chief of Police, Yeshurun Shiff, did all he could to mediate between the rival sides. The strange and exotic world of Jerusalem's orthodoxy in which he suddenly found himself, offered him a fascinating break from the gray police routine. "Under no circumstances will I let such a sacred matter provoke disorder," he wrote to the Sabbath Guardians, and proposed, somewhat solemnly, that they address themselves to the City Council, or even to "His Honor, the Mayor, himself," to ask him to intervene in the conflict and try "to entreat the cinema owners not to violate the Sabbath lest the sacred feelings of a good many, be injured." It was a "precious and holy matter," he said. The Mayor of Jerusalem was Daniel Oster, a Galicia-born jurist, businessman and politician, very conscious of his own merit, popular among both Jews and Arabs. He undertook to mediate the issue, together with the District Supervisor, A. Bergmann. Bergmann noted after one of the meetings that the representatives of the Rabbinate and the Agudat Israel had agreed that the early show on Saturday nights would begin at 7.30, although the Sabbath ended only at 8, but that the tickets would be sold the previous day. The cinema owners, however, replied that this arrangement would not do in Jerusalem, which is not like any other city in Israel. For Jerusalemites to come to the second show, they said, it would have to start early, because Jerusalemites go to bed early and the bus service to the far-flung neighborhoods ends early, too. Nor was it conceivable to have only one show on Saturday night, for with the division of the city in the recent war the cinema owners had lost the public that used to come from the eastern, non-Jewish part of the city, and they could afford no more losses; their Sunday revenues had always come from the Arabic-Christian public. Moreover, Jerusalemites would not buy the tickets on Friday, because Jerusalemites always decide to go to the cinema at the last moment. "It isn't easy to change the habits of the Jerusalemites," grumbled Israel Gutt, owner of the Zion cinema, and he was sure to know, for his was the oldest cinema in town.

The government ordered an official investigation into the Jerusalem cinema riots. It was determined that some of the policemen had used excessive violence in handling the demonstrators. Some time later Minister of Police, Behor Shalom Shitrit, wrote to the Chief of Police and asked him "to instruct the force, while preserving public order, to persuade the cinema owners not to sell tickets before the Sabbath was over, because it was best not to arouse the public against it, while a bylaw was being drafted for the Interior Minister's signature, which, once enacted, would have to be enforced by the police." Police Commissioner Sahar replied that the police had tried several times to persuade the cinema owners to refrain from ticket sales on the Sabbath, but had failed: "It is enough for us to have to enforce the law, and the Sabbath watchers will have to direct their demands to the legislative institutions so that the law will be enacted quickly." Shitrit wrote in red ink, "This is no answer. Have the police tried to use its influence as I have directed?!" According to Shitrit, he was under heavy pressure from the religious ministers and various orthodox groups. Meanwhile summer was drawing to a close and the Jerusalem District Officer, S.B. Yeshaya, made a note to himself: "Next year—no daylight saving time, and that will solve the whole problem."*

In 1949 the road to the "Mandelbaum Gate"—the passage between the Israeli and Jordanian halves of Jerusalem—still led through the ultra-orthodox Meah Shearim quarter, and traffic passed there on Saturdays. The residents saw this as an intolerable provocation which directly harmed their way of life. So they began to demonstrate against it.† But it was not only their own

---

*However, the following year the police recorded ten Sabbath demonstrations; in 1954—fifteen; in 1965—nineteen, one of which also led to an investigation, as one of the demonstrators was killed, and became the Sabbath zealots' martyr—Pinhas Sigalow.[2]

*M.D. Levinstein, MK, of the Agudat Israel protested to Ben-Gurion that men in army uniform had supposedly thrown a bomb into a synagogue in Meah Shearim on a Saturday. He asserted that it was done in order to offend the worshippers. Ben-Gurion explained the incident: It was a vehicle which

communal interest they were seeking to preserve. As far as they were concerned, the public violation of the Sabbath was graver than its violation in private. "Whoever violates the Sabbath in public must be made aware that he is piercing the heart of the observant Jew as though with a sword," said Rabbi Shaag. "The public domain belongs to all of us, and you must not prevent me from breathing the air in the public domain, to which I am entitled as much as yourself."[4] The observance of the Sabbath was, of course, a biblical commandment, and its violation might bring a frightful retribution upon the city, as written in the Book of Jeremiah: "Then will I kindle a fire in the gates thereof, and it shall devour the palaces of Jerusalem, and it shall not be quenched" (Jer. 17:27). They believed that it was their duty to reprove the violators, and some of them believed that "reproof" might be extended to physical violence. Thus the battle for the Sabbath became a religious duty, unto bloodshed. The police would not stand for it. Behor Shalom Shitrit complained, "Those people hit everybody, Jew or Gentile. . . . They attacked them in ways which are not to be tolerated by civilized people—spitting in faces, throwing rocks, scattering glass on the road. They went so far as to attack foreign diplomats and the staff of the UN. . . ." Rabbi Levin, MK, tried to explain, "Why will you not understand our anxiety. When one sees the state of religion in the country, and the violation of the Sabbath, which we have been taught to observe by our prophets for thousands of years, [one can understand] when Jews, men and children, go out into the street and see the Sabbath publicly violated they cry out, *Sabbath!* with the tradition of Israel speaking from their throats—and then the soldiers of Israel see fit to beat them till they draw blood. . . ." Shitrit countered, "They were not content to cry, *Sabbath!* They went up on their balconies and threw rocks, they entered houses and smashed glass and scattered it on the road. . . . Five policemen were injured. We have medical certificates to prove it. Some were bitten on their hands and ears, some had their clothes torn. What were the police to do? What if it had been

---

was carrying food to one of the advance border posts, "and when it approached the outpost it was attacked by a group of local residents who called the commander 'Hitler' and the soldiers 'Nazis.' They attacked the vehicle and damaged army property. The commanding officer kept his head, and after trying in vain to explain to the attackers what the vehicle was doing there, he lit a smoke signal. This enabled him to proceed behind the smoke-screen."[3]

the other way around? The Communists, too, demonstrated once. Why didn't you say then that we must not beat? We beat them too." Levin replied exhortingly, "Can you not understand that for us the Sabbath stands for the very existence of the Jewish people, and its violation means the end of the state and the destruction of the nation?. . . . For us it is a matter of life and death."[5]

His voice reflected genuine distress, because the State of Israel permitted its citizens to violate the Sabbath, both publicly and in private, and the state itself violated it, in operating the water and electricity supplies, as well as various industries, radio broadcasts, telephone services, diplomatic activities, the police and the armed forces on the Sabbath. The orthodox could, of course, resist, and they did, but they were well aware that the State of Israel would not and could not be a theocratic state. Most Israelis did not want it that way, and the religious Law made it impossible, because it conflicted with the order of life in the country. It was a difficult problem. Yeshayahu Leibowitz expressed the opinion that for Israel to live by the Law, the Law would have to be adapted to its needs. He also considered the possibility that the religious Law would be amended so that the state and the public would be permitted to do what the private individual was forbidden to do—just as, for example, the state is allowed to kill whereas the individual is commanded not to do so.[6]

Throughout the years certain adjustments were made in order to make orthodoxy more compatible with the modern state. Rules for religious observance in the armed forces were laid down by the Chief Army Chaplain, Rabbi Shlomo Goren, and some technological innovations made modern life possible without violating the Law. But the main problem remained unsolved—the observant Jews did not produce a great religious reformer, and the Law was not adjusted to the needs of the state. Some, such as the "modern orthodox," learned to compromise with reality, without feeling that they were compromising their faith or their conscience. Others refused to compromise.

The most extreme were the Neturei Karta, "The Guardians of the City," a small congregation of zealots who had split off from Agudat Israel in the late 1930s, and rejected the very idea of the Jewish state. They fought against the Zionist movement, which they viewed as an outright heresy, because it broke the three vows which the Almighty had imposed upon the Jews before they were exiled: not to rebel against the Gentiles among whom they lived; not to attempt to seize the Holy Land by force; and not to attempt to hasten the End of Days. To them, the Declaration of Independence was a direct violation of the Law, so they refused to acknowledge the existence of the state or to obey its laws, and went so far as to declare that they would not defend it if it were attacked. Their refusal to fight, declared Rabbi Amram Bloy, their flamboyant, red-headed spiritual leader, might cause the downfall of the state, but, as he put it, "we undertake this in advance, before any war, and declare that we surrender unconditionally. . . ."[7] Bloy announced that Neturei Karta would accept "the rule and protection of any nation which the United Nations would choose, or the rule and protection of all of them together, for it was Providence that sent us into exile, and this is the way that our fathers have lived throughout the exile to this very day, and the way we wish to go on living . . . until the Hour comes to which the eyes of all Israel look with longing. . . ." In an appeal he sent the UN Secretary General in July 1949, Bloy demanded that Jerusalem be placed under international jurisdiction, and that the ultra-orthodox Jews who wished it should receive "UN passports." He announced that the Neturei Karta community was willing to move from Jerusalem to any place where they might live in accordance with the Law.[8] The zeal of the Neturei Karta was genuine, uncompromising and wholehearted. They were a small minority in the religious camp, but they had considerable influence over Agudat Israel and indirectly over the relations between the religious and the secular communities, because the Agudat Israel leadership dared not ignore them and was often drawn into a more extremist position so as not to lose their support.

The Agudat Israel, too, rejected Zionism, but in the late 1930s, with Hitler in power in Germany and Arab riots in Palestine, some of its leaders began to cooperate with the Zionist institutions in the country. At this point the Neturei Karta split off, and since that time attacked Agudat Israel with the utmost fury, charging it with all kinds of abominations for joining the Zionist establishment. "Agudat Israel pretends to be trying to save the Torah and our faith," they wrote in one of their leaflets, "but it is all a lie, and its deeds speak more loudly than words. All its deeds conflict with the Torah and our Law, and as for its

'Council of Sages' [supposedly the party's supreme spiritual authority]—it is completely subservient to Aguda's political interests and aims. . . ."[9]

There was a good deal of party politicking in this conflict, whose origins lay in far older disputes—between Rabbi A.I. Kook and Rabbi Y.H. Sonenfeld, both of Jerusalem; between the Chief Rabbinate and the ultra-orthodox congregation; between Jerusalem, on the one hand, and Warsaw and Frankfurt, on the other; between the Hassidic movement and its opponents, the Mitnagdim; between the joyful Hassidic rabbis surrounded by their "courts," and the austere heads of Talmudic *yeshivot* (colleges); and numerous other intense conflicts whose source lay in the non-Zionist orthodox movement, in both Israel and Europe, for generations. An outsider can hardly ever understand them.

To begin with, the Agudat Israel movement was a worldwide, pluralistic federation of orthodox congregations. Its founding conference, held in Katowitz in 1912, was a response to the anxiety felt by Jewish orthodoxy in view of the increasing popularity of secular movements among Jews, including the Zionist movement. "Not only Frankfurt, Berlin and Hamburg," lamented an Agudat Israel chronicler, "but Kovno, Cracow, Warsaw and Lemberg, and the rest of the Jewish communities in Eastern Europe, which were holy congregations for hundreds of years, have suddenly become hornets' nests of aggressive heresy and atheism, shaking the very foundations of traditional Judaism. Journals, books and pamphlets full of hatred for the Jewish way of life are cropping up everywhere, like mushrooms after the rain. . . ." Agudat Israel considered itself the bulwark against the new Jewish identity, which it viewed as a profane threat.

It was no easy matter to bring together the Hassidic rabbis and the rival heads of Talmudic schools in Eastern Europe, and to have them collaborate with the new German orthodoxy, which followed Rabbi S.R. Hirsch's innovative thought. At the first great Synagogue Council, the ultra-orthodox, International, the Rabbi of Gor emphasized that customs varied from country to country: "What is correct in one country may be wrong in another, and may act against us like venom. . . ."[10] Henceforth, they made a point of preserving the pluralistic nature of the overall movement. In Israel, too, they were organized in many different congregations and movements, preserving a lost Jewish

past. Tchibin, Sadigora, Presburg, Ludek and Torda, all East European centers of Jewish learning—recalling a universe which
had been destroyed—represented a very real political map in the
Agudat Israel's world, including conflicts and hatreds which
they carried along from days—even centuries—past. Their many
publications abounded in the heart-felt vituperation, of the true
believer.

Rabbi Itzhak Meir Levin was born in 1894 in Gora Kalvaria,
called Gor or Gour by the Jews, a famous Hassidic town not far
from Warsaw. His grandfather had been the Hassidic rabbi of
Gor, and upon his death the title passed to his son, Levin's uncle
and later his father-in-law. Levin married the rabbi's daughter
Devorah, when he was fifteen years old. After spending a few
years in his uncle's "court," he settled in Warsaw and engaged in
commerce and banking, spending most of his time dealing with
the affairs of his community. A clever and energetic person, he
was one of the founders of the Polish branch of Agudat Israel,
and one of the principal opponents of the Zionist movement. After the outbreak of World War II, the Gor Hassidim in New York
managed to arrange exit visas for their rabbi and his family and
enabled them to escape from Nazi-occupied Poland with Italian
visas. Levin was among them. He arrived in Palestine in 1940
and became the leader of Agudat Israel there after the deaths of
Moshe Bloy and Itzhak Breuyer, its longstanding leaders. Thus,
when the state was founded he was still relatively new to the
country. Indeed, throughout all his years in the Knesset and in
the Cabinet—as Minister of Welfare—he never quite learned to
speak modern Hebrew.

Neturei Karta used to accuse Levin of having once uttered
the monstrous heresy that the State of Israel was the first step
toward the Deliverance. Agudat Israel denied the charge: "All
this is vile libel and slander," its spokesmen declared, "founded
on abominable lies."[11] Agudat Israel favored mass immigration,
in the hope of creating a sizeable autonomous, religious Jewish
community, but unlike the Zionist movement it did not deny
the legitimacy of the Diaspora, and did not believe that Israel
alone could preserve the physical existence of the Jewish people.
No less than Neturei Karta, it fought against the Zionist movement on account of the secular character that it sought to give
the Jewish State. The bold Binyamin Mintz, leader of the *Poalei*

Agudat Israel movement, once admitted that the creation of the State "might" be considered the first step toward Deliverance, but Rabbi Levin never did.[12]

On a visit to Palestine in the 1930s, Levin saw a kibbutz, which, he said, aroused his pity. His meeting with the Mizrahi aroused his rage. Returning home to Warsaw he wrote:

> The Mizrahi people witness the destruction and havoc which the antireligious, secular and nationalistic Zionism is wreaking upon the souls of Israel, how it detaches many young people from the Torah and Judaism and leaves them deprived of any Jewish content— and they remain silent. They even presume to call themselves a religious party, while collaborating with antireligious elements. Instead of declaring open war on the antireligious who are destroying Judaism, they act in loving concert with them. They direct their arrows at the ultra-orthodox, who are fighting for their lives, with the argument that one must compromise with reality and that the first task is to build up the country. Which is the reality that they seek to compromise with? The one of today, which tells you to do this one day, and to do another thing tomorrow? Is this to be called building, or destruction? Can Israel be built on the ruins of Judaism and the Torah?[13]

The beginnings of religious Zionism could be discerned at the turn of the century, but the Mizrahi federation was created only in 1920, upon the initiative of Rabbi Yaakov Reines. Mizrahi is an acronym for *Mercaz Ruhani*—a spiritual center. It began as a national-religious Zionist movement. Later a "leftist" group, with Labor leanings, arose in its ranks, and was called *Hapoel Hamizrahi*; a similar development took place in Agudat Israel—*Poalei Agudat Israel*.

Agudat Israel attacked the Mizrahi with the same fervor as the Neturei Karta attacked them. And just as it was drawn to more extreme positions by Neturei Karta, so Poalei Agudat Israel were drawn to more extreme positions by Agudat Israel, and were followed by the Mizrahi who, in turn, drew Hapoel Hamizrahi after them. Every religious politician had a more extreme religious politician peering over his shoulder, seeking to dictate his positions. This situation affected the relations between the religious and the secular communities—the former adopted the positions of their more extreme flanks, whereas the latter were content to follow the moderate, or even indifferent, elements among them.

Orthodox demonstrators attacked a bookshop which displeased them, because it sold books that they considered abominable; they set a meatshop on fire because it sold pork, and then they began to attack vehicles seen moving on the Sabbath, recording their numbers with the help of the page numbers in their prayerbooks, and smashing them during the week. Twenty such vehicles were burned. Late in 1949, or early in 1950, Ben-Gurion received a report which had apparently been prepared by the secret service, with the following reference to the Sabbath zealots: "Until a few years ago the organization lacked political motivation. It represented all segments of the old Jerusalem community. In the last few years the Neturei Karta have become predominant among the Sabbath zealots."[14]

On May 14, 1951, the Knesset was about to debate the conscription of women. The Minister of Police, Behor Shalom Shitrit, later claimed that a group of ultra-orthodox activists had planned to cut off the electricity and then throw a scare-bomb into the hall. The Minister identified them as members of an underground group called "Brit Hakanaim"—"The Zealots' Alliance." The secret service knew about this group, having planted an agent in it.[15] The Knesset Chairman, Yosef Shprintsak, had been warned that an attempt was planned, and he hastened to close off the session, in opposition to the security people, who had hoped to catch the zealots red-handed. Some 40 of the ultra-orthodox were arrested as suspects, including one woman, and, according to the Minister of Police, they were caught in possession of three hand guns, two machine guns, several grenades, ammunition and two home-made bombs. According to Shitrit, they had planned to enforce the Sabbath laws by violence, first in the public domain and then in private.[16] The detainees were taken to a detention camp where they were humiliated and mistreated, which caused a scandal. The Knesset appointed a special parliamentary investigating committee, which strongly criticized the police. One of the orthodox detainees—Shlomo Lorinz, the future MK for Agudat Israel—made considerable political capital out of the affair, to the point of reaching the top leadership of his movement. The security forces greatly overstated the danger to the state from the ultra-orthodox underground at the time, which was just before general elections. Also in May 1953, the police arrested two young ultra-orthodox men and charged them with planning to place an explosive charge at the entrance to the Ministry of Education, by way of protest against the State Education Law.

As tension rose between the religious and the secular camps, there were warnings that it could lead to bloodshed. Eri Jabotinsky, MK for Herut and son of the late leader of the Betar movement, warned that "facing the fanatical, irate camp of Neturei Karta, a no less fanatical camp of aggressive atheists is forming."[17] But this was not quite true. Atheists were always rare in Israel; the nonreligious Israelis were not real fanatics.

One Saturday in the late 1920s, three young men sat on a bench on Allenby Street in Tel Aviv, talking and smoking in violation of the Law. An orthodox Jew passed by and reproved them. Two of the young men put out their cigarettes. The third refused: "I am not a Jew," he said. His name was Uriel Halperin, who would later become famous as the poet Yohanan Ratosh, and the prophet of the "Canaanite" movement. "That man did not know how to take my remark," recalled Ratosh years later. "Nor did I, perhaps, fully understand what I was saying. I only knew that I was not in the least religious. I did not even have any respect for religion. . . ."[18] Ratosh and his "Hebrew Youth," or "Canaanites," as their opponents styled them and as they too later called themselves, held the most explicit antireligious position ever known in Israel. But they, too, regarding themselves as "Hebrews," not Jews, fought against Zionism more than they fought against Judaism. Paradoxically, they found themselves close to the anti-Zionist Neturei Karta.

Ratosh was associated with Jabotinsky's movement, as well as with the right-wing anti-British and anti-Arab terrorist organizations, Irgun Zvai Leumi (IZL) and Lehi (the "Stern Gang"). As a "Canaanite," he made a distinction between "the Jewish community"—i.e., believers in the Jewish religion and observers of its tenets—and the "Hebrew nation," meaning the people of the Fertile Crescent, which supposedly included the Christians, Moslems, Druze and other ethnic communities in the Middle East. As a boy, Ratosh believed that "the Jewish Problem" would eventually solve itself: "It's only a question of time before the Jews of Meah Shearim, the black-frocked Jews, disappear from the world. . . . There is not a human community in the world which does not include some retarded, backward groups. Their precise numerical ratio is without significance." Even in 1949, when he wrote about "God's cossacks," Ratosh was inclined to dismiss the influence of the ultra-orthodox. "They are a negligible minority in the country," he wrote, "an old, retarded, backward and vanishing minority. They have gone so far as to project rural ghettoes, in order to preserve their existence." Ratosh asserted that he felt "a stranger's respect" for them, and stated, "We rise up against Judaism only when it tries to impose its values upon us."[19] If, indeed, Judaism was a religious community, and the Hebrews were a nation, like the French, for example, then somewhere in the landspace between the Mediterranean and the rivers of Iraq there would be room for Hebrews of the Jewish faith, as much as for "Hebrews" of the Christian, Moslem or Druze faith—the way a Frenchman might also be a Catholic, Protestant, atheist, agnostic or believer in any religion he wanted. Thus the "Canaanite" movement was not atheistic—in the Fertile Crescent there was also room for believers.

Most Israelis, however, saw themselves as Jews, even if they did not know exactly what they meant by it. The problem had first arisen in the nineteenth century, when some Jews ceased to define themselves in terms of their religion and sought a new kind of Jewish identity. This problem was a constant preoccupation for them wherever they found themselves, and it continued to be in Israel. The most "antireligious" position ever to be heard in the Knesset was for legislating the separation of church and state. Eri Jabotinsky, MK, was considered the most militant of the fighters against religion. Once he demanded to be served a ham sandwich at the Knesset buffet. But even Jabotinsky did not completely deny the place of religion. He promoted the idea of creating a "*Sanhedrin*" (a religious high court), which would take care of religious affairs, and would be financed by the orthodox. "I believe that Judaism has a great and important part to play," he said in the Knesset. "I think its task is to Judaize the world. I do not think that its task is to Judaize the institutions of the State of Israel, but to bring the ideals of Judaism and Jewish morality to the entire world."[20]

Although only 16 of the members of the first Knesset belonged to the religious parties, the majority of the members of the secular parties had received some kind of religious education in their childhood. Many had rebelled against their Jewish past. It was an interesting transformation, intellectually speaking, but they did not change completely. Even the few who regarded themselves as atheists retained some of their early training. They either did not wish, or were unable, to break away completely from religion. Many of them made a point of stating that they respected religion and felt close to it in their own way. Shmuel Dayan, father of Moshe Dayan, put it this way: "Many of us often envy the religious, because man sometimes feels helpless, insignificant, in the face of fate and a higher power." Dayan told the Knesset of a religious experience which, he said, was "engraved in his being" when he visited a church in Rome. "In the deep silence and gloom inside the church a woman and a girl were kneeling and shedding tears before the Almighty. . . ." The communion of Man and his God, he said, was an expression of pure feeling which one respects. Dayan feared the consequences of its loss. He feared that an "unbridgeable gulf" would set apart "the small Jewish tribe which we have raised on this soil," i.e., the Israelis who knew neither religion nor tradition, and never experienced exile, like the Jews of the Diaspora.[21]

Something of this sentiment was beginning to be felt even in the kibbutzim of the left-wing *Hashomer Hatsair*. During the twenties and thirties they had led an almost totally secular life. The members were quite indifferent to Judaism, and some even called themselves atheists. Yet, with very few exceptions, they had their sons circumcised, though no one compelled them to do so. Irrespective of how estranged they were from Judaism, they still needed to feel somehow connected. In the fifties, following the Holocaust, the creation of the state, the War of Independence and the mass immigration, these kibbutzim, too, began to lose their secular quality and very gradually began to find ways of introducing Judaism into their values and way of life. Their leader, Yaakov Hazan, still complained that the men of religion in Israel were no different from clerics throughout the world: "They are completely incapable of understanding other people and showing a human regard for anyone who is not like them." His conclusion was—"There can be no compromise with them."[22] Yet even in his own kibbutz, Mishmar Haemek, they began to consider how to bring the new generation closer to the "spirit of the Diaspora"; in 1948 the subject was discussed at some length in their school's jubilee book.[23]

In March 1951 "The League for the Prevention of Religious Coercion" was founded in Jerusalem. Its charter described it as a response to the "anxiety which has seized broad segments of the public in the face of the attempt by religious organizations and persons to prevail over the public and private domains of life, while declaring openly their intention of continuing the religious coercion and even intensifying it, aided by gangs of hoodlums who do not stop at acts of violence."[24] At that time Jerusalem was rocked by a series of violent outbreaks by Neturei Karta and some Agudat Israel youth who joined them. The League declared that it would devote its efforts "mainly" to fighting religious legislation by the Knesset, but warned: "We do not propose to overlook attempts of religious coercion by force." In practice, there were hardly any acts of violence against the religious. The bomb placed near Pincas' residence was an exception. There were provocative motorcades through Meah Shearim on Saturdays, and occasionally during demonstrations by the ultra-orthodox fist fights broke out between them and the secular. But these things happened very infrequently.

The League included people from the political Left, from the Center and from the Right. "We are united by a single idea," stated their founding charter, "that matters of religion and faith are the private affairs of each person." Among them were university teachers, lawyers and journalists; many were people who harbored rather eccentric opinions such as Eri Jabotinsky, Itzhak Greenbaum, Yohanan Ratosh and his energetic brother, Uzi Ornan, the League's secretary. They emphasized that they were fighting neither religion nor religious people. On the contrary—they respected all religious beliefs and defended the religious man's right to observe his religion's precepts and customs. "We do not stop you from praying, from eating kosher food and studying in your rabbinical schools," stated the League in a leaflet addressed to the religious community. "Don't you bother us. Keep the Sabbath in your homes and let every man live according to his own conscience."[25]

The League published ads in the papers, distributed leaflets, held meetings, cultivated the press, and tried to influence politicians, mayors and government officials as best it could. The activities of the League helped to ensure that the problem of religious coercion remained a permanent topic in Israeli politics. But it achieved little and eventually vanished from the scene. In fact, the Leaguers had begun too late—the decision not to separate church and state had been made long before they organized. Furthermore, the strong link between the Jewish religion and Jewish national feeling, and the great multitude of religious rit-

uals that Judaism imposes on the individual and the congregation, meant that the strict separation of church and state and the
complete avoidance of all religious coercion could only have
come about as a result of the secular public defeating the religious; most Israelis did not wish to go that far.

Following the Sabbath demonstrations around the cinemas
in Jerusalem, the local Labor Council published a large poster on
a red background, warning that "Whoever breaks the laws of the
state or acts against its constitution, will be strongly resisted.
. . . Down with the horror propaganda of the forces of darkness in
the country. Down with the hoodlums' attempts to impose a religious regime on the country. The working class and the progressive forces, which make up the majority of the people of Jerusalem, will close ranks to resist these plots."[26] But when the
League, together with the "Canaanites," MAPAM and the Communist party, called for mass demonstrations against the Sabbath laws, including Pincas' traffic stoppage, only several hundred demonstrators turned out—not thousands. The Israeli
public violated Pincas' regulation restricting private transportation on the Sabbath until it was dropped, but they did not come
out and demonstrate against it. They drove to the beaches on
Saturdays, but they would not fight for public transportation on
Saturdays. They flocked to the soccer games on Saturdays, but
they would not rebel against the prohibition of movies on Friday
nights. This, then, was the chief difference between the camps—
the orthodox were willing to fight for their way of life; the nonreligious would not fight for their own. The majority did not observe the rules of religion, and in that sense they were secular.
But the great majority had not gone so far as to separate their
Jewish identity from Judaism. They felt attached to the Jewish
heritage and kept up some vestige of its ritual laws. Eri Jabotinsky explained: "From earliest childhood we have been accustomed to take a certain attitude toward religion—the attitude of each one of us toward Grandmother who lights the
candles and Grandfather who goes to the synagogue."[27] And this
was what made coexistence possible.

Before the UN Partition Resolution of 1947, the Agudat Israel opposed the idea of a Jewish state, but it did not publicly
oppose its creation.[28] Various alternative plans were discussed
inside the movement—prolonging the British Mandate, the creation of a Jewish-Arab federation, cantonization of the country,

with autonomy for the ultra-orthodox community, and so forth. Anything was better, they felt, than a sovereign Jewish state which does not abide by the Law. But the Council of Sages advised the leaders of Agudat Israel to avoid expressing their views in public, not to say yea or nay, "for fear of the consequences to individuals and the community," if it were said "that the orthodox Jews are the ones who oppose and hinder the creation of the state." And though they knew that the state would not live by the Torah, they exerted themselves in trying to shape its character. In November 1946 Rabbi Levin met with MAPAI's Moshe Sharet and Eliezer Kaplan, but the two would only promise autonomy to the religious educational system, and to establish Saturday as the general day of rest. They negotiated for several months. Ben-Gurion, too, was involved in these negotiations, as were many others, religious and secular. One of them was Moshe Sne. He, too, the future Communist leader, had studied at the rabbinical school as a child, and in the period just before the creation of the state, being then the national commander of the Haganah, he was anxious to keep the rifts in the Jewish community to a minimum.

In 1947, the United Nations Special Committee on Palestine, UNSCOP, visited Jerusalem. Its recommendations would lead to the UN Partition Resolution and the creation of the state. The heads of the Jewish Agency were naturally anxious that the Jewish community would appear before the Committee in a body, and they sought to prevent the leaders of the orthodox movement from expressing to the Committee opposition to the creation of a Jewish state. A few days before Rabbi Levin was due to appear before the Committee, he and some of his associates met with Ben-Gurion and demanded guarantees that the future state would carry out a list of their demands. Ben-Gurion replied that "the Constitution of the state would be the work of the elected legislative assembly, and until a constitution was enacted nothing could be guaranteed." But the ultra-orthodox would not give up. They demanded that there should be no civil marriage, that the Sabbath and the kosher laws should be kept, and that there be autonomy for the religious education system and freedom of religious conscience. The last demand reveals how deeply they feared the secular Jewish regime. Ben-Gurion only promised to take these demands into consideration. Levin noted, "He spoke very nicely, but in fact he did not commit himself to anything."

For the next few days a draft of a letter was worked on from the Jewish Agency to Agudat Israel, arguing over every sentence and measuring every word. In the final draft they took pains to point out that the Jewish Agency was not empowered to determine in advance the kind of constitution the future Jewish state would have, and added that the state would not win the recognition of the United Nations if it were a theocratic state, "and it is plainly essential to ensure in advance equal rights for all the citizens and the absence of any coercion or discrimination in matters of religion as in other matters." The preamble held a few more phrases of this kind, but in the body of the text they undertook the following:

A. *The Sabbath.* Obviously the day of rest in the Jewish state will be Saturday, while Christians and people of other persuasions would of course be free to rest on their own weekly holiday.

B. *Kosher Food.* All necessary steps would be taken to ensure that any government kitchen catering to Jews would serve kosher food.

C. *Laws of Matrimony.* The members of the Executive are all aware of the gravity of the problem and the many difficulties involved, and all the bodies represented in the Executive will do everything possible to satisfy the profound need of the religiously-observant in this matter, in order to eliminate the danger of dividing the House of Israel in two.

D. *Education.* The full autonomy of every education system will be guaranteed (as, by the way, it is right now), and the government will not jeopardize the religious feeling and conscience of any part of the people of Israel. The state will, of course, determine the minimum obligatory studies, such as Hebrew, history, sciences, etc., and supervise this minimum, while at the same time giving each educational system the freedom to conduct its education in accordance with its convictions, and will refrain from any constraint against religious conscience.

Ben-Gurion signed this document himself, and made Rabbi I.L. Maimon put his own signature right beside his, so that he would not later be able to retract his commitment. He got Itzhak Greenbaum to add his signature on the other side, to ensure that the most extreme anticlerical elements would also be committed to the guarantees. The first paragraph did not promise to prohibit violation of the Sabbath; the second paragraph did not promise to prohibit nonkosher food; the third paragraph was equally ambiguous, though it did suggest that the State of Israel would not introduce civil marriage; the fourth paragraph suggested that agreement would be possible on the subject of education. Altogether, the document expressed goodwill and readiness to meet the orthodox halfway. In years to come it would be described as the basis of the status quo in religious matters. In reality, it was merely the first step, a preliminary basis for negotiations. When Rabbi Levin appeared before UNSCOP, he did not express support for the Jewish state, but he was careful not to oppose it. Before Agudat Israel would agree to join the government formed by Ben-Gurion after the first general elections, it was necessary to hold further negotiations. Ben-Gurion wrote:

> MK Meir David Levinstein of Agudat Israel came to see me prior to their decision to join the government. He wanted to know what I had meant in speaking about equal rights for women, and whether the promises that Fishmann (Maimon), Greenbaum and I gave, concerning the Sabbath, kosher food and laws of matrimony were still in force. I told him that women's equality meant the same rights as men, in secular matters such as inheritance, property, the right to give evidence, etc. We would not touch the laws of marriage and divorce. He asked if, when it came to matters of principle, the legislative assembly or the Knesset would agree not to decide on its own but to consult the Council of Sages. I answered with a categorical No. Let them choose the rabbis to represent them, and let them express their opinions, and the majority will decide.[29]

A month later he talked with Rabbis Maimon and Levin, together with Moshe Shapira, about the final draft of the government's basic platform. "They agreed to the statement that the government will provide for the religious needs, but objected to the final phrase, 'will prevent religious coercion.' I told them to choose—either accept the whole thing or reject the whole thing. They chose to accept it all."[30]

Another month passed, and Ben-Gurion began to draft a new letter to Rabbi Levin. In it he repeated, in different words, what he had promised with regard to the Sabbath and the kosher laws, and added that the state would provide for the public religious needs, and would prevent religious coercion. This letter, too, was discussed at great length and went through at least two drafts. Finally they agreed on the following:

> Freedom of religion and conscience will be guaranteed—to wit, every citizen in the state will be able to remain faithful in his own way to the customs of his religion, and in this mater there will be no coercion on the part of the government. Similarly, each person will have the freedom of conscience to act in accordance with his understanding, provided he does not violate the laws of the state or the rights of others. The legal status of women in Israel will be equal to that of men, in all civil, social, political, economic and cultural matters, and this equality will be upheld by the rabbinical courts when deciding issues of personal status, inheritance, alimony, etc. This government will not introduce a provision for civil marriage and civil divorce in Israel, and will continue to uphold the existing law. The various educational systems will retain their autonomy within the state's educational system in accordance with Section 7 of the government plan, as approved by the Knesset. . . .[31]

This was scarcely an improvement over the previous letter. Indeed, from the orthodox viewpoint, the statement regarding freedom of religion and conscience represented a certain loss of ground. But by this time they no longer feared that the government would force them to violate the Law—now they wanted it to force the rest of the country to keep it.

It was also agreed to exempt religious women from military service, the secular establishment thereby abandoning the principle that all citizens must share equally in the burden of security, as well as the principle of the equality of women. It was also an implied acknowledgement of the armed forces' moral deficiencies, as understood by the orthodox. Before the end of the year a delegation of Hapoel Hamizrahi came to Ben-Gurion to ask him to create special religious units in the army, as well as to reserve certain posts in the Ministry of Defense for religious persons. Ben-Gurion rejected both requests.

> I told them: "A. Our army will be unified, without any factions; B. To keep it unified we shall make it kosher throughout; C. We shall have a Jewish atmosphere on the Sabbath; D. We will impose mutual respect, so that the soldier who does not pray will not mock the soldier who does."[32]

In the meantime, the battle for the Sabbath continued almost everywhere: local rabbis, religious councils and the representatives of the religious parties in local councils and municipalities, all took careful note of every public violation of the Sabbath and did their best to stop it. Before long it became a thorough and systematic operation, coordinated by a central "Public Council for the Sabbath," which was associated with the Ministry of Religious Affairs. It concentrated its activities in nonreligious communities. Its purpose was to strengthen the religious character of life throughout the country. Most members of the Council belonged to Hamizrahi. Their activities consisted of enforcing various local bylaws, such as those enacted in Tel Aviv in 1937 but never enforced. Now the Sabbath guardians proposed to recruit students of rabbinical schools to act as Sabbath watchmen. The Council did not try to impose the observance of the Sabbath in the private domain, nor did it try to impose it in excess of the law, but wherever local bylaws were lacking, it did all it could to get them enacted. It also strove to tighten the existing laws and to have them strictly enforced. It worked ceaselessly on a local level, day by day, using personal contacts, and before long the cumulative effects of its wide-ranging efforts became noticeable. At one point the Council reported nearly 300 cases where it had prevented Sabbath violation in a few communities—an average of two a week. About a quarter of the cases concerned public transportation—urban and interurban buses, trains and the national airline's flights.

In September 1952 the Council's publication reported: "When it was learned that the management of El Al [the national airline] had failed to keep its written and verbal promises not to fly on the Sabbath, the Council protested to the Ministry of Transport and demanded that the Sabbath flights be stopped." The Ministry reported that El Al did not fly on the Sabbath except in "unavoidable" cases. About another quarter of the cases dealt with by the Council had to do with movies, theaters and other forms of entertainment on Friday nights. Another quarter had to do with Sabbath work in industry, and the rest with miscellaneous matters, such as peddlers, shops, restaurants, and so forth.

The mayors who did not depend on coalitions with religious parties attempted to resist the Council's interferences. They did not bother to enact Sabbath laws or to enforce their observance in any other way. When Hapoel Hamizrahi's Shapira was not Minister of the Interior, the recalcitrant mayors enjoyed the

Ministry's backing: Ministers Gruenbaum, Rokah and Bar-
Yehuda tended to delay the ratification of Sabbath bylaws. There
were also some local police chiefs who were less than eager to
help the Sabbath guardians. Moshe Reich, Director of the Council for the Sabbath, sent his men instructions on how to press
charges in a private criminal suit: "A chief of police may not
refuse to press charges when presented with a properly argued
appeal, if he does not want to be accused of contempt of court,"
Reich wrote, adding: "If you follow these instructions carefully,
you are sure to obtain a thorough handling of your complaints
against Sabbath violators . . . and with God's help you will succeed in restraining the transgressors, if not entirely, then at least
partially. . . ."[33]

In 1949 "The Sabbath Covenant," the organization which
had led the Sabbath demonstrations in Jerusalem, among other
activities, and whose members included the two Chief Rabbis,
drafted a Sabbath law which it tried unsuccessfully to have
passed as a bylaw in Jerusalem, with the intention that eventually it would become the law of the land. The proposed law read
as follows:

> On Saturdays and holy days all traffic, whether of motor vehicles,
> carts or any other kind of vehicle, is prohibited. The Jerusalem ra-
> dio station will cease broadcasting on Saturdays and holy days. The
> following activities will be considered violations of the Sabbath
> and liable to punishment and fines as listed below: any form of
> work or labor, turning on of lights, kindling fire, smoking, produc-
> ing sounds from machines, instruments and musical instruments.
> Arrangements such as professional gatherings, conferences, balls,
> parties, performances, exhibitions, sports activities, entertainment
> and so forth, will be permitted only with the Sabbath Committee's
> license. . . . Half the members of the Sabbath Committee will be ap-
> pointed by the Municipality and the other half by the Chief Rabbis.
> Only people who observe the Sabbath in their private lives may be
> appointed to the Sabbath Committee. . . . A person who fails to
> obey the rules enacted by the Sabbath Committee will be liable to a
> fine of up to 100 *lirot* or three months in prison, or both.[34]

This, then, was the ideal. The Provisional Council of State had
determined that Saturday and the Jewish holidays would be days
of rest, but did not state what acts were permitted and what was
forbidden, nor did it determine any punishment for violators.
The Sabbath law was never enacted, despite repeated attempts

to get it passed by the Knesset in various guises, and despite an explicit promise by Ben-Gurion that there would be a Sabbath law in Israel. Industry and business (for Jews) on the Sabbath were eventually outlawed, however, by a law whose purpose was to fix legal working days, hours and rest.

The first Knesset spent more time debating the Sabbath than any other religious issue, including education, military service for women and the Constitution. Discussions in the Knesset rambled on for hours.

> *Question:* "Why do new immigrants who arrive in Israel on Saturday have to remain on board until the end of the Sabbath, instead of being received at once?" (*Answer:* "To ensure the Sabbath rest of the port workers and to avoid upsetting those of the immigrants who observe the Sabbath.")[35]

> *Question:* "Why do the police discriminate against Sabbath-observing officers?" (*Answer:* "There is no discrimination. There is an order that the Sabbath must be observed by the police. Since an officer on duty must be clean-shaven, Sabbath-observing policemen must be instructed to shave on Friday afternoon, so that when they turn up for duty on Saturday they will be clean-shaven.")[36]

> *Question:* "Why was the Israel-Transjordan Armistice Commission convened on a Saturday?" (*Answer:* "Israeli Embassies are closed on the Sabbath and are instructed to avoid diplomatic meetings on the Sabbath, as much as possible. The Armistice Commission acts as a consequence of the war and is therefore subject to the rules of war.")[37]

> *Question:* "Is Mr. Ben-Gurion aware that in Beersheba, the cradle of Judaism, the place where the Covenant with Abraham the Patriarch was renewed, volunteer soldiers from abroad are building a cinema on the Sabbath?" (*Answer:* "An order has been given to investigate the matter and stop all construction work on the Sabbath, since there are no war measures involved. The description of Beersheba as the cradle of Jewish civilization is a dubious one.")[38]

The government adhered to the spirit of the Jewish Agency's letter to the Agudat Israel.

In order to sustain his party's standing among his ultra-orthodox constituents, Levin had to keep pointing to the party's achievements, yet if he wanted to achieve anything, he had to continue claiming that the ultra-orthodox were not getting a fair deal. This necessitated a certain acrobatic facility. Once he admitted that "for tactical reasons we had to protest repeatedly against discriminations and injuries and ignore all our achievements."[39] His supporters vehemently defended his participation in the government. "And if Rabbi Levin were to quit the government, would Sabbath violation come to an end?" they asked rhetorically in a special pamphlet distributed among their adherents. "Would smoking on the Sabbath be prohibited? Would the Sabbath be observed throughout the country? What was it like before the creation of the state, and before Rabbi Levin became a Minister? Did the kibbutzim keep the Sabbath?"[40] In July 1949 Levin sent a long apologetic letter to Rabbi Yaakov Rosenhein in New York. "Without the ultra-orthodox Ministers in the government we would not have achieved anything," he asserted, and listed a long series of achievements, including a substantial budget allocated to the ultra-orthodox educational system. "It's inconceivable that we would have been able to exist without this government subsidy,"[41] he noted.

One of the rabbis on the Council of Sages, Meir Karlits, gave Levin a letter in which he recalled that Agudat Israel always had a "lobbyist" to look after the interests of the ultra-orthodox Jews in every country's government. "And if it is possible to introduce such a lobbyist into the Israeli Government, it should be done unhesitatingly," he concluded.[42] Agudat Israel had had in fact lobbyists in various parliaments, including the Polish Sejm. When the United Nations Organization was created, they sent a delegation to represent them in its forums, and did not recall it after the creation of the state. Rabbi Levin had served in the *Judenrat*, the Council of Jews, which the Nazis had created after they conquered Warsaw in World War II—as a lobbyist for the ultra-orthodox Jews. Now Agudat Israel sought to represent its relations with the Israeli Government as if it were just another lobby under Gentile rule.

Levin was a pragmatic and clear-eyed politician in his own way. He was aware of the difference between the desirable and the feasible, and knew how to dodge, when necessary, the rigid dogmas dictated by his faith. In the course of lengthy heart-to-heart talks with Ben-Gurion, he revealed an open mind concerning Zionism, in contrast not only to Neturei Karta, but also to his own Council of Sages, his movement's spiritual leaders. Levin's letters to Ben-Gurion reveal respect and friendship:

> In the time that I have had the opportunity to work with you I have learned to respect your love and devotion to the people of Israel, to the state and the Jewish values. "I see you as a man who in his own way endeavors to seek out what is authentically Jewish (for me the source of our authenticity is clear and present). . . . Optimally, ultra-orthodox Jewry would demand that all the affairs of the state be conducted according to the Law of the *Torah*. But so long as this demand may not be realized, minimally we must protect the interests of the ultra-orthodox community in Israel, and our participation in the coalition government was made possible by the acceptance of our minimal demands. . . .[43]

Moshe Shapira, another of the religious bloc Ministers and soon to be the leader of the Mizrahi, maintained that Ben-Gurion preferred the Agudat Israel to his movement, because the former tended to be insular and content to protect its own community, whereas the Mizrahi fought to introduce religion into all spheres of life in the state.[44] But Shapira, too, was able to establish businesslike, and in time even amicable, relations with Ben-Gurion, beginning with the period of the struggle against the British. At that time Ben-Gurion and Moshe Sne brought Shapira into some of their practical deliberations.

A graduate of the famous rabbinical institute founded by Rabbi Azriel Hildesheimer in Berlin, Shapira could find the common ground between the Jews of Eastern Europe, whose world he came to know when he was a rabbinical scholar in Grodno, and German Orthodox Jewry, as well as Western civilization and the Zionist outlook. He had engaged in public activities since his youth, eventually becoming a politician, which began with his position as assistant to Rabbi Meir Bar-Ilan. Politically moderate, authoritative, almost charismatic, he was a distinguished gentleman who looked like an old-time Hollywood movie star. "I can't say that I have never given you a hard time," Ben-Gurion wrote him on his fiftieth birthday, "and perhaps you too reciprocated in kind, nor is there any guarantee that such doings will not recur from time to time. But it seems to me that our disagreements, over the years, only served to demonstrate the basic common view, of idea and vision, which underlay our friendship and common work."[45]

Ben-Gurion wrote in a similar vein to the other Ministers of the religious bloc, Maimon and Levin. "I can promise you both that with all our disagreements in spiritual matters—and they are not negligible—there is one issue on which there can be no disagreement—any antireligious coercion or provocation is inconceivable (just as in my opinion religious coercion is inconceivable)."[46] Earlier he had written that the government had done more to give a Jewish character to the population and the army "than all the religious organizations, including the Mizrahi and Agudat Israel, among all the Jewish communities throughout the world." Therefore, he stated, no government could be more amenable to the religious aims in his Cabinet. He wrote:

> This government did not undertake to turn the State of Israel into a theocratic state and it will not impose the Law upon the people. On the contrary, this government, with your participation, has declared that there would be no religious coercion. But I cannot imagine any alternative government which would show a greater understanding for your religious feelings and those of others, and which would be as devoted to the values of Judaism (though not necessarily in the terms of the Mizrahi or Agudat Israel) as this government.[47]

The religious Ministers were inclined to agree. "Our ways differ in many great and small matters," wrote Rabbi Maimon, "but many are the matters which link us and lead us along the same path. One of these is undoubtedly the gauging of all issues in a measure of honesty, and an objective evaluation of controversial matters. . . ."[48] He might have added, a sharply political view, sober and pragmatic, inspired by a sincere anxiety that a cultural conflict "would explode the Jewish people into two peoples," as Rabbi Levin put it, "and cause such a deep rift as we should never be able to bridge."[49]

When in the afternoon of May 14, 1948, they were still arguing about the final draft of the Declaration of Independence, Moshe Shapira, leader of Hapoel Hamizrahi, demanded that the Declaration mention "the Lord of Israel." The representatives of MAPAM objected. Had they not stopped the argument in time, they might have had to postpone the Declaration of Independence, as this was a Friday afternoon and it was agreed that the signing ceremony would end before the Sabbath, at sundown. This, too, caused an argument: MAPAM demanded at first that the Declaration be signed at midnight that night, when the British Mandate of Palestine came to an end. But everyone else thought that this was a deliberate provocation against the religious, and ignored the demand. Yet they all realized that they would never agree on a text if the Almighty were not mentioned in it. Finally it was agreed that the Declaration would be signed "with faith in the Rock of Israel" (*Tsur Israel*), a biblical phrase generally used to designate God. Ben-Gurion approved the compromise, which he described as a "nice compromise of Jewish fellowship." In time to come, he said, he would have no difficulty explaining to his children, "who are not religious," how he could have endorsed such a phrase with an easy heart and a clear conscience. He told his comrades in the People's Administration that the entire argument was "not practical," and that on the eve of Independence it was best to avoid carrying such disputes to extremes.[50] With an equally easy heart and clear conscience he let Rabbi Maimon read out the traditional thanksgiving prayer in the course of the ceremony, yet he sat through the prayer with his head uncovered, presumably also with an easy heart and a clear conscience. A few days later he had no difficulty stating that Israel had only itself and "our Father in heaven" to rely on, for which Rabbi Maimon was duly grateful.[51]

Ben-Gurion respected Maimon and Maimon respected him, ever since the days when the Ottoman government that ruled the country before the British, deported them both, along with Ben-Tsvi and some others. After they reached the United States, Maimon, who already had a well-established organization behind him, helped them both out. Maimon was a highly literate man and a devout Zionist, and had been arrested by the British authorities as a Zionist leader. His sister Ada was a MAPAI member of Knesset. He used to interrupt her speeches and she would protest, "I beg my Honorable brother not to interrupt me!" His son-in-law was Itzhak Refael, to whom Maimon once said, "If it had not been for Ben-Gurion, it's very doubtful if we would have lived to see the state." To which Refael replied: "But we believe that the state was given by God. Could God have chosen as His messenger a man who violates the Sabbath and does not keep the Law?" Maimon grew thoughtful and finally said: "It's miraculous that Ben-Gurion is not an observant Jew, or people might have mistakenly believed that he was the Messiah, who has not yet come."[52]

Ben-Gurion was not a religious man. A little before the first session of the Knesset, he obliged Rabbi Meir Bar-Ilan by going to the Yeshurun synagogue in Jerusalem to attend a thanksgiving prayer. "This is the first time that I attend a synagogue service in the Land of Israel," he noted later in his diary.[53] He had been in the country more than forty years. The precepts of Judaism and the Jewish way of life in the Diaspora repelled him. He sought his roots in the Bible, and tended to link the statehood of Israel with the biblical Hebraic nation: "The Rock of Israel," he once wrote, "is to be found in the State of Israel and in the Book of Books."[54] Among other things, he found in the Book the yardsticks of prophetic morality which he ascribed to the state. Ben-Gurion was not an outstanding scholar and the extensive use to which he put the Bible did not derive from profound knowledge. His habit of politicizing the Bible for contemporary purposes infuriated the orthodox, but he enjoyed arguing with them, deliberately downgrading the importance of the post-biblical *Mishnah, Talmud* and the rabbinical responsa. "I do not value the Talmud," he once said. "I cannot compare it with the Bible."

On that occasion Ben-Gurion was asked whether he believed in God. His answer was:

> The question is, who is God? The Jews, most Jews, see him as an old man with a long beard sitting on the heavenly throne, and believe that he spoke to Moses. I don't believe that God spoke to Moses. Moses heard a human voice in his heart and knew that he had to do this thing. But I do not believe that there are only physical forces in the world. I have read Darwin's theory, and there is a good deal of logic in it. But I cannot assume—and I asked one of the greatest scientists about it—that the mind is only the product of a natural process. By what physical process could Newton have reached his theory, or Darwin his theory, or Einstein, or any other discovery? There is something above it all. Above the physical forces. Niels Bohr was here and I asked him this question, 'Is there a difference between the physical processes of the brain and those of this table?' And he answered: 'The brain thinks.' Why assume that the cosmos does not think? One can't assume that the cosmos does not think and I don't assume that there are only physical processes in the universe. Once when I was in Sweden I was taken to see a machine which measures the millionth part of a second. The millionth part of a second! How is it done?! They explained that there was one disk and another disk and a ray of light and another disk. No, I don't believe that nothing governs all this. It can't be merely a physical process.[55]

But there was a certain kind of Polish Jewishness which adhered to him and which he could not shake off. He, too, like the others, retained something of his childhood *Yiddischkeit*.

When he had to lay the foundations for the co-existence of religious and secular Jews he was guided by political considerations and national responsibility, not by Jewish sentiment. Menahem Parosh, MK of Agudat Israel, put it thus, "Ben-Gurion gave us more than anyone else, because he understood that if the state did not make concessions to us we would have to leave the country, and this he did not want."[56] He understood that religious needs, such as education, religious services and the like, were national needs, and insisted that the state subsidize them out of its budget. Once it undertook the responsibility to finance religious services, the state would also be the source of its authority. "I want the state to hold the religion in the palm of its hand," he once said to Yeshayahu Leibowitz, and the irate scholar interpreted this as "a prostitution of religion for the sake of power, political, factional and personal interests."[57] Ben-Gurion did a great deal to give the religious a share in the government, and not only for reasons of convenience—he believed that sharing in the national responsibility would restrain them from rebelling and would reduce the tensions between them and the secular public. Fear of the consequences which might be created by these tensions also led Ben-Gurion to consider the separation of church and state an inconceivable option.

"The very existence of a religious party," he once wrote, with distaste, "inherently implies, consciously or not, a desire to impose rabbinical laws and tradition upon the country. The freedom of religion and conscience, which the religious party demands for itself, it is neither willing nor capable of granting to others."[58] This was a highly realistic assessment, suggesting the awareness that there would be no compromise between the religious and the secular. Not everybody understood this. Years later, Dr. Zerah Warhaftig, MK, stated that "Ben-Gurion hated the religion," but he praised him for knowing how "to penetrate religious psychology" better than anyone else. "He did argue that we were unwilling to make concessions, but he understood that we could not make concessions."[59] Rabbi Kalmann Kahana, MK, speaking with Ben-Gurion, put it this way, "For you it would not be a tragedy if your son should be religious. For me it would be a tragedy if my son were irreligious."[60] Ben-Gurion did, nevertheless, realize that the religious were capable of making certain concessions and that in certain circumstances they would be willing to make them.

Having laid the groundwork for the cooperation between the religious and the secular, Ben-Gurion felt that the ideological conflict between them should be put off. "There is no need at this time to resolve problems of opinion and belief, over which we shall remain divided for a long time to come," he wrote. Uncompromising argument about the status of religion in the State of Israel, or attempts at coercion in matters of religion, may become a "national powder-keg," he feared.[61] Speaking to his party's leaders he said that such argument was "idiotic."[62] Following one of the most fascinating discussions ever held in the Knesset, it was decided to put off the writing of a Constitution for the state and to make do with the so-called Basic Laws, in time to become part of a constitution, leaving civil rights inadequately protected. Perhaps this was the intention, but, had they undertaken to write a Constitution, they would have had to choose between two diametrically opposed truths. "As a socialist and an atheist I could never endorse a program that included a religious model," said one of MAPAI's MKs. "Only the *Torah* Law and tradition are sovereign in the life of Israel," responded another MK, of Agudat Israel. Rabbi I.M. Levin wanted to postpone the debate on the Constitution for the same reasons and almost in the same words as Ben-Gurion.[63] So they decided not to decide and were left without a Constitution, but the *"Kulturkampf"* they had all feared was avoided.

PART IV

Between Vision
and Reality

9

The Quest for a National Identity

EARLY IN THE MORNING of May 4, 1949, the final preparations were being made in Tel Aviv for a military parade scheduled to take place that afternoon, to commemorate one year of Independence. Soldiers polished their boots and belt buckles, while carpenters drove the last nails into the guest podium—a wooden structure as high as a one-story building. Municipal workers hung flags over it and placed chairs upon its tiers, while policemen stretched ropes around it. All through the year there had been many celebrations—in every town and every village there had been displays and parades of all sorts. On May Day, 40,000 workers were brought to Tel Aviv by bus from all over the country.

The Day of Independence parade was supposed to be the most impressive of all. It had been eagerly anticipated, though the previous evening had been disappointing. Crowds filled the streets but did not find any way of celebrating the occasion. The loudspeakers did not work and the fireworks were less than spectacular. "People ask each other what to do. How to celebrate," wrote *Haaretz*'s Haifa correspondent. "Those who looked forward to real, heartfelt celebration were disappointed."[1]

By midday some 300,000 people had reached Tel Aviv, about
a third of the country's entire population. Thousands moved on
to the guest podium, like a mighty wave, breaking down fences,
ripping and even cutting them with knives, breaking through
courtyards and passages between buildings, and even jumping
from roof to roof. The area grew more and more crowded, almost
to the point of suffocation. The policemen and ushers were helpless. In the meantime Ben-Yehuda Street had been opened to
traffic—or perhaps they had forgotten to close it in the first
place, or perhaps they had closed it but nevertheless the drivers
drove through. One way or another, the solid mass of people was
suddenly blocked by a tremendous traffic jam. In a little while a
general scuffle broke out, men fighting with their fists, women
with their nails, and everybody with their elbows. Among the
scufflers were some who held tickets to the guest podium—
government Ministers, Members of the Zionist Executive,
Members of the Knesset and foreign diplomats. A judge was seen
to climb over a barrier, a foreign ambassador leapt over benches.
By the time they all reached the platform, it was already filled. A
senior officer was seated in the place of an Ambassador's wife
and refused to vacate it. A Consul took the place of a Minister's
wife. The Minister's Director General tried to help her, but the
Consul was stronger than he. Everybody was shouting and cursing and waving their invitations. The heat and humidity were
overpowering. And all that time Chief of Staff Yaakov Dori sat
on the podium, waiting for Prime Minister Ben-Gurion. Ben-
Gurion waited at home, a few streets away, receiving continuous reports on the situation. When it became clear that the parade route could not be cleared except by use of force, he sent
word to the Chief of Staff that the parade would not take place.
"The holiday was ruined," he wrote later in his diary.[2]*

The following day *Maariv*'s chief editor, Azriel Karlebach,
wrote that people wept like children with bitter disappoint-
ment, fury and shame "about the disgrace, about the impression
abroad, about the disorders and the failure, the demonstration of
our incapacity on the day of our strength." He found some con-
solation in the idea that "perhaps there was some sublime

---

*A committee, which investigated the causes of the fracas, recommended
dismissing some of the officials responsible for organizing the parade. *Haaretz:*
"Much of their failure may be attributed to their inexperience. Who in this
country has ever organized a military parade?"[3]

beauty in this failure, and it is to our glory and honor that the parade did not take place for such a stupid reason." In Hitler's Germany, he stated, such a thing could not have happened, "and it may be that it was supposed to be the essence of the day that the people and not the army filled the road." He thought it was highly symbolic: "The parade failed because while we wanted a military parade with all our hearts, we are, nevertheless, Jews."[4]

Some time after these events, "Army Day" was celebrated with a parade which was of exemplary discipline and order. The honor guards stood like tin soldiers, with leather straps across their chests, and the guests on the podium were suitably solemn and elegant, the women in fancy hats, as if at Ascot. Now Herzl Rosenblum, the editor of the competing evening paper, *Yediot Aharonot*, paid his rival back with the following:

> "Jewish order" was what our enemies used to call the Jewish lack of discipline, and in time the Jews themselves came to believe in their own ineffectuality. Yesterday it became plain to all that it is a lie. ... What took place yesterday, in the parade, in the stadium and in the streets, could well have served as an example even to the Gentiles, and I heard one foreign attaché comment to another, that this is unquestionably the only European army in the Middle East.[5]

At that time Ben-Gurion believed that a real Israeli army did not yet exist. "We are now about to organize the army of Israel," he said to the leaders of MAPAI in the summer of 1949. "So far we have not done it. Up to now we have had a fighting force with which to resist the Arabs. Now we are about to create a real army, with a military system and law."[6] A few months later the army was still, according to Ben-Gurion, in its early stages. "We must start everything almost from scratch," he wrote.[7] The Prime Minister was dissatisfied with the standard of fighting, with the quality of the military equipment and the level of training. "Given the means, the forces and the methods of the past year," he stated, "we will not win again."[8]

Among other things, he frequently complained about the poor discipline during the war and after. "The situation in the army is very bad," he noted, following a talk with two senior officers, Haim Laskov and Mordehai Makleff. "Orders are not given, Headquarters makes no final decisions."[9] Aside from the heavy losses and the defeats in battle, the looting, rape and murder, which had taken place in the course of the war, the army also suffered from careless expenditure, neglect and general lack of discipline. Ben-Gurion wrote, "At Tel Litvinsky [Tel Hasho-mer] there is a training camp for 1,200 men. The number of trainers is 500![10] . . . The airfields are left unguarded. A week ago a stranger entered the Herzlia airfield at six o'clock in the morning, started an airplane and flew off with it. . . ."[11] He was also troubled by the many road accidents caused by army drivers, and the information he received that "officers and instructors used foul language and obscenities when addressing their subordinates (junior officers, sergeants and privates)." When he heard about it he sent a "private and personal" letter to Haim Laskov: "The Jewish people should not be contaminated with this kind of military style. . . ."[12]

Ben-Gurion envisioned the Israel army as "a pioneering, educating force, nation-building, wilderness-redeeming . . . molder of the nation's leaders, the cultural instrument of the ingathering of the exiles, their unification and spiritual uplifting."[13] Yet at a closed session with the heads of his party Ben-Gurion also said, "The very existence of an army is a danger to the state, a danger to democracy, because it is a group of people with power. Twenty thousand armed men are more powerful than 20 million unarmed people. If in a country there are 20 thousand men who can seize power, who wish to seize power, they can rule over 10 million unarmed people, who will be completely helpless." He believed that this had been and still was Menahem Begin's intention. "I don't think that Begin has changed. That is Begin's program, that is Sne's program [MAPAM], and that is Mikunis' program [the Communist party]." Ben-Gurion warned of the danger that the left-wing MAPAM would seize power with the help of its followers in the army. He felt this to be a real and present danger, stemming from the absence of national tradition and the emotional intensity of the political conflicts. "Among us the disputes are not like those of more-or-less normal people," he said, "but like those of zealots."[14]*

To insure that the army would be loyal to the state and obey any elected government, Ben-Gurion decided to make it a non-

---

*He did note, however, that the individualistic character of the Israelis would make it difficult to bring off a military coup in Israel:

I am sure that our boys are not like the boys in Germany. In Germany there were 5 million Communists and 7 million Socialists. But when a gang of adventurers came and declared, "We are the government," both Communists and Socialists stood to attention. But here, if Moshe Sne [MAPAM] were to take a battalion, in opposition to the will of the government and the Knesset, and lead it in a march on Tel Aviv, to seize the Headquarters, some of the boys will not obey.

political army of national unity. In the meantime, he banned all political activity in the army and ordered that all "party systems" be eliminated from the armed forces, just as he sought to eliminate them in the national educational system, thereby strengthening not only the concept of statehood, but also eliminating the influence of MAPAM and reinforcing that of MAPAI, his own party being the ruling party.

On the eve of the first Knesset elections David Ben-Gurion indulged in a little game—he wrote down what he thought would be the results on a sheet of paper and gave it to his aide, Nehemiah Argov, to deposit in the Defense Ministry's safe. After the elections the paper was returned to him. "All my guesses were right except one," Ben-Gurion noted proudly. "MAPAM has received far fewer votes than I had expected."[15] A few months later Ben-Gurion described the struggle between MAPAI and MAPAM as the struggle "between Socialist Zionism and Jewish Communism, both in domestic affairs and in international relations."[16]

In addition to the impassioned ideological and political disagreements—on such issues as negotiations with the Arab countries, the orientation between East and West in the Cold War, and the political structure of the army—there were other disputes: MAPAM demanded the nationalization of the country's major industries, and preferential treatment for the cooperative and kibbutz movement, leading gradually to a socialist economy. MAPAI encouraged private initiative and investments of foreign capital. MAPAM organized demonstrations in demand of higher wages. MAPAI was reluctant to respond, being concerned with the cost of living index, premiums and production quotas. MAPAM demanded a constitution—MAPAI delayed it; MAPAM opposed the concessions made by MAPAI to the religious parties.

David Ben-Gurion always viewed the *Palmah* elite fighting units as a MAPAM stronghold. This motivated him to dismantle the *Palmah* and have their functions transferred to the General Army Headquarters in November 1948. Most of the Palmah people were indeed MAPAM supporters and did view themselves as a separate ideological pioneering unit.* The Palmah

---

*A third of MAPAM's voters in the first general Knesset elections were soldiers, as against a fifth of MAPAI's.[17] Some months later Ben-Gurion looked into the party allegiance of six army brigades. He found that "of 36 senior

had a special life-style which made it difficult to integrate its units into the state's regular army establishment. Ben-Gurion suspected, and not without justification, that some Palmah fighters would place obedience to their party before obedience to General Headquarters. This caused a prolonged and painful conflict between MAPAI and MAPAM, partly political, partly psychological—it was a confrontation between different world views and political interests, opposing theories of warfare and philosophies of life. Ben-Gurion wrote to a soldier by name of Shmarya Rapaport:

> I agree with you that Palmah brigades must continue to exist but it is not clear to me what is their special quality. I spent a whole day trying to get to the bottom of it, in company with Palmah commanders—some sixty of them—in kibbutz Naan. I asked them to clarify for me their special ideological, political, professional, technical and partisan quality, and I did not get an authoritative or satisfactory reply. Clearly, the Palmah veterans are distinguished by some important and unique qualities, but . . . I know many people in other brigades who are equally devoted to the high values of pioneering, agricultural settlements, the Hebrew language, have respect for spiritual values, moral courage and so forth. And I know many in the Palmah who are not especially devoted to these values.[19]

A few months later Ben-Gurion invited Israel Galili of MAPAM, the former Commander of the Haganah National Headquarters, to come and see him. Galili had some painful things to tell him. Ben-Gurion later wrote in his diary:

> I invited Galili to explain to me, if he would, what were the ideological, political, and any other differences between us that keep us in two different parties. He said he would explain another time. Instead he told me what he knew about the disorder in the army—the extravagance, careerism, the publicity-chasing, the competition for rank. The good ones don't want to stay on. . . . People want to leave for party reasons, and there is partisan preference. Haim Laskov [later the Chief of Staff] admitted eighty officers for partisan reasons.[20]

A few days later Ben-Gurion asked Laskov if it was true that officers were given commands because they were loyal MAPAI

---

commanders 19 were MAPAM supporters, 5—MAPAI, 9—non-partisan, 2—MAPAM sympathizers and 1—*Hapoel Hamizrahi*."[18]

members. Laskov replied: "In many cases yes, in many cases no."[21]

With the approach of the first anniversary of the dissolution of the Palmah, in October 1949, its former commanders organized a great farewell rally for its fighters, a few hundred of whom were still in the armed forces. At first Ben-Gurion allowed the officers still serving to take part, but later he changed his mind and forbade them to go. He assumed that it would be a MAPAM antigovernment power display. The order placed the Palmah veterans in a difficult situation. "It was a serious conflict," Itzhak Rabin recalled many years later. "An officer does not disobey an order. But my participation in a farewell rally with comrades in arms was a matter of conscience and also filled a deep spiritual need." He decided to disobey the order and attend. A few hours before the rally Rabin was summoned by Ben-Gurion to report to him about some sporadic fighting which had then taken place near Beit Govrin. They met at the Prime Minister's house in Tel Aviv. Ben-Gurion was relaxed and ready for a long, general chat. Rabin: "The hours passed and time was running out, and there I was in uniform, and I still had to change into civilian clothes, since I could not really appear at a Palmah gathering in uniform. I was on pins and needles." Finally he asked Ben-Gurion boldly, "Why put me and my comrades, who have remained in the army, in such an embarrassing position—caught between the desire to maintain discipline and the duty of comradeship, the fraternity of arms and the great partnership with the men with whom we had gone such a long way? Why force us to choose between two rotten alternatives: either to take part in the rally and disobey orders, or not to take part and violate a sacred rule of camaraderie, namely, not to betray your friends?!" Ben-Gurion did not reply. Instead, he asked Rabin to stay for dinner, and Rabin suspected that he was trying to detain him until after the rally. He thanked the Prime Minister but hurried to join his comrades. "I got there late," he recalled, "and the looks people gave me showed what would have happened if I had accepted Ben-Gurion's invitation to have dinner with him...."[22]

There were several hundred officers and men at the rally, all in violation of orders. Ben-Gurion considered it an attempt to "build up an independent military force and accustom the men to put their party's orders above those of the army and prove to the government that it could do nothing to stop it." As far as Ben-Gurion was concerned, the officers who took part in the rally had "betrayed their oath," and he wanted them punished.[23] Indeed, many senior commanders associated with MAPAM were discharged or left, but Ben-Gurion discovered that even after the dissolution of three out of the six brigades which had been formed in the course of the War of Independence, there would still remain MAPAM supporters and sympathizers in the upper echelons of the army.[24] The leaders of MAPAI urged him to reduce their number. "Those are not our officers," they complained, warning that they represented "a great danger to the state." Soon MAPAI began to prepare several hundred cadres of its own people to serve as military instructors.[25]*

Along with the steps taken by Ben-Gurion to cleanse the army of MAPAM people, he also devoted much of his time during those months to the reorganization of the army. His diary is replete with figures: brigades, regiments, service lists, costs. By July he was in a position to present his party with a general outline of the plan, whose execution, he estimated, would take eight to nine months: "We shall have a minimum standing army and a maximum of well-trained and equipped reserves," he announced. At first, Ben-Gurion considered a regular service of three years, but later compromised on two, the first to be devoted to agricultural training and the second to military training. In addition to compulsory national service, he also proposed a voluntary service by professional and scientific cadres who would serve a further three to five years in the armed forces, or as much as a lifetime.[27]

Ben-Gurion hoped to be able to reduce the number of people serving in the armed forces to 20,000. This was not easy: "Once again I have tried to put an army together," he wrote at the end

---

*Among the officers who were wondering at this time whether they would be able to remain in the army was Lt. Colonel Israel Baer. In September 1949 he told Ben-Gurion that he was a member of MAPAM, and asked if he could remain in the army. Ben-Gurion told him that his membership of MAPAM was not a drawback, but warned him that "whoever works in the army may not consult with his party on military matters, neither provide information nor receive orders from it." Baer replied that he accepted these restrictions.[26] A few months later he wrote Ben-Gurion that he was thinking of resigning from the army because people close to the Minister of Defense doubted his loyalty. "You have no reason to fear anybody's doubts," Ben-Gurion reassured him, and perhaps at that time there was indeed no reason. In 1962 Baer was sentenced to 15 years' imprisonment for spying for the USSR.

)f June 1949. "I got down to 25,000."[28] At the beginning of the year there were still nearly 100,000 men in the army. All this was part of what Ben-Gurion described in his diary as the "Fred Plan."

Ben-Gurion was referring to "Fred Harris," but when he was asked about him in the Knesset Foreign Affairs and Security Committee, he admitted that this was not his real name: "Like his friend David Marcus, who changed his name when he was here to Mickey Stone, so Fred Harris is a *nom de guerre*. He is an American citizen, and like Marcus and the rest of the volunteers from the United States, he was not required to swear the oath of loyalty to the Israel Defense Forces."

When the war broke out, several thousand foreign volunteers of many different nationalities, not all of them Jews, came to the country. Most of them were motivated by sympathy for the Zionist struggle, but there were some who were essentially adventurers and misfits. Some had acquired military experience in the armies of the United States, Canada, Britain, South Africa and the Soviet Union, among others. Some of these men were very useful, as infantrymen, naval and airforce personnel. The best known of these volunteers was the American Jewish Colonel David Marcus, who was killed four months after his arrival. He was then the Commander of the Jerusalem front, with the rank of Major General. Ben Dunkelmann, a Jewish-Canadian officer, became the Commander of the Seventh Brigade, which captured Nazareth and got as far as the Litani River in Lebanon.

In a letter Ben-Gurion wrote to Itzhak Ben-Aharon, MK for MAPAM, he stated that "Fred Harris helped the army's Chief of Operations and in that capacity he helped to prepare the firing line and fortifications plan for all the outposts in the country. He also helped with the training of recruits and took part in courses and tests. From time to time I seek his advice and views on various military questions and I have a high regard for his knowledge, experience and understanding in military matters; I don't think there is anyone in the country superior to him."[29]

From time to time Ben-Gurion invited him to take part in meetings of the General Staff. He often met with "Harris," and his diaries reveal that he accepted some of his proposals. At the beginning of January 1949, he recorded the American's findings of various inadequacies that he had discovered in the army, including waste of manpower, as well as faults in administration, acquisition of material, intelligence services and field security.

Ben-Gurion encouraged him to submit written proposals for improvement. He also noted "Harris'" personal estimates of the army's top staff: "Not one of the front commanders is suited for his post," Harris once told Ben-Gurion. Describing Yigael Yadin, Harris wrote: "brilliant, but depends too much on improvization and does not always think all the way through." Harris on Moshe Dayan: "Excellent, very promising, but also needs additional training."[30]

The man who, according to Ben-Gurion, was superior to all the military experts he had ever met, was never known by any name other than Fred Harris, which was what the heads of the army called him.* His real name was Fred Grunich, a native of New York, the son of Jewish immigrants from Austria, a geologist by training but a soldier by inclination and occupation. When he arrived in Israel, a few weeks after the Declaration of Independence, he was 32 years old, and had recently left the US army with the rank of colonel. During World War II he had for a time been attached to Dwight Eisenhower's headquarters. He was a staff officer and also engaged in intelligence work. Years later he related:

> Two men encouraged me to come here, David Marcus and Teddy Kollek [at that time one of Ben-Gurion's aides and head of Israel's diplomatic mission in Washington]. They said my experience would be useful. They didn't tell me exactly what I'd have to do. I was a bachelor, I had just left the army, I still didn't know what I wanted to do. The suggestion to come and help the Israeli army appealed to me greatly. I was a Zionist, in my own way, like everybody else. By the time I arrived, in the latter half of June 1948, David Marcus was no longer alive. Nehemiah Argov met me at the airport and took me straight to Ben-Gurion. Ben-Gurion knew I was coming, but didn't know just what to do with me. He sent me to help Moshe Dayan check the outposts along the Partition line in Jerusalem. I organized a patrol course for them. Then it was decided that I should help Haim Laskov. I went everywhere with him, and I saw at once that the army was not worth much, professionally speaking. Everything was makeshift, many soldiers were killed needlessly. They wouldn't have been killed if the army had been organized as it should be. I understood that I had something to contribute in all that relates to the organization of the army. Ben-Gurion understood this too.[31]

---

*Even 35 years later, the editors of Ben-Gurion's war diaries did not state the man's real name, but only noted that "Fred Harris" was a *nom de guerre*.

He talked to Ben-Gurion about the manpower organization, the weapons systems and the training programs, but also about the rights of the soldier as a citizen and of the citizen as a soldier. Ben-Gurion questioned him a good deal about the defects that he had found in the army and he told him what he had seen: the horrors of the seizure of the Arabic village of Jish, including the massacre of civilians, and the expulsion of the civilians from Rama, and "criminal negligence" in the battle of Faluja. "I told Ben-Gurion that it [the Israeli army] would get bogged down, and it did." Ben-Gurion used to draw him into long conversations about the relative merits and disadvantages of various military doctrines, and about the function of the army as an educational force. He took him along to agonizing sessions with officers of the Palmah, and he took him along to the Knesset, to consult him in the course of the debate about the national service law. He had previously had him take part in the consultations on the wording of that law. Grunich, years later, commented, "Ben-Gurion erred when he took me along to the meeting with the Palmah people. It was a serious error. I sat in the first row, I stood out like a red cow, and as an American I stood for everything that they loathed."

Before leaving the country Grunich tried to persuade Ben-Gurion to end the military rule in the Arab areas. Ben-Gurion rejected his advice, partly due to Igael Yadin's influence. Grunich: "Yadin did not care for my presence. Our disagreements were professional, but perhaps he also thought of me as a rival. I warned Ben-Gurion not to rely on Yadin overmuch. During my service in the American forces I knew some great generals, and I realized that Yadin was not a great general. Ben-Gurion asked me what I thought about the possibility that Yadin would be appointed Chief of Staff. I opposed the idea. One day Ben-Gurion telephoned me from Tiberias and told me that he had decided to appoint Yadin Chief of Staff. I understood that henceforth I would have nothing more to do here, so I went back home."

During his stay in Israel Grunich lived in a rented room in Tel Aviv, and even his landlady did not know his real name. When touring the front lines, and when taking part in the meetings of the General Staff, he wore khaki clothes, without any insignia, and an American-style peaked cap. He spoke English, and at General Staff meetings had to have the proceedings interpreted for him. In every brigade and on all the fronts it was known that he was part of Ben-Gurion's entourage, but nothing more. Some respected his experience and abilities, but many disliked and distrusted him. Being an American, Grunich was despised by the left, both in and outside the army. Before long a rumor spread that he was in Israel on behalf of the Pentagon, or of the CIA—possibly as an advisor, possibly as an agent, perhaps even as a spy. The Palmah chiefs suspected that his mission was to draw Israel into the American strategic system. Grunich stated, "I was neither a spy nor an agent, but I certainly did hope that as a result of the advice I gave Ben-Gurion the Israeli army would be so organized, trained and equipped as to be able to fit into the overall strategic system of the United States in the future. I believed that it would serve the interests of Israel as well as of the United States, because Israel would be unable to stand alone. It did not belong in the Communist bloc and France was not to be relied on. West Germany was yet to be [a world power], Britain was an enemy. That left the United States."

The secret of his stay in Israel was kept for about a year. In July 1949, when the bitterness over the breakup of the Palmah was at its height, Itzhak Ben-Aharon, as member of the Knesset Foreign Affairs and Security Committee, sent Ben-Gurion a parliamentary question off the record in which he demanded to know if it was true that "Fred Harris" was acting as principal military advisor to the Minister of Defense and the Chief of Staff, and was it true that nothing was kept from him? Ben-Gurion confirmed this and added: "I must express my profound regret at this attempt to disqualify (not to use a stronger term) a Jewish soldier, just because he was born in America. . . . I have no reason to doubt Fred Harris' loyalty. On the contrary, I greatly respect him and his service and I view with profound concern the attempt made by your associates in the army to disqualify the help given by persons whose only sin—to the best of my knowledge—is that they know more than those who are trying to find fault in them." According to Ben-Gurion, everything that Ben-Aharon had written about "Harris" could just as well have been written about David Marcus. "I see no basic difference between the two men, except the fact that one has fallen and is no longer with us, so there is no need to undermine him." Ben-Gurion was very angry: "I am filled with anxiety about the methods used by some of your comrades in the army . . . against anyone who is not approved of by MAPAM."[32]

A few days later the matter was leaked to the Communist

daily *Kol Ha'am*. The newspaper extracted from the scanty information at its disposal the conclusion that "General Harris" had come to Israel "to harness our army to the aggressive chariot of the American imperialists and to investigate the conditions prior to establishing American military bases on the soil of our country."[33]* And so Grunich became a part of the debate about the relations of Israel with Washington and Moscow. This was another struggle over principles, and like the others, it was charged with emotions and ideological arguments. Ben-Aharon maintained that the presence of an American officer in Israel violated the government's undertaking to steer a neutral course in the Cold War between the two superpowers. Ben-Gurion replied, "I am a member of a Zionist government and am myself a Zionist and I still believe that I am part of the Jewish nation and that this state belongs to all of it. Every Jew has a share in this state, and it seems to me that spiritual slavery to an anti-American attitude goes too far, if it ends by disqualifying the Jews of America."[35]

A few days later Ben-Aharon published an article in his party's daily *Al Hamishmar*, in which he stated:

> The State of Israel is at present undergoing an intense process of transforming the army, modeling it upon the British and American armies, and this reorganization is not only costing us vast sums of money, but is also losing us some of the finest commanders. . . . This "reorganization" is not motivated by reasons of security. It is dictated not by the interests of the country, but by political and international considerations, and the desire to deprive MAPAM of a decisive role in the army. . . .[36]

Thirty-five years later Grunich denied that the State Department knew about his activities in Israel. Only once, he said, did he meet US Ambassador McDonald at a cocktail party. He introduced himself by his real name and said he was a journalist. Ac-

---

*Toward the end of the year, and in a different context, that newspaper had to answer charges of slander against Ben-Gurion, having accused him of treason. In their efforts to substantiate their accusation, the defendants referred to the withdrawal from El Arish as a result of American pressure, and to "Harris'" presence in Israel. Their counsel interrogated Ben-Gurion himself: "Does not the presence of a foreign espionage officer in the General Staff Headquarters of the army, and the passing of secret information to a foreign power by this means, constitute treason?" The witness Ben-Gurion declined to answer. The court decided that "Harris'" presence in Israel did not suggest that the Prime Minister had committed treason.[34]

cording to him, it was years before the Ambassador discovered that Grunich was Harris. When the truth became known, Grunich was called to Washington and, he said, reprimanded for his activities in the Israeli army without prior permission and without coordinating them with the US military attaché in Tel Aviv. He confirmed, however, that there were some people in Washington who knew what he was doing, including some officials of US Intelligence. During his 18 months in Israel he went twice to the United States in an attempt to persuade the Administration to send a group of military advisors to Israel. He talked one of his acquaintances, Major General Ralph Smith, into agreeing to head such a group, on the condition that Chief of Staff Lawton Collins would approve the mission. Smith approached Collins, but the answer was negative.

Teddy Kollek had previously discussed the matter with Ben-Gurion, who was less than enthusiastic. "I doubted if it was worthwhile bringing in an American general to help with the reorganization of the army," he noted in his diary.[37] Two days later he had already made up his mind unequivocally, following discussions with Golda Meir and Moshe Sharett: "As for inviting an American general, I said I was entirely opposed to it. We cannot reveal all our secrets to an American soldier. They will reach the British and perhaps the Arabs. Best to make do with loyal Jews and to send young men abroad for training."[38] Grunich commented: "I believe that in the end the Old Man would have bought the idea, if only we had got the green light from Washington. He was very keen on American involvement." About a year after he first met Grunich, Ben-Gurion asked Haim Laskov what he thought of him. "He knows a lot," said Laskov. "No less than Marcus, though he is less than Marcus intellectually." "Is he loyal?" Ben-Gurion asked. "Yes," said Laskov. "So long as Israel and the United States are on friendly terms."[39]

Thirty-five years later Ben-Aharon had this to say of him: "David Marcus was also an American colonel. But he was a good buddy, a colorful and humane man, a fighter and a Palmah type. Fred Harris was a dubious character, and he came here on a mysterious and menacing mission. Perhaps some circles in Washington did oppose his mission in Israel, but there were certainly some that encouraged him to come here. In Israel there were elements which tried drawing the country into a complete involvement with the Americans' strategic system, as well as their imperialistic aggressions. The whole thing was sickening."[40] According to Teddy Kollek "Fred came here to help us and did a good job. It was his misfortune that he did not get killed like David Marcus, or he would have been remembered as an even greater hero."[41]*

As the Cold War grew hotter, the ability of small countries to remain neutral and avoid aligning themselves with one or the other of the two superpowers was all but lost. Israel confronted a difficult choice which entailed not only a division between the parties of the Left and those of the Center and Right, but a genuine conflict within MAPAI itself. The Soviet Union had originally supported Israel—Andrei Gromyko's speeches at the UN in favor of the creation of the Jewish state had warmed all Israeli hearts. The Communist countries of the Eastern bloc had sold Israel a good portion of the armaments it used in the War of Independence, and opened their gates to let out Jews of military age, who reinforced the Israeli armed forces. Hundreds of thousands of Jews were still there. Moscow was the capital of Socialism; sympathy for Stalin's USSR involved certain problems, but served MAPAI as an indication of her ideological credibility as a socialist party. It was not easy, in view of the socialist radicalism of MAPAM and the Communist party.† Contrasting with these ideological discussions was Ben-Gurion's pragmatic statesmanship.

The United States applied heavy pressures on Israel, demanding—and sometimes compelling—it to give in on issues Israel considered vital. On the other hand, the biggest and most prosperous Jewish community in the world lived in the United States, and it was an essential source of economic aid and political support. Ben-Gurion tended to express disdain for the American Jews who would not immigrate to Israel, but he took care not to drive them to turn their back on a state whose regime was

*After his return to the United States, Grunich went into the movie business. Thirty years later Jerusalem's Mayor Teddy Kollek still knew how to put him to good use: he got him to support the creation of the Jerusalem Cinemathèque.

†The Israeli CP sought to create a Stalin-type regime in Israel. MAPAM believed in democratic socialism, yet its leader, Yaakov Hazan, is on record as saying, "For us the USSR ... is our second socialist homeland. . . ."[42] On May 1, 1949, MAPAI's Golda Meir promised that a socialist regime would be established within a year by next May Day.[43]

socialistically minded and maintained relations with the Communist bloc. In the first government's basic platform it was said that Israel's foreign relations would be based on friendship with all peace-loving states, "and especially with the United States and the USSR."[44]

For several months, Ben-Gurion tried to maneuver the state through this diplomatic minefield. In a letter to Foreign Minister Sharett, he instructed him to support peace and cooperation between the democratic world and the Communist countries: "Israel avoids joining the Cold War," he stated, "because of vital interests of the state, and out of hope that peace can be maintained." He added that the "democratic bloc" could assure Israel's vital interests in the spheres of immigration, security, the borders, the problem of Jerusalem and relations with the neighboring countries, and allowed for the possibility that if the "totalitarian world" should attack democracy, Israel would come to the latter's defense. Ideologically speaking, the choice had already been made: "The State of Israel is neither passive nor neutral in the great debates raging in the world—in the ideological debate it is democratic and anti-Communist."[45]

Encouraging Israel to enter its sphere of interest, the United States sought to strengthen MAPAI. A few days before the first general Knesset elections it was announced that the American Import & Export Bank was about to lend Israel 100 million dollars to help finance the absorption of immigrants and various development projects. This was a very large sum of money in those days. Negotiations for the loan had been going on for some time—Haim Weizmann, Eliezer Kaplan, Moshe Sharett and others had been engaged in them for some time—but the timing of the announcement, just before the elections, enabled MAPAI to point to a concrete and essential achievement and damaged the credibility of MAPAM's pro-Soviet orientation. The United States emissary, and later Ambassador, to Israel, James McDonald, had initiated this intervention in Israel's internal affairs, on the premise that MAPAI might not otherwise win all the votes it needed to withstand MAPAM's "pro-Soviet subversion." "The Soviets may be planning a few election tactics of their own," the diplomat warned in a letter to Secretary of State George Marshall, which he asked the latter to convey to President Truman. "The Soviet Union enjoys widespread public sympathy in Israel," he added. He described MAPAI as a pro-Western party that upheld a Western-style regime ensuring political rights, and economic and social justice. He recommended that the United States strengthen MAPAI's position by announcing its formal, *de jure*, recognition of Israel even before the elections, or at least approval of the loan. "MAPAM is equally aware of the need to obtain this loan," he pointed out, "but it will object to any political strings that might be attached to it. It is therefore highly important for MAPAI that the announcement should emphasize that the loan does not entail any political commitments."[46]* Three months later the head of the Middle East and Africa Section in the State Department recommended that the US respond favorably to another request which had in the meantime been made by Tel Aviv—to enable a number of Israeli officers to train with the American armed forces. The State Department official wrote that this would help strengthen Israel's link with the West.[48]†

In the latter half of 1950 the tension between the two blocs reached an unprecedented climax, and the Korean War broke out. At this point Israel aligned itself openly with the United States. The USSR had already withdrawn its warm support for Israel and begun to seek friends in the Arab world. In effect, Israel had begun to enter the American sphere of influence a long time before it admitted as much, and some of the neutralists in Israel—including Foreign Minister Sharett and the higher echelons in his Ministry—did not become aware of it at once. This was a crucial decision, but it was not made by an authorized government forum; rather, it was the outcome of circumstances and various steps taken by the pragmatic aides of David Ben-Gurion, following his lead which was more pro-American than neutralist. The American loan, the request for military aid from the United States, and Fred Grunich's mission were largely the results of these pragmatic concerns. In addition, there were already in Israel many American experts and advisors of various sorts. Some time later, the US created a special fund for the dis-

---

*The American loan was indeed criticized as an attempt to rope Israel into serving US interests. Moshe Sne (MAPAM): "The first stage is aid, the second stage is subjugation, the third stage is military bases, and from here on the road is open for the final stage: a world war."[47]

†The US Ambassador in London sent Washington a highly secret report suggesting that the Soviet Union might win greater influence in Israel through Menahem Begin, in part because of their shared hatred for Britain.[49]

tribution in various countries, including Israel, of American books, periodicals, movies and records, in order to counteract the propaganda which was pouring in across the Iron Curtain. All these were early stages in the Americanization of Israeli society.[50]

Israel's pro-American orientation led to a deterioration of the relations between the pragmatists of MAPAI and leftists of MAPAM and impeded the negotiations between them after the first general elections. Had the two parties come to an agreement they could between them have controlled 65 out of the 120 seats in the Knesset, and together with the two Arab MKs who were committed to MAPAI they would actually have enjoyed a majority of 67 as against 53. MAPAM was very eager to take part in the government—its leaders dreamed of a "Labor hegemony."[51] In MAPAI, too, there were many who were eager to see such a partnership—at meetings of the party Center, the Secretariat, and the party's MKs, it was constantly depicted as an ideal of "working class solidarity" and "the ideological solidarity of sister parties."

But MAPAI had no wish to see its political power dependent on MAPAM's support. The latter's political path had led it down a too-leftist course and the price it demanded for participation in the government was too high. In the negotiations, it demanded, among other things, the Ministry of Defense.[52] Partnership with the religious bloc, on the other hand, ensured MAPAI's dominant status in the government, and the religious tended to confine their demands to religious matters. In fact, they did not demand much more than they would have obtained if they had not supported the government, since Ben-Gurion considered the rift between the religious and the secular more dangerous for the country than a rift between MAPAI and MAPAM. And so MAPAM remained in the Opposition and as time went by adopted very radical positions, some of them not far from those of the Communist party.

While negotiating with MAPAM, MAPAI also studied the possibility of including the General Zionists in the government. They had participated in the provisional government prior to the creation of the state and their presence in the coalition, along with the religious bloc, would have served to isolate Herut in the right wing of the Opposition. Neither MAPAI nor the General Zionists had any difficulty in bridging the ideological and emotional differences between "workers" and "management." What they were unable to bridge was their dispute over the ministries they both coveted. The General Zionists demanded much more than MAPAI was willing to give, and in the end they, like MAPAM, remained in the Opposition for the time being.[53] Like MAPAM, the General Zionists were a very active Opposition, and often fought the government tooth and nail. Yet they never forgot that the time might come when they would renew their partnership with MAPAI—and so it came to pass.

The same was not true of Herut and the Communist party. These were ostracized and kept outside the camp, as it were, on the fringe of political legitimacy. The Communist party was very small. Three of its four MKs were very young, under 30, and one of them was an Arab. The slogan "without Herut and the CP" was not meant to exclude the Communists from potential participation in the coalition, since there was no question of including them in the Cabinet, but rather to ostracize Herut while tainting it by bracketing it with the Communists. The rift between MAPAI and Herut was so deep that violence between the two groups was not out of the question. One could trace the rift back to the twenties when the Labor Zionist movement was already at loggerheads with the nationalist "Revisionist Zionists" whose leader was Zeev Jabotinsky. In the forties, the "Revisionists" operated anti-British terrorist organizations. Before the establishment of Ben-Gurion's government, they attempted to smuggle in a ship filled with weapons, the *Altalena*, which was sunk by order of Ben-Gurion himself. They also assassinated the Swedish UN emissary, Count Folke Bernadotte. As Ben-Gurion put it, the *Altalena* was "an attempt to destroy the army and murder the state."[54] The assassination of Bernadotte he described as a frightful and disgraceful act.[55] Those two affairs revived the image of the underground organizations as terror groups. Menahem Begin's fiery, chauvinistic speeches in the country's public squares, surrounded by gangs of young men in uniform, reinforced his image in the eyes of his opponents as a potential fascist dictator. The year 1949 was not a good one in Begin's career: his party, Herut, organized in time for the first general elections, won only 14 seats in the Knesset, a disappointing return. "Yet it was our tremendous power which defeated

Britain!" wrote Yohanan Bader. "We are wholly justified, and no other factor in the country wishes to serve the nation as wholeheartedly as we served it in the days of the underground."[56]

Herut prepared itself dejectedly for a long stay in the Opposition. Begin proclaimed: "We have a great responsibility and we shall do the best we can."[57] He was then 36 years old. A native of Brest-Litovsk, he described himself as a journalist, having served as a private soldier in General Andres' Free Polish army, and later as the commander of *Irgun Zvai Leumi* (the National Military Organization), an anti-British terror organization commonly referred to as the IZL or "Irgun." After the creation of the state he took great pains to shed the image which had been attached to him and his party as a result of their acts of terrorism. At the Knesset he appeared as a proper gentleman, meticulous in his dress and style of speech—"Your Honor, the Speaker of the House; Honorable Members!" He frequently cited fine points in the law, laced with many Latin phrases. Before long he shaved off his mustache. In September 1948 Begin told the members of his party's Secretariat that it was essential to maintain cordial relations with Ben-Gurion's government, yet without blurring the party's Opposition character. But MAPAI did everything it could to prevent Herut from joining the legitimate parliamentary process. Its heads simply refused to believe that Herut had really outgrown its underground behavior. As late as April 1949 Ben-Gurion noted a report by Isser Harel, head of the Secret Service, stating that "the underground plans to assassinate Abdullah Tall . . . and blow up the walls of Jerusalem."[58] Six months later Harel reported that Herut was planning to set up "a small underground" in the army.[59]

Menahem Begin did a great deal of travelling around the world, going wherever he was honored more than he was in Israel, including a visit to the Argentine dictator, Juan Perón. He did not often make speeches in the Knesset, but when he did he spoke only about the headline-making issues, deliberately adopting the role of a statesman and historian, a national, nonpartisan, heroic figure. He was worshipped by his followers, and popular among the religious and Oriental Jews, as a leader who exemplified national dignity and pride, an impressive alternative to the "defeatism" of the government, whose "conciliatory" attitudes had, according to him, caused the loss of half the country. "Frightful bloodshed still awaits us," he said following the armistice agreement with Jordan. "This is not a tactical error, nor is it a strategic one, but an historic crime, and we must demand that those who conduct our foreign policy pay for the defeat they have inflicted upon our people."[60]

While he was ostracized as a leper by MAPAI and most parts of the political establishment, his actions and speeches carried little weight, and neither did the speeches of his comrades, but they did contribute to the development of Israel's parliamentary democracy; it was difficult and frustrating to lead the Opposition against David Ben-Gurion. MAPAI's secure coalition led many of its leaders to identify their party with the state, and to view any struggle against its rule as an attack upon the state itself. "Ours is a strange party," said MAPAI's Secretary General, Zalman Aran: "The party is the Histadrut, the state, and the Jewish Agency; it's everything!"[61] Ben-Gurion and the leaders of his party did feel, however, a genuine commitment to the restrictions of democracy and the rule of law, but they often interpreted them in their own way—"for the good of the state," "for security reasons," or even "for the good of the party." Ben-Gurion's giant shadow possessed certain quasi-totalitarian characteristics. *Dvar Hashavua*, a weekly magazine published by the Histadrut and representing the views of MAPAI, demanded once that "mediocre and bad artists" be forbidden to leave the country, for fear that they would hurt the reputation of Israeli art, and thus damage Israel's good name. The weekly asked why "the state, which for its own sake and ours has imposed supervision over all aspects of life, cannot see to it that the arts should not be a wide open territory which anyone can come and plow at will."[62] It warned against "excessive criticism" of things that happened in the country, which might give the state a bad name and weaken its international standing. "We must appear before the world as a nation-state, and we must learn to live like a nation-state," it declared.[63] Ben-Gurion too tended to demand that the press be "responsible" to the nation. "The journalist, if he is not to be a mere hireling who sells himself to the buyer, is the public educator and instructor," he once wrote to Gershom Schocken, the Editor-in-Chief of *Haaretz*. The Prime Minister protested that "a large number"—"too many"—journalists "were not doing their duty in these grave times."[64] His suit against the Communist daily *Kol Ha'am* was, in his own words, meant to put an end to it.[65] The chief of the Secret Services, Isser

Harel, often engaged in political investigations, and military censorship was often used to prevent the publication of matters that MAPAI found inconvenient, such as a poem by Nathan Altermann, protesting the breaking up of the Palmah. Itzhak Ben-Aharon read it in the Knesset, where it went into the *Knesset Record*.[66] Furthermore, Ben-Gurion, on the subject of "unjustified strikes" in the civil service, stated, "In my opinion such a thing is no less dangerous than the threat of war, military coups and the like."[67]

Party politics were filled with spite. Years later Yohanan Bader of Herut wrote of MAPAI, "They hated us. They were wolves."[68] The feeling was mutual. Menahem Begin said that Israel was being "governed from a den of iniquity."[69] All these served as tests of the capability and readiness of the first Israelis to live together in a democratic law-abiding state. They wanted to do so and they succeeded, which was the great achievement of that year of genesis. The verbal violence—in speech and in writing—which often verged on hysteria, tarnished the image of the political scene, but, paradoxically, it may have been one of the reasons why the violence almost never became physical, rather like steam being let off and evaporating.* Beyond the everyday rivalry, and even beyond what looked to many of the first Israelis of all parties like an eternal enmity between the forces of good and the forces of evil, most Israelis agreed with the basic aims of Zionism and felt a deep commitment to the national struggle, a commitment which was intensified by the Holocaust and the War of Independence. Israeli politics had learned a good deal from 50 years of Zionist activity, and the Israeli administration had learned a good deal in the 30 years of British rule. Both the Zionist movement and the mandatory government were heirs to a tradition of parliamentary democracy.

The first Israelis often indulged in soul-searching arguments, where they tried to mold their national and cultural identity as

---

*The exception was on September 12, 1949, when a young man by the name of Avraham Tsfati entered the public gallery of the Knesset, pulled a machine gun from under his overcoat and aimed it at the seats of the Cabinet. The Prime Minister and several of the Ministers were present at the time. Tsvi Ziegler, the usher, managed to push the man aside seconds before he pressed the trigger. Tsfati said he wanted to punish the government for refusing to meet his demand to build a temple dedicated to the United Nations in Jerusalem.

Jews and Israelis. It was not easy; almost every news event led to long, repetitive, discussions, all of which eventually led back to the basic question: Who are we; what do we strive to be? Toward the end of March 1949—and again in mid-October—Ben-Gurion found time to hold a lengthy discussion with several dozen writers and intellectuals. "The government wishes to learn from you," he told them. It was a gathering of highly respected thinkers, who were struggling with the modern definition of a national Jewish identity.

Philosopher S.H. Bergmann: ". . . It has been said that we are in difficulties because of the mass immigration which we must forge into a nation. I believe that the difficulty is amongst ourselves no less than between us and the newcomers. I feel that we are in the throes of a great crisis of values, a profound spiritual crisis. . . . Zionism has given the people of Israel, the Jewish people which had been severed from its spiritual resources, a new content and purpose. Zionism filled the hollow space which had opened in the Jewish people, and enabled it to go on existing spiritually for several generations, because it was a goal for which it could strive. And now this goal has been achieved, in its first and most important phase. And once again we have to face the question: What is Judaism, what does it stand for, and what is a Jewish State? . . . And I see a fearful danger facing us. It is precisely among ourselves, in the second generation, that I perceive a danger of dehumanization, a loss of human values among the young people. I see a tendency to xenophobia, a kind of self-segregation—which is no doubt a psychological, historical and sociological effect of the Holocaust and all that has happened to us. It is a frightful thing. Go through the streets of Jerusalem . . . and you will see that all the signs in Latin characters have been removed. This is a dreadful illustration of how our young people are turning inward, of a generation that does not know what the founders of this state fought for, the great human values which they had in mind. . . . This year they reduced the hours of English lessons in the primary schools. We may assume that this was done as a temporary measure, resulting from the shortage of teaching staff. But I see it as part of the tendency to sever our links with the outer world. Instead of creating a Hebrew environment which would also be humanistic and cultivate relations with the outer world—and I don't care if we teach our young people Russian or English or German, as long as they will know the outer world—we have been cultivating the opposite tendency. . . ."

Writer Eliezer Steinmann: ". . . The question is, what are we carrying over from Judaism into Israeliness? What do we consider
the solid values and what is secondary, which of the old things
are we willing to give our lives for, and which are we not? . . .
We are deeply stirred and anxious to discover the new form that
we are taking, the new, Israeli, core which is forming inside us,
what links us to the Jewish culture and what to that of other nations, how far can we go from our sources without endangering
our distinction and even our existence? . . ."

Poet Haim Gouri: ". . . At the Sharon Hotel in Herzlia our young Israeli snobbery has been enjoying itself in luxury in the best 'international' tradition, which is rapidly growing here, while the
soldiers at the front, and the state, are facing the fire, in the gray
austerity of bread, clothing and a roof over the head. . . . What
should have been created here is a socialist culture deriving
from the depths of this soil, a culture which would emerge from
the conquered wilderness, and the struggle for the smells and
landscapes of this land. . . ."

In the course of this discussion various proposals were made
for a greater involvement of intellectuals in the shaping of society, including a suggestion to create a *"Sanhedrin"* of intellectuals—parallel to the Knesset—to guide the people. At the second meeting there was also the following dialogue: ex-Minister
and columnist I. Gruenbaum said, "The Messiah has come,
though in fact he is not here. We have a state, but no Messiah. I
use the word Messiah to indicate liberation. For the Jews of Morocco, Yemen and North Africa, when the Exodus began, the
idea of the Jewish State awakened dreams and hopes that the
Messiah had come. And then they came here—and there was no
Messiah. . . ." And S. Yavniely, one of the founding fathers of the
Labor movement said, "The time of the Messiah is here. In every
one who fell in battle and in every soldier who remains alive, in
the government, in the entire independent system of administration, the Messiah is realized. . . ." To which Ben-Gurion re-
torted:

I say the Messiah has not come, and I do not await the Messiah.
The moment he arrives, he will cease to be the Messiah. When you
find his address in the telephone directory, he will no longer be the
Messiah. The greatness of the Messiah lies in that his address is unknown and one cannot reach him, and no one knows what sort of
car he drives, or if he drives a car at all, or rides on a donkey or flies

on the wings of eagles. The Messiah is needed so that he will not arrive, because waiting for the Messiah is more important than the Messiah himself and the Jewish people lives awaiting him and believing in him. Which is the reason why the Jewish people exists at all.[70]

Some of these discussions reflected a growing tension between the national vision and the day-to-day routine, between inner emotion and the requirements of national policy. Most painful among them was the debate concerning Israel's relationship with West Germany. Negotiations over the reparations agreement had begun, and the government had to discuss the possibility of trade relations between the two countries.[71] At first, the issue overlapped with the argument over Israel's relationship with the superpowers, as the Federal Republic, headed by Chancellor Adenauer, was clearly part of the Western bloc, and thus viewed by the Israeli Left as an alliance between American imperialism and German neo-Nazism. But there was more to it. Gershom Schocken, the liberal, German-born editor of *Haaretz*, demanded that the Knesset pass a law forbidding Israelis to settle in Germany or even to enter it, except on a specific national mission. The law he proposed would also have prohibited any social contact between Israeli and German citizens, beyond accidental meetings, such as might take place in hotels outside Germany.[72] The awareness of the Holocaust and the means of preserving its memory were still in their embryonic stages—at this time they reflected hatred and vindictiveness, not yet a national mythology of heroic resistance, which characterized Israel's later attitude toward the Holocaust. "We must inculcate hatred for Germans in our young children and in their offspring to come," asserted an article in the evening paper *Yediot Aharonot*. "Vengeance must come, and it will come when we are stronger."[73] The first Israelis did not quite know how to deal with the problem. The slightest hint of a possible connection with Germany, and especially visits by Germans to Israel, aroused violent reactions in the press. Yet when Hilmar Schacht, who had served in Hitler's government, stopped at Tel Aviv airport in transit, he was interviewed by Israeli newsmen about the state of the world economy. The press later entered a long debate on whether or not it was OK to interview an ex-Nazi. While still searching for the proper way of commemorating the Holocaust, a kibbutz was established and named Buchenwald, after the concentration camp. Later it was renamed Netser Sereni, after an Israeli agent who was dropped behind the German lines during the war and perished. In the spring of 1949 "The Seven Dwarfs from Auschwitz," two brothers and five sisters, Hungarian-born survivors of the death camps, who were dwarfs, toured the country singing and dancing, before full houses. At the same time, the Knesset debated laws against genocide as well as a law to bring Nazis and their accomplices to justice.

The intense confrontation between different values and ideologies gave rise to a tremendous flood of literature. In the months preceding, during and after the War of Independence, the country was inundated with new newspapers and magazines. Everywhere there were poetry readings, literary evenings and political symposiums. There were books, including novels and collections of poetry, which sold tens of thousands of copies. The theaters staged original plays before packed houses. A new generation of authors appeared, to be named "The 1948 Generation." There was great uniformity in their writings. Most of them produced documentary-style novels whose main subject was always the nation and the country rather than the individual. They wrote and thought in the first person plural, seeking to express the ethos of a reborn nation. Their main subject was the mythical *Sabra*, the native-born soldier boy. Handsome, upright, honest, bold and hounded by none of the complexes of the Diaspora, he was always ready to die in defense of his home and the life of his "girl." He was always ready to kill too, but whenever he had to shoot he would cry in self-pity, for of course he hated war more than anything else. Tough on the outside and tender on the inside, his hair was always blowing in the wind as he rode his jeep, part cowboy in a Western movie, part epic hero in a great Soviet novel; these novels were quite popular in Israel in those days.

Everybody talked about "new horizons," but the writers of 1948 were no rebels or revolutionaries; in fact there was something distinctly conservative and nostalgic about them. They identified with the goals and struggles of Zionism and shared the values of their fathers who had come to Israel as pioneers to build the country and be rebuilt in it. Like their fathers many of them belonged to the Labor movement, having been brought up that way at home, in the Labor schools and in the Labor youth movements. Many of them had fought in the War of Independence. According to writer Ehud Ben-Ezer, the War of Independence left a deep trauma in the mind of the generation that fought it. Returning from the front, many of them felt alienated in the face of the profound changes that had taken place in the landscape, both physical and human, with the flight of the Arabs, the mass immigration and the stepped-up construction everywhere, which lacked even the smallest touch of romance. They had been dreaming of "new horizons" and fighting for them, but having returned from the war they were yearning for the land of their childhood and, yes, even for the Arabs. The Arabs were the enemy, but they were also regarded as the ones who kept up the real biblical nature of the country. Now that they were gone, it was no longer the same. All this ambivalance was also echoed in their writings.[74]

Baruh Kurzweil, a noted and feared critic, had little use for the writers of 1948, because as he put it they tended to ignore the "historical connection between the thousands who died here and the millions who died over there," namely the victims of the Holocaust. Kurzweil resented what he regarded as false Israeli sentimentalism and lack of genuine Jewish emotion.[75] The real debate, however, raged between the literary establishment, including the generation of 1948–1949, and another type of literature which also grew out of the war, but which was skeptical and at times nihilistic, anti-Zionist and in a sense "non-Jewish." Emerging out of the "Canaanite" movement and its fringes, this literature questioned some of the most basic values and ideologies upon which Israeli society was built—notably, the conception of Jewry as a national entity.[76] The leader of the "Canaanites," Yohanan Ratosh, postulated in 1949 what might lie ahead for the young state.

> Now it is possible for a new Hebrew nation to arise, young and strong and mighty, the liberator of its homeland . . . hand in hand with all its inhabitants . . . Jews, Christians, Moslems, Druze and others. Or there will be a Jewish State in the Holy Land, part of the Jewish Diaspora, a latter-day Second Temple kingdom, an insular entity, its existence submissive, depending on force of arms and money in a hostile world . . . leaning on the communities of the Diaspora, using them to obtain for it the support of the world at cut price. . . .[77]

Few people were attracted to this anti-Zionist literature, since most Israelis viewed themselves as Jews and Zionists. Yet the

"Canaanite" philosophy was more than an intellectual freak; some of its ideas found their way into Israeli poetry and fiction, and here and there into the press. Some were even compatible with David Ben-Gurion's own philosophy.

Ben-Gurion, like the "Canaanites," set the Land of Israel at the center of the national existence: "It was here that the histori- cal Jewish nation was forged,"[78] he wrote, ignoring the Jewish culture which had flourished elsewhere in the world. He sought to link Zionism to the civilization of the ancient Hebrews. The first Zionist immigrations from Eastern Europe had created, in his opinion, "a new human type," "a bold and creative man whose purpose in life was work and defense . . . such as had not been seen among the Jews in all the lands of the Diaspora."[79] At the first meeting with the writers Ben-Gurion said, "This nation will be built from many tribes. It is necessary to melt down the debris of Jewish humanity which is scattered throughout the world and will come to Israel, in the melting-pot of Indepen- dence and national sovereignty. It is necessary to create a He- brew character and style, which did not exist, which could not have existed, in the Diaspora, among a people without a home- land, without Independence and national freedom."[80]*

These "Canaanite" elements in Ben-Gurion's outlook greatly impeded relations between the state and the Jewish Diaspora. Ben-Gurion could not sever the connection, nor did he want to, but his relations with the Jewish communities abroad were com- plex and full of inner contradictions. "The real business is here," he determined, "and ten Herzls could not change this."[82] In the latter half of 1949 he formulated a number of basic rules to regu- late relations between Israel and the Diaspora, principally the Jewish community in the United States:

> No Jew in the Diaspora, be he Zionist or non-Zionist, can take part
> in the government of Israel. The state is sovereign, and its regime,

*Many others thought so too. In the first 18 months after Independence, some 20,000 of the first Israelis changed their surnames for Hebrew ones, seek- ing a new Israeli identity. This practice had begun in the first decades of the century and reached its climax in 1949. Ben-Gurion (formerly Green) encour- aged this development. On some occasions he made a change of name a condi- tion for promotion in the army or the civil service.[81] When it was decided that the Tel Aviv municipality would include Jaffa, the question arose what the joint entity would be called. Some said Jaffa took precedence, being a biblical town—Ben-Gurion also thought so. Others preferred Tel Aviv, the Hebrew ti- tle of Theodor Herzl's *Altneuland*. It was agreed to call the city Jaffa–Tel Aviv. However, in time the Jewish-Zionist approach won, and the city came to be known as Tel Aviv–Jaffa.

constitution and government will be determined only by the will of its citizens. . . . On the other hand, the State of Israel does not represent the Jewish people in the world, nor is the Government of Israel entitled to speak on behalf of world Jewry. . . . A Jew in the State of Israel has no particular prerogative to deal with [worldwide] Jewish matters in preference to any other Jew elsewhere.[83]

The Controller of the Zionist Federation, Dr. Emile Schmorak, a man of integrity, believed that the Prime Minister had made things perfectly plain. He therefore proposed that the State of Israel repay the Zionist Federation all the sums it had received to finance the War of Independence and immigrant absorption. Ben-Gurion lost no time in setting him straight: "The State of Israel is not just the business of its inhabitants," he said. "We, the Jews of the Land of Israel, do not need, for our own defense, to settle the entire country. We sit in Tel Aviv and Haifa, and that is quite enough for us."[84]

The Israeli interpretation of Zionism placed a heavy emphasis on agriculture as a human and moral value which also reflected an obvious anti-Diaspora sentiment, almost Canaanite. The writer Yehuda Bourla sought to identify the nation's very existence with the cultivation of the land, and the Jewish Agency reprinted some of his ideas in its official publications:

> It is quite plain that only large-scale agricultural development can serve as a healthy foundation for the Homeland, and indeed, for creating the Homeland, and with its creation, the nation itself will follow. In the lands of the exile the Jewish people was denied the privilege and joy of suckling at the breast of the soil, of merging its soul with the soil. Strange and alien, hated and persecuted, the Jew moved around the world mentally harassed and spiritually embittered. The whole Jewish people was an invalid, an abnormality, and it is therefore its greatest ambition that the major part of the people should be rooted in the soil of the Homeland, linking heart and soul with the labor of its cultivation, for there is no more marvellous a cure to restore the Jewish people to national health, homely simplicity and human naturalness, than the cultivation of the soil.[85]

Ben-Gurion told the Knesset that in the opinion of military experts whom he had consulted, including "important experts from abroad," there would never be an effective army in Israel unless the youth, and most particularly those who had recently arrived, first received training in agriculture, "which would make them become rooted in the life of their Homeland."[86] The schools, too, devoted much time to introducing children to the life of the farmer. In one of the most popular textbooks for young children, the theme of "Daddy" began with the words, "In the morning Tamar did not see Daddy—he was in the fields."[87] At midday Daddy was still in the fields. "When I grow up I shall be a farmer, and build a little house in the country" read one of the rhymes in the same book, under the heading "When I Grow Up."[88] "Yossi saw his brother Shlomo plowing the field. In the evening he went up to him and whispered in his ear: 'Shlomo, when I grow up I should like to plow, too.'"[89] About 20 percent of the text in that reader contained similar material, in accordance with the national educational program.*

The children hoed and sowed in the school gardens, and once a year, on *Tou Bishvat* (The 15th of the month Shvat is the Jewish calendar), they were taken to plant trees.† Once a year, on the feast of *Shavuot* (Pentecost), the children put garlands on their heads and went on parades, bearing fruit and vegetables which they had brought from home, preferably in straw baskets. The teachers accompanied them, beating tambourines. When, in February 1949, it was decided to impose a luxury tax on musical instruments, they exempted tambourines, concertinas and flutes—to protect the performances of so-called folk music and dance, which were largely derived from rural Eastern Europe. In Israel's new national myth, the cities, in contrast to the country, represented morbid decadence and corruption; Tel Aviv was ruled by the bourgeois General Zionists. Many of the country's

---

*At this time *Dvar Hashavua* depicted this youthful Israeli ideal:

> Our children start going to kindergarten almost as soon as they learn to walk. In another few years they begin to attend school. They ride bicycles, join the youth movement, go on hikes throughout the country, engage in sports and swim in the sea. They pass their exams, and now they are adults, at the service of the nation. Our children go to the front and defeat the enemy. Many of them are joining agricultural settlements. May there be more like them in Israel![90]

Not an academic career, then, nor any other professional training—agricultural settlement was the goal.

†The forestation of the country was one of the most important enterprises of the state. It, too, was an idea that occupied Ben-Gurion's mind obsessively. One day he called Yosef Weitz, head of the Jewish National Fund, which was in charge of forestation, and ordered him to plant one billion trees in the next 10 years. Weitz thought the Prime Minister was joking, or going out of his mind.[91] Some time later Ben-Gurion called him again and asked if it was possible to transfer a 5,000-year-old cedar from Lebanon—"from the time of Abraham the Patriarch"—to plant on Mount Herzl, thus fulfilling the prophecy of Ezekiel in Chapter 31. Weitz replied that it was impossible. Ben-Gurion said that nothing was impossible, no matter how much it cost.[92]

politicians came from kibbutzim, or at any rate felt committed to the "working settlements," as they called the rural population, as though the urban population did not work. As a result, considerable budgets were allocated to agricultural development, and the cities were neglected. Nevertheless, the overwhelming majority of Israelis preferred to live in the cities, disregarding the "decadence of exile."

10

Codfish with Everything

After the Declaration of Independence, it was estimated that the cost of absorbing each immigrant—including housing, and employment—would range between 2,000 and 3,000 dollars. Thus, in order to absorb 230,000 immigrants in 1949, a sum of between 460 and 690 million dollars would be required. According to David Horowitz, at that time Director General of the Finance Ministry, "This was more money than we had and more than we could hope to raise."[1] In the fiscal year 1949–1950, the government spent about 170 million *lirot*, equivalent then to about 700 million dollars—at the then current rate of exchange of four dollars per *lira*.[2]* The Israeli balance of pay-

---

*In September 1949 the British government devalued the pound sterling. It had stood at about 4 dollars, and was now set at about 3. Until 1952 the Israeli *lira* was linked to sterling, and thus was devalued at the same time. Ben-Gurion wrote:

Finance Minister Kaplan informed me that he had an urgent matter to put before the Cabinet. It met at nine-thirty. . . . England informed us that it was devaluing the pound sterling and setting it at 2.8 dollars. Kaplan and Horowitz proposed postponing our decision, because they thought they would want to devalue our *lira* down to 2.4 dollars later on. I proposed that we decide forthwith on a reduction to 2.8 dollars, or else there would be confusion and currency speculation would begin. All the members of the Cabinet agreed, except Kaplan.[3]

ment deficit in 1949 reached 220 million dollars, and the following year rose to 282 million dollars.* In the course of the year Israel received some 320 million dollars, one third from the Jewish community of the United States, and the rest as loans. Prolonged negotiations with the British government produced the thawing of Jewish sterling reserves, which had been frozen in London during World War II, including funds belonging to the Jewish Agency, the Jewish National Fund, *Keren Hayesod*, chief financial instrument of the Zionist organization, the Histadrut and the Anglo-Palestine Bank (later *Bank Leumi Le-Israel*). But since about 25 percent of the government's budget was allocated to defense, the entire annual budget was much smaller than the sum required for immigration absorption. In addition, it was necessary to invest in housing and employment for tens of thousands of veterans. At this time total unemployment in Israel including the new immigrants, stood at 14 percent. Among the veteran Israelis the figure stood at 10 percent. Horowitz wrote: "The waves of immigration and the economic problems fell upon us with a force which could have broken the backs of those who were responsible for the absorption of the immigrants."[5]

There had been Jewish immigration to Palestine before Independence, but those immigrants had brought with them capital, means of production, skills and education. Most of the immigrants who arrived after Independence were destitute, and their level of education was lower than that of the established population. Thus the chief burden of absorbing them fell upon the public, through the government and the Jewish Agency. In the short run it was necessary to finance both the immigrants' passage to Israel and their basic needs, such as housing (in the camps), food, clothing and medical services. In the long run it would be necessary to provide permanent housing—urban and rural—sources of employment, an educational system, and so forth. Part of the public investment needed to finance absorption, mainly that in settlement and housing, the government financed by inflationary means, including the printing of money. At the same time, an austerity program was initiated, which included strict price

---

*About 30 percent of imports were finished consumer goods; the rest was raw materials, fuel and finished investment products. The total value of Israeli exports in 1949 was a mere 40 million dollars. Israel's principal exports were citrus fruit and cut diamonds, which between them accounted for 80 percent of the exports in 1949.[4]

controls, rationing of food and services, raw materials and foreign currency. The program was designed to ensure a minimum
standard of living for the entire population, locals and newcomers alike.

The austerity regulations were copied principally from the
rationing methods which had been enforced in Britain during
World War II. The Hebrew name for the program, *Tsena*, was a
translation of the English word "austerity," an innovation
coined by the linguist Reuven Alkalay, when he was still working for the British Mandatory Press Office. He had considered
several possibilities and even consulted the poet Avraham
Shlonsky.[6] Poet Uri Tsvi Greenberg, who was then a Member of
Knesset, proposed to call it "pioneer poverty." He not only favored the austerity plan—he wanted it to be the country's "life-
long constitution."[7] "There is no other alternative," stated
Golda Meir, single-minded as ever: "There is no avoiding this
simple choice: either ration immigration, or ration food and
clothing." She infused even this economic debate with heavy
emotion. "After all, what is demanded of us?" she asked, addressing the Knesset. "A little less extravagance, so as not to dis-
sipate the inheritance for which our dear ones gave their lives.
They did not die for the sake of prosperity, but for the state and a
great immigration."[8] From the Opposition benches came the
cry, "But the people are hungry!" and Menahem Begin went so
far as to argue that the austerity program endangered the state's
security, as hungry children would not grow into stalwart war-
riors. "You are bringing up a generation of invalids!" he cried.[9]

The people were not hungry, but they had to make do with
frozen codfish and dehydrated eggs, obtained in exchange for
coupons after standing in line for hours. The coupons and lines
frayed people's nerves. The austerity program threatened the
country with economic tyranny, but in effect it proved to be a
boon to both speculators and bureaucrats, who fought one another through the grotesque labyrinth of bylaws, regulations and
orders, licensing and supervision, in which both sides lost their
way.

Dov Yosef, "Minister of Austerity," as he was called, asserted that control would not succeed in opposition to the people's will. He recalled the American experience of prohibition:
"The American people didn't want it, and so eventually the government had to abolish that law, though it was a good law, for

the good of the people and to save them from harm."[10] The Israelis did not want Dov Yosef to impose upon them what was good for them, despite all his achievements, and he never forgave them for it: "They wanted beef," he recalled, disgustedly, in his memoirs.[11] The austerity program was, like many other measures, a product of compromise among parties and politicians.[12]

The debate around it also reflected a genuine conflict of social outlooks. "The State of Israel is not a capitalist state," declared David Ben-Gurion in the course of one of those debates, defending the imposition of government control in the austerity program. "Less than half its workforce is employed by private enterprise. Nor is this a socialist state, because it does have—at the government's encouragement—private enterprise and private capital and hired labor."[13] The other disputants also reverted to ideological arguments of one kind or another, as was the style of the times. The austerity program reflected a measure of puritanism, a profound dislike of shopkeepers and all that they stood for, and an almost mystical belief in the power of bureaucracy to solve problems. Dov Yosef reported:

> When the fighting ended the government realized that the historic undertaking of our generation, the ingathering of the exiles, could only be carried out with huge efforts and sacrifices on the part of all sections of Israeli society. This was the reason for the decision to impose austerity—ensuring food for everyone, controlling, and if possible reducing, prices. Only thus could the country produce the income of hard currency which it desperately needed to develop our agriculture and industry.[14]

Dov Yosef's first austerity speech, in April 1949, was, like the man himself, very matter-of-fact. Yohanan Bader, MK for Herut, himself an economist and a shrewd parliamentarian, commented many years later that those MKs who heard the speech did not at once grasp its significance.[15] Ben-Gurion had preceded the Minister with a dramatic announcement in which he spoke about "the tremendous difficulties and dangers" facing the state in its effort to carry out the three undertakings, each of which was "all but impossible"—defense, immigration absorption and the maintenance of an acceptable standard of living.[16] The business-like tone adopted by Dov Yosef appeared milder than Ben-Gurion's announcement and blurred the impression it had left.

... We shall determine a modest and rational diet which alone will
be available to the public. ... We shall permit the production of
luxury goods only for export, and stop the importation of all luxury
goods. ... All imports will require licenses from the Ministry of
Supplies and Rationing. Importers will be allowed to sell their
goods only to wholesalers licensed by the Ministry of Supplies and
Rationing. Each wholesaler will be allowed to sell his goods only to
a fixed number of retailers. ... Every retailer will have on his books
a given number of consumers, who will be allowed to buy only
from him, according to the coupon books which will be issued to
the entire population. ... The consumer will give the retailer the
appropriate coupons, and the latter will turn them over to the Ministry of Supplies and Rationing. ... [17]

Dov Yosef was the right man for the task of organizing rationing and supervising its execution. He believed in the system
wholeheartedly and did not hesitate to link his name with it, until it became a contemptuous byword and he himself the object
of loathing and scorn. He knew that he had been called upon to
serve in Ben-Gurion's first government on account of his experience in emergency rationing when serving as the military governor of besieged Jerusalem in the War of Independence. He had
been respected for the way he carried out that mission, but he
was not liked. The Montreal-born attorney was reserved, author-
itarian and cold. There was something reminiscent of the mandatory period about him, a little out-of-date, always dressed in a
dark, heavy tailored suit. He looked as if the British had forgotten to take him with them when they left the country. He was a
pedantic formalist, very proper and dry as a crust. People who
knew him well described him as a man of taste, a lover of art and
music. Once in a while he made an attempt to put a touch of hu-
mor into his speech, but he remained sour, flat, stuffy and cheer-
less.[18]

The newspapers called him "Yosef the Provider," but his du-
ties went beyond mere purveyance of food. The government had
determined what could be imported from abroad, in what quantities and at what prices. It also undertook to arrange much of
the importation at its own expense, chiefly of raw materials and
food products. The government organized, carried out and financed the transport and the warehousing, and it sold the goods
according to its own criteria to agriculturists and industrialists.
It was the government which determined what the agricultur-

ists would grow, as well as the quantities and prices of the produce, and similarly it regulated industry, its production, quantities and prices. The government also took part in the process of
production, as for example in the case of grains—in March 1949
the government took possession of the grain and flour, and all
the mill owners had to do was to supervise the milling, in return
for a fee. Thus the government acted as both employer and client. To bring the price of wheat flour down, the government sold
it directly to the bakeries, avoiding wholesale middlemen.[19] Beginning in September 1949, they saved time and increased pro-
ductivity by baking only a standard round loaf. From then on, all
Israelis ate only standard round "black bread," by order.[20]

The government undertook to determine who would sell
what to whom, in what quantities and at what prices, and
through which agents, wholesalers and retailers. It decided who
would buy from whom, exclusively—whether grocery stores,
greengrocers, butchers, milkmen, fish and chicken shops. Every
individual and every family were tied to certain shops in their
neighborhood; only there could they receive their food rations.
The grocers, greengrocers and butchers were entrusted with the
distrubution of the coupon books, according to a list of consumers. The books were made up of sheets of detachable coupons of various values. The distribution of the coupon books and
the correct clipping of coupons to match the rations turned the
small retailers into agents of the government administration and
made the customers dependent upon them. After a while
the restaurants, too, were ordered to demand coupons from their
customers, tourists as well as Israelis. The rations sold to the
public were determined as often as once a day, on the basis of
availability, and with an effort to maintain a minimal daily ration of calories, approximately 2,600 per day. The time of distribution was announced in the newspapers thus: "Carrots being
distributed in area 8 (Tel Aviv). Individual ration—250 grams.
Price—95 *mils* per kilogram. Coupons—page N, number 24."[21]

Prices were low, but the shortage oppressed the public. The
daily burden of it fell primarily on the women, who spent much
of their time standing in line. The columnist Shulamit Lev-Ari
wrote:

In most of the city's greengrocers which do not carry *Tenuvah* or
Tenneh products, there was hardly any fresh produce in the morn-

ing. Since everyone had to do all their shopping at the same time, there was crowding and long lines. The produce was marketed little by little, and the official announcements were issued several times a week, and so one day was spent buying 200 grams of carrots and the next one a quarter of a kilogram of bananas, and so forth. Thus, the women had to return to the shop several times a week, though during the winter the produce would have kept for a few days. The repeated visits to the grocery stores made the long lines an everyday occurrence. From the beginning of May, with the weather turning warm, the women had to go to the store every day, since few people had refrigerators and even in the ice-boxes the produce would not keep more than a day or two. Thus, paradoxically, as fruit and vegetables became more plentiful and varied with the onset of summer, the lines in front of the stores grew still longer. . . ."

The retailers had a hard time of it too. Shulamit Lev-Ari reported from Room 13 in the Tel Aviv wholesale produce market:

They rush over here to get the merchandise for their shops. First they go to the notice-board on the ground floor and study the lists which the officials of Room 13 had pinned up. The retailers look for their names and serial numbers on the lists, which have no more than ten names at a time. The lists emerge from Room 13 in a slow trickle, because the produce also reaches the city in a slow trickle, truck by truck, and then the inspectors in the warehouses must check it and fill in their forms before the office can take over the distribution to the retailers. Two, three, even four hours pass this way. Scores, if not hundreds, of greengrocers have already arrived. There are 300 greengroceries in Tel Aviv. The grocers go up and down the stairs, between the notice-board and Room 13. They crowd the corridor and wait. . . . In the meantime, the shops are standing empty. The women who went to buy vegetables for the midday dinner look in and go back home. The grocer's wife or helper keeps repeating that the produce has not yet arrived.[22]

Something of the sort took place in the lines for eggs and milk, meat and fish. It often took as long as two hours, and sometimes it was all in vain—by the time the housewife's turn came the rations had run out and she had to go home empty-handed. For example, Haim Kimhi wrote:

On the Thursday before *Rosh Hashanah* my wife went to the market in Hadera. She stood in line at the butcher's for an hour, to get a chicken. When she got inside there was not a chicken left. She could not go elsewhere, because there were two children waiting for her at home. At 5 in the afternoon, after work, I went to another butcher shop and could not get anything. On Friday my wife went to the butcher shop again, and again returned empty-handed. She applied to the local inspector of food distribution and he reassured her very politely, saying that she would get the ration the following week, after the holiday. My wife returned home tired and angry, and I tried to look into the matter at the local supplies office, but there I found a notice saying that the office was open only on week-days between 9 a.m. and 1 p.m. I can't get there during those hours, because I work outside Hadera.[23]

Bureaucratic arbitrariness hurts people no less than the shortage. "This Friday many people who stood in line," wrote a reader to *Davar*, "found that they had waited in vain. They had lost coupon number 20. This was not an accident—it was the result of carelessness on the part of those who decided to issue rations for coupon number 21 before number 20. The result was that number 20 was cut out of the coupon sheet and got lost. Citizens lose their rations and then grow angry with the whole government. . . ."[24] Moreover, the coupon books were forever falling apart, sheet by sheet, which was intolerable.*

Dov Yosef pointed out years later, in his typical style of enlightened absolutism, that the Israeli workers received three times as much bread as the workers in the USSR, twice as much milk, ten times as much sugar and four times as much meat. "People made do with the rations and accepted the austerity regime in good spirits," he stated. "They grumbled, made jokes and sang songs about it."[26] Some of the jokes were no funnier, and some of the songs no more amusing, than their counterparts in the USSR.† The Ministry of Supplies and Rationing made efforts to help people cope with the austerity system, among other means by distributing recipes such as porridge made from

---

*Characteristically, the bureaucracy set out to eliminate the long lines by setting up a Committee for the Abolition of Lines.[25]

†A public opinion poll conducted in 1950 revealed that most Israelis felt that their economic conditions had worsened since the creation of the state. Most of the people questioned attributed it to external causes, the difficulties faced by the state, but they also ascribed them to many other factors, such as poor planning, inefficiency, "politics," "corruption," etc. Industrialists, merchants and the free professions felt their conditions had worsened a good deal. Civil servants and workers generally felt no worse off, some, even a little better off.[27]

crushed *matzot*, herring in yogurt, sardine dumplings in diluted milk and similar delicacies.[28]

In August 1950, some 15 months after the imposition of the austerity measures on food, they were widened to include textiles and leather goods. The consumers were not tied to given stores, but from here on could buy limited quantities of clothes and footwear, for which they also received coupons, marked as "points"—85 points for clothes per person per year, and 45 for shoes. "Every citizen will receive his due," announced Dov Yosef, and like a strict teacher castigating his pupils, he added: "If the public had not rushed to buy more than they needed for the past year and a half, we might not have had to do this now." The principal reason given was, as before, the foreign currency deficit and the demands of immigration. Yosef cautioned, "If we want the immigrants who will come here next year to be able to obtain clothes and shoes too, we must start to cut down what we take for ourselves right now, to ensure that we shall have enough for the immigrants."[29]

At the same time, production quotas for the *Lacol* ("for everyone") standard goods were increased. The goods were of low quality and uniform design, and the prices were low, reduced by as much as 50 percent, and were subject to close supervision in every industry. The Ministry of Supplies and Rationing determined the quality of the product—generally lower than before—and the range of standard designs. Once the quality and the basic model were established, each plant was allotted its quota of raw materials at official, minimal prices. The Government Annual Report stated that "between May 1949 and March 1950, 2,155,819 *Lacol* clothing items and 4,210,288 meters of textile were produced."[30] There were *Lacol* shoes and *Lacol* schoolbags, *Lacol* furniture and *Lacol* ice-boxes, every item marked with the *Lacol* label—kitchen sinks, notebooks, writing-paper and envelopes, toilet paper and cardboard suitcases, ladies' handbags and men's hats, brooms and buckets, prams and strollers, all listed in meticulous proud detail by the Government Annual Report, together with their retail prices. "Garbage *Lacol*" was *Maariv*'s description of it.[31]

Satirist Amos Keynan wrote the following monologue for his regular character, Uzi:

"At long last we have moved into our new apartment, two rooms in a new house on pillars on 23rd Street, Block 12, Entrance 5, Apart-

ment number 7. I took a truck and loaded it with all our belongings—*Lacol* table, *Lacol* wardrobe, *Lacol* chairs, *Lacol* bookcase,
Lacol armchairs, *Lacol* sofa, radio, Herzl's picture and the map of
Eretz Israel. My wife was very happy. So were the two children. My
wife arranged the furniture in the two rooms, spread the carpet on
the floor and said we would now start a new life. I went to work
happy. I came back late at night. I was tired. I remembered that I
was now living in the new housing development, on 23rd Street,
Block 12, Entrance 5, Apartment number 7. I went upstairs, rang
the doorbell. I could hear the children shouting, and I took the
candy which I had bought them out of my pocket. The wife opened
the door. I kissed her on the forehead. She asked me how my day at
the office was. I sat down in the *Lacol* armchair and the children sat
on my knees and started to pull my hair. Ben-Gurion was speaking
on the radio about increasing production and reducing consumption. In the *Lacol* bookcase stood in neat rows the complete works
of Bialik, the complete works of Berl Katsenelson, the complete
works of Herzl, the Hebrew Encyclopedia and the writings of Ben-
Gurion. There were flowers on the *Lacol* table. There was a shining
new *Lacol* cover on the *Lacol* bed and another on the floor. The
wife talked about the hardships of the lines at the greengrocer's,
and I talked about my chances of getting a raise. Then the wife said,
'Yossi, I'm tired.'

'What kind of nonsense is this?' I asked. 'Since when am I
Yossi?' 'What do you mean, since when are you Yossi?' said the
wife. 'You are Yossi—you've been Yossi ever since we met, since
the day when we went to the park and fell in love. Since the day
you married me.' 'I'm sorry,' I said to the wife. 'There has been a
misunderstanding. I live on 23rd Street, Block 12, Entrance 5,
Apartment number 7.' 'What an unfortunate mistake,' said the
wife. 'This is 22nd Street, Block 11, Entrance 4, Apartment number
6.' 'Actually, it's not too bad,' I said to the wife. 'I'm tired and I'm
willing to stay here forever.' 'All right,' said the wife. 'I don't mind
either. What's your position in the office?'

'The same,' I said.

'Fair enough,' said the wife. 'Only remember that from now on
you live on 22nd Street, Block 11, Entrance 4, Apartment number 6.'

Life goes on as usual, but just to make sure, I put a note on the
door saying, 'Please ring twice.'"[32]

Dov Yosef had to address the Knesset repeatedly to defend
his austerity program. All his speeches were like the first—laden
with statistical data and incessant details. He often quoted the
various experts he had consulted, most of them British. At times

he sounded as if he were reading out a warehouse inventory, and at other times, a cookbook. His speeches reflected not only his pedantic character, but also the philosophy behind the system, and above all, the penetration which the regime sought to effect into the everyday life and privacy of every home. Here are some excerpts:

> "... The absence of butter does not mean a thing, since we provide margarine at a sixth of the cost and enrich it with vitamins, so that it is in no way inferior to butter. It is known to all the scientists in the world ... and I hereby declare with all due responsibility that the diet is perfectly adequate and that no one will starve, but everyone will remain in good health ..."[33]

> "... There are countries such as France which are known for their fine food, and where people prefer small fish. They think that its flesh is finer and tastier. Jews like a big fish, and if you don't give it to them they're disappointed. When you come to sell them small fish they don't want to pay for it. It's a problem. ..."[34]

Menahem Begin, MK: "Can the public eat statistics?"

Dov Yosef: "You can eat unlimited amounts of available bread, of the available codfish, lentils, oats, yogurt, skim cheese. You can eat the kilogram and a half of sugar you get every month. ..."[35]

> "... We shall have to reduce the meat ration to 540 grams per month. This is not the average amount, because sick people, people employed in hard physical labor and other special cases get more. ... We shall also have to ration chocolate and toilet soap. We hope not to have to reduce the amount of soap, but only to regulate its use, so that everyone will get as much as he needs. ..."[36]

> "... MK Nahum Nir's statement that a small child cannot subsist on 150 grams of meat and 5 eggs a week is without foundation. A child certainly can. ..."[37]

> "... When a couple gets married we shall issue them enough 'points' to enable them to buy sheets, pillowcases, etc., with which to start their married life. ..."[38]

> "... People have said to me, 'What, only 70 'points' for pregnant women? It won't be enough for a dress and diapers. Gentlemen, I reject this argument. A diaper costs 2 'points,' so the woman can buy 10 diapers, or 12 diapers at 24 'points.' (Interjections: 'That's not enough!') She will still have 46 'points' left, and will be able to buy 3 dresses for the baby, a blanket for the baby and even a dress for herself. ..."[39]

"... A dress made in the most fashionable style and costing much more than a plainer dress, will not cost more 'points' than the plain one, if the amount of fabric used is the same. Provided the two dresses contain the same amount of fabric...."[40]

"... MK Landau asks what can a man buy for 85 'points' for clothes and 45 'points' for shoes. ... Short khaki pants, sir, are 11 'points,' and you can also get them for 9. 2 khaki shirts—14 'points'; 2 undershirts—6 'points'; 2 pairs of socks—6 'points'; pyjamas—12 'points'; and it does not have to be flannel; you can make do with cotton pyjamas. ... MK Mazor says he will have to spend 72 'points' on a pair of pants. Not at all, sir, that is not true...."

MK Landau: "We'll have to go without pants at all!..."[41]

Dov Yosef: "I have not seen anyone going naked or barefoot. ... They are making a fuss about shoes. Someone says he will be able to buy only one pair of shoes. (Interjection: Only one shoe!) But that is not so. In a family of four, if the father is in urgent need of a pair of shoes, and needs 33 'points,' he can take the entire family's allowance and buy the shoes. Next month he will be able to take half the family's allowance and buy shoes for his wife and one of the children, and the next month after that buy a pair for another child, and this way they will all have new shoes by winter, even if they don't all need them. ..."[42] The wealthy people among us will get what the rest of the people get, and no more...."[43]

"... I have in mind the new doctors, as well as the new lawyers, who will have to buy gowns. An attorney who already has a gown, even if it is ten or twenty years old, will not be able to buy a new one. An old gown is a respectable symbol, a sign of experience. But the newly-made lawyer will get a new gown...."[44]

"... Some honorable members have attacked me on the subject of the dish-cloth. 5 'points' for a dishcloth. Yes, gentlemen, 5 'points' are needed for a dish-cloth, which is nothing less than a crime today, because it is made of wool and pure cotton. Why can't it be made from remnants? In the future we shall not permit the production of such dish-cloths, and then it will not be necessary to charge more than one 'point' for them, and I am told by the experts that they will be even more absorbent...."[45]

All this necessitated an immense apparatus for supervision. Dov Yosef was forever complaining that the number of inspectors his Ministry's budget enabled him to employ was insufficient. "We have less than a fifth of the number of officials required for our work," he protested. "We work like slaves. In my Ministry hardly anyone works less than 10 or 11 hours a day. The inspectors often work all night, and then come to the office in the morning to complete their 8, 9 or 10 hours of work, because we have but 350 inspectors for the whole country."[46] Theirs was a thankless job, because the Israelis cheated as much as they could. They diluted the milk with water and filled the ground beef with bread. Thousands, if not tens of thousands, got their doctors to give them certificates that entitled them to various extra rations. After the imposition of the austerity regime, the number of people registered as chronically ill rose to 15 percent in Tel Aviv.[47]

In his memoirs Dov Yosef noted some of the methods used to beat the system:

> We found out that when a certain quantity of leather was allocated to an industrialist to produce a given quantity of shoes, he would change the style of the shoes to use up less leather, and thus produce more than his quota of shoes, the difference being sold on the black market. We had to issue orders limiting the models and the number of different models that we allowed them to produce. Some food producers used less sugar in their products than they had agreed on with the Ministry, and sold the difference, or used it to produce other foodstuffs.

In addition to supervising the factories, warehouses and stores, they also stopped vehicles for inspection and sent inspectors to search private homes. Yosef reported, "The inspectors discovered a trailer belonging to a margarine production plant with 35 chickens hidden in it, for sale on the black market. They found a hiding place in a bus, and in it a live calf, 6 hens and 200 eggs."[48]

From time to time Yosef reported such doings to the Knesset, in his usual meticulous and humorless style: "In one house we found 40 kilograms of meat, and 3 customers, who were in the apartment when we came in to search. . . . In another house were found 18 kilograms of meat, in another 15 chickens, in another a crate with 150 packets of tea. . . . In one house there were 10 hens and 87 eggs. In another apartment . . . there were 3 kilograms of meat and one-and-a-half kilograms of liver. In one house 30 kilograms of meat were discovered, as well as 20 liters of cream, a product which is altogether banned by law. . . ."[49]*

---

*Military censorship, imposed upon all incoming and outgoing mail, was used to trace illegal possession of goods.[50]

That year there were two murders connected with black-market operations. One victim was a Tel Aviv butcher and the other smuggled "Camel" cigarettes.* But these were, of course, exceptional cases. Most Israelis knew how to manage without getting too deeply involved with lawbreaking. Some kept laying hens on their balconies, others bred rabbits in the backyard, and some had their connections—a brother-in-law in the import office, a cousin who lived on a farm or a child who was sick and thus entitled to an extra ration of eggs, yet was not allowed to eat eggs at all, and so the extra ration could be exchanged for butter or meat. Cleaning women often brought produce to their employers. The family of a cleaning woman who worked in the house of one of *Maariv*'s correspondents had twelve people, eight children and four adults. It was thus entitled to a total of 52 eggs a week and 15 kilograms of sugar a month. "This family has never used and never will use such a quantity of eggs and sugar," wrote the journalist. "It sells much of its legitimate rations to the daughter's employers."[51] There were some who could not afford the rations to which they were entitled, and sold them on the black market.

Surplus money increased as a result of the government's inflationary financing of its operations. The money available on the market increased by 35.5 percent in 1949, as against the previous year, and in the years 1949–1951 it grew at an average annual rate of 34 percent. Nadav Halevi and Ruth Klinov-Maloul of the Hebrew University have calculated that while the amount of money available increased by 140 percent, the cost-of-living index (which did not include the prices on the black market) rose by only 16 percent. In other words, people had money, but the system of rationing prevented them from spending much of it, for prices were kept at a low level, so they turned to the black market.[52]

Much of the merchandise available reached the black market because of the policy of distributing everything uniformly, as Pinhas Lavon, Minister of Agriculture, pointed out in an exceptional statement in which he detailed—for the first time openly and systematically—the sources which supplied the black market. Some of the merchandise came directly from the producers, he said, and mentioned the kibbutzim among them. Some of it

---

*The men who murdered the cigarette smuggler—two Haifa Arabs—were sentenced to death by hanging, the first sentence of its kind in Israel. The sentence was later commuted.

came from the wholesalers, and both were the results of deliberate deceit. Some quantities were lost in the process of weighing, counting, packaging, transport and so forth, and even if it came to no more than one percent, the amount was considerable. The "lost produce" was found and made its way to the black market. There was also smuggling from abroad and inside the country. Lavon played down that aspect: "One cannot smuggle a thousand cows for slaughter," he said, but confirmed that there was a certain amount of smuggling, and it did create "some black marketeering." He admitted that it was he who had abolished the restrictions on food packages from abroad. He said:

> I did it knowing that a certain percent would make its way to the black market. But if today 120,000 food packages arrive each month, and even if at the highest estimate—a gross exaggeration—ten thousand packages are sold on the black market, and ten thousand packages are a huge black market—we are still faced with the basic question of policy: ... What is better—additional food for 100,000, or 150,000 families, that is, about 400,000 people, or the risk that something will be affected by the trickling of a certain number of such packages to the black market.[53]

Those packages, like the coupons and the lines and the codfish, became symbols of the times. Sent to Israel by friends and relatives abroad, they were sent through a commercial agency and contained a standard choice of goods. They were not rationed. They could also be picked up in exchange for a special yellow tab, generally known as Scrip. Sent from abroad, good for standard packages to be collected in Israel, they soon became synonymous with sausages and tinned goulash, cocoa and condensed milk—fabulous delicacies.*

In late September 1950 Ben-Gurion dropped all other matters and concentrated for three whole days on the problem of the black market and possible ways of eliminating it.† The Prime

---

*The head of the Economic Department of the Police reported that "investigations of several of the firms specializing in food imports of this kind have shown that 99 percent of the food they import are destined not for genuine customers but intended for the black market. ... Various charity organizations, and political parties, used to hand out goods which they had obtained through the 'Scrip' system."[54]

†In addition to the Prime Minister and the Ministers Dov Yosef and Golda Meir, the consultations on the subject included Attorney General Haim Cohen, the Chief of the Secret Service Isser Harel, the Chief of Police Yehezkel Sahar, several MKs, a number of Jewish Agency leaders, including Levi Eshkol, several Histadrut officials and numerous civil servants.

Minister studied the subject in the finest detail, for hours on end. He wanted to know everything he could about building materials, iron, and timber; would the price of apartments go down if the government built them? (The answer was yes.) What about meat, vegetables, tea? Could rice be grown in Israel? (The answer was no.) Why has the price of bathtubs gone up? (They told him it was part of the general hysteria.) Do people like codfish? (They replied that the Oriental Jews preferred carp.) From the minutes:

> Haifa Mayor, Abba Houshi: "The Jewish Agency is the largest importer of building materials. It gives the kibbutzim building materials instead of money. We have information about 22 cases of black-marketeering by the kibbutzim. The Histadrut investigated 14 of them and sued some of them. Some of the 22 kibbutzim sold the materials they had received from the government or the Jewish Agency. It came to light in a curious way: The bookkeeper of the village of Kfar Shmaryahu, where there were mostly German Jews, noted in his books, 'I bought 3 tons of grain for the poultry at the official price, and 6 tons at black-market price.' He also noted the name of the kibbutz where he had bought that grain.* . . . In France and in Italy there are merchants who export food to Israel through the immigrants. The immigrants sell the products upon landing in the country, near the camp. When I heard about it I said I wanted to go there at night so as to see what was going on. I was warned to be careful, or I might get knifed. So I didn't go alone. When I got there I saw an open market with hundreds of people, carrying on business quite freely."†

*In October 1950 Attorney General Cohen reported to the Prime Minister that 3 kibbutzim—Beit Hashita, Maoz Haim and Sdeh Eliyahu—had been charged with violations of the marketing restrictions, including price manipulations. The three kibbutzim hired Attorney Yaakov Shimshon Shapira, the former Attorney General and future Minister of Justice, to defend them, and he argued that the court was not empowered to try a kibbutz, since it is not "a natural entity." Cohen said to Ben-Gurion: "I am especially pained by this act, which I cannot justify either on legal-technical grounds or on any other, because it was done by people who claim that they are supporting you and your government in our struggle to put an end to this evil."[55] Until that time such affairs had always been dealt with "in the family," the kibbutzim being tried by the Histadrut, rather than in open court.

†Minister of Agriculture Pinhas Lavon confirmed in the Knesset that he had signed orders not to search the immigrants' baggage for smuggled food products. He said that the danger that some foodstuffs would reach the black market was not as grave as the danger that there would be "rows and scuffles" with the immigrants at the moment of their arrival at "our country's port of liberation. . . ."[56]

Dov Yosef: "The owners of the chocolate factories *Lieber* and *C.D.* are being charged. Charges are also being drawn up against the *Elite* chocolate factory. . . ."

Ben-Gurion: "How come such big industrialists go in for black marketeering?—Surely they are millionaires!"

Houshi: "They made their money by such methods when the English were here. Sometimes it takes fifteen months before the person charged with black marketeering has to stand trial. And then the sentences are so mild that it pays to sin."

Ben-Gurion: "Could Mr. Lieber be fined 20,000 *lirot*?"

Yosef: "He can even be sent to prison! . . ."

Police Commissioner Yehezkel Sahar: "When you ask in a Tel Aviv store how much a thing costs . . . they tell you, so much with 'points' [official price] and so much without."

Yosef: "We send our people to catch such cases."

Ben-Gurion: "We can get 500 Histadrut members in Tel Aviv to go to the stores and investigate this."

Sahar: "A man came to our house and offered extra eggs at black-market prices. Fortunately for him, I was out at the time."

Yosef: "If we could jail a dozen such merchants it would be a tremendous blow to the black market. . . ."

Sahar: "If you arrested 100 Jews for such crimes, you'd never have enough room in the prisons for them."

Ben-Gurion: "It's not the small fry we have to deal with, but the rich ones. . . . I want you to get a few thieves to work for us. . . . I've heard that when stuff is being transported from place to place some of it is often stolen. I'd like a few thieves to try to steal for us, so that we'll know where the goods are going."

Sahar: "Most of the thieves are now in prison."

Houshi: "We recently caught a Kosher food supervisor who smuggled pork. . . ."

Ben-Gurion: "I want people in the country to know that a real war is going to be waged on the black market, and it would be a good thing if a few stalwart community members who are also wardens of their synagogues and respected in their circles, were punished for black marketeering and spent a few months in prison."*

---

*Reports of the Central Police Headquarters show that it was in fact the small fry who were caught: A Jaffa waiter who served a meal and did not collect coupons, an electrical appliances shop owner who sold a boiler at an exorbitant price, a Haifa warehouseman who hid 182 eggs, a Tel Aviv resident who transported 9 kilograms of hard cheese, and the like, a total of a few score a day.[57] In October Ben-Gurion asked the President of the Tel Aviv District Court to place "the very best men" at the disposal of the war on the black market, and set

Amos Landman (of Haifa port): "There are two problems here which are not easy to overcome. One is that a Jew does not like to betray another Jew to the authorities, even in the State of Israel and to the Israeli police. We run into this with our own workers, who are supposed to be responsible for the warehouses and sheds. When they catch one of the dock workers stealing, they are reluctant to turn him over to the police. They say that the police should be on the spot and do their own thief-catching."

Ben-Gurion: "This attitude is the product of hundreds of years of exile."

Landman: "There is another thing, which is also an inheritance of the British Mandate days, and that is that public property is nobody's property."

Ben-Gurion: "This whole phenomenon worries me greatly. If the navy goes in for stealing, how will they guard anything?"

Landman: "I propose that the navy loan some of its personnel to the police for a while, and that a single authority be put in charge."

Ben-Gurion: "But even if there was a policeman in every boat, how can we make sure that he does not steal? . . . How are the goods stolen from the ships?"

Landman: "The sailors steal during the passage and when the ship docks somewhere they sell the goods or unload them somewhere. Or, if they get here with the stolen goods, they try to smuggle them through the port."

Yosef: "We have heard recently that merchants have begun to take out bigger insurance policies on their homes. Some think that this shows that they are hiding goods in their homes."

Ben-Gurion: "I assume that such things don't happen on Swedish ships, for example, because the sailors are honest and no such established methods of this type exist."

Landman: "It's a matter of established methods, and it's also a question of tradition."

Ben-Gurion: "It will be a long time before we create a tradition that Jews are not thieves. But how to ensure this before we educate them? . . ."

---

aside at least one day a week for hearing such cases. Minister of Justice Rozen urged the judges to impose harsh sentences on speculators. But on the whole this did not happen: Between May 1949 and June 1950 the police apprehended 8,387 cases of speculation and black marketeering; of these only 3,530 were charged. The courts completed the trials of only 1,613 of these cases—86 were given prison sentences, 1,191 were fined. The average prison sentence was 27 days and the average fine 41 *lirot*.[58]

Yosef: "It's not so easy to make the arrangements on board ship. A ship is a tiny place. There is a crew of 25 or 20 men and they would know immediately that so-and-so is supposed to prevent thefts, and they will make his life a misery."

Sahar: "They steal the belongings of immigrants. We discovered this when we found Italian bricks in crates."

Ben-Gurion: "It's not so much the stolen goods which bother me, as the shame of Jewish sailors being thieves."

Landman: "Workers are also thieves. At first the Histadrut would not help us fight it. In 1948, when we began to catch dock workers stealing and started to fire them, the Histadrut didn't support us."

Ben-Gurion: "This is frightful. It's our flag and our honor. And these are people with regular work and an income. This phenomenon dishonors the name of Israel. . . ."

Yosef: "Sometimes peddlers sell produce and announce the official price, and add 'plus a contribution to the Jewish National Fund,' as a joke, because what they mean is a contribution to the black market."[59]*

While maintaining a collective willingness to sacrifice for the sake of the common good, everyone strove to make their own concession as small as possible. Soon it was generally agreed that there was no recourse but to cheat the authorities. Everybody condemned the black market, but everyone saw its prices as the true standard. A reader of *Dovar* wrote to the editor: "We had hoped to get something for the High Holy Days, but we did not get a chicken either for *Rosh Hashanah* or for *Yom Kippur*. And so, despite my adherence to the austerity regime and my opposition to the black market, I had no choice but to buy fish and meat on the black market."[62]

"The fact is that mothers can't get enough food for their children and have to turn to the black market," asserted Yeshayahu Foerder, MK of the Progressive party.[63] The evening paper *Yediot Aharonot* quoted a Tel Aviv merchant who described the

---

*Minister of Agriculture Lavon tended to think of the black market as part of the system of rationing: "If tomorrow cockroaches were rationed, there would soon be a shortage of cockroaches," he said to the Knesset Economic Committee.[60] A true politician, Lavon tended to blame the press, saying:

"I should be the last to try to cover up facts or paint a rosy picture," he said, "as if everything was all right. But, gentlemen, the disease which has affected our public, the tendency to pathological exaggeration, the loss of all sense of proportion in describing and defining the facts, the tendency to seize on a detail and regard it as the whole picture, that is a characteristic which the political parties and the newspapers are cultivating, and it is becoming a dangerous national disease."[61]

multitude of luxury items which were being offered to him on the black market—refrigerators, stoves, mixers, some of them brought in by Israelis who had been abroad on an official mission. "And who can withstand such temptation?" asked the paper sympathetically.[64] "The sun had not changed/Nor its radiance/," wrote poet Nathan Altermann, "But in their exchange, the buyer/ Avoided the seller's gaze/ For theft was in their eyes." Theft, said Altermann, had become "a tolerated flavor of life, a kind of tacit understanding."[65]

Minister of Justice Rozen confirmed this: "Black marketeering has not only remained with us," he said in the Knesset, "there are signs—we are getting a lot of complaints—that the black market is spreading over all branches of commerce in this country, and that all walks of society are involved with it, regardless of association or political or economic affiliation. . . ."[66] In the latter half of 1950 the Knesset economic committee created a subcommittee to investigate the sources of the black market. When the committee began its investigations it appealed to the general public through the press and over the radio, asking for information about the black marketeers. The appeal remained virtually unanswered, as the public was not inclined to cooperate with the committee.[67]

At one stage, special courts were established to deal with the offenders against the austerity regime, using a jury-like system (an exception to the normal judicial procedure in Israel). Justice Minister Rozen explained:

> The idea was to take the judicial process out of the hands of a single judge, who normally deals with ordinary criminal cases, and bring these special cases before the judgment of men and women whom these violations and their harmful results directly affect. We believed that those voluntary judges would express the public anger with the black market. . . . However, experience showed us that in those courts the representatives of the public tended to be lenient rather than severe, and instead of giving expression to the victims' anger they tended to show excessive understanding for the accused.

Rozen also had to admit that some of those representatives of the people were themselves guilty of similar offenses.[68]

The Ministry of Supplies and Rationing tried to involve the public in the work of the supervisory staff, but only in half the areas which were earmarked in this project were there any citizens who were willing to help.[69] The Government Annual Report recorded that about 100 mass meetings had been held to explain the system of rationing and supervision, as well as over 100 other gatherings and conferences, and scores of lectures and seminars providing information and instruction on issues related to the supervision. The results were pathetic—in Jerusalem only 200 people agreed to help the Ministry, in Tel Aviv some 300 and in Haifa 150.[70] "The public shows no awareness that speculation in rationed commodities is a crime," stated MAPAM's MK Hannah Lamdan ruefully. On the contrary, "the inspectors are generally disliked; they are viewed as informers. . . . Whenever an inspector enters a shop to supervise the shopkeeper's practices and make sure that he does not sell at extortionate prices, he gets beaten up. . . ."[71]

Searches conducted in private homes caused an uproar in the Knesset and forced Dov Yosef to apologize at great length for what Arye Ben-Eliezer of Herut described as "a basic violation of the citizen's minimal rights—a violation of his home."[72] Perets Bernstein, MK, asked the Attorney General Haim Cohen to drop the charges against one of the "Scrip" companies. "Legal action against this company would create a very bad impression in America," he later explained in the Knesset.[73] Not long before he died, Dov Yosef revealed the following: "During the days of austerity some of my staff paid an unexpected visit to a Rumanian restaurant in Jaffa, which was known as a place where one could eat without 'points.' Among the customers who were dining there at the time was MAPAI's Levi Eshkol, later Minister of Finance and Prime Minister. When I heard about it I brought it up at a Cabinet meeting and demanded that Ben-Gurion condemn this act explicitly, and forbid the members of the government and the leaders of the public to eat in places which violate the austerity regulations. Otherwise, I said, I would give the story to the press."[74]*

*There was another notable scandal, this time involving a government Minister. Attorney A. Meridor in his speech for the defense on behalf of his client, Tsvi Gintsburg, a fish merchant in Jerusalem: "On the last day of Passover 1949 the Minister of Welfare, Rabbi I. M. Levin, asked my client to reserve for him a certain amount of fish for the holiday, as he was receiving guests from England and the United States. My client thought that it was his duty to oblige the Minister and he set aside the amount of fish requested. As it happens, two inspectors entered the premises and found the fish. They ordered Mr. Gintsburg to sell the fish and wrote a complaint against him." The Minister's holiday fish became a subject of lengthy correspondence between the Attorney General and several Cabinet Ministers.[75]

When he first proposed his austerity program to the Cabinet, Yosef ran into opposition, and it took a long debate before the government undertook to place the program before the Knesset. What the Ministers feared was a political, rather than an economic, repercussion. They thought that the program would be described as an attempt to destroy the middle classes, and in fact this is what happened.[76] The General Zionists and Herut were the chief proponents of this claim, while the Communists and MAPAM attacked the program from the left, maintaining that the burden would fall chiefly on the poorer people. Everyone sought to protect this or that sector of the public from exploitation and discrimination: women and cobblers, soft-drink sellers and retired citizens, Arabs, Oriental Jews and religious people (some of the meat which was imported for distribution as rations was not kosher). The debate combined ideological conflict with party-politicking.

> Haim Landau MK (Herut): "I am convinced that one of the purposes of the austerity program is to squeeze the small businessman out of business. Our government can't stand the small businessman, whom it regards as a middle-man, an obstacle to be removed, and so it dispossesses the artisan, the small manufacturer, the merchant. . . ."[77]
>
> Yosef: "I shall not enter into argument with MK Landau. I know that he disapproves of the government's economic system, the system of supervision and rationing. He doesn't believe in it. He believes in what he calls freedom and liberty. I call it anarchy. Even in the economic field, Mr. Landau, if we followed your ideas we would not now be sitting here, because we would have died of hunger."
>
> Landau: "We'd be in the Old City of Jerusalem, sir. . . ."
>
> Yosef: "MK Landau wishes to defend the black market. . . ."[78]
>
> Yosef Sapir (General Zionists): "The way that this government runs the state, it will either become a dictatorship or go bankrupt. And given our circumstances, the first will lead to the second."[79]
>
> Ben-Gurion: "The austerity program is not devised for the purpose of imposing equality. Our government does not yet presume to undertake such a mission, not because it is not important or desirable, but because its time has not yet come. Whoever tries to achieve it now is either a crook or a saboteur. . . .[80] We say, give everyone the necessary minimum before we give plenty to the few. The General Zionists say, let free enterprise take over and it will provide plenty for everyone. We have yet to see a country

which provides plenty for everyone. America is the land of plenty and the richest country in the world, but after the establishment of free private enterprise by President Hoover in the 1930s, there were millions of hungry and unemployed workers and all the banks were about to close down, until Roosevelt imposed government intervention and planning and saved big and rich America from total bankruptcy. We too did not want to trust the free enterprise of a few speculators. . . ."[81]*

But politics were stronger than Dov Yosef. In 1950–1951 strikes and demonstrations broke out everywhere, some by workers and some by merchants and manufacturers. Both groups enjoyed the support of one or the other party, Left or Right. The Opposition reaped considerable benefit from the situation. As people grew bitter, the coalition began to crack. Dov Yosef would later complain that his standing in the government was "hopeless": Some of the Ministers gave him no support. Minister of Police, Behor Shalom Shitrit, "secretly opposed the system of control" and was disinclined to act against the merchants who broke the law. The judiciary was also inefficient in trying the violators. According to Yosef, Minister of Justice Rozen was under constant pressure from his centrist Progressive party. Minister of the Interior Shapira (Hapoel Hamizrahi) fought in the Cabinet for the right of industrialists and merchants to conduct their businesses without restriction.

At the same time, there were some people in MAPAI who feared that the austerity program would adversely affect their party's chances in the forthcoming elections for local councils.[83] All these pressures made an impact. To start with, "tax-free import" was allowed to enable people to transfer their capital to Israel without having to exchange it at the official rate-of-exchange. The Ministry of Supplies and Rationing was abolished—its functions were divided between the Ministry of Agriculture and the Ministry of Trade and Industry, thus putting an effective end to the supervisory system. In October 1950 there

*David Horowitz suggested that the austerity program appealed to Ben-Gurion because its control of the economy through administrative regulation matched his conception of national power. "Ben-Gurion detested the belief in economic laws and the autonomy of the economic mechanism," wrote Horowitz. "He never understood them and he thought of them as a deliberate obfuscation and an impediment to man's will. He wanted to force the laws of economics, break their power and reveal their uselessness."[82]

was a government crisis—Ben-Gurion resigned, tried to form a minority government and failed, then contrived to re-establish the former coalition. The Ministry of Trade and Industry was given to an inexperienced person, Yaakov Geri, of the *Ata* textile industry, and Dov Yosef was given the Ministry of Transport. In the general elections for the second Knesset MAPAI succeeded in retaining its predominance, largely due to its influence in the immigrant camps. The centrist General Zionists received 16 percent of the votes, three times as many as they had won in the previous elections, two and a half years before. The message was plain to all. Enforcement of the austerity regulations slacked off, and before long the program was dropped altogether.*

The aims of the austerity program were to a certain extent reasonable, but its execution was inept. It attained its principal objective, a system of rationing which ensured the minimum necessities of life for everyone at a reasonable price. The products available were distributed among all the citizens, old-timers and newcomers alike, according to their needs rather than their income, in a most progressive fashion—the poorest families who were also the ones with the largest number of children, pregnant women and people who did hard physical work, all received extra rations. There were some well-off people who purchased coupons and 'points' and rations from the badly-off, but minimum sustenance was accessible to all. Between May 1948 and February 1950 the cost-of-living index went down 14 percent, thanks to the 20 percent reduction in the price of controlled products. But as prices went down, so the demand for the goods went up, the sense of shortage grew more acute and with it the tendency to oppose the system and undermine it. To stop the inflationary development it would have been necessary to adopt certain fiscal measures which would have absorbed the excess money in the hands of the public, such as increased taxation, a wage-freeze or even wage reduction.

Dov Yosef: "The Ministry of Finance did not follow up the

---

*1951 was also a time of crisis, due to the drought and the consequent poor harvest of local agriculture, combined with the worldwide increase in prices as a result of the Korean War. Dov Yosef tried to reinstate the austerity program under the aegis of the Ministry of Trade and Industry, but in February 1952 a new economic program abolished most of the rationing and control provisions. US loans and UJA monies started to come in, as well as reparations from West Germany. Immigration also slowed down—in 1953 there were only 10,000 immigrants.

achievements of the austerity program with economic and fiscal measures, which it should have done as a natural procedure to absorb the excess money that the public had as a result of the austerity program."[84] This was an accepted view: "It appears that the Ministry of Finance was not willing to give whole-hearted support to the policy of Dov Yosef's Ministry," commented *Haaretz*.[85] Years later, David Horowitz, who at the time was General Director of the Ministry of Finance, confirmed this, but maintained that the austerity program was altogether a mistake. He himself proposed other measures, but the government rejected them—in his view, on political grounds. Among the measures he proposed were some dramatic and obviously unpopular ones, such as restraining the increase in the standard of living and consumption by means of wage restrictions and heavy taxation. A memorandum he submitted to Ben-Gurion in late 1950 protested against the government's acquiescence in the investments in consumer goods industries, and the construction of grandiose structures such as the *Binyanei Hauma* concert hall in Jerusalem and the Histadrut executive building in Tel Aviv. "We are creating an economy of *consumption*," he wrote, using the English word because, he explained "in English 'consumption' means both what people consume and tuberculosis. I think that both meanings fit our system." Once in a Cabinet meeting he said: "Of course, technically speaking, and without considering the price, everything is possible. One can even grow coffee on the roofs of Jerusalem. But is it wise? We live in a fool's paradise. It seems that the general philosophy adopted by members of the government is that if you hit your head against the wall time and time again, eventually the wall will be broken. . . . We are not living within our means, and many of our actions are like a permanent wave on a bald head."[86]

Nathan Gross, of the Hebrew University in Jerusalem, has tried to explain the fact that the Ministry of Finance did not accompany the austerity program with the appropriate monetary and fiscal policy by suggesting that the people in charge of the economy did not fully understand the nature of the inflation. By analyzing the statements of policy made at the time, Gross reached the conclusion that the only symptom by which the government gauged the inflationary pressure was the fluctuation of prices. The Treasury was inclined to view the reduction in prices as an indication that the inflationary pressure had diminished, without taking into account the amount of money in the hands of the public. In other words, they believed that the problem was an inflation of expenditure, and ignored the effects of demand. Gross also points out that the system of taxation was inefficient, and so the Ministry of Finance was unable to absorb the excess money, if it actually wished to do so.[87]

Toward the end of 1951 the country was still in the grip of severe unemployment, and tens of thousands were still living in immigrant camps. Despite aid from the United States and the income from the Government Development Loan, there was a grave shortage of hard currency. Inflationary pressures continued, and the price structure was as lopsided as ever. "The new economic policy" put a stop to the inflationary government financing and the attempts to restrict credit to the public. An obligatory loan from each citizen to the government, which was to be returned by the government at a later date, was imposed upon the money in circulation and even on the current accounts in the banks. The income tax department was brought up to date and the importance of that tax as a source of government income steadily increased. Some government-owned lands were sold to the public, as a way of absorbing funds, and government expenditure was reduced. The *lira* was devalued and price controls were removed from certain commodities, which went up as a result. All these were economic measures.

At the same time the government also took a step that a year or two before would have been unmentionable—it reduced to a minimum the attempts to step up immigration. In 1951 there were still over 173,000 new immigrants; in 1952 only a little over 23,000 arrived, and the following year just over 10,000. The government had come a long way since the time when it argued about "regulation" and "selection" of immigration, and then resolved to bring in 250,000 immigrants in one year.

Most Israelis understood that austerity was a part of the national revolution and were willing to bear part of the burden, as after all, they had wished for the revolution. What they could not abide was the constant meddling with their normal everyday life. They rebelled against the distortions that developed from the system, the discrimination, the preferential treatment, the arbitrariness, corruption and bureaucratic muddle. They beat the system and it was a fine demonstration of their democratic awareness. With the abolition of the austerity system certain clearcut limits were drawn for the intervention of the authorities in the country's economy, and certain interventionist Marxist tendencies prevalent in MAPAI were rejected, a salutary lesson for years to come. At the same time a certain sense of dependency on the government could never be abolished. Ever since the days of austerity Israelis often tended to demand from their government more than they demanded from themselves.

The habits of bad conduct from the black market days also survived for many years in, for example, the poor service given the customer in Israeli stores, even when plentifully stocked, as though the customer were still dependent on the shopkeeper's good grace, as in the days of austerity. There was also the notion that life outside Israel was somehow better—a notion which existed partway between the dream and the daily routine, remained as a hangover of the austerity. "Abroad" meant quality, plenty and economic security, so the urge to go and obtain goods from abroad inevitably became a frustrated heart's desire—in 1949 it was necessary to obtain an exit permit to leave the country, in order to prevent the loss of hard currency; only two, later three, out of four applicants obtained it, most of them on official missions on behalf of the state and its institutions. Thus "abroad" became integrally associated with "good connections"—like "good connections," "abroad" was part of a whole concept, a reflection of the first Israelis' doubtful and ironic attitude toward the country and themselves.

The everyday routine of the first Israelis was thus less pioneering and heroic than they had dreamed it would be, and the society they shaped was less enlightened, less idealistic, less altruistic and less Ashkenazi than they had hoped. It promised neither justice for all, nor equality for all, nor peace. Perhaps the first Israelis never recognized this—absorbed in euphoria, they failed to see the reality as it was. Their dream was the fuel that powered their action, the cement which bound them together, the myth and the consensus. At times it also served as an excuse for the mistakes they made. The dream gave them the strength and the courage to start a new life after the horrors of the Holocaust. Dreaming, they struggled against the British, fought against the Arabs and won a war. The dream brought many of them to Israel and gave the immigrants the patience to withstand the appalling conditions in the camps. The dream gave birth to plans of action, policies, ethics, values and ways of life. It restrained the hatred between opposing camps and moderated the conflicts which threatened Israeli society. Perhaps it was their common dream that curbed the first Israelis when civil war might have erupted between old-timers and newcomers, Ashkenazis and Oriental Jews, or the religious against the secular, just as war had been the outcome of the tensions and conflicts of interest between Jews and Arabs. Above all, it was that dream that gave them so much confidence in themselves. They argued, struggled with themselves, hesitated, and sometimes changed their minds, but the road they took was the road they believed to be right, and they followed it with wholehearted confidence and belief in their cause. For that, they are to be envied.

Notes

Introduction

1. *Maariv*, 2.9.49
2. *Knesset Record*, Vol. III, p. 5, 11.7.49
3. *Davar*, 8.2.49
4. *Maariv*, 8.16–17.49
5. *Dvar Hashavua*, 9.22.49
6. 2.12.49, Labor Party Archive,
7. Quoted in Horowitz, p. 18
8. Horowitz, p. 26
9. Political Consultation, 4.22.49, State Archives, Foreign Ministry, 2447/3
10. Ben-Gurion *Diaries*, 3.11.49
11. Ben-Gurion to the editor of *Hador*, 11.18.48, Ben-Gurion Estate
12. Ben-Gurion to Ronnie Baron, 9.28.49, Ben-Gurion Estate
13. The question was put to the residents of Haifa in the course of a public opinion poll conducted by the *Haganah* command in the city. By courtesy of Mr. Rehavam Amir, who was one of the poll organizers.
14. *Yediot Aharonot*, 1.13.49 (unsigned)
15. Abu Iyad, p. 25

16. *Haaretz*, 1.13.49
17. Ibid., 2.13.49
18. Ibid., 8.9.49
19. Uri Avnery, *Haaretz*, 2.11.49
20. Zionist Executive, 8.18.49
21. Writers' meeting with Ben-Gurion *(Divrey Sofrim)*, 3.27.49, State Archives
22. *People's Administration Record*, p. 107, 5.12.48, State Archives
23. *Haaretz*, 1.16.49
24. Ben-Gurion, *Medinat Israel*, p. 184
25. Ben-Gurion *Diaries*, 7.1.48

1. The Green Line

1. *Foreign Relations of the US*, 1948, p. 1705; McDonald, p. 117
2. Ben-Gurion *Diaries*, 1.6.49
3. Ibid.
4. Ben-Gurion *Diaries*, 1.5.49
5. S. B. Yeshaya Report, 1.3.49, Ben-Gurion Estate
6. Ben-Gurion *Diaries*, 1.7.49
7. Ibid., 1.8.49. Allon wired the next day that the British had had time to photograph the aircraft wreckage before it was possible to remove it to Israeli territory.
8. Weizmann, p. 70
9. Ben-Gurion *Diaries*, 1.8.49
10. Ibid., 1.7.49
11. Haaretz, 9.18.48
12. Bernadotte, p. 79
13. Dayan, p. 86
14. Rabin, p. 76
15. Eitan, p. 34.
16. Political Consultation, 4.12.49, State Archives, Foreign Ministry, 2447/3
17. Ben-Gurion *Diaries*, 1.18.49
18. Eitan, p. 33
19. Eitan to Sharett, 1.22.49, *Israel Documents*, Vol. III, p. 54; also Eitan, p. 36. In these pages I have also made use of the introduction to the volume by Yemimah Rosenthal.
20. Ben-Gurion *Diaries*, 2.24.49

21. Rabin, p. 77
22. Eitan to Sharett, 2.22.49, *Israel Documents*, Vol. III, p. 266
23. Rozen to Robinson, 3.6.49, Ibid., p. 293
24. Rozen to Sasson, 3.13.49, Ibid., p. 311
25. Yadin to Eitan, 3.11.49, Ibid., p. 309
26. Rozen to Sharett, 3.16.49, Ibid., p. 312
27. Ben-Gurion *Diaries*, 3.17.49
28. Ibid.
29. Ben-Gurion *Diaries*, 5.24.48
30. Sharett *Diary*, Vol. 4, p. 996
31. Dayan to Yadin, 3.12.49, *Israel Documents*, Vol. III, p. 405
32. Ben-Gurion *Diaries*, 1.17.49
33. Tevet, p. 328
34. Eitan to Sharett, 3.23/24.49, *Israel Documents*, Vol. III, p. 468
35. Ibid., 4.3.49, Ibid., p. 500
36. *Yediot Aharonot*, 5.29.59; 6.4.59, 6.11.59 and 6.19.59
37. Ben-Gurion *Diaries*, 1.26.49
38. Sasson to Sharett, 3.10.49, *Israel Documents*, Vol. III, p. 377
39. Ben-Gurion to Dr. S. Gross, *Haaretz* 3.23.62; Bar-Zohar, Vol. 2, pp. 823–826.
40. Ben-Gurion *Diaries*, 5.24.48
41. Ibid., 6.18.48
42. Ibid., 6.21.49
43. Ibid., 3.11.49
44. Ibid., 1.16.49
45. Ibid., 4.16.49
46. Ibid., 4.30.49
47. The Minister to Secretary of State, *Foreign Relations of the US*, 1949, p. 965
48. Ben-Gurion *Diaries*, 5.7.49
49. Secretary of State to US Embassy in Israel, 5.9.49, *Foreign Relations of the US*, 1949, p. 990
50. Ben-Gurion *Diaries*, 5.16.49; Rozen to Ben-Gurion and Sharett, 5.18.49, *Israel Documents*, Vol. III, p. 581
51. Eban to Rozen, 5.18.49, *Israel Documents*, Vol. III, p. 584
52. Minister to Secretary of State, 5.19.49, *Foreign Relations of the US*, 1949, p. 1030
53. Eban to Sharett, 6.1.49, *Israel Documents*, Vol. III, p. 594
54. Sharett to Eban, 6.2.49, Ibid., p. 595
55. Sharett to Eban, 6.5.49, Ibid., p. 596

56. Sharett to Eban, 6.8.49, Ibid., p. 597
57. Ben-Gurion *Diaries*, 7.9.49
58. Sharett to Eban, 5.25.49, *Israel Documents*, Vol. III, p. 589
59. Shiloah to Sharett, 5.31.49, Ibid., p. 592
60. *Davar*, 1.8.49
61. *Herut*, 1.25.49
62. *Knesset Record*, Vol. I, p. 65, 3.8.49
63. Ibid., p. 107, 3.9.49
64. Ibid., p. 289, 4.4.49
65. *Al Hamishmar*, 1.14.49
66. *Knesset Record*, Vol. I, p. 306, 4.4.49
67. Ben-Gurion *Diaries*, 1.18.49
68. Ibid., 2.1.49
69. Ibid., 12.14.49
70. State Archives, Foreign Ministry, Security Section, A/1/2442. Details about negotiations also in *Foreign Relations of the US*, 1949, pp. 1545, 1558, et al.
71. Sharett in MAPAI Secretariat, 7.28.49, Labor Party Archive
72. Ben-Gurion *Diaries*, 6.16.49
73. Sasson to Sharett, 8.21.49, State Archives, Foreign Ministry, Reconciliation Conference, 2447/13
74. Ben-Gurion *Diaries*, 11.28.49
75. MAPAI Council, 2.7.48, Labor Party Archive; Ben-Gurion, *Behilahem Israel*, pp. 68–69
76. Ben-Gurion, General review at first session of National Council, 4.5.48, *Yoman Hamilhama*, p. 387
77. Michaeli, *Yeshuvim Shenitshu.*
78. Ben-Gurion, *Behilahem Israel*, p. 65. Among the masses of material on the refugee issue there is special interest in an article by Marie Syrkin, "The Arab Refugees—A Zionist View," *Commentary*, January 1966, and one by Uri Avnery, "The Birth of a Problem," *Etgar*, 11.28.63
79. Ben-Gurion *Diaries*, 11.10.48
80. Minutes of Cabinet Meeting, 11.17.48, Kibbutz Meuhad Archive (A. Cizling), section 9, container 9, file 3
81. Ben-Gurion to Shapira, 11.19.48, Ben-Gurion Estate
82. Government Resolutions, 12.5.48, Kibbutz Meuhad Archive (A. Cizling), section 9, container 9, file 1
83. Ministerial Committee for Abandoned Property, 7.13.48, State Archives, Foreign Ministry, A/21/2401
84. Ben-Gurion *Diaries*, 7.15.48

85. *Haaretz*, 10.24.79/2.10–11.79 (by Dan Margalit); Minutes of Cabinet Meeting, 7.21.48, Kibbutz Meuhad Archive (A. Cizling), section 9, container 9, file 3. For further details about expulsion, or "evacuation," of Lydda and Ramlah Arabs, see Oren.

86. Order of Tsvi Ayalon, 7.6.48, Kibbutz Meuhad Archive (A. Cizling), section 9, container 9, file 1

87. Ministerial Committee, 11.5.48, State Archives, Foreign Ministry, A/21/2401

88. M. Sela Report, 11.4.48, State Archives, Ministry for the Minorities, section 49, container 114, file 302

89. Ben-Gurion at MAPAI Central Committee, 3.16.49, Labor Party Archive

90. Political Consultation, 4.12.49, State Archives, Foreign Ministry, 2447/3

91. Sharett in meeting of MAPAI MKs, 4.26.49, Labor Party Archive, Section 2, 11/1/1

92. Eitan to Sharett, 4.3.49, *Israel Documents*, Vol. III, p. 449

93. Sharett to Eitan, 6.6.48, State Archives, Foreign Ministry, Arab Refugees, 2444/19

94. Sharett to Goldman, 6.15.48, *Israel Documents*, Vol. I, p. 163

95. Sharett to Bernadotte, 8.1.48, Ibid., p. 441; Ben-Gurion *Medinat Israel*, p. 167

96. Bernadotte, p. 163

97. Ben-Gurion *Diaries*, 9.8.48

98. Ibid., 9.26.48

99. Ibid., 10.26.48; a later report estimated their number at 600,000. State Archives, Foreign Ministry, Arab Refugees, 2444/19. The Arabs claimed their number was close to 900,000.

100. Ben-Gurion *Diaries*, 10.31.48

101. Yosef to Sharett, 2.1.49, State Archives, Prime Minister's Office, Reconciliation Conference, C/221/5578

102. Ethridge to Foreign Minister, 4.13.49, *Foreign Relations of the US*, 1949, p. 913

103. Middle East Information, The Problem of Arab Refugees, State Archives, Foreign Ministry, Refugees, 2444/19

104. Ben-Gurion to Shapira, 4.10.49, Ben-Gurion Estate

105. Sharett to Weitz, Lifshitz and Danin, 3.14.49, State Archives, Foreign Ministry, Refugees, 2444/19

106. Cabinet Meeting, 7.21.48, Kibbutz Meuhad Archive (A. Cizling), section 9, container 9, file 3

107. Weitz to Sharett, 5.27.49, State Archives, Foreign Ministry, Refugees 2444/19

108. Weitz *Diary*, 7.27.49

109. McDonald to Foreign Minister, 6.10.49, *Foreign Relations of the US*, 1949, p. 1111

110. Ibid., 7.27.49, p. 1265

111. Sharett before Foreign Affairs and Security Committee, 8.1.49, State Archives, Foreign Ministry, A/3/2451

112. *Knesset Record*, Vol. II, p. 1227, 8.2.49

113. Chargé d'affaires to Secretary of State, 8.9.49, *Foreign Relations of the US*, 1949, p. 1292

114. Burdett to Acheson, 8.15.49, *Foreign Relations of the US*, p. 1314

115. MAPAI MKs with party Secretariat, 8.1.49, Labor Party Archive, 11/2/1

116. Weitz *Diary*, 8.18.49

117. State Archives, Foreign Ministry, 2442/6

118. Yosef Tkoa to Yehoshafat Harkabi, 8.9.49, State Archives, Foreign Ministry, Arab Refugees, 2444/19

119. Ben-Gurion *Diaries*, 7.14.49

120. Sharett to Eban, 9.26.49, State Archives, Foreign Ministry, 2447/1

121. The US Minister to the Secretary of State, 5.19.49, *Foreign Relations of the US*, 1949, p. 1032

122. Ethridge to Truman, 4.11.49, *Foreign Relations of the US*, 1949, p. 905

123. Acheson to the Ambassadors, 8.16.49, *Foreign Relations of the US*, 1949, p. 1317

124. Ben-Gurion *Diaries*, 6.30.49

125. Ibid., 5.29.49

126. The Government of Israel to the Government of the United States, 6.8.49, *Foreign Relations of the US*, 1949, pp. 1075 and 1005; Truman letter, p. 1074

127. Ethridge to the Secretary of State, 6.2.49, *Foreign Relations of the US*, 1949, p. 1085

128. Sasson to Sharett, 8.15.49, State Archives, Foreign Ministry, Conciliation Commission, 2447/1

129. Eitan to Sharett, 1.23.49, *Israel Documents*, Vol. III, p. 52

130. Ben-Gurion in MAPAI Central Committee, 7.22/23.49, Labor Party Archive

131. Political Consultation, 12.30.48, State Archives, Foreign Ministry, 2447/3

132. Sasson to Sharett, 2.24.49, *Israel Documents*, Vol. III, p. 271

133. Ibid., 2.25.49, p. 247

134. Political Consultation, 12.30.48, State Archives, Foreign Ministry, 2447/3

135, Political Consultation, 4.12.49, State Archives, Foreign Ministry, 2447/3

136. Ibid.

137. Ibid., 12.30.48, State Archives, Foreign Ministry, 2447/3

138. Ben-Gurion to Valley Committee, 3.8.49, Ben-Gurion Estate

139. Political Consultation, 4.22.49, State Archives, Foreign Ministry, Lausanne Conference, 2447/3

140. Ben-Gurion *Diaries*, 6.3.49

141. Ibid., 7.9.49

142. MAPAI Secretariat, 7.28.49, Labor Party Archive

143. Ben-Gurion *Diaries*, 7.18.49

144. Consultation, MAPAI Members of the Knesset, 12.18.49, Labor Party Archive, 11/1/1

145. Ben-Gurion *Diaries*, 12.14.49

146. Ibid., 12.16/17.49

147. Ibid.

2. Face to Face

1. Weitz *Diary*, 2.14.49

2. Ibid., 2.8.50

3. *Knesset Record*, Vol. I, p. 85, 2.28.49

4. "Problems of Histadrut in the State," February 1948, Labor Party Archive, 7/69/48

5. "Problems of Education in the State," Tel Aviv, June 1948, Labor Party Archive, 7/1/48

6. "Problems of Histadrut in the State," February 1948, Labor Party Archive, 7/69/48

7. Party MKs with Secretariat, 8.1.49, Labor Party Archive

8. Minutes of Ministerial Committee for Abandoned Property, 7.26.48, State Archives, Foreign Ministry, 2401/21/A

9. State Archives, Ministry for Minorities, 1319/42, attempt to prevent expulsion of Tarshiha residents; 1319/66, attempt to prevent expulsion from village of Igzim, et al.

10. Ben-Gurion *Diaries*, 5.8.48

11. Ben-Gurion *Diaries*, 3.22.49

12. Ibid., 11.10.48

13. Ibid., 10.9.48

14. Ibid., 3.24.49

15. Ibid., 6.22.49

16. Committee for Evaluating Question of Arabs in Israel, State Archives, Prime Minister's Office, C/5593

17. *Hapraklit*, February 1946, pp. 58–64

18. *Haaretz*, 7.1.49. For more moderate version, see *Herut*, 7.1.49

19. Herzl Kook and Zipporah Vinirsky *versus* Minister of Defense et al., Petition to High Court of Justice, 1 + 2/48, *Hamishpat* Vol. 3, 1948, p. 307

20. Ismail Ali *versus* Commissioner of Police, et al., *Piskei Din Verdicts*, Vol. 7, p. 913; Alioubi *versus* Minister of Defense et al., *Psakim*, Vol. 6, p. 105; Abu Ali et al. *versus* Verbin et al., *Psakim*, Vol. 13, p. 473

21. Ben-Gurion *Diaries*, 8.26.48

22. Minutes of Ministerial Committee for Abandoned Property, 7.13.48, State Archives, Foreign Ministry, A/21/2401

23. Ben-Gurion *Diaries*, 10.9.49: "I told Avner to be strict about corruption, and if he has well-founded suspicion, dismiss mercilessly."

24. Several of these actions were discussed in the Knesset: *Knesset Record*, Vol. I, p. 753, 6.30.49 (Nazareth); Vol. II, p. 906, 7.5.49 (Ramlah); Vol. III, p. 71, 11.16.49 (Shfaram), etc.

25. Ben-Gurion *Diaries*, 1.5.49

26. Minutes in possession of Rehavam Amir, quoted with his permission

27. Ibid.

28. Interview, 6.14.83

29. Ibid., 6.15.83

30. Ben-Gurion to Knesset Speaker, 4.12.49, Ben-Gurion Estate

31. Ben-Gurion *Diaries*, 11.22.49

32. "The reprimand to Tewfik Toubi," *Hatoor Hashevii*, Vol. I, p. 276

33. Burdett to Acheson, mentioned in *Foreign Relations of the US*, 1949, p. 1320. Quoted here from original in Washington DC 867N, 48/4, 1949

34. Atallah Mansour, *Haaretz*, 9.23.77

35. *Haaretz*, 8.11.72

36. Ben-Gurion *Diaries*, 11.16.48

37. Rehavam Amir to Moshe Yatah, January 1949, State Archives, Ministry for Minorities, 1319/47

38. Arab refugees in northern villages, Intelligence Report, 10.14.48, State Archives, Ministry for Minorities, section 49, container 114, file 302

39. Ben-Gurion *Diaries*, 5.1.49

40. Commander of Haifa Region to Ministry for Minorities, 12.1.48, State Archives, Ministry for Minorities, Ein Hod, 1319/54

41. Ben-Gurion, *Yoman Hamilhaura*, Vol. 3, pp. 833 and 926

42. Minutes of Ministerial Committee for Abandoned Property, 12.17.48, State Archives, Foreign Ministry, 2401/21/A

43. Ibid.

44. *Al Hamishmar*, 12.10.50

45. Ben-Gurion *Diaries*, 1.4.49

46. Ibid., 2.7.49

47. State Archives, Foreign Ministry, Arab Refugees, 2444/19

48. *Knesset Record*, Vol. I, p. 85, 3.9.49

49. Burdett to Acheson, 4.19.49, *Foreign Relations of the US*, 1949, p. 1320. Secretary of State Acheson instructed the Consul to send him the names and identity numbers of the deportees, Acheson to Burdett, 4.26.49, Ibid. These documents are mentioned in the FRUS but quoted here from the original 867 N, 48/4–1949; State Archives, Ministry of Minorities, 1319/40, expulsion of residents from village of Milya; 1319/53 ban on return of Hawassah residents to their homes; 1319/66, argument between security forces and the Ministry for Minorities regarding the expulsion of residents from the village of Igzim, etc; Dayan, p. 95

50. Minutes of Ministerial Committee for Abandoned Property, 12.31.48, State Archives, Foreign Ministry, 2401/21/A; Weitz *Diary* 2.23.49; Dayan, p. 96; *Ner* No. 3–4, 1.12.50

51. Ibid., Vol. II, p. 1513, 9.1.49

52. *Haolam Hazeh*, 6.22.50, photo by Maxim Solomon, and 6.29.50

53. Ben-Gurion *Diaries*, 7.6.49

54. Weitz *Diary*, 8.17.49

55. Ibid., Vol. 4, p. 358 (No Date)

56. *Knesset Record*, Vol. II, p. 1189, 8.1–3.49; expulsion of residents of village of Rebassieh, petition to High Court of Justice, 288/51; 33/52, *Piskei Din*, Vol. 2, pp. 689–696

57. *Haaretz*, 8.9.49

58. Moshe Sharett to Cabinet Ministers, 2.24.50, State Archives, Dov Yosef Archive, correspondence and memoranda, 703/16

59. Labor Party Archive, section 2, temporary number 901
60. Kollek, p. 121
61. Interview, 6.6.83

3. Dividing the Spoils

1. State Archives, Prime Minister's Office, Custodian of Abandoned Property, 5440/C, 210/05
2. Ben-Gurion *Diaries*, 16.6.48
3. Minutes of Ministerial Committee for Abandoned Property, 11.5.48, State Archives, Foreign Ministry, 2401/21/A
4. Shafrir, p. 224
5. Ben-Gurion *Diaries*, 11.11.48
6. *Haaretz*, 9.1.49
7. Yosef to Ben-Gurion, 12.9.48, Ben-Gurion Estate
8. Ben-Gurion to Yosef, 12.16.48, Ben-Gurion Estate
9. Ben-Gurion, *Yoman Hamilhama*, p. 591
10. State Archive, Prime Minister's Office, Custodian, 5440/C, 210/05
11. Shafrir, p. 242
12. Ibid.
13. Minutes of Cabinet Meetings: 6.9.48 (Shitrit); 7.4.48 (Bentov); 7.21.48 (Cizling); Kibbutz Meuhad Archive (Cizling), section 9, container 9, file 3.
14. *Knesset Record*, Vol. III, p. 37, 11.14.49
15. Ibid., Vol. III, p. 156, 11.22.49
16. Custodian's Report, State Archives, Prime Minister's Office, Custodian, 210/05 5400/C
17. Ben-Gurion *Diaries*, 6.7.48
18. Cizling to Ben-Gurion, 6.16.48, State Archives, Foreign Ministry, 2401/21/A
19. Custodian's Report, State Archives, Prime Minister's Office, Custodian, 210/05, 5440/C; Minutes of Cabinet Meeting, 7.21.48; Kibbutz Meuhad Archive (Cizling), section 9, container 9, file 3
20. Minutes of Ministerial Committee for Abandoned Property, 7.13.48, State Archives, Foreign Ministry, 2401/21/A
21. Minutes of Ministerial Committee for Abandoned Property, 11.5.48, State Archives, Foreign Ministry, 2401/21/A
22. Ben-Gurion to Zalman Mishari, 11.11.48, Ben-Gurion Estate
23. Lufbann, p. 117
24. Ben-Gurion *Diaries*, 6.16.48

25. Central Zionist Archive, S/41 248; Lufbann, p. 199; In September 1948 the government created a four-member Ministerial Committee to determine the order of distribution of apartments in Jaffa. Minutes of Cabinet Meeting, Kibbutz Meuhad Archive (Cizling), section 9, container 9, file 1

26. Shafrir's report, State Archives, Prime Minister's Office, 210/05, Custodian, 5440/C

27. Central Zionist Archives, S/41 248

28. *Haaretz*, 7.3.49

29. Ibid., 4.8.49; on this and similar affairs, see State Archives, Minorities Ministry, section 49, container 83, file 309.

30. Letters to *Haaretz* editor, 9.20.49 and 2.25.49

31. Shafrir's report, State Archives, Prime Minister's Office, 210/05, Custodian 5440/C

32. Ben-Gurion's statement, *Knesset Record*, Vol. I, p. 399, 4.26.49

33. Lufbann, pp. 122–3

34. Zionist Executive Minutes, 4.29.49

35. Lufbann, p. 122–3

36. Ibid., p. 123

37. Ibid., p. 125

38. Central Zionist Archives, S/41 247 I. The decision to resettle Beersheba, Ramlah and Lydda was taken by the Ministerial Committee for Arab Affairs, 12.5.48, State Archives, Foreign Ministry, 2401/21/A. Amendment to decision, in Minutes of Ministerial Committee for Abandoned Property, 2.17.48. Settlement of Migdal Gad and other places, ibid., 12.31.48

39. Yoseftal to Greenberg, 4.13.49, Central Zionist Archives, Absorption Department, S/84/71

40. *Davar*, 10.6.49

41. Central Zionist Archives, Absorption Department, S/84/71

42. Minutes of Zionist Executive, 11.15.49

43. Report of the Committee of Investigation on Compensation for Absentee Property, State Archives, Foreign Ministry, Compensation and Absentee Property, 2451/18

44. Ben-Gurion *Diaries*, 5.6.48

45. Ibid., 8.4.49, also Memorandum of Meeting on Abandoned Property, 8.4.49, State Archives, Prime Minister's Office, 5431/17

46. State Archives, Prime Minister's Office, 5431/17

47. *Knesset Record*, Vol. III, p. 144, 11.22.49

48. Quoted by Jiryis, p. 66

49. *Knesset Record*, Vol. III, p. 164, 11.23.49

50. Report of Committee of Investigation on Compensation for Absentee Property, State Archives, Foreign Ministry, 2451/18

51. Custodian to Finance Minister, 2.11.51, State Archives, Foreign Ministry, Custodian Council, 1949–53, 5431/19

52. Memorandum of Meeting on Abandoned Property, 8.4.49, State Archives, Prime Minister's Office, 5431/17

53. Yehoshua Palmon, Problems of Absentee Property, 6.15.49, State Archives, Foreign Ministry, 2401/21/A; Committee on Absentee Property, 1.8.52, State Archives, Prime Minister's Office, Absentee Property file #2, 5431/18; Aharon Liskovsky, The Present Absentees in Israel, reserved internal document of Advisor on Arab Affairs, August 1959, State Archives, container 386, 3/9959/27

54. Foreign Minister to Attorney General, 1.11.50, State Archives, Foreign Minister, 2401/21/A

55. Shabtai Rozen to Foreign Minister, 7.27.48, State Archives, Foreign Ministry, Compensation and Absentee Property, 2451/18; Correspondence with Immigration Organization in Iraq, in files of Immigration Department of Jewish Agency, package #365/57, original designation 2421/53

56. *Knesset Record*, Vol. III, p. 40, 11.14.49; similar charges, Vol. IV, p. 674, 1.31.50

57. Minutes of Zionist Executive, 6.5.49; Department of Assistance to Immigrants, to Tsvi Herman, 10.6.49, Central Zionist Archives, Absorption Department, S/84/71; State Archives, Dov Yosef Archive, Correspondence and Memoranda, 703/16, 12.5.49

58. State Archives, Minorities Ministry, section 49, container 1314, file 49, February 1949, Lengthy Correspondence between the custodian and an Arab guard in one of the abandoned villages.

59. Quoted by Bein, pp. 80–81, and Korn, p. 26

60. Ibid.

61. Zionist Executive, 11.22.48

62. Minutes of Cabinet Meeting, 6.27.48; Kibbutz Meuhad Archive (Cizling), section 9, container 9, file 3

63. Ben-Gurion to Cizling, 9.13.48, Kibbutz Meuhad Archive (Cizling), section 9, container 9, file 4; also ibid., Minutes of Ministerial Committee on Absentee Property, 9.17.48.

64. State Archives, Dov Yosef Archive, section 69, 714/4

65. Settlement Plan, Kibbutz Meuhad Archive (Cizling), section 9, container 8/A

66. Weitz *Diary*, 1.26.49

67. Ibid. 1.27.49; 2.24.49; 6.24.49

68. Ibid. 6.7.49; 8.9.49

69. Ibid. 3.15.49

70. Kibbutz Meuhad Archive (Cizling), section 9, container 9, file 1

71. Minutes of Ministerial Committee on Absentee Property, 8.27.48, 12.27.48, State Archives, Foreign Ministry, 2401/24/A

72. Central Zionist Archives, Immigrant camp Givat Shaul 2, Deir Yassin, S/84/28; S/84/30; S/84/32; S/63/51; S/84/70; S/84/71

73. Ibid.

74. State Archives, Prime Minister's Office, Absorption of Immigrants in Agriculture, 7133 5559/C

75. *Knesset Record*, Vol. II, p. 1201, 8.1.49

76. Ibid. Vol. II, p. 1219, 8.2.49

77. *Davar*, 7.27.49

78. *Haaretz*, 5.31.49

79. *Dvar Hashavua*, 8.4.49

80. *Knesset Record*, Vol. III, p. 303, 12.14.49

81. *Haaretz*, 2.11.49

4. The First Million

1. Alterman, Vol. 1, p. 120

2. Twenty-Third Zionist Congress, p. 178 ff. There are other statistical tables, but they do not vary greatly. The differences stem from the various definitions of origins, according to country of birth or last country of residence. See Sikron, p. 7

3. On the problems of immigration and absorption in the first two years of statehood, April 1948, Labor Party Archive, 7/36

4. 1949—230,900; 1950—169,000; 1951—174,000; 1952—23,375

5. *Haaretz*, 4.13.49

6. Ben-Gurion, *Knesset Record*, Vol. I, p. 54, 3.8.49

7. Ben-Gurion, *Netzah Israel*, p. 16

8. Consultation, 4.12.49, State Archives, Foreign Ministry, 130. 02/ 2447/3. His statement before the MAPAI Secretariat, 4.22.49 (Labor Party Archive, section 2, 24/49), and a meeting of the party Central Committee, 7.22–23.49 (Labor Party Archive, section 2, 11/2/1); In his diary Ben-Gurion noted the components of Israel's security in the following order: 1. Immigration; 2. Settlement; 3. Economic power; 4. Foreign policy (Ben-Gurion *Diaries*, 5.12.49

9. Barzilai to Sharett, 9.30.49, State Archives, Foreign Ministry, 2397/19

10. Sharett's report, 12.12.48, State Archives, Foreign Ministry, 130.11/2502/8

11. Zionist Executive, 12.13.48

12. Ibid. 1.16.49

13. State Archives, Dov Yosef Archive, Correspondence and Memoranda, section 69, 703/16

14. Ibid.

15. Israel Consulate in Warsaw to Foreign Ministry, 8.21.49, State Archives, Foreign Ministry, 2397/19

16. State Archives, Dov Yosef Archive, Correspondence and Memoranda, section 69, 703/16

17. Barzilai to Sharett, 10.19.49, State Archives, Foreign Ministry, 2397/19

18. Interview, 3.22.83

19. Avriel to Sharett, 8.14.49, State Archives, Foreign Ministry, 2397/20. The material in the file suggests that the Joint acted on its own initiative

20. Zionist Executive, 11.9.49; also files of Immigration Department, package #56, file 352, original designation 2421/34 (emigration permits from Hungary); package 410, original designation 2437/40, including a series of letters from the Agudat Israel leader I.M. Levin

21. Protocol of the Immigration to Israel of Hungarian Citizens, 10.20.49, in the files of the Organization for Immigration, (Mossad) Israel Army Archive, 14/79. Some of the files that deal with the financial transactions between Israel and the Eastern European countries have not yet been opened for inspection, and certain documents have been removed from some of the files which are available. Sources for the present text are the files of the Foreign Ministry and the Jewish Agency's Immigration Department, including the State Archives. Files of the Foreign Ministry: Israel-Czechoslovakia relations, 2381/19; Immigration permits for Bulgaria, 21/34, file #2246; Immigration from Hungary, 2397/20; Immigration from Rumania, 2411/7. Files of the Jewish Agency's Immigration Department: Immigration Permits for Bulgaria, package #56, file 354, original designation 2421/43; Immigration Permits for Hungary, package #56, file 352, original designation 2412/34; Immigration Permits for Poland, package #56, file 349, original designation 2421/12. Also files of the Central Zionist Archive: immigration by country, S/41 256. The files of the Immi-

gration Department are not kept in the Central Archive. Some of them are in the possession of Dr. Refael. The Jewish Agency permitted me to inspect the files which are still kept in the department. I discovered them in a dark and mouldy cellar in the Russian Compound in Jerusalem. They have, since then, been transferred to another store. My thanks are due to Zeev Mahnai, Yehuda Dominitz and Aryeh Golz of the Jewish Agency for their assistance. Some of the material in these files, as well as additional information on the subject, are to be found in the files of the Organization for Immigration (Mossad), in the Israel Army Archive.

22. Gruenbaum, Zionist Executive, 8.18.48

23. Newman, Zionist Exeutive, 8.19.48

24. Zionist Executive, 8.19.48

25. Ibid.

26. Zionist Executive, 9.27.48

27. Ibid., 9.19.48

28. Ibid. 9.28.48

29. Ibid. 3.21.49

30. Refael, pp. 50–52

31. Ibid. p. 51

32. Zionist Executive, 11.28.49, and Refael, p. 147

33. Ibid., 4.22.49

34. Ibid. 5.2.49

35. Ibid. 10.4.49

36. Interview, 3.22.83. Irregularities, among other matters in the transmission of funds by Rumanian Jews to Israel, with the connivance, *inter alia*, of Israeli diplomats, and likewise "embezzlements in the immigration from India"—files of Immigration Department, package #59, file 411, original designation 2139/55. Embezzlements in immigration from Iran, package #63, file 410, original designation 2429/54, and others. In this connection, see also report of Jewish Agency Controller in files of Mossad for Immigration, Israel Army Archive 14 (Zim), 3–4, the Zion Ezri affair and 14/10. Other irregularities, such as private use of foreign currency, negligence, possible corruption, in handling immigrants' baggage, ostentatious parties thrown by Jewish Agency officials, their extravagant way of life, presents they received on the Agency's behalf—see files of Immigration Department, Controller's Office, package #19, file 81, original designation 1006

37. Milstein, *Kadmon* and Klieger

38. Refael, p. 66

39. Zionist Executive, 6.22.49. Also, "The Mossad is an auxiliary to the Immigration Department," Refael to Zerubavel, 6.22.49, Central Zionist Archive S/20/95

40. Levin to Director of Immigration Section Shai, Ministry of Immigration, 3.8.50, Immigration Permits for Austria, Immigration Department package #56, file 33, original designation 2421/35

41. From Iraq to the Mossad, 3.26.49, Israel Army Archive, 28/14

42. State Archives, Foreign Ministry, Jews in the Arab countries, 2.27.50; also, Central Zionist Archive, S/20 538, about the escape from Arab country by boats, including details about the sinking of one such boat

43. For example, in Libya. Meir Shilon's report, 3.19.52, State Archives, Foreign Ministry, 21/721 52/C, container 2246

44. Interview, 1.4.83

45. Ben-Gurion *Diaries*, 6.16.49

46. Immigration Department files, package #57, file 365, original designation 2421/53

47. Refael to the Coordination Institution, 8.27.50

48. The company to Binyamin Yerushalmi, Jewish Agency representative, 3.21.49, files of Mossad for Immigration, Israel Army Archive, 14/635

49. Refael, p. 65

50. Letter from Consul Israel Carmel, 9.22.49, Central Zionist Archives, Immigration by Country, S/41/256I

51. Shilo to the Mossad, 7.24.49, Israel Army Archive, 14/123

52. Gileadi report, 5.2.50, Central Zionist Archives, Immigration by Country, S/41/2561

53. On the immigrants from Shanghai, Zionist Executive, 4.22.49

54. Refael's statement, Zionist Executive, 8.28.49. The letter from Johannesburg and similar letters, all bearing censorship stop stamps, in the Mossad for Immigration files in the Israeli Army Archive, 14/451. Among them also a letter from the Organization's agent in Turnis, asking that "negative" letters from immigrants be held up

55. Zionist Executive, 3.21.49. The full quote runs: "I forbade the publication of this matter because it would have weakened the Jews' will to emigrate, and the whole thing is now under a cloud and we don't know what the situation with regard to immigration will be like tomorrow. Right now we can get them out of there."

56. Mordecai Ben-Ari to Moshe Shapira, 7.6.50, in Immigration Department files, package #65, file 353, original designation 2421/35

57. Sharett to Members of Cabinet, State Archives, Dov Yosef Archive, Correspondence and Memoranda, Section 69, 703/16

58. Ben-Menahem, p. 179

59. Zionist Executive, 11.28.49, According to one estimate, if the Italians returned to Libya it would cause the Jews to remain there. It was therefore proposed to hasten their emigration from that country, lest they feel too comfortable there. Dr. J. Weinstein of the Immigration Department to Zeev Shind, of the Mossad, concerning a meeting between Dr. S.A. Nachon and the Italian Consul in Jerusalem, 3.13.49. Files of Mossad for Immigration, Israel Army Archive, 14/123

60. Zionist Executive, 4.22.49

61. The Organization for Youth Immigration in Morocco and Algeria, 2.25.50, files of Immigration Department, Immigration permits for North Africa, package #61, file 398, original designation 2421/73

62. "Maxie," the agent in Egypt, to the Mossad's Executive, 11.18.49, files of Immigration Department, Immigration permits for Egypt, package #60, file 389, original designation 2421/71

63. Zionist Executive, 4.22.49

64. Refael, p. 51

65. The entire report is kept in the files of the Immigration Department, Controller's Office, package #19, file 81, original designation 1006, report for the year 1951. Some parts are also kept in the files of the Mossad for Immigration, Israel Army Archive, 14/10

66. Ibid.

67. Zionist Executive, 3.21.49

68. Ibid., 4.29.49

69. Dr. Einhorn on the transport of immigrants from Poland, 1.17.50, files of Mossad for Immigration, Israel Army Archive, 14/444. More about transport conditions, Mossad files, Army Archive, 14/118; "Two old people passed away," Kadmon to the Mossad, 1.24.49; Dr Y. Goldin to the Mossad, 8.31.48, 14/362, "The sanitary conditions and air circulation are very poor"; N. Wachsmann to Barpal, 3.23.49, Zim 14/28, "the air is suffocatingly close"; Ministry of Health to Immigration Department, 4.15.49, 14/372, "rats."

70. Finance Department to the Mossad for Immigration, 6.20.49, Mossad files, Israel Army Archive, 4/10

71. Zionist Executive, 4.29.49. Meir Grossmann, too, charged that

the Mossad was acting without due supervision. Likewise, Moshe Kol: "In Munich questions of immigration are decided not by the immigration officers nor by the Jewish Agency delegation, but by the Mossad's people" (Zionist Executive, 8.19.48). Some weeks later the Jewish Agency decided to take certain steps to increase the supervision over the Organization (Zionist Executive, 6.19.49). But there is some evidence that Refael himself did not get a full report on the activities of the Mossad and its expenditures. Immigration Department files, Joint, package #23, file 122, original designation 1092

72. *Haaretz*, 4.15.49, Barpal's response: "We won't tolerate their talking about us like this!" He got so carried away as to make the following, highly significant, remark: "We are in control of millions . . . it's an immense economy!" Zionist Executive, 4.22.49

73. Memorandum, 3.21.52, Central Zionist archives, S/41 263

74. Concerning the dispute over the closing down of the Mossad for Immigration, see Israel Army Archive, 14/648

75. Report of Jewish Agency Controller, Department of Immigration files, Controller's Office, package #29, file 81, original designation 1006, Report for the year 1951. Parts of the report are also found in the files of the Mossad for Immigration, Israel Army Archive, 14/10

76. Immigration officer Gileadi to Ministry of Immigration, 3.2.49, Central Zionist Archives, S/41 256I

77. Barzilai to Sharett, 10.30.49, State Archives, Foreign Ministry, Immigration from Poland, 2397/19

78. Eisenstadt, Chapter 2, p. 34 ff.

79. The Consul to the Immigration Ministry, 11.2.49, State Archives, Foreign Ministry, The Situation of Jews in Germany, 2387/22

80. Barzilai to Sharett, 9.20.49, State Archives, Foreign Ministry, 2397/19

81. Vaad Hapoel, p. 118

82. Ben-Gurion's meeting with writers (*Divrei Sofrim*) 10.11.49, State Archives

83. Zionist Executive, 11.15.48

84. Ben-Gurion, *Netsah Israel*, p. 37

5. Working and Fighting Hands

1. Lufbann, p. 94
2. Zionist Executive, 6.19.49

3. Ibid., 8.19.49

4. Yosef Barpal at conference of directors of Eretz Israel offices in Europe, Paris, 3.18.49, Central Zionist Archive, 12413/C. "In the countries where they're eliminating the Jews by emigration we have to take them all in."

5. Summary of meeting, 3.30.49, State Archives, Prime Minister's Office, Immigrant camps, 5558/C

6. *Knesset Record*, Vol. V, p. 1745, 6.19.50

7. Arye Dissenchik, *Maariv*, 7.1.49

8. His series of reports bore the title "I was a New Immigrant for One Month." It was published in fifteen instalments between 4.13.49 and 5.20.49

9. On September 7, 1949, Dr. Yaakov Weinstein of the Immigration Department wrote Giora Yoseftal: "I went with a delegation of people from Tunisia to visit the immigrant camp in Beer Yaakov, where I saw with my own eyes how the immigrants refused to eat the soup because of the maggotty vegetables in it." Department of Immigration files, Immigrant Homes, Kiryat Shmuel, package #49, file 236, orignal designation 215/4912

10. Concerning the camps constructed without kitchens or sanitary facilities, see Zionist Executive, 4.11.49. Correspondence with Minister Shapira regarding the mixed accommodation for men and women, in view of the concern over venereal disease and the impossibility of maintaining the ritual purity of family life—see files Jewish Agency Immigration Department, package #49, file 232, original designation 215.

11. Zionist Executive, 3.29.49

12. Ibid., 8.12.49

13. Yoseftal to Locker, 6.9.49, Central Zionist Archives, S 41/2471

14. *Knesset Record*, Vol. I, p. 662, 6.7.49

15. Ibid., Vol. II, p. 1302, 8.10.49

16. Ibid.; concerning shortage of doctors and ambulances, see also files in State Archives, Prime Minister's Office, 5558/C, Immigrant camps

17. *Haaretz*, 3.10.49

18. Ruth Klieger's report, September 1949, State Archives, Prime Minister's Office, Division 43, 333/5: severe criticism of the administration in immigrant camps—inefficient, thereby aggravating suffering of residents: "Most of the efficient workers in the Jewish Agency were transferred to the civil service after the creation of the state. Consequently, the functioning of the Jewish Agency has deteriorated to the point of absolute chaos." Levando

report, 4.22.49, State Archives, Prime Minister's Office, 5558/C. Concerning corruption in food distribution, see Central Zionist Archives, Immigration Absorption, S 41/247I

19. Zionist Executive, 4.22.49. See also Klieger report, State Archives, Prime Minister's Office, Division 43, 333/5: "The immigrant is not conscious of being a full citizen of the State of Israel. He feels like a second-class human being, etc."

20. Zionist Executive, 3.29.49

21. Interview, published in *Haaretz*, 12.25.81

22. Zionist Executive, 3.29.49

23. MAPAI—Problems of Immigration and Absorption in the first two years of statehood, April 1948, Labor Party Archive, 7/36

24. Quoted by Bein, pp. 80–81

25. Koren, p. 22

26. Ibid., p. 27

27. Report on tour of villages with a North African settlement group on Wednesday and Thursday, 12–13 October 1949, Central Zionist Archives, S/20 479

28. Koren, pp. 28–29

29. Prime Minister's Office, State Archives, Absorption of Immigrants in Agriculture, 7133 5559/C

30. Central Zionist Archives, S/63 42

31. Asaf to Ben-Gurion, 1.23.51; Eshkol to Ben-Gurion, 1.13.51; Elkanah Gali to Asaf, 2.9.51, State Archives, Prime Minister's Office, Absorption of Immigrants in Agriculture, 7133 5559/C

32. Interview, 5.20.83

33. Koren, p. 36

34. Ben-Gurion in Knesset, *Knesset Record*, Vol. III, p. 536, 1.16.50. Aharon Cizling, *Al Hamishmar*, 1.27.50. Goldstein report, State Archives, Prime Minister's Office, Absorption of Immigrants in Agriculture, 7133 5559/C

35. *Haaretz*, 4.26.49

36. Ibid., 5.9.49

37. *Knesset Record*, Vol. II, p. 1137, 7.26.49

38. Zionist Executive, 3.7.49; also 4.29.49

39. *Knesset Record*, Vol. III, p. 618, 1.24.50

40. Ibid., Vol. II, p. 1278, 8.8.49

41. Ibid., Vol. I, pp. 633–34, 6.1.49

42. Ibid. Vol. II, p. 1276, 8.8.49

43. Ibid., Vol. II, p. 1275, 8.8.49

44. Ibid., Vol. I, pp. 633–34, 6.1.49

45. *Haaretz*, 8.21.49

46. *Knesset Record*, Vol. I, p. 609, 5.31.49

47. Ibid., Vol. II, p. 1244, 8.3.49

48. Dov Givon, Director of Housing Department, to Golda Meir, 11.30.49, State Archives, Prime Minister's Office, Immigrant Housing, 7135 5559/C

49. MAPAI Secretariat, 4.22.49, Labor Party Archive, 24/49, Div. 2

50. Zionist Executive, 3.24.49

51. Grossmann's statement, Zionist Executive, 5.2.49

52. Zionist Executive, 3.29.49

53. Ibid., 5.2.49

54. Yoseftal to Kaplan, 9.6.49, Central Zionist Archives, Immigration Absorption, S 41/247

55. MAPAI Secretariat, 4.22.49 Labor Party Archive, Division 2; 24/49

56. *Knesset Record*, Vol. III, p. 32, 11.9.49

57. Zionist Executive. For the following pages I made use of a study by Devorah Bernstein, as well as the report of the interministerial committee to coordinate the social services in the immigrant camps, State Archives, Division 43. File 3903, container 5558/C, and the Labor Ministry's Housing Plan, State Archives, 16/957/24

58. Yoseftal, p. 148

59. Michael, p. 21

60. Appelfeld, p. 61

61. This was the basic thesis of the study by sociologist S.N. Eisenstadt. It matched the widely-held concept of the political establishment, and also laid the groundwork for an entire school in Israeli sociological research. The common phrase was "Absorption through modernization."

62. Ben-Gurion's Meeting with writers, 10.11.49, *Divrei Sofrim*, State Archive

63. MAPAI Central Committee meeting, 7.22–23.49, Labor Party Archive, Division 2, ll/2/1

64. *Haaretz*, 4.21.49

65. Alterman, Vol. 3, p. 236

66. Zionist Executive, 4.22.49

67. Meir Shilon's report, 3.19.52, State Archives, Immigration from Libya, 21/721 (52)C, container 2246

68. *Knesset Record*, Vol. I, p. 54, 3.8.49

69. Zionist Executive, 12.10.48

70. Ibid.

71. Ibid., 4.29.49

72. Ibid., 3.29.49

73. Ibid.

74. Ibid.

75. Ibid., 10.6.49

76. Ibid., 11.28.49

77. Ibid., 12.11.49

78. Ibid., 1.2.50

79. Ibid., 4.29.49. Concerning the dispute with the "opponents of immigration," see Refael, pp. 133–166, including the charge that Dr. Nahum Goldmann proposed returning 100,000 immigrants to their countries of origin

80. Zionist Executive, 4.22.49

81. *Haaretz*, 2.11.49, M. Kramer (Keren)

82. Ibid., 4.13.49

83. *Hamashkif*, 3.25.49

84. *Dvar Hashavua*, 4.21.49

85. *Hatzofeh*, 4.13.49

86. Zionist Executive, 4.29.49

87. Ibid., 3.21.49

88. *Knesset Record*, Vol. III, p. 128, 11.21.49

89. *Haaretz*, 4.19.49

90. Ibid, 2.11.49

91. Zionist Executive, 4.29.49; also Hermon, Zionist Executive, 3.21.49. "Very poor human material from the point of view of absorption."

92. Ibid., 3.29.49

93. Ibid., 10.4.49

94. Ibid., 10.10.48

95. Ibid., 3.29.49

96. Ibid., 12.10.48

97. Ibid.

98. Dan to the Mossad for Immigration, 1.2.49, Files of Mossad, Israel Army Archive, 570/14

99. 2.17.50, Files of Immigration Department, package # 60, file 839, original designation 2421/71

100. Minister of Immigration to immigration officers, 8.20.48, Mossad Files, Ministry of Immigration, Israel Army Archive, 14/362

101. Zionist Executive, 3.29.49

102. Ibid., 6.19.49

103. Barpal at conference of Eretz Israel Offices' directors, Paris, 3.18.49, Central Zionist Archives, 12413/C

104. Files of Immigration Department, Joint, package #23, file 1122, original designation 1092; also Central Zionist Archives, Social Welfare cases among immigrants, S 41/246

105. Department of Immigration, Emigration permits from Egypt, package #60, file 839, original designation 1421/71; State Archives, Foreign Ministry, Immigration from Egypt, 2397/16/C, and Mossad files, Israel Army Archive, 14/372

106. Files of Immigration Department, Permits from North Africa, package #61, file 393, original designation 2421/73. Date of letter 6.8.49

107. Schmidt to Department, 5.13.50, Central Zionist Archives, Immigration office in Aden, S 27 II

108. Files of Immigration Department, Immigration permits for US, package #60, file 380, original designation 2421/62

109. Attorney General's intervention, State Archives, Division 21/43, file 2246, Immigration permits for Bulgaria

110. Refael, pp. 90–91; see also argument between M. Sharett and M. Vilner, MK, in Knesset, *Knesset Record*, Vol. I, p. 866, 6.29.49

111. Yellin-Mor, MK, *Knesset Record*, Vol. I, p. 671, 6.8.49

112. Files of Immigration Department, Immigration permits for Austria, package #56, file 353, original designation 2421/35

113. Circulars of Immigration Department, Central Zionist Archives, S/41/240

114. Minister of Immigration to his Ministry's delegates: "Every case having to do with a newspaperman, to be referred to our decision," 9.20.48, files of Immigration Organization, Israel Army Archive, 14/362

115. Circulars of Immigration Department, Central Zionist Archives, S/41 240; pamphlet of Absorption Department, No. 4, Central Zionist Archives, S/20/103. See also Refael's request to Eshkol to give special consideration to group of activists, 11.20.49, Eshkol's Office, Central Zionist Archives, S/43/260

116. Meir Shilon's report from Libya on work of emissary Baruch Duvdevani, 3.19.52, State Archives, 21/721(52)/C, container 22.6

117. *Haaretz*, 4.21.49

118. Klieger report, State Archives, Prime Minister's Office, Division 43, 333/5

119. Public Opinion Research Institute, Report No. 5

120. Kramer, *Haaretz*, 4.15.59

121. Gelblum, *Haaretz*, 5.20.49

122. Shimon Gurevitch, *Yediot Aharonot*, 9.30.49; Eliezer Kaplan, *Knesset Record*, Vol. III, p. 122, 11.21.49; M. Kramer, *Haaretz*, 4.15.49

123. Ben-Gurion's Meeting with Writers, 10.11.49, *Divrei Sofrim*, State Archives

124. Gruber, 8.12.49, State Archives, Prime Minister's Office, Immigrant camps, 5558/C

125. Pamphlet of Jerusalem Scouts, No. 2, Nahum Levin Archive, Central Archive for History of Jewish People

126. Rivkah Sapir, Operation Roof Over Immigrant Children's Heads, *Megamot*, Vol. III, 1951

127. Zionist Executive, 10.12.48; 3.21.49

128. Ibid., 1.2.50

129. Central Zionist Archives, Department of Jews in the Near East, S/20/538

130. State Archives, Prime Minister's Office, Division 43, 333/5

131. Ariav to Minister of Justice, 6.15.50, State Archives, Prime Minister's Office, Division 43, 333/5

132. Ostrovsky to Yoseftal, 1.5.50, Central Zionist Archives, S/41/247I

133. *Vaad Hapoel Hazioni*, p. 128

134. Gelblum, *Haaretz*, 4.12.49

135. Public Opinion, No. 5

136. B. Minkowsky, *Dapei Alya*, 14

137. *Haaretz*, 4.22.49

138. Minkowsky, *Dapei Alya*, 14

139. Ben-Gurion in MAPAI Secretariat, 4.22.49, Labor Party Archive, 24/49, Division 2

140. Avnery, p. 324

141. Public Opinion, No. 1.

142. *Maariv*, 1.13.49

143. Ibid., 3.1.49

144. Public Opinion, No. 1

145. *Maariv*, 4.17.49

146. Shalom Cohen in MAPAI Central Committee, 8.4.49, Labor Party Archive, Division 2, 23/49

147. Letter to *Haaretz* editor, 2.25.49

148. Ben-Gurion in MAPAI Secretariat, 4.22.49, Labor Party Archive, Division 2, 24/49

149. State Archives, Prime Minister's Office, Immigrant camps, 5558/ C

150. Koren, p. 56

151. Almogy, p. 82

152. Conclusions of committee to investigate possibility of organizing immigrants in labor brigades and companies, State Archives, 1/ 160

153. Zionist Executive, 12.18.49

6. Nameless People

1. Zionist Executive, 4.29.49, also Zionist Executive 4.10.49: "We certainly would not wish this to be the only source of immigrants."

2. Ibid., 3.21.49

3. Ibid.

4. Reuven Hirsch to the Mossad, 9.2.49, Mossad files, Israel Army Archive, 14/123

5. Pragai (Foreign Ministry) to Cherbinsky-Carmil, the Mossad, 10.2.49, Mossad files, Israel Army Archive, 14/372

6. *Knesset Record*, Vol. IV, p. 940, 3.6.50

7. Weitz *Diary*, 9.19.50

8. Zionist Executive, 6.5.49

9. Ben-Gurion's Meeting with Writers, 10.11.49, *Divrei Sofrim*, State Archives

10. Ben-Gurion, *Netsah Israel*, p. 17

11. Ibid., p. 9

12. Ibid., p. 14

13. Ibid., p. 34

14. *Vaad Hapoel Hatsioni*, p. 118

15. Ben-Gurion, *Netsah Israel*, p. 37

16. Ibid., p. 23

17. Knesset Constitution, Law and Justice Committee, 7.13.49, Ben-Gurion Estate

18. Ben-Gurion *Diaries*, 7.20.49

19. Ben-Gurion to Etsioni, 8.3.59, Ben-Gurion Estate

20. *Megamot* B/3, (April 1951), also in issues B/4 & C/1. Relative distribution of immigrants into Ashkenazi and Arab-country Jews, by month—Eisenstadt, p. 28. The change began to be perceptible in the middle of 1949.

21. Shiran, *Hatiyug Hamahtim.*

22. *Yediot Aharonot*, 4.13.49

23. Ibid., 5.3.49. Concerning immigrants from Rumania who had grown accustomed to an idle life at public expense—see *Yediot Aharonot*, 3.30.51. Likewise on reports of lung disease and tuberculosis among Ashkenazi immigrants. For favorable reports, as for example about new settlements of Ashkenazi immigrants, see *Haaretz*, 5.18.49; *Yediot Aharonot*, 6.12.49; *Haaretz*, 12.15.50

24. *Haaretz*, 3.22.51. *Haaretz* published reports about immigrants from Tunis (5.5.52), Afghanistan (5.21.52) and Iran (6.2.52), emphasizing their poverty, diseases and degeneracy: "A considerable number of Persian Jews smoke opium and hashish. . . . There are syphilitics, including children. There is a congenital element in this." In April 1952 a *Haaretz* editorial stated that mass immigration from backward countries endangered Israel's future as a modern state (4.11.52). Similar statements were made in other publications, as for example, with reference to immigrants from Iraq, who had previously worked as officials in British companies, the postal services and the railroad: ". . . Although they all have some experience in administration, their standard, as compared with the European standard, is below average. . . . There is reason to fear a decline in the administrative standard in Israel," *Yediot Aharonot*, 3.31.51. There were reports about industries who requested the Labor Exchanges to send them "civilized workers," not of the Eastern communities, *Yediot Aharonot*, 2.23.51; *Haaretz*, 5.27.52.

25. Ibid., 4.22.49. Responses, including an article defending Arye Gelblum's right to "present the facts as he saw them"—4.25.49 (editorial); 4.27.49 (Minister Shitrit's letter); 5.8.49 (article by Efraim Friedmann; 5.16.49 (readers' letters); 5.19.49 (more readers' letters); 5.20.49 (Gelblum's response). See also K. Shabbetai, "The Truth About Those Moroccoan," *Davar*, 11.18.49, 12.1.49, 12.12.49. There were other replies, and even some thirty years later this article still served as the point of departure for the debate on intercommunal relations. See also Amos Eilon "Two Weeks in the Other Israel," *Haaretz* Publications, 1951, and E. Wiesel, series of articles, in *Yediot Aharonot*, November 1950

26. Report of the Chairman of the Association of Immigrants from North Africa, 3.4.50, in Immigration Department files, package #62, original designation 2421/73

27. Concerning the situation of Jews in French North Africa, 2.3.49, Central Zionist Archives S/20/550/5

28. Political consultation, 4.12.49, State Archives, Foreign Ministry, 130.02/2447/3

29. "The Day of the Million," Alterman, Hatur Hashvii Vol. 1, p. 120

30. Central Zionist Archives, S20/555

31. For details about pogroms, persecutions and kidnapping of Jewish girls in Libya, see Yaakov Kraus, The Situation of Jews in Libya, 4.18.49, files of the Mossad for Immigration, Israel Army Archive, 14/5/A

32. Yaakov Kraus, The Situation of Jews in French North Africa, 2.3.49, Central Zionist Archives, S20/5550/5

33. Refael to Zionist Executive, 6.5.49, Central Zionist Archives S/41/256

34. Kraus to the Mossad for Immigration, 4.18.49, Mossad files, Israel Army Archive, 14/5/A

35. Ibid.

36. Immigration and escape from Morocco, (undated), Mossad files, Israel Army Archive, 14/5/A

37. Ibid.

38. Department of Immigration files, Immigration permits for North Africa, package #61, file 393, original designation 2421/73

39. Immigration and escape from Morocco, (undated), Mossad files, Israel Army Archive, 14/5/A

40. Yany (Avidov) to Barpal, 12.30.48, Organization files, Israel Army Archive, 14/5/A

41. Refael to Executive, 9.9.49, Central Zionist Archives, Immigration, S/41/256/II; for details about the negotiations, see report on immigration and escape from Morocco, (undated), Mossad files, Israel Army Archive, 14/5/A. In that file, see also long letter from Gershuni to Governor of Morocco, 3.9.49

42. Ibid.

43. Tsvi Hermon, Zionist Executive, 3.21.49

44. Zionist Executive, 10.6.49

45. Settlement between Mordehai Ben-Porat (Plaintiff) and Barh Nadel (Respondent), Civil Court in Herzlia, Civil Lawsuit 63/81

46. The files of the Foreign Ministry, the Mossad and Department of Immigration contain many reports and telegrams which suggest that the Jewish community in Iraq enjoyed a measure of security and prosperity—even after the creation of the State of Israel and the War of Independence—with the exception of individuals who were suspected of Zionist activity

47. "Berman" to the Mossad, Mossad files, Israel Army Archive, 14/28

48. Cherbinsky of the Mossad to Moshe Sharett, 10.10.49, Mossad files, Army Archive, 14/29/C

49. Civil Court of Herzlia, Civil suit 63/81

50. "Berman" to the Mossad, 1.14.51, and the Mossad to "Berman," 1.15.51, Mossad files, Israel Army Archive, 14/389; Iraq to the Mossad, 3.4.50, files of Department of Immigration, package #57, file 365, original designation 2421/53

51. Refael to Executive, 10.28.48, Mossad files, Israel Army Archive, 14/372

52. Bahar to Immigration officers, 10.25.48, Mossad files, Israel Army Archive, 14/444

53. Klieger report, September 1949, State Archives, Prime Minister's office, Division 43, 333/5

54. Barpal to the Mossad, 10.3.48, Mossad files, Israel Army Archive, 14/123

55. Rabinowitz to Department of Immigration, 12.22.48, Department of Immigration files, package #61, file 393, original designation 2421/73

56. 12.48, Central Zionist archives, S20/550I

57. Ben-Gurion *Diaries*, 5.3.49

58. Ibid., 8.8.49

59. Central Zionist Archives, S20/550I

60. Dr. Goldmann to Dr. Kornblit, 12.31.48, Central Zionist Archives, S20/550I; likewise other letters by Goldmann. A very grave report about conditions in the Marseilles camps, also in Central Zionist Archives, S20/562 (Eli Peleg's report). Somewhat more positive view in Controller's report, Department of Immigration files, package #19, file 81, original designation 1006. Dr. Israel Goldstein also denounced discrimination against North African immigrants in the Marseilles camps, Zionist Executive, 7.18.49

61. Undated, Department of Immigration files, package 61, file 393, original designation 2421/73

62. Artsieli report, 8.9.49, Central Zionist Archives, S20/555

63. Eli Peleg's report, 7.24.49, Central Zionist Archives, S20/562. Likewise, Zionist Executive, 7.31.49; Eliyahu Dobkin: "There is a new phenomenon—they don't want to move. In June–July there was a quota of 1,500 which was not filled. I know of a transport of 112, but only 80 arrived. The people in the Marseilles camps say, let's wait a little, until the housing situation in Israel improves.

There are also cases of people leaving the Marseilles camps and returning to Morocco." A report by a delegation of observers from Tunis who came to Israel to study the conditions of immigrant absorption and left with very adverse impressions, Central Zionist Archives, S41/256, file 6-7

64. Grossman report, undated, files of Immigration Department, package #61, file 393, original designation 2421/73

65. Concerning the image and the sense of strangeness, see Rivkah Sapir, "A Roof Over One's Head," *Megamot* C, 1951

66. The cobbler sent Ben-Gurion several heart-rending letters. Central Zionist Archives, S41/498

67. Files of Immigration Department, package #61, file 393, original designation 2421/73

68. Zionist Executive, 10.24.48

69. Nini, p. 284. Likewise, statement by A. Agasi, in committee that studied future relations with Arab labor: "If we look closely, we will find that in fact the principle of 'Hebrew Labor' was not used as a barrier to cheap labor—for, after all, we ourselves imported cheap laborers from the Yemen—but as a barrier against a tide of alien laborers. . . ." MAPAI, the Center for Histadrut and State Problems, Labor Party Archive, 7/69/48

70. Interview, 5.20.83

71. Weitz *Diary*, 7.7.50

72. Ibid., 9.19.50

73. Sharett report, 12.12.48, State Archives, Foreign Ministry, 130.11/2502/8

74. Ben-Gurion *Diaries*, 9.2.49

75. MAPAI central committee, 12.18.49, Labor Party Archive

76. M. Grabowsky, MAPAI central committee, 2.21.49, Labor Party Archive

77. Ibid.

78. Ibid.

79. Ibid.

80. Absorption Department in Jerusalem to D. Tenneh, Tel Aviv, 1.11.53, Central Zionist Archives, S84/77

81. Zionist Executive, 10.9.49

82. Ibid.

83. Zionist Executive, 12.26.49

84. Ibid., 1.2.50

85. Barzilai to Sharett, a series of letters between September and November 1949, State Archives, Foreign Ministry, 2397/19

86. Ben-Gurion to Gruenbaum, 3.28.50, Ben-Gurion Estate
87. Central Zionist Archives, S41/247
88. *Haaretz*, 11.8.49
89. *Knesset Record*, Vol. III, p. 31, 11.8.49
90. *Haaretz*, 9.9.49
91. Frumkin Report, p. 127
92. Concerning their immigration, see Nini and Levitan
93. Concerning the negotiations, see Kubovitzky to World Jewish Congress, 4.24.49, files of the Mossad for Immigration, Israel Army Archive, 14/49. There were some other meetings in this connection: the Jewish Agency's emissary, Yosef Tzadok, even met with the Imam in person. The Mossad's agent, Ovadiah Tuvia, contacted the Sultan Audli. See Tuvia to the Mossad, 5.14.49, Mossad files, Israeli Army Archive, 14/49
94. Shreiboim report, 7.21.49, Central Zionist Archives, S20/487II. Concerning the role played by the US Consul in Aden in bringing about these contacts, see State Archives, Foreign Ministry, 2397/15; also Zionist Executive, 6.5.49 and 8.28.49.
95. Tsadok to Eretz Israel office in Aden, 12.20.49, Central Zionist Archives, L27, file 4. File includes Tsadok's journal and letters.
96. Tsadok to Immigration office in Aden, 12.31.49, Central Zionist Archives, L27
97. Ibid.
98. Zionist Executive, 8.28.49
99. Refael, p. 73
100. Refael to Locker, 1.22.51, Central Zionist Archives, S41/256I
101. Tsadok, p. 233
102. Klieger report, State Archives, Prime Minister's Office, Division 43, 333/5
103. Ministry of Health, internal memorandum—not for publication—following a visit to Aden, September 1949, State Archives, Foreign Ministry, 2397/15
104. Yosef Tsadok to D. Menahem, 7.21.49, Central Zionist Archives, S20/457II
105. Barer
106. Levitan, p. 133; Tsadok, pp. 23–30; Sternberg, pp. 78–104
107. Report of the investigating committee for the discovery of the missing Yemenite children, March 1968, p. 183, State Archives, 968/1
108. Ben-Tsvi report, 12.18.49, Central Archive of Jewish History, Nahum Levin Archive

109. Menahem Ben-Yosef to Avraham Hadar, 10.9.49, Central Zionist Archives, Section of Jews of the Middle East, S/20/600; likewise, Central Zionist Archives, S20/109, S20/547II

110. Ibid., S20/457II, including references to rivalry between MAPAI, MAPAM and Hamizrahi, as well as the investigation by the Security Forces into past of IZL representative

111. Central Zionist Archives, Aden Immigration office, L27

112. S.K. (student at Hebron Rabbinical School) to Minister Y.M. Levin, State Archives, Prime Minister's Office, 347/15

113. Tsadok, p. 232; Refael, p. 75; and 23rd Zionist Congress, p. 209.

114. Refael, p. 72; Levitan, p. 167

115. Ben-Gurion *Diaries*, 9.28.49

116. *Knesset Record*, Vol. III, p. 128, 11.21.49

117. Central Zionist Archives, 7.18.49. A few moments later Gruenbaum asked that it be recorded in the minutes that he had not spoken against immigration from the Yemen. With reference to his doubts on the subject, see also Ben-Gurion *Diaries*, 9.28.49

118. Zionist Executive, 11.8.48

119. Ibid., 9.11.49

120. Ibid., 11.28.49

121. Ibid., 9.4.49

122. Ibid., 10.6.49

123. Ibid., 6.5.49: "There's no need to fear the arrival of many chronically ill persons, as they have to trek on foot for two weeks. People who are gravely ill won't be able to do it." Also Zionist Executive, 9.30.49: "There is no stopping the immigration from Yemen. I can stop all those who are living in their towns and even in the European camps. The Yemenites are out in the streets and in the desert."

124. *Dvar Hashavua*, 11.10.49;

125. Ben-Gurion *Diaries*, 9.28.49

126. *Knesset Record*, Vol. III, p. 128, 11.21.49

127. Ibid.

128. Ben-Gurion to Yadin, 11.27.50, Ben-Gurion Estate

129. *Knesset Record*, Vol. VIII, p. 1102, 2.14.51

130. Leaflet issued by Absorption Department, #7, Central Zionist Archives, S20/103

131. Levitan, p. 164, and Zionist Executive (Hermon), 12.26.49

132. Levitan, p. 237

133. Ibid., p. 243

134. Ibid., p. 245

135. Ibid., p. 246 (map)

136. *Haaretz*, 10.13.50, letter from Yemenite Association concerning exploitation of Yemenite workers, while sidestepping Labor Exchanges, and a promise by the Prime Minister's Secretary that the matter would be properly dealt with—Yemenite Association to Central Chamber, 5.8.50, State Archives, Prime Minister's Office, Immigrant camps, 5558/C

137. Glouska, *Knesset Record*, Vol. II, p. 1041, 7.18.49. Aso Vol. I., p. 441, 4.27.49; Vol. II, p. 1305, 8.10.49; and Vol. III, p. 84, 11.16.49. In April 1950, Glouska sent Levi Eshkol a long and significant letter, listing a long record of discriminations against Yemenites during the Mandate period, including discrimination in immigration permits, etc. Glouska to Eshkol, 4.20.50, Central Zionist Archives, S34/272. Concerning Yemenites in the armed forces: "Despite the excellence of young Yemenites, 90 percent of them have remained private soldiers," *Knesset Record*, Vol. II, p. 1559, 9.5.49

138. Glouska, p. 275

139. *Haaretz*, 12.18.50 Regarding the attempt to teach Yemenite women to put diapers on their babies and feed them properly: "They feed them bread and coffee," (*Haaretz*, 11.21.50). The parents were frequently described as if they did not leave any food for their children (*Haaretz*, 12.19.50; 5.20.52)

140. *Knesset Record*, Vol. II, p. 1550, 9.5.49

141. Report of the committee appointed to study the situation in the new settlements of Yemenite immigrants, plus related material, State Archives, Prime Minister's Office, (9012), 5581/22 4

142. Perets Cohen, "Community & Stability in Immigrant Township," Social Studies, Ministry of Welfare, Department of Research & Planning, Jerusalem 1959. For impressions of visit to Yemenite immigrant camps, see also in Immigration leaflet #7, Central Zionist Archives, S20/103. A visit to Yemenite immigrants in Jaffa, Central Zionist Archives, S20/104. A shocking report by Esther Badihi about the condition of Yemenite immigrant women, Central Zionist Archives, S20/457III, 1.14.49. Hagit Riger, "The Adjustment Problems of Yemenite Youth in Israel," *Megamot* C, 1951; Ovadiah Shapira, "Gadish—A Yemenite Immigrant Village in the Jerusalem Hills," Jerusalem, 1960

143. MAPAI Central Committee, 1.4.49, Labor Party Archive

144. Ben-Gurion *Diaries*, 1.20.49

145. A. Tabib and others to MAPAI Central Committee, 12.21.48, Ben-Gurion Estate.

146. Levitan, p. 313ff.

147. Yemenite Association to Minister of Police, 4.11.50; 4.18.50; 5.8.50. State Archives, Prime Minister's Office, Immigrant camps, 5558/C

148. Yosef Tsuriel, "Twelve Families in Search of their Children," *Maariv*, 4.1.66

149. Report of the investigating committee for the discovery of the missing Yemenite children, March 1968, State Archives, 1/968/1. The Haifa District Attorney, Y. Bahalul, and Superintendent Reuven Minkowsky of the State Police Headquarters, were in charge of the investigation. Concerning the police and Ministry of Health investigations in the years between the "Magic Carpet" immigration and the creation of the investigating committee, and the attempts to suppress knowledge of the existence of the investigations and their findings, see Levitan, p. 270 ff.

150. Minister of Police Shitrit to Cabinet Ministers, 4.24.50, State Archives, Dov Yosef Archive, Correspondence and Memoranda, Division 69, 703/16. See also Prime Minister's Office, 5558/C

7. Each in the Name of His God

1. Report of the investigating committee on the state of education in the immigrant camps, p. 10, State Archives, 1/152 (hereafter—the Frumkin Report)

2. At his death Nahum Levin left an ancient valise packed with various files, documents and a series of personal notes, resembling a diary. The material was kept for years by Levin's widow, who kindly permitted me to study it, for which I am very grateful. She has since divided it between two archives—the Central Archives of Jewish History, which has marked the material P161, but at the time of writing has not yet sorted it out. The quotes in this text are taken from the material in this set, unless otherwise noted. Some of the material is kept at the *Yad Vashem* Archives, whiere it is marked (5814), Z/36-2, Z/36-1. Still more material, including letters, is in the possession of Mrs. Bronya Bendek, who was Levin's secretary. She too let me see it, for which I wish to thank her. Eviatar Levin, who has since died, helped me with information about his father's life.

3. Frumkin report, p. 21

4. These pages are based on Bentwitch, the Educational Encyclopedia and an article by Zvi Lamm, "Ideological Tensions—Conflicts over Aims of Education," in Ormian.

5. *Knesset Record*, Vol. IV, p. 892, 2.38.50

6. State Archives, 43/5558/C/3885

7. *Knesset Record*, Vol. II, p. 1165, 7.27.49

8. *Hatzofeh*, 6.30.49; 10.25.49; 12.12.49

9. *Davar*, 1.10.50; 1.24.50; *Maariv* 11.7.49

10. Correspondence between Ben-Gurion and Avner, June 1949, Ben-Gurion Estate

11. Pincas to Ben-Gurion, 1.6.50, State Archives, Prime Minister's Office, 3633/C/5543

12. *Knesset Record*, Vol. II, p. 1153, 7.26.49

13. Ibid., p. 1101, 7.20.49

14. Ibid., Vol. IV, p. 894, 2.28.50

15. Ibid., Vol. II, p. 1144, 7.26.49

16. Ibid., Vol. II, p. 1103, 7.20.49

17. Ibid., Vol. IV, p. 936, 3.6.50

18. These pages are based on a paper by Eliezer Don Yihya, "Cooperation and Conflict Between Political Camps, the Religious Camp and the Labor Movement, and the Crisis of Education in Israel," submitted as a doctoral thesis to the Hebrew University Senate in 1977

19. Interview, 11.2.82

20. Yad Vashem Archives, Z, 36-1

21. State Archives, Prime Minister's Office, 347/15

22. Frumkin Report, p. 40

23. Yad Vashem Archives, Z, 36-2

24. All the speakers at the party's MKs' meeting in Knesset, 1.24.50 Labor Party Archive

25. Yad Vashem Archives, Z, 36-2

26. Frumkin Report, pp. 78–80

27. Bendek documents and Frumkin Report, p. 40

28. Interview, 10.27.82

29. *Davar*, 6.12.50

30. Bendek documents, State Archives, Prime Minister's Office, 347/15

31. Frumkin Report, pp. 82 ff.

32. State Archives, Prime Minister's Office, 3634/C/5543/43, and *Knesset Record*, Vol. V, p. 1699, 6.13.50, and pp. 1723–25, 6.14.50

33. State Archives, Dov Yosef Archive, Correspondence and Memoranda, 703/16

34. Central Zionist Archives, S 41/340; for other complaints, see Rabbi Yitzhaki of Rish Haayin to Ben-Gurion, 12.12.49, State Archives, Prime Minister's Office, C/5543/3631, including reference to cutting off of sidelocks and attempts against religious education; Ben-Gurion to Y.M. Levin 7.11.50, Ben-Gurion Estate

35. Frumkin Report, p. 40

36. *Knesset Record*, Vol. IV, p. 855, 2.27.50

37. Report of visit to immigrant camps in Ein Shemer and Pardesia, State Archives, Prime Minister's Office, 3885/5558/C/43

38. Ben-Gurion to Maimon and Levin, 2.20.50, State Archives, Prime Minister's Office, 3633/5543/C

39. State Archives, Prime Minister's Office, 3885/C/5558/43

40. MAPAI MKs directorship in Knesset, 1.24.50, Labor Party Archive, 11/1/1

41. Don Ihye, p. 635

42. Interview, 10.21.82

43. Ben-Gurion *Diaries*, 2.28.49

44. *Knesset Record*, Vol. IV, p. 884, 2.28.50; also S.Z. Shragai, ("Inquisition"), Zionist Executive, 12.4.49

45. Minutes, 2.1.50, State Archives, 347/15

46. More in Don Ihye, p. 658

47. *Knesset Record*, Vol. IV, p. 885, 2.28.50

48. Karlebach, p. 278

49. MAPAI MKs, 1.24.50, Labor Party Archive

50. Ibid.

51. Ben-Gurion to Rabbi Maimon, 1.2.50, Ben-Gurion Estate

52. MAPAI MKs, 1.24.50, Labor Party Archive

53. Ibid.

54. Frumkin Report, p. 17

55. Ben-Gurion to Maimon and Levin, 2.20.50, Ben-Gurion Estate

56. Ben-Gurion to Maimon, 1.12.50, Ben-Gurion Estate

57. Ben-Gurion to Aran, 2.19.50, Ben-Gurion Estate

58. Ibid.

59. State Archives, 347/15

60. Interview, 12.5.82

61. Ibid., 12.10.82

62. *Knesset Record*, Vol. V, p. 1758, 6.19.50

63. Interview, 11.11.82

64. Ibid., 10.27.82

65. Ibid., 11.3.82
66. *Knesset Record*, Vol. V, p. 1761, 6.19.50
67. State Archives, 43/5558/C/3885; 43/5543/C/3633; and Bendek documents
68. Interview, 11.4.82
69. Ben-Gurion to Shapira, 7.7.50, Ben-Gurion Estate
70. Rozen to Cabinet Ministers, 8.20.50; State Archives, 43/5543/C/3633
71. Dania Levin to Ben-Gurion, 11.21.50; Nahum Levin to Ben-Gurion, 2.13.51, State Archives, 43/5543/C/3633
72. Interview, 12.16.82
73. Ibid., 9.30.82
74. Frumkin Report, p. 104
75. Ibid., p. 177
76. Ibid., p. 116
77. *Knesset Record*, Vol. IV, p. 889, 2.28.50
78. Levitan, p. 199
79. *Knesset Record*, Vol. III, p. 262, 12.17.49

8. The Battle for the Sabbath

1. All quotes about the affair of that demonstration and its aftermath, State Archives, Ministry of Police, Section 119, 24/160, 3331/C, unless otherwise stated.
2. Report of the Committee of Investigation of the Sabbath Demonstrations, 1956, State Archives, 1/157
3. *Knesset Record*, Vol. II, p. 907, 7.5.49,; see also Milstein
4. Ibid., Vol. IV, p. 794, 2.14.50
5. Ibid., Vol. V, p. 2509 ff, 8.8.50
6. Leibowitz, pp. 140–141
7. *Neturei Karta* leaflets, Report of the Committee of Investigation of the Sabbath Demonstrations, 1956, State Archives 1/157; Leaflet collection at National Library and Friedmann
8. Ibid.
9. Ibid.
10. *Agudat Israel* World Federation, "Removing Disguises, A Clarification," Jerusalem 1951; "Who put an end to the conflict?"—A short review of the conflict between the organized ultra-orthodox community and the free parties. A Plain Reply to the attacks of

Neturei Karta on the *Agudat Israel*, organized by *Agudat Israel* in Jerusalem, in the month of Av, 1964

11. Ibid.
12. *Shearim*, 11.13.47
13. Levin, p. 44
14. State Archives, Prime Minister's Office, 5585/C/4468
15. Bar-Zohar, *Hamemune*, p. 94 ff.
16. *Knesset Record*, Vol. IX, p. 1779, 5.16.51
17. Ibid., Vol. IV, p. 932, 3.6.50
18. Ratosh, p. 9 ff.
19. Ibid.
20. *Knesset Record*, Vol. VI, p. 2398, 8.1.50
21. Ibid., Vol. IV, p. 1013 ff., 3.14.50
22. Ibid., p. 1011, 3.14.50
23. Golan, p. 204
24. The League for the Prevention of Religious Coercion, Newsletter #1 ff.; The "peace conference,"—Jerusalem City Archive, 1856-21/13/1
25. Ibid.
26. State Archives, Prime Minister's Office, 5593/C/4681
27. *Knesset Record*, Vol. IX, p. 1777, 5.16.51
28. These pages are based on Menahem Friedmann's article, "Relations Between Religious and Secular Groups Prior to the State," in the series "Problems in the History of Zionism and the Yishuv," 2 (The religious movement in Zionism), published by Am Oved and Tel Aviv University, 1983
29. Ben-Gurion *Diaries*, 2.7.49
30. Ibid., 3.7.49; *Knesset Record*, Vol. I, p. 55, 3.8.49
31. Ben-Gurion to Levin, 4.10.49, Ben-Gurion Estate
32. Ben-Gurion *Diaries*, 9.23.49
33. The Sabbath Council Information, 1954
34. State Archives, Ministry of Police, 3331/C/24/160; A more moderate proposal by the Ministry of Religious Affairs (1949), Ben-Gurion Estate
35. *Knesset Record*, Vol. I. p. 326, 4.6.49
36. Ibid., Vol. III, p. 373, 1.2.50
37. Ibid., Vol. I, p. 703, 6.14.49
38. Ibid., Vol. I, p. 572, 5.24.49
39. *Agudat Israel Federation*, "Removing Disguises," A clarification, Jerusalem, 1951

40. Ibid.

41. Ibid.

42. Ibid.

43. Levin to Ben-Gurion, 1.15.50, State Archives, Prime Minister's Office, 5543/C/3633

44. Daniel, p. 189

45. Ben-Gurion to Shapira, 3.31.52, State Archives, Prime Minister's Office, 1122/5385/22

46. Ben-Gurion to Maimon and Levin, 2.20.50, Ben-Gurion Estate

47. Ibid., 1.12.50, Ben-Gurion Estate

48. Maimon to Ben-Gurion, 1.15.50, State Archives, Prime Minister's office, 5543/C/3633

49. Frumkin Report, p. 16

50. State Archives, The People's Administration, Minutes, p. 120 ff.

51. However, in the *Knesset Record*, Vol. I, p. 136, 3.10.49: "Kahana asked why I made no reference to our Father in Heaven. In this connection I should like to state once and for all, that in this forum I do not speak about anything that cannot be put to the vote, and I am certain that Rabbi Kahana would agree that the subject of the Almighty can hardly be put to the vote in the Knesset."

52. Refael, p. 359

53. Ben-Gurion *Diaries*, 2.4.49

54. Ben-Gurion, *Netsah Israel*, p. 43

55. The day before the 20th Day of Independence, I interviewed Ben-Gurion, together with Yosef Avner and Avraham Kushnir. His remark concerning his attitude to the Talmud as compared to the Bible, and his comments about God, are quoted from the tape of that interview, which was held at Sde-Boker and lasted over three hours.

56. Interview, 11.1.82

57. Leibowitz, p. 173

58. Ben-Gurion, *Netsah Israel*, p. 20

59. Interview, 10.29.82; Rubin's statement, *Knesset Record*, Vol. III, p. 261, 12.7.49

60. Interview, 11.11.82

61. Ben-Gurion, *Netsah Israel*, p. 23

62. Meeting of party's MKs with Secretariat, 6.14.49, Labor Party Archive, 11/2/1; also *Knesset Record*, Vol. IV, p. 812 ff., 2.20.50

63. Tavori (MAPAI), *Knesset Record*, Vol. IV, p. 722, 2.13.50; Levenstein (Agudat Israel), *Knesset Record*, Vol. IV, p. 742, 2.7.50; Levin, *Knesset Record*, Vol. IV, p. 808, 2.20.50

9. Quest for a National Identity

1. *Haaretz*, 5.5.49
2. Ben-Gurion *Diaries*, 5.4.49
3. *Haaretz*, 5.15.49
4. *Maariv*, 5.5.49
5. *Yediot Aharonot*, 8.16.49
6. Meeting of Party's Central Committee with party's MKs, 7.23.49, Labor Party Archive, 11/2/1
7. Ben-Gurion *Diaries*, 12.31.49
8. Meeting of MAPAI's Central Committee with party's MKs, Labor Party Archive, 11/2/1
9. Ben-Gurion *Diaries*, 8.26.49
10. Ibid., 1.4.49
11. Ben-Gurion *Diaries*, 6.20.49
12. Ben-Gurion to Laskov, 4.27.50, Ben-Gurion Estate
13. Ben-Gurion, *Yehud Veyeud*, pp. 130–131
14. Meeting of MAPAI Central Committee with party's MKs, July 22–23, 1949, Labor Party Archive, 11/2/1
15. Ben-Gurion *Diaries*, 2.4.49
16. Meeting of MAPAI Secretariat, 10.20.49 Labor Party Archive, 24/49
17. Ben-Gurion *Diaries*, 2.7.49
18. Ibid., 7.3.49
19. Ben-Gurion to Rapaport, 11.10.48, Ben-Gurion Estate
20. Ben-Gurion *Diaries*, 6.16.49
21. Ibid., 6.23.49
22. Rabin, p. 86
23. Ben-Gurion *Diaries*, 10.16.49
24. Ibid., 7.3.49
25. Aran in MAPAI's Center, 2.24.49, and Secretariat, 6.5.49, Labor Party Archive
26. Ben-Gurion *Diaries*, 9.11.49; Ben-Gurion to Baer, 10.14.49
27. Meeting of Party's Central Committee with party's MKs, 7.22–23.49, Labor Party Archive, 11/2/1
28. Ben-Gurion *Diaries*, 6.28.49
29. Ben-Gurion to Ben Aharon, 7.28.49, Ben-Gurion Estate
30. Ben-Gurion *Diaries*, 1.4.49
31. Interview, 7.13–17.83
32. Ben-Gurion to Ben Aharon, 7.28.49, Ben-Gurion Estate

33. *Kol Ha'am*, 8.18.49

34. The Israeli Communist Party, *Kol Ha'am*–Ben-Gurion lawsuit, June 1951, *Kol Ha'am*, 8.29.51

35. Ben-Gurion to Ben Aharon, 7.28.49, Ben-Gurion Estate

36. *Al Hamishmar*, 9.23.49

37. Ben-Gurion *Diaries*, 4.23.49

38. Ibid., 4.25.49

39. Ibid., 6.23.49

40. Interview, 7.15.83

41. Ibid., 7.13.83

42. *Knesset Record*, Vol. I, p. 125, 3.10.49

43. *Davar*, 5.3.49

44. *Knesset Record*, Vol. I, p. 55, 3.8.49

45. Ben-Gurion to Sharett, 9.15.49

46. McDonald to Marshall, 12.20.48, *Foreign Relations of the US*, 1948, p. 1674

47. *Knesset Record*, Vol. I, p. 155, 3.17.49

48. Sotherwit to Acheson, 3.24.49, *Foreign Relations of the US*, 1949, p. 863

49. Douglas to Marshall, 8.6.48, *Foreign Relations of the US*, 1948, p. 1292

50. Kollek, p. 162

51. Meir Yaari, "For Labor Hegemony in a Progressive Government," *Al Hamishmar*, 1.24.49

52. Zeev Tsur, "Between Collaboration and Opposition," Yad Tabenkin, Studies, 8, 1983

53. Ben-Gurion to Weizman, 3.4.49, Ben-Gurion Estate

54. Minutes of Cabinet meeting, Ben-Gurion, "The State of Israel Reborn," p. 184

55. The Council of State, Vol. I, 9.23.48

56. *Herut*, 1.26.49

57. Ibid., 2.4.49

58. Ben-Gurion *Diaries*, 4.27.49

59. Ibid., 10.12.49

60. *Knesset Record*, Vol. I, p. 728, 6.15.49

61. Aran to MAPAI Secretariat, 6.5.49, Labor Party Archive

62. *Dvar Hashavua*, 5.8.49

63. Ibid., 7.17.49

64. Ben-Gurion to Schocken, 1.4.49, Ben-Gurion Estate

65. Ben-Gurion to Y.S. Shapira, 10.16.49, Ben-Gurion Estate

66. *Knesset Record*, Vol. I, p. 515, 5.17.49

67. Ben-Gurion to Dov Yosef and others, 12.29.49, Ben-Gurion Estate

68. Bader, p. 25

69. *Herut*, 1.16.49

70. Meeting with Writers, 10.11.49, *Divrei Sofrim*, State Archives

71. Minutes of Cabinet meeting, 3.2.49, Kibbutz Meuhad Archive (Cizling) section 9, container 9, file 1

72. "We and the Germans," *Haaretz*, 9.2.49; see also *Haaretz*, 9.4.49, against trade relations with Germany

73. Ora Shem-Or, *Yediot Aharonot*, 9.6.49

74. Ehud Ben-Ezer, *Portzhim Unetzurim*, *Keshet*, No. X, #7, 1968

75. Kurzweil, p. 168 ff.

76. Discussion of this issue: *Proza*, August–September 1977, "The Literary Failure of 1948," including discussion between Dan Omer and Amos Keynan, notes and documentary material

77. Ratosh, p. 218

78. Ben-Gurion, *Netsah Israel*, p. 22

79. Ibid.

80. Meeting with Writers, 10.11.49, *Divrei Sofrim*, State Archives

81. A series of articles about this issue by Mordehai Kassover appeared in the Jewish-American periodical *Bitzaron*, No. 13, Vol. XXVI, continuing in XXVII.

82. Zionist Executive, 8.19.48

83. *Vaad Hapoel Hazioni*, p. 153

84. Ibid.

85. *Dapei Aliyah*, No. 14, p. 46, 1949

86. *Knesset Record*, Vol. II, p. 1339, 8.15.49

87. Gavrieli & Avivi, p. 30

88. Ibid., p. 62

89. Ibid., p. 52

90. *Dvar Hashavua*, 7.7.49

91. Weitz *Diary*, 8.18.49

92. Ibid., 1.10.50

10. Codfish with Everything

1. Horowitz, p. 30

2. Halevi–Klinov-Maloul, p. 148

3. Ben-Gurion *Diaries*, 9.18.49

4. Halevi–Klinov-Maloul, p. 121

5. Horowitz, p. 23

6. *Maariv*, 5.13.49

7. *Knesset Record*, Vol. I, p. 417, 4.27.49

8. Ibid., Vol. VI, p. 2469, 8.7.50

9. Ibid., Vol. III, p. 22, 11.9.49

10. Ibid., Vol. XII, p. 2130, 5.27.52

11. Yosef, p. 235

12. These pages are based on a paper by Uri Weiss, "Price Control in Israel, 1939–1963," submitted as M.A. Dissertation to the Hebrew University in Jerusalem, July 1964

13. *Knesset Record*, Vol. VI, p. 2503, 8.8.50

14. Yosef, p. 228

15. Bader, p. 31

16. *Knesset Record*, Vol. I, p. 399, 4.26.49

17. Ibid., p. 401, 4.26.49

18. Yosef, *Kirya Neemana*, p. 9

19. Government Annual Report, 1951, p. 42

20. Ibid., p. 44

21. *Haaretz*, 1.13.49

22. Shulamith Lev-Ari, "Why We Stand in Line," *Haaretz*, 7.1.49, first article in series

23. *Davar*, 10.6.49

24. Ibid., 9.7.49

25. State Archives, Ministry of Supplies and Rationing, Section 196, 2/4/7

26. Yosef, p. 236

27. Institute for the Study of Public Opinion, The War on the Black Market, 1950, State Archives, Prime Minister's Office, 5512/17

28. State Archives, 22/950/6; 22/950/7; 22/956/8

29. *Knesset Record*, Vol. VI, p. 2425, 8.2.50

30. Government Annual Report, 1951, p. 46

31. *Maariv*, 9.19.49

32. Keinan, p. 247

33. *Knesset Record*, Vol. II, p. 951, 7.11.49

34. Ibid., p. 953, 7.11.49

35. *Knesset Record*, Vol. III, p. 117, 11.21.49

36. Ibid., Vol. V, p. 1783, 6.20.50

37. Ibid., p. 1775, 6.20.50

38. Ibid., Vol. VI, p. 2425, 8.2.50
39. Ibid., p. 2491, 8.8.50
40. Ibid., p. 2429, 8.2.50
41. Ibid., p. 2495, 8.8.50
42. Ibid., p. 2428, 8.2.50
43. Ibid., Vol. I, p. 492, 5.11.49
44. Ibid., Vol. VI, p. 2427, 8.2.50
45. Ibid., p. 2495, 8.8.50
46. Ibid., Vol. V, p. 1943, 6.28.50
47. Yosef, p. 235
48. Ibid., p. 247
49. *Knesset Record*, Vol. V, p. 901, 3.1.50
50. State Archives, Dov Yosef Archive, Section 69, 713/11, 728/4
51. *Maariv*, 5.10.49
52. Halevy–Klinov-Maloul, p. 221
53. *Knesset Record*, Vol. VI, p. 29, 9.11.51
54. Ibid., Vol. XVII, p. 958, 3.1.55
55. Cohen to Ben-Gurion, 10.26.50, Prime Minister's Office, State Archives, 5512/10
56. *Knesset Record*, Vol. X, p. 9.11.51
57. State Archives, Prime Minister's Office, War on the Black Market, 5512/11
58. Ben-Gurion to Israel Levin, 10.9.50, State Archives, Prime Minister's Office, 5512/9
59. State Archives, Dov Yosef Archive, The War on the Black Market, 714/16
60. *Knesset Record* (Sapir's statement), Vol. X, p. 260, 10.8.51
61. Ibid., Vol. X, p. 26, 9.10.51
62. *Davar*, 10.16.49
63. *Knesset Record*, Vol. X, p. 29, 9.11.51
64. *Yediot Aharonot*, 8.24.49
65. Songs of the Black Market, *Davar*, 10.27.50
66. *Knesset Record*, Vol. VI, p. 2201, 7.17.50
67. Committee's report, State Archives, Dov Yosef Archive, Section 716/69
68. *Knesset Record*, Vol. VI, p. 2218, 7.17.50
69. Ibid., Vol. XII, p. 2130, 5.27.52
70. Government Annual Report, 1953, p. 122
71. *Knesset Record*, Vol. VI, p. 2238, 7.18.50

72. Ibid., Vol. IV, p. 898, 3.1.50
73. Ibid., Vol. XVII, p. 959, 3.1.55
74. Interview with Dan Almagor, *Yediot Aharonot*, 1.18.80
75. State Archives, Prime Minister's Office, 5512/20
76. Yosef, p. 230
77. *Knesset Record*, Vol. V, p. 1559, 5.30.50
78. Ibid., Vol. VI, p. 2236, 7.18.50
79. Ibid., p. 2452, 8.7.50
80. Ibid., p. 2499, 8.8.50
81. Ibid., Vol. X, 251, 10.8.51
82. Horowitz, p. 14
83. Yosef, p. 251 ff.
84. Ibid.
85. *Haaretz*, 8.4.50
86. Horowitz, 65
87. Halevi–Klinov-Maloul, p. 211

Bibliography

All sources are quoted from Hebrew original, except when otherwise stated. Books also published in languages other than Hebrew are listed in parentheses.

ABU, IYAD—*Lelo Moledet*. Jerusalem: Mifras, 1979 (Palestinien Sans Patrie, Entretiens avec Eric Rouleau, Paris: Fayolle, 1979)

ALMOGY, YOSEF—*Beovi Hakora*. Jerusalem: Idanim, 1980

ALTERMAN, NATHAN—*Hatur Hashvii*. Tel Aviv: Hakibbutz Hameuhad, 1980

APPELFELD, AHARON—*Mihvat Haor*. Tel Aviv: Hakibbutz Hameuhad, 1980

AVNERY, URI—*Bisdot Pleshet 1948*. Quoted from the 11th edition, Tel Aviv: Alef Lamed, 1975

BADER, YOHANAN—*Haknesset Veani*. Jerusalem: Idanim, 1979

BARER, SHLOMO—*Al Kanfei Nesharim*. Tel Aviv: Masada, 1966 (*The Magic Carpet*, New York: Harper, 1952)

BAR-ZOHAR, MICHAEL—*Ben-Gurion*. Tel Aviv: Am Ored, 1977 (*Ben-Gurion*, London: Weidenfeld and Nicolson, 1978)

BAR-ZOHAR, MICHAEL—*Hamemune*. Jerusalem: Weidenfeld and Nicolson, 1940 (*Spies in the Promised Land*, Houghton Mifflin, 1972)

BEIN, ALEX—*Aliya Vehityashvut Bimdinat Israel*. Tel Aviv: Am Oved, 1982

BEN-GURION, DAVID—*Behilahem Israel.* Tel Aviv: MAPAI Publishing House, 1951

BEN-GURION, DAVID—*Diaries,* 1948–1949. Quoted from the original manuscript held at the Ben-Gurion Estate in Sde-Boker as well as from *Yoman Hamilhama.* Tel Aviv: Ministry of Defense, 1982

BEN-GURION, DAVID—*Medinat Israel Hamehudeshet.* Tel Aviv: Am Oved, 1969

BEN-GURION, DAVID—*Netsah Israel.* Jerusalem: Shnaton Hamenshala, 1954

BEN-GURION, DAVID—*Yehud Veyeud.* Tel Aviv: Maarahot, 1971

BEN-MENAHEM, ITZHAK—*Adam Velohem.* Tel Aviv: Amihay, 1975

BENTWICH, YOSEF—*Hahinuh Bimdinat Israel.* Tel Aviv: Chechik, 1960

BERNADOTTE, FOLKE—*Lirushalaim.* Jerusalem: Ahiasaf, 1952 (*To Jerusalem,* London: Hodder and Stoughton, 1951)

BERNSTEIN, DVORA—*Hamaabaroth Bishnot Hahamishim.* Haifa: Mahbarot Lemehkar Ulebikoret, 1980

DANIEL, S.—*Hasar Shapira.* Tel Aviv: Don-Yad Shapira, 1980

Dapei Aliya—Current monthly publication of the Jewish Agency

DAYAN, MOSHE—*Avnei Dereh.* Jerusalem: Idanim, 1976

Divrei Sofrim—See Meeting with Writers

DON IHYE, ELIEZER—*Shituf Vekonflict.* Ph.D. Dissertation, The Hebrew University, 1977

EISENSTADT, S. N.—*Klitat Aliya.* Jerusalem: The Jewish Agency and The Hebrew University, 1952

EITAN, WALTER—*Bein Israel Leamim.* Tel Aviv: Masada, 1958

ENCICLOPEDIA HINUHIT.—Jerusalem: Mosad Bialik, 1959–1969 (5 vols.)

Foreign Relations of the United States—Vol. V (1976) and Vol. VI (1977). Washington vs. Department of State

FRIEDMANN, MENAHEM—*Hevra Vedat.* Jerusalem: Yad Ben-Tsvi, 1978

FRUMKIN REPORT—*Din Veheshbon shel Vaadat Hahakira Beinyanei Hahinuh Bemahanot Haolim* (Report of Investigation Committee on Education in the Immigrant Camps). State Archives 1/152

GAVRIELI, HANUM AND AVIVI, BARUCH—*Mikraa Layeled.* Tel Aviv: Yavne, 1944

GLOUSKA, ZEHARYA—*Sefer Lemaan Yehudei Teiman.* Tel Aviv: n.p., 1974

GOLAN, SHMUEL (ED.)—*Dor Ledor.* Kibbutz Mishmar Haemek, 1948

HALEVI, NADAV AND KLINOV MALOUL, RUTH—*Hitpathuta Hakalkalit Shel Israel.* Jerusalem: Akademon, 1968

HOROWITZ, DAVID—*Haim Bamoked.* Tel Aviv: Masada, 1975

ISRAEL DOCUMENTS—Documents of the Foreign Policy of Israel 1948–1949. Jerusalem: State Archives, 1983

JIRYIS, SABRI—*Haaravim Beisrael.* Haifa: Al Itihad, 1966 (*The Arabs in Israel,* New York: Monthly Review Press, 1966)

KARLEBACH, AZRIEL—*Sefer Hadmuyot.* Tel Aviv: Maariv, 1959

KEINAN, AMOS—*Beshotim Uvearkabim.* Tel Aviv: Israel Press, 1948

KLIEGER, RUTH (ALIAV)—*Hamiflat Haaharon.* Tel Aviv: Am Oved, 1976

KOLLEK, TEDDY—*For Jerusalem.* London: Weidenfeld and Nicolson, 1978 (Quoted from the English original)

KOREN, ITZHAK—*Kibbutz Galuyot Behitnahluto.* Tel Aviv: Am Oved, 1964

KURZWEIL, BARUH—*Hipus Hasifrut Haisreelit.* Tel Aviv: Bar Ilan University Press, 1982

LEIBOWITZ, YESHAYAHU—*Yahadut, Am Yehudi Umedinat Israel.* Tel Aviv: Schocken, 1979

LEVIN, ITZHAK MEIR—*Haish Upoalo.* Jerusalem: Yad Harav Meir, 1972

LEVITAN, DOV—*Aliyat Marvad Haksamim.* M.A. Dissertation, Bar Ilan University, 1983

LUFBANN, HEZY—*Ish Yotse el Ehav.* Tel Aviv: Am Oved, 1969

MCDONALD, JAMES C.—*My Mission to Israel.* New York: Simon and Schuster, 1951 (Quoted from the English original)

MEETING WITH WRITERS—Quoted from *Divrei Sofrim.* Tel Aviv: Prime Minister's office, 1979

MICHAEL, SAMI—*Shavim Veshavim Yoter.* Tel Aviv: Am Oved, 1974

MICHAELI, BEN-ZION—*Yeshuvim Shenitshu.* Tel Aviv: Milo, 1980

MILSTEIN, URI—*Hatiun Hadati Betahalih Hahakika.* Ph.D. Dissertation, The Hebrew University, 1972

MILSTEIN, URI—*Kadmon Vehavurato.* Tel Aviv: Am Oved, 1974

NINI, YEHUDA—*Teiman Vetsion.* Tel Aviv: Tel Aviv University Press, 1982

OREN, ELHANAN—*Badereh el Hair.* Tel Aviv: Ministry of Defense, 1976

ORMIAN, HAIM (ED.)—*Hahinuh Beisrael.* Jerusalem: Ministry of Education, 1973

PUBLIC OPINION—*Daat Hakahal Al.* (A Series of Opinion Polls published by the Government Information Office) 1949

RABIN, ITZHAK—*Pincas Sherut.* Tel Aviv: Maariv 1979

RATOSH, YOHANAN—*Reshit Hayamim.* Tel Aviv: Hadar, 1982

REFAEL, ITZHAK—*Lo Zahiti Baor Mehahefker.* Jerusalem: Idanim, 1981

SHAFRIR, DOV—*Arugot Haim.* Tel Aviv: Hamercaz Hahaklai, 1975

SHARETT, MOSHE—*Yoman Ishi.* Tel Aviv: Maariv, 1978

SHIRAN, VICCY—*Hatiyug Hamahtim*. M.A. Dissertation, Tel Aviv University, 1978

SIKRON, MOSHE—*Haaliya Leisrael 1948–1953*. Jerusalem: Mercaz Falk, 1957

STERNBERG, AVRAHAM—*Behikalet Am*. Tel Aviv: Hakibbutz Hameuhad, 1973

TEVET, SHABTAI—*Moshe Dayan*. Tel Aviv: Schocken, 1971

TSADOK, YOSEF—*Bisearot Teiman*. Tel Aviv: Am Oved, 1957

Vaad Hapoel Hatsioni—Meetings of the General Council of The Zionist Movement 1949. Jerusalem: Zionist Executive, 1949

WEISGALL, MEIR—*Ad Kan*. Jerusalem: Weiderfeld and Nicolson, 1972 (*So Far*, New York: Random House, 1971)

WEISGALL, MEIR AND CARMICHAEL, YOEL (EDS.)—*Haim Weizmann*. Jerusalem: Hasifria Hatsionit, 1964

WEITZ, YOSEF—*Miyomani*. Tel Aviv: Masada, 1965

WEIZMANN, EZER—*Leha Shamaim Leha Arets*. Tel Aviv: Maariv, 1975

YOSEF, DOV—*Kirya Neemana*. Tel Aviv: Schocken, 1964 (Yosef, Dov—*The Faithful City*, New York: Simon and Schuster, 1960)

YOSEF, DOV—*Yona Vaherev*. Tel Aviv: Masada, 1975

YOSEFTAL, GIORA—*Hayav Upoalo*. Tel Aviv: MAPAI Publishing House, 1963

ZIONIST EXECUTIVE—Minutes of the Meetings of the Zionist Executive (*Hanhala Tsionit*) held at The Central Zionist Archive, Jerusalem, 1948–1949

Index